Water Supply and
Environmental Management

Studies in Water Policy and Management
Charles W. Howe, Series Editor

Water Supply and Environmental Management: Developing World Applications, Mohan Munasinghe

Farmer Participation and Irrigation Organization, edited by Bradley W. Parlin and Mark W. Lusk

Water Resources Management in Latin America and the Caribbean, Terence R. Lee

Social, Economic, and Institutional Issues in Third World Irrigation Management, edited by R. K. Sampath and Robert A. Young

Irrigation Development in Africa: Lessons of Experience, Jon R. Moris and Derrick J. Thom

Congress in Its Wisdom: The Bureau of Reclamation and the Public Interest, Doris Ostrander Dawdy

Water Supply and Environmental Management

Developing World Applications

Mohan Munasinghe

Foreword by Donald Lauria

Westview Press

BOULDER • SAN FRANCISCO • OXFORD

Studies in Water Policy and Management

This Westview softcover edition is printed on acid-free paper and bound in library-quality, coated covers that carry the highest rating of the National Association of State Textbook Administrators, in consultation with the Association of American Publishers and the Book Manufacturers' Institute.

Copyright © 1992 by Westview Press, Inc.

Published in 1992 in the United States of America by Westview Press, Inc., 5500 Central Avenue, Boulder, Colorado 80301-2877, and in the United Kingdom by Westview Press, 36 Lonsdale Road, Summertown, Oxford OX2 7EW

A CIP catalog record for this book is available from the Library of Congress.
ISBN 0-8133-8414-1

Printed and bound in the United States of America

The paper used in this publication meets the requirements
of the American National Standard for Permanence of Paper
for Printed Library Materials Z39.48-1984.

10   9   8   7   6   5   4   3   2   1

To Neela

CONTENTS

TABLES

FIGURES

FOREWORD

Since the International Drinking Water Supply and Sanitation Decade ended in 1990, the focus of world attention on the environment has shifted from water supply to sanitation and, more generally, to environmental management. The rapid changes in Eastern Europe and the former Soviet Union, with their myriad other environmental problems, have all but eclipsed water as a pressing global issue. However, as Dr. Munasinghe stresses, water resource and environmental issues are inextricably linked. His introductory chapter indicates that nearly twenty percent of the urban population in developing countries and more than one-third of rural dwellers are still without adequate water supply. This shortfall will be further exacerbated by the inexorable growth of demand and the increasingly complex interactions between water availability and environmental degradation.

Approximately 1.2 billion persons in the developing world are in need of water systems. Tens of millions of individuals are walking long distances and spending hours each day trying, often unsuccesfully, to collect adequate amounts of water from natural sources of dubious quality. Tens of millions of families are spending inordinate fractions of their incomes on water they purchase from vendors, paying more each month than most households in industrialized countries spend for their modern and reliable piped supplies. The numbers of people who lack this basic need are staggering and beyond comprehension. What is a billion? Fifty cities each of the size of Tokyo or São Paulo? A file of persons 50 abreast stretching from New York to San Francisco? By no means has the global water supply problem been solved or gone away. It continues to loom as a major challenge in humanity's quest for dignity, health, and well being.

It is fitting and timely for Dr. Munasinghe to offer the profession new knowledge to help guide water supply planning and environmental management into the 21st Century. Never have the issues surrounding water supply been as pressing as they are today. Household water supply in many parts of the world is in a life-or-death struggle with competing demands, principally agriculture. The costs of water supply are rising, especially as it becomes necessary to go farther afield for adequate sources. Water resources are increasingly in short supply or environmentally degraded and must be used efficiently if needs are to be met. The traditional planning process wherein decisionmakers decide what is best for the beneficiaries without even consulting them must be replaced by a process that is more demand driven and which takes account of willingness-to-pay. Flat-rate tariffs that give rise to waste and uneconomic water use must be replaced by efficient price structures and metered supplies. The list of important planning issues seems endless.

Indeed, more than ever before the present situation calls for new approaches to planning, new policies, new techniques, and a holistic mindset that rightly sees the interconnectedness of water with the rest of the global economy and environment.

Mohan Munasinghe has written a book that addresses these issues from a comprehensive, sound, and practical perspective. At the outset, he lays the foundation for integrated water resources planning for sustainable development. He then addresses the evaluation of water projects in developing countries, covering such topics as benefit estimation, shadow pricing to deal with economic distortions, and alternative criteria for assessing public investments. Next, he deals with water system optimization, including water supply quality issues and the massive problem of unaccounted-for water. This is followed by rigorous treatment of environmental issues and their incorporation into water-sector decisionmaking as well as water pricing, demand forecasting, and rural water supply. Throughout the book, there is a generous distribution of case studies -- so often lacking in other texts dealing with issues and principles -- that anchor this volume in the real world and demonstrate the application and practicability of theory.

Dr. Munasinghe is best known for his work in the energy area, having done research and published extensively on such topics as demand forecasting, pricing, investment analysis, and policy design for developing countries. His award-winning work and authorship of numerous books and hundreds of technical articles have made him a renowned leader in that field. While his reputation in energy is outstanding, water resources and environment are certainly not "secondary" interests. In fact, his record of accomplishments in the areas of water and environment would be the envy of scholars who specialize in these same fields. Thus, he is well qualified to offer the profession this new work on water supply and environmental management.

For over 18 years, Mohan has worked at the World Bank, where he is presently division chief for environmental policy and research. From 1982 to 1986 he was senior advisor to the president of Sri Lanka, his native land. He has served on international committees and expert panels, often as chair, in the fields of energy, water, and environment. He has held professorial positions and has wide teaching experience.

A wide range of readers including students, practitioners, and experts will find this book a major resource in understanding and applying the wealth of latest knowledge that pertains to this important field.

Donald Lauria
Professor, Department of
Environmental Sciences and Engineering
University of North Carolina
at Chapel Hill

ACKNOWLEDGMENTS

During the past two decades, many distinguished colleagues and mentors who are too numerous to list here have contributed generously to the ideas developed in this volume.

I would like to thank especially Walter Buydens, Chitru Fernando, and Michael Lee, whose inputs and assistance greatly enhanced the quality of the book. I am indebted also to Ramesh Bhatia, Joseph Callaghan, John Dixon, Robert Dorfman, Kevin Fitzgerald, Mike Garn, Robert Goodland, Ron Hoffer, Charles Howe, Shailu Iyengar, Ian Johnson, Charles Kolstad, Donald Lauria, M. Manolaysay, Geoffrey Matthews, Alex Mcphail, Anusha Munasinghe, Ranjiva Munasinghe, Emilio Rodriguez, Adelaida Schwab, Mary Sheehan, Karl Steininger, Richard Tabors, Carlos Velez, Jeremy Warford, Dale Whittington, and Guillermo Yepes for valuable comments and help at various stages. Ellen McCarthy, Deborah Rich, and the staff of Westview Press provided crucial guidance in the closing stages. The responsibility for any errors or omissions is, of course, mine alone.

I am most grateful and privileged to have the Foreword contributed by a leading international scholar and authority in the field -- Donald Lauria, and the Introduction written by another eminent expert -- Charles Howe. Last but not least, thanks are due to my wife, Sria, and children, Anusha and Ranjiva, for their patience and understanding.

Mohan Munasinghe

SERIES EDITOR'S INTRODUCTION

This comprehensive book on potable water supply in the developing world is a very welcome addition to the Studies in Water Policy and Management series. Dr. Munasinghe is a world-renowned scholar in the areas of water and energy, combining research talents, experience, and an ability to communicate difficult concepts to a broad audience of practitioners.

The Water Policy and Management series has, in the last several years, featured studies relating to irrigation and related issues of farmer participation in developing countries. This volume is the first in the series to address the crucial issue of potable water development. It provides broad coverage of the state of Third World potable water development, methodologies for project optimization and evaluation, and excellent illustrative case studies. It will stand as a classic alongside <u>Drawers of Water</u> (by Gilbert White, David Bradley, and Anne White, 1972), <u>Impact and Economics of Community Water Supply</u> (by I.D. Carruthers, 1973), and <u>Village Water Supply</u> (by Robert Saunders and Jeremy Warford, 1976).

Chuck Howe

1

Introduction and Overview

Historically, water has played a critical role in every facet of human activity. In more recent times water has emerged as a key natural resource to be efficiently managed for environmentally sustainable development. Water is vital in a modern economy, not only in the urban-industrial context, but also in rural areas through its more widespread use in productive activities, and its potential to improve living conditions.

The foregoing underlines the importance of more efficient analysis, planning and management of water sector programs. The purpose of this volume is to outline such an approach by describing the concepts and tools of integrated water resources planning and management, with special reference to drinking water. Faced with a shortage of capital, as well as the need to improve the economic efficiency and environmental sustainability of projects, the role of the water supply and sanitation decisionmaker is becoming increasingly more demanding. Of critical importance also is the identification and prevention or amelioration of a growing range of environmental factors, which impose economic and social costs throughout the economy. It is clear that successful and sustainable development can be achieved only by a rational and systematic integration of water-related socioeconomic, environmental and technical considerations within the broader framework of national macroeconomic and multi-sectoral policymaking. The recent emergence of transnational and global environmental concerns suggest that water resource analysts should develop an even wider perspective.

During the past few decades, significant progress has been made in the manner in which we comprehend, analyze and resolve conventional water resource issues. In this context, one central message of this volume is the importance of an integrated approach. Better management of water resources requires a comprehensive framework that systematically takes into account, multiple actors (ranging from multinational companies and international organizations to local citizens groups); multiple criteria (such as economic efficiency, basic needs-poverty, etc.); multiple levels of analysis (global, national, sectoral, and subsectoral); multiple constraints (including inadequacy of institutions and human resources); and so on.

The economic efficiency objective plays a key role in conventional water management. Thus, the efficient development of freshwater sources relies on least-cost investment, optimized water losses, and efficient operation of the enterprise (especially the physical plant). At the same time, on the demand side, the economic allocation of scarce water supplies should favor the highest value added users of water. Pricing water at marginal cost is an important decentralized market mechanism by which this efficient matching of multiple sources with multiple uses may be realized. We recognize the existence of other criteria or constraints, such as providing subsidized, affordable water to targeted poverty groups, that might lead decisionmakers to deviate from such a strictly efficient approach.

Environmental concerns of more recent origin, have given rise to two main corollaries. First, improving the management of water resources in the conventional sense, especially through the better implementation of recognized techno-economic principles outlined earlier, will already make a major contribution towards resolving the environmental issues. Thus, the more efficient development, conservation and use of freshwater will automatically reduce pressure on this scarce resource -- resulting in less overuse and pollution of water sources.

Second, certain specific aspects of the conventional water resource management framework summarized earlier, become even more important. The need for an integrated approach is strengthened by recognizing the holistic nature of water resources (e.g., river basin, watershed, or aquifer), and the practical complications that arise when such a complete physical system cuts across national, administrative, or sectoral boundaries. The efficiency theme also requires reinforcement. For example, the consequences of overpumping, pollution, and other types of mismanagement, for both surface- and ground-water sources, should be incorporated into the least-cost decisionmaking process. This in turn requires better understanding of the physical, biological, and social consequences of exploiting water sources, as well as improvements in the economic valuation of the costs and benefits of such impacts. Meanwhile, water quality and health impacts, sewerage, industrial discharges, and other environmental issues relating to water use, must be addressed also. All these environmental considerations could be incorporated into the water allocation process, either through pricing or other policy and regulatory instruments. More research, policy and implementation experience is crucial to systematically internalize these environmental impacts, along the lines described in this volume.

The International Drinking Water and
Sanitation Decade

The importance of the rational development of water resources and provision of adequate water supply services has been recognized worldwide. Thus, in 1980, the UN General Assembly proclaimed 1981-90 as the International Drinking Water Supply and Sanitation Decade. Governments were urged to provide all their citizens with clean water and adequate sanitation by 1990. The task was recognized as formidable. In 1980 some two billion people lacked adequate water and sanitation. Global coverage of water supply (defined as access to a safe and adequate water supply) stood at about 40 percent. Sanitation coverage (defined as access to a facility for the storage, transportation, or processing of waste) was lower, at about 25 percent. Coverage was lower in rural areas than in suburban areas and for lower income people wherever they lived (World Bank 1988).

During the course of the decade 1,348 million more people were provided with safe drinking water supply, of which 368 million resided in urban areas and 980 in rural areas. Similarly, 748 million more people (314 million urban dwellers, and 434 million people in rural areas) were provided with suitable sanitation services. Overall, the number of people without safe water decreased from 1,825 million to 1,232 million, while the number of people without suitable sanitation remained virtually the same at 1,740 million (United Nations, 1990). However, at the end of the Decade, it became clear that the original goal of supplying safe water and sanitation for all by 1990, had been reached only by a few countries. Indeed, there have been significant variations among geographic regions, both in levels of service coverage and progress during the course of the Decade.

From the viewpoint of environmental sanitation, the inadequacy of safe drinking water and sewerage disposal has dire consequences in the developing world (World Bank 1992). Currently, at least 5 million people -- mainly children under five years of age -- die annually of diarrhea, and among the general population almost a billion episodes of intestinal disorder occur. Some of the basic measures discussed in this volume could save about 3 million lives per year and reduce by up to 1 billion cases, the incidence of illness due to diarrhea, roundworm, schistosomiasis, trachoma, and guinea worm.

Water Supply Status in Developing Countries

General Characteristics

Tables 1.1 and 1.2 present coverage information for both water supply and sanitation, by developing region, from 1980 to 1990. They also contain

TABLE 1.1   Percentage of Total Population with Access to Urban Water Supply and Sanitation Services, and Average GDP per Capita in Developing Countries

Region	Water Supply			Sanitation			Urban Population (1990)	GDP/capita (1989 US$)
	1980	1990	2000*	1980	1990	2000*		
Africa	83	87	76	65	79	73	203	350
Latin America and Caribbean	82	87	89	78	79	79	324	2,000
Asia and Pacific	73	77	71	65	65	58	761	450
Western Asia (Middle East)	95	100	100	79	100	100	44	2,200
Total	77	82	77	69	72	77	1332	

* Most recent estimates.
Sources: United Nations, 1990. World Bank Data for GDP per Capita.
Note: The definition of adequate urban and rural water supply and sanitation varies across countries since it is related to local conditions.

projections for the year 2000. Because of data constraints, these numbers are indicative estimates. Given the wide differences in the characteristics of the developing countries, with populations varying from a few hundred thousands to over one billion, gross national product (GNP) per capita ranging from under US$ 150 to several thousands per annum, and a great variety of resource endowments and sociopolitical structures, it is rather difficult to generalize. However, some interesting points may be deduced from the tables.

At first glance, there may be some evidence to support a commonly held hypothesis -- that the extent of water sector services might be related to the GNP per capita, because higher incomes imply greater availability of resources not only for governments to provide water services, but also for consumers to purchase water. For example, the relatively low-income African countries rate rather poorly in terms of service in rural areas. However, this is not necessarily always the case. The Asia and Pacific region, which has substantially lower per capita incomes than Latin America or Western Asia, nevertheless had superior access to water supply and sanitation in rural areas, in 1990. Even within regions, the correlation between economic output and progress in water supply and sanitation is not very clear-cut.

Table 1.1 shows that overall, the level of urban water supply rose only from 77 to 82% between 1980 and 1990. Clearly, greater percentage coverage would have been achieved if not for the rapid rate of urban population increase -- which reached almost 60% in Africa and over 25% in the Americas and South and East Asia. However, even after the efforts of the Decade, the increase in urban population was such that the absolute number

TABLE 1.2 Percentage of Total Population with Access to Rural Water Supply and Sanitation Services, and Average GDP per Capita in Developing Countries

Region	Water Supply			Sanitation			Rural Population (1990)	GDP/capita (1989 US$)
	1980	1990	2000*	1980	1990	2000*		
Africa	33	42	47	18	26	31	410	350
Latin America and Caribbean	47	62	77	22	37	52	124	2,000
Asia and Pacific	28	67	99	42	54	65	2099	450
Western Asia (Middle East)	51	56	57	34	34	32	26	2,200
Total	30	63	89	37	49	58	2659	

* Most recent estimates.
Sources: See Table 1.1

of unserved persons increased by almost 15%. This means that in 1990, there were about 250 million urban dwellers who did not have access to safe drinking water supply. Assuming that the efforts of the Decade will continue, the number of unserved people will increase to around 500 million in the year 2000, and over 1.5 billion by the year 2020. Despite the rapid urban population expansion, the proportional levels of urban population with access to sanitation rose from 69% in 1980 to 72% in 1990.

For rural residents it is estimated that an additional 1 billion received access to an adequate and safe water supply (United Nations, 1990). However, this still leaves approximately 1 billion unserved. Nevertheless, there has been a rise in the overall level of service coverage over the 10 years up to 1990, from 30% to 63%. At the current rate of progress the coverage is estimated to attain a level as high as 89% by the end of the millennium (Table 1.2).

In 1990 it was estimated that there were still nearly 1.5 billion people in rural areas without access to an appropriate means of excreta disposal. Table 1.2 shows that the relative gain over the decade, as well as the projected increase in coverage is clearly below the progress made in rural water supply.

A general observation is that the urban sector remains better served than the rural sector for both water supply and sanitation. Coverage for water supply is generally superior to that for sanitation for both urban and rural subsectors.

Regional Conditions

An intra-region comparison reveals that in Africa, significant progress has been made in extending urban water supply and sanitation by 1990. However, the rural coverage is still poor and well below the global average.

Urban water supply and sanitation services provide relatively high coverage in the urban regions of Latin America and the Caribbean. However, the level of rural supply remains low, particularly in the sanitation sector.

The Asia and Pacific region has had to face the difficulties of rapidly rising urban populations. This phenomenon to some extent accounts for the fact that despite the achievement of extending services to an additional 180 million urban residents, urban water supply coverage has risen only 4 percentage points during the 1980s and is likely to drop 6% by the year 2000. Urban sanitation just kept pace with the population increase. The greatest achievement in the region has been in rural water supply, where coverage rose from 28% to 67% over the decade, and is estimated to reach near full coverage by the year 2000. Progress with rural sanitation coverage has not been so impressive, although it compares favorably with other regions.

The Western Asia region managed to provide all its urban dwellers with adequate water and sanitation services. However, the region is definitely underperforming as far as coverage of its rural population is concerned. The expansion of rural services barely matched the population increase.

Future Prospects

Population Projections and Resource Potential

Between 1990 and the year 2000, the population of developing countries is expected to grow by an amount greater than the total additional population served by the water and sanitation sector during the last water decade. Consequently, the level of both internal and external financing of investments in the water sector will need to be significantly increased if a sustained rise in coverage levels is to be achieved. As populations levels grow, communities already served by water and sanitation will place a greater strain on the water resources supplying their water needs and receiving their waste. Supply and treatment systems will need to be expanded and upgraded to cope with the increased demands made on them. In many cases, the resource potential of regions are already heavily exploited. In some of these cases there is over-exploitation, resulting in an accelerating deterioration of both the quantity and quality of service that can be provided. Most often, additional sources of supply are available, or alternative technologies for the collection, treatment and disposal of wastewater can be applied, but often they impose significantly higher economic, social and environmental costs at the local, regional and national level.

Table 1.3 gives a grim picture of projected water shortages in various parts of the globe. Falkenmark (1989) indicates that societies generally experience water shortages when annual renewable supplies become less than about 2000

TABLE 1.3   Examples of Water Scarcity

Region	Observations
Africa (North and East)	-Ten countries are likely to experience severe "water stress" by the year 2000, as growing demand will invoke increasing user conflicts. -Egypt, already near its limits, could lose part of the currently available freshwater from the Nile, as upper-basin countries develop the river's headwaters.
China	-Fifty cities face acute shortages, related to the increased difficulties of obtaining groundwater, given a 1 to 2 meter annual drop in the water table.
India	-Tens of thousands of villages face water shortages. -Large portions of New Delhi have water only a few hours a day. -Plans to divert water from Brahmaputra River have heightened Bangladesh's fear of freshwater shortages.
Middle East	-With Israel, Jordan, and the West Bank expected to be using all renewable resources by 1995, shortages are imminent. -Syria could lose vital supplies when Turkey's massive Ataturk Dam comes on line in 1992.
Soviet Union	-Depletion of river flows has caused the volume of the Aral Sea to drop by two-thirds since 1960.
Mexico	-Over-exploitation of groundwater, with pumping exceeding recharge by 40 percent, causes land subsidence in parts of the valley containing Mexico City.

Source: Postel, 1989.

m^3 per person while water demands are increasing as part of the development process.   Recent World Bank information indicates that in 1990, all Middle Eastern and North African countries fell short of this critical level, as well as five East African and four Southern African nations (WDR 1992).   In China, the East-West Environment and Policy Institute (1988) projects that the water demand for Beijing will increase by 50% over the next decade, at a time when most of the accessible water sources on the North China Plain have already been tapped.   In the Indian subcontinent, deforestation and denuding of critical watersheds, have destabilized the natural hydrological water cycle.   The results are that more rainfall runs off rapidly causing devastating inundations, and less of it percolates to recharge the aquifers which fulfil a natural buffering role in water management.   This loss of recharge, according to Bandyopadhyay (1989), explains why high rainfall areas now have to petition for drought relief. The World Bank (1987) predicts that, at the rate of current consumption growth, water demands in Israel and Jordan will exceed all renewable sources within six years. This will leave both countries with the politically difficult choice of shifting water away from farmers to supply domestic and industrial needs, or exploiting far more expensive sources of water.

Water shortages are seriously affecting many industrialized nations as well. The situation in certain parts of Easter Europe is precarious. For example, the annual renewable water available per capita was below the critical 2000 m^3 value in four of these countries (WDR 1992). Former Soviet planners hoped to save the Aral Sea (one of the largest fresh water bodies, which has shrunk to 40% of its original area during the last few decades), by reducing losses due to poor irrigation efficiency. Preventing further ecological havoc will require authorities to take some prized farmland in Central Asia out of production (Perera 1988). The Western US (especially California) has experienced unprecedented shortages of fresh water for both urban and agricultural in the late 1980s and early 1990s. In 1991, rationing measures were introduced by many water suppliers in California for their residential, industrial, commercial and irrigation customers. Residential rationing was as high as 50% in some urban areas, with households limited to a lifeline level of 50 gallons (190 liters) per day per person above which tariffs increased considerably. Cutbacks for irrigation customers varied between 30% and 100% over previous use. Industrial consumers received lower cut-backs of around 5%-10%. As an example of an urban conservation program, the City of Los Angeles introduced a six-phase mandatory conservation scheme in 1991 designed to curtail water use and impose penalties for non-compliance (LADWP 1991). Different percentage allotments of prior consumption are allowed at different phases (depending on water shortage severity) and lump-sum and pro-rata fines may be charged on consumption over these allotments (typically 15%-75% of a total bill, plus US$ 3-4 per billing unit of 100 ft^3 or 2.8 m^3). Phase Five imposes a cut-back of 25% over the 1986 base year consumption.

A good recent survey of urban water resource issues (Bhatia and Falkenmark 1992) shows that many developing countries have not developed policy instruments (either regulations or economic incentives) for either encouraging conservation of water or including effects which arise when one user affects the quantity and quality of water available to another. More specifically, the opportunity costs of using water are generally ignored, as are the costs of environmental degradation. As a result, from an economic viewpoint excessive quantities of water are used, and high levels of pollution are produced. In the absence of a policy framework which takes account of such externalities, human activities both cause and are affected by closely related water quantity and quality problems. There are many representative examples.

The surface and groundwater supplies used by the city of Bogota, Colombia are often contaminated by both microbiological, organic chemical and heavy metal pollutants. In most cases the culprits include agriculture, industry and human settlements in the watershed, and homes and industries in the city itself. In Tianjin, China, about 80% of the total wastewater flows untreated into open water bodies. As a result, surface and groundwater sources are very much polluted and cannot be used for domestic water supply. The cost involved in treating this water is much higher than the cost of bringing water from other sources (Leitmann 1991).

In the Ciliwung river in Indonesia, the average level of biochemical oxygen demand (BOD) was about 15 mg/liter, 150% higher than the norm (Budirahardjo and Surjadi 1990), while in the Sunter river, the level of BOD was about 28 mg/liter in 1985 -- at the confluence with the Cipinang (Binnie & Partners 1986). Moreover, at the river mouths to the Jakarta Bay, the level of BOD in some rivers exceeds the value of 90 mg/liter (Clarke et al. 1991). In the case of Ciliwung river, the water quality in the upstream area is acceptable for all purposes except drinking; however, in the downstream area after the river has passed Jakarta, the water cannot be used at all. The situation becomes even worse during the dry season when the flow is lower, since the amount of discharge going into the river remains constant all year round. A review of the water pollution levels in selected rivers in Java indicates that the level of fecal coliform is, in some cases, above 4,000 times the conventional standard. In the Cisadena river near the Tangerang Industrial Zone, the level of mercury was registered as 100 times the allowable level, and also excess levels of other toxic metals (cadmium, chromium and selenium) were observed (World Bank 1988).

In Tunisia, the largest surface-water reservoir in the country, which provides about half of the total available water resources (Sidi Salem), is suffering from pollution. Sewerage effluent and municipal waste dumped directly into this water body and the nutrients from agricultural run-off, are the causes for the insufficient penetration of solar rays, the reduced quantity of oxygen, and further eutrophication. All these effects help to propagate parasites, viruses and bacteria, and endanger fish and bird species, as well as other living organisms (Krause and Krist 1986).

Such environmental problems give rise to two distinct health problems. The "old" problems are the high rates of transmission of communicable diseases resulting from the use of inadequate quantities of poor quality water. The "new" problems are the health risks arising from contamination of water sources by synthetic organic chemicals, heavy metals, pesticides and other modern pollutants. These risks -- both old and new -- are particularly high for the poor, and constitute an important cause of the wide mortality differentials between the poor and rich in urban areas of developing countries.

Many other examples exist in which similar environmental and economic problems are emerging as a result of the unsustainable exploitation of water sources. The next section provides an insight into the complex interaction of water resources and environmental factors in Egypt and the Mediterranean.

A Case Example: Water Shortage and Environmental Degradation Effects in Egypt

The freshwater resources of the Mediterranean region are currently experiencing water stresses (or shortages) that are likely to afflict many other developing countries in the 1990s. This diverse region includes the coastal areas of North Africa, the Levant and southern Europe, and encompasses levels of economic activity which range from heavy manufacturing to traditional agriculture. Factors responsible for the area's precarious state of freshwater availability also vary. In the northern part of the region, for example, the heavily industrialized countries of southern Europe are faced with the problem of industrial pollution, which may jeopardize the future of major sources of potable water. In the south, tremendous population growth and agricultural pollution threaten to overwhelm a sustainable water supply. The situation in Egypt is quite typical, where water resource scarcity has been identified as the most serious environmental constraint to that country's urban and agricultural growth.

Although Table 1.4 shows Egypt's present water supply exceeding demand by a margin equal to 10% of supply, growing demand, uncertainty of future supply and increasing pollution make water stress a priority issue. Projections for the year 2000 claim that supply will be augmented by storage in coastal lakes, efficiency gains in agriculture, reduced outflows to the sea and operation of the Sudan Jonglei Canal. Supply will increase relative to demand, bringing the reserve margin (i.e., the fraction of excess supply capability over demand) to over 13%. But while these figures convey a sense of security, they generally fail to pay sufficient attention to implied infrastructure and other investment costs. According to the World Bank, the availability of water for further use by the year 2000 is contingent on substantial infrastructure investments and institutional efforts which are still at an early stage, and which have significant technical constraints and fiscal implications. Already, the proposed storage of 3.3 billion m^3 of water in the coastal lakes has been found infeasible for environmental and cost reasons, and some other methods of enhancing supply may in fact ultimately decrease the availability of usable water. In particular, there are minimum amounts of water which must be released into the sea, to prevent salinization of groundwater sources. In addition, uncertainty about completion of the Jonglei Canal because of civil

TABLE 1.4   Egyptian Water Supply and Demand (billions m^3)

	1987	1991	2000
Supply:			
Nile water quota	55.5	55.5	57.5
Underground water	3.1	4.0	7.9
Reuse of drainage water	4.6	6.5	7.0
Water management		0.5	1.0
Saving of releases to sea through storage			2.3
Total:	63.2	66.5	75.7
Demand:			
Agriculture	46.7	50.7	55.0
Dom., Commer., Industry	7.4	8.8	10.0
Navigation	2.7	2.7	0.6
Total:	56.8	62.2	65.6

Source: Abu-Zeid, 1988.

war, and escalating demands from upstream countries for increased use of Nile waters, cast doubt on optimistic estimates of future supply.

The demand side of the Egyptian water balance equation is also unclear. Future industrial and municipal demand is uncertain, as projections range from 3 to 10 billion m^3 in 2000. The country's water supply network is aging and inadequate, and water losses in some areas exceed 60% of gross production. As tourists consume over three times as much water per capita as urban Egyptians, conservative estimates expecting the tourist industry to host 72% more visitors in 1999 than in 1987, are cause for concern. A potential crisis is foreseeable in Alexandria, where World Bank estimates show that demand will far exceed supply by 2000, and that the freshwater balance will also be negative. In an effort to accommodate an expanding population, prospering tourist industry and agricultural efforts in the Sinai Peninsula, additional infrastructure including five pipelines is currently being planned or built.

But exploiting more water from the ecosystem in an attempt to satisfy a growing economy must take into account environmental effects. In fact, the fastest growing and most unpredictable threat to sources of water seems to be environmental degradation throughout the Mediterranean region. This is caused by overuse of naturally replenished water resources and can lead to saltwater intrusion, brackish groundwater, falling water tables, and chemical imbalance (see Section 4.4). This in turn raises the cost of water reuse as increasingly sophisticated and expensive technology is required to maintain the quality and usability of water resources.

A rapid increase in the use of fertilizers and pesticides is causing severe environmental damage. Fertilizer use has soared since the 1960s, when the

Aswan Dam was completed and began depriving Egypt's soil of the fresh silt which had previously traveled downstream. The rate of fertilizer and pesticide application is already one of the highest in the world, and total use is expected to increase about 50% in the next decade. Due to run-off and leaching, high levels of nitrate from these agricultural inputs and from animal and human wastes have been found in surface and groundwater. Present laws do not prohibit the use of some particularly dangerous pesticides, and enforcement is often weak where a legal framework exists.

Industrial pollution is also a cause of environmental degradation of water resources in Egypt. Several studies and surveys estimate that industrial effluent will increase about 2.5 times between 1985 and 2000, at an average annual rate of 8.8%. Water use by the chemical, steel and iron companies, which produce the most toxic wastes, accounts for over half of total industrial use and is expected to increase ten-fold by 2000. Because there is no provision for industrial sludge disposal, it is released directly into drains, lagoons, sewers or the ground. As a result, chemical pollution can easily reach surface and groundwater sources.

Domestic wastewater is discharged along with industrial wastewater into available water bodies without treatment. In 1985, the total volume of such wastewater totalled around 986 million m^3 adding considerable weight to the organic and inorganic loading of water sources.

Generalizing from the above information, most of the issues challenging Egypt's water resources are found throughout the Mediterranean region. Groundwater is being locally exploited in excess of natural rates of recharge, and in several urban and industrial areas this has led to saltwater intrusion and land subsidence. The supply of groundwater and surface water is also limited by pollution, which acts as a type of invisible constraint. In the southern Mediterranean countries, the use of fertilizers and other chemical inputs in the agricultural sector has doubled over the past fifteen years and is likely to increase as population expands, and demand for agricultural products and water increases.

More than 75 percent of the increase in the region's demand for fresh water in the near future will be in the southern countries. A study based on national statistics of the 1980s shows that the consumption index (the ratio of water consumption to estimated total water resources) was 7 percent in the North, compared with 51 percent in the South. Indeed, as water becomes more scarce and the environment is compromised, costs to consumers will rise. In turn, in Algeria, Egypt, Israel, Libya, Morocco, and Syria, the scarcity of freshwater resources is likely to become a significant constraint on development unless resources are allocated toward meeting current and future water demand and water stress planning.

The Changing Nature of Water Development Costs

According to the World Bank Water and Sanitation Sector Review for 1990, decisionmakers in developing countries in the coming decade will be faced with a number of problems. Because of the increases in water sector development costs, the effectiveness of available investment capital in terms of population reached or service level achieved will be increasingly reduced. According to the review, the main areas for concern are:

- the increasing demand pressure for water and sanitation services due to the high rates of population growth;
- the decreasing water availability and quality and attendant increases in supply costs;
- the inadequate mobilization of domestic financial resources and the limited international capital available; and
- the record of unsound investment and ineffective operational management and maintenance of existing facilities by sector institutions.

The real costs of meeting rising demands for all water users at an environmentally acceptable quality level is dramatically increasing throughout the developing world (Falkenmark et al. 1990). The three main symptoms are:

- the increase in the long-run marginal costs of supply resulting from the added expenditure necessary to maintain supply and sanitation services at their existing quality for those communities already covered;
- the incremental cost of upgrading and expanding existing supply and sanitation systems and bringing additional systems on line to satisfy the greater demands of growing communities already included within the coverage; and
- the increased per capita costs of supplying communities not yet covered due to the more complex technical, social and environmental factors affecting the exploitation of remaining water sources.

Since the incremental (or long-run marginal) costs of additional water supplies and methods of waste disposal will be considerably higher in most future projects, it follows that the number of people that can be reached with the same level of investment will decrease. A considerable proportion of these increased costs will be a product of growing environmental pressures exerted on water resources which makes it more difficult to obtain reliable, potable water. Clearly the most convenient and cost effective sites for water development have already been exploited and what remains are the technically or environmentally more difficult (and hence more expensive projects). While in most developing countries, water is not yet a scarce commodity (in absolute terms), the fact is that the technical solutions required to make the various unexploited sources available are increasingly expensive.

The most dramatic examples of rising costs are in growing urban areas, where the development of water resources cannot keep pace with the growth of demand (Cesti 1989). The costs of providing services increased in most regions between 1980 and 1985 despite the development of less expensive technologies. For example, the median costs of providing urban house connections rose 16% overall. The costs of supply though standposts rose by between 20% and 110% (WHO 1987). As indicated in Table 1.5, depletion of groundwater reserves has led to increases in production costs in diverse cities such as Amman (Jordan), Lima (Peru), and Mexico City (Mexico). Furthermore, groundwater depletion around the metropolitan area of Mexico City has resulted in severe problems of land subsidence and deterioration in water quality (see also Chapter 5). Groundwater contamination is the cause of increasing production costs in Shenyang (China) and in Manila (The Philippines--see also Chapter 13). Over-exploitation of the least-cost sources of surface water has led to the development of progressively more costly dams and reservoirs for the provision of urban water supply in Tunis and Sfax (Tunisia). These studies have shown that the average incremental costs of new supplies is typically more than twice that of existing supply sources.

As shown in Figure 1.1, in many developing country cities, new supplies have to be obtained from long distances (ranging between 50 to 180 kilometers), involving high investment costs for pipelines and pumping (Bhatia and Falkenmark 1992). Both the quantity and quality problems (pollution of surface and groundwater sources) have raised the costs of water supplies of adequate quality. Thus, the cost of a unit of water from the "next project" is often 2 to 3 times the cost of a unit from the "current project" (Figure 1.1). Increasing unit costs and scarcity of funds imply that an increasing number of urban poor will continue to depend on unreliable public supplies (piped sources or handpumps), or have to use surface and groundwater sources often contaminated by both "old" (microbiological) and "new" (organic chemical and heavy metal) pollutants. As a result, health problems and mortality rates will worsen. Further, the poor (mainly in peri-urban areas) have to either pay a high percentage of their income in obtaining water for basic needs, or reduce their already meagre consumption of water.

More than 130 million of the developing world's poorest lived in urban areas in 1988. About two-thirds of this total occupied squatter settlements -- 63 million in Asia, 28 million in Latin America and 9 million in Sub-Saharan Africa (Leonard et al. 1989). Most of these people depend on traditional sources of fresh water which are getting increasingly contaminated due to human waste, industrial effluent, and agricultural pollutants. As a consequence, many of them have to purchase safe household water for meeting their basic needs, from water vendors, at exorbitant prices.

TABLE 1.5   Examples of Increasing Long-Run Marginal Costs of Water Supply

City (Country)	Marginal Cost in US$ per Cubic Meter	Water Source	Reason for Increase in Marginal Cost
Shenyang (China)	0.04 0.11 (a)	Groundwater Distant sources	Poor water quality
Amman (Jordan)	0.41 1.33 (a) 1.50 (p)	Groundwater Reservoir Distant sources	Depletion of aquifer Insufficient surface water
Mexico City (Mexico)	0.53 0.82 (p)	Groundwater Distant sources	Poor water quality and land subsidence
Lima (Peru)	0.25 0.53 (p)	Surface/Groundwater Distant sources	Depletion of aquifer
Manila (The Philippines)	0.13 0.22 (p)	Groundwater Groundwater	Depletion of aquifer and saline intrusion
Tunis and Sfax (Tunisia)	0.21 0.54 (a)	Distant sources Distant sources	Insufficient surface water

(a) = actual cost
(p) = projected cost

Sources: Cestti 1989; Munasinghe 1990.

In general, the urban poor pay relatively high prices for water, and therefore spend a much higher proportion of their income on this basic need (compared with those in higher income brackets).   For example, in Port-au-Prince, Haiti, it was found that the poorest households sometimes spend 20% of their income on water (Whittington et al. 1987); in Onitsha, Nigeria, the poor were estimated to be paying 18% of their income on water during the dry season versus 2% to 3% for upper income households; in Addis Ababa, Ethiopia, and Ukunda, Kenya, the urban poor spend up to 9% of their income on water (Whittington et al. 1989).   Only 14% of the 8 million population of Jakarta received water through direct connections to the municipal system in 1988.   Another 32% bought water from street vendors who charged around US$ 1.5 to US$ 5.2 per cubic meter depending on the distance from the public tap.   In some cases, households purchasing from private vendors paid as much as 50 times more per unit of water than households connected to the municipal system (Lovei and Whittington 1991).

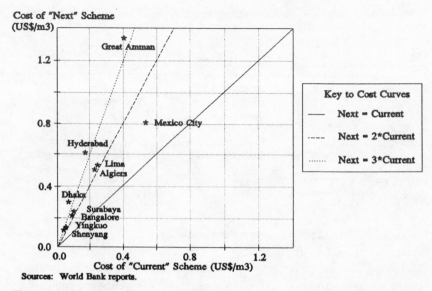

Figure 1.1 The Rising Costs of Water Supply -- Current Scheme Vesus Next Scheme (Costs in mid-1988 US$)

Allocation of Scarce Resources

The water supply and sanitation sector must also anticipate significant and growing clashes over allocation of water among competing uses like human consumption versus industrial and agricultural use. Intense competition will lead to significant increases in the real cost of water. As summarized in Table 1.6, the largest user of water currently is irrigated agriculture (WRI 1990). In the 1980s, this sector accounted globally for about 69% of all water withdrawal, whereas the share of industrial usage was 23%. Domestic water use was only 8% of the total. While middle income economies seem to conform to the average global numbers, the situation is distinctly different for the low-income countries. Here, more than 90% of all water resources are used for irrigation, while industry and domestic use only account for about 5 percent each. Meanwhile, in high-income countries, industry has the major share (47%).

However, incremental water demand for industrial use is growing much faster than agricultural demand in the developing world. Table 1.7 summarizes data on the relative growth rates of industrial and agricultural output. These rates can be used as rough indicators for water demand increase, since the demand for water is related to output. For all developing countries, industrial growth rates were twice as high as growth rates for agriculture. As would be expected, the largest relative differences are for

TABLE 1.6   Relative Water Withdrawals by Sector in the 1980s

Country Group	Water Consumption as a Share of Total Use		
	Domestic	Agriculture	Industry
Low Income	4	91	5
Middle Income	13	69	18
High Income	14	39	47
World	8	69	23

Source: World Resources Institute 1990.

countries with the lowest incomes. Table 1.8 gives an overview of the relative water scarcity in relation to the needs of crops, the human population and the total actual demand for 38 developing countries (Falkenmark et al. 1990).

The foregoing vignettes of existing water scarcities and rising supply costs suggest that the overall strategies for water supply and sanitation should be shaped by sound water resource and environmental principles -- although the focus for the 1990s and beyond must be on those still without services. In particular, increasing water demand and consequent discharge of greater volume of waste, threaten the quality of limited water resources.   One important challenge of the 1990s will be the large-scale implementation of water and sanitation programs in poor communities in cities and rural areas worldwide, using appropriate technologies and service levels.

Investment Prospects for the 1990s

In addition to the growing shortage of physical water resources, there are also serious issues concerning the   availability of financial resources to expand services. Table 1.9 shows the projected investment (in 1990 US$) for the six year period 1985-90 to meet national coverage targets for the urban and rural sectors. A total of US$ 86.50 billion (or almost US$ 15 billion per year, on average) was the estimated investment for attaining national goals by the Water Decade's end. These national target levels were, in most cases, significantly below the United Nations' official target levels of coverage. By comparison, the World Bank loaned a total of only about US$ 4.5 billion for water and sewerage projects over the six fiscal years ending June 30, 1990, as illustrated in Figure 1.2. If contributions from other bilateral and multilateral sources are included, the total foreign aid that flows to the water sector in the developing countries would not have greatly exceeded US$ 1 billion per year (or less than 10% of the above investment needs). Thus the bulk of the required investment

TABLE 1.7 Relative Growth Rates in Industrial and Agricultural Output in Developing Countries (1965-1987)

Country Group	Industrial Output (1) %	Agricultural Output (2) %	Ratio (1)/(2)
LOW INCOME	8.7	3.1	2.8
China/India	9.3	3.6	2.6
Other	6.9	2.3	3.0
MIDDLE INCOME	5.0	3.1	1.6
Lower middle	4.7	3.1	1.5
Upper middle	6.7	3.1	2.2
ALL DEVELOPING COUNTRIES	6.7	3.1	2.2

Source: Garn (private communication).

(now and in the 1990s) would have to be mobilized internally. The most recent data on this aspect indicates significant shortfalls.

Thus, investment in the water supply and sanitation sector continues to reach well short of the level required to provide services to all those currently unserved as well as the new population in developing countries. The World Bank (1990) recently summarized the public investment levels in 34 developing countries through the second half of the 1980s. These figures provide a broad impression of the degree of internal mobilization of capital. Investment in the sector averaged at a relatively consistent but low level of about 10% of total public investment or 0.5% of GDP. Whilst water sector investment held its absolute level as total public investment declined, this amount represents an investment of only around $20 per capita, a figure which includes expenditures on public sector, commercial, and industrial supplies as well as domestic coverage.

Contemporary barriers to achieving water supply and sanitation goals are generally no different from the traditional difficulties of the past (WHO 1987). The broad themes are:

- funding limitations;
- inadequate cost recovery;
- lack of trained personnel; and
- inadequate operation and maintenance.

TABLE 1.8   Water Scarcity in Relation to Plant Need, Population and Actual Demand

Country	Plant Need (a)	Human Need (b)	Actual Demand (c)
Algeria	x	x	x
Argentina	x		
Botswana	x	x	
Cape Verde		x	
China	x		
Colombia			
Costa Rica			
Cuba			x
Cyprus		x	x
Egypt	x	x	x
El Salvador			
Ghana		x	
Guatemala			
Honduras			
India	x	x	x
Iran	x	x	x
Iraq	x	x	x
Israel	x	x	x
Jordan	x	x	x
Lebanon	x	x	
Libya	x	x	x
Madagascar		x	x
Mauritania	x	x	
Mexico	x		
Morocco		x	x
North Yemen	x	x	x
Oman	x	x	x
Peru		x	
Saudi Arabia	x	x	x
South Africa	x	x	
Sri Lanka			
Sudan	x	x	
Syria	x	x	x
Thailand		x	
Togo		x	
Tunisia	x	x	x
Turkey			
Yemen	x	x	

x indicates water scarcity as follows:
(a) Water deficit exceeding 1000 mm/year in combination with interannual variability of rainfall of more than 40 percent.
(b) Annual water availability approaching 2000 cubic meter per person at year 2000. At that level societies typically experience "water stress".
(c) Actual demand beyond 20 percent of overall availability. According to European experience, large water management and investment problems tend to emerge when demands grow beyond that limit.

Source: Falkenmark et al., 1990.

TABLE 1.9   Estimated Capital Investment (as at December 1985) to Attain National
Decade Targets by 1990 (US$ millions)

Region	Urban		Rural		Total
	Water Supply	Sanitation	Water Supply	Sanitation	
African	2930.2	4765.0	2911.2	2301.3	12907.7
Americas	8625.7	8293.8	2257.6	807.2	19984.3
South and East Asia	5530.6	5234.2	2827.4	2405.3	15997.5
Eastern Mediterranean	11065.3	13158.8	6035.6	1824.2	32083.9
Western Pacific	1998.2	1624.0	1576.5	324.7	5523.4
GLOBAL	30150.0	33075.8	15608.3	7662.7	86496.8

Source: World Health Organization, 1987.

The shortfall in available capital investment for water and sewerage systems
is significant, and for all practical purposes this is not a problem that can be
adequately addressed even in the medium-term. Inability to generate revenues
within the water sector, coupled with rising costs partly caused by
inefficiencies of supply, exacerbate this problem. Inadequate cost recovery
and inefficiency due to lack of trained personnel are to some extent linked
because it is cost recovery that makes possible the adequate salaries and
improved working environments which attract and retain trained personnel
(Munasinghe 1988).   Thus, in many ways, the key to improving the
performance of the water and sewerage sector over the short- and
medium-term lies in the ability of public utilities to recover from their
customers an increasing percentage of the cost of providing services. This is
especially true since most developing country governments are so
overburdened with debt and persistent budgetary deficits that they are unable
to subsidize chronic shortfalls in the water sector.

The macroeconomic and water sector outlook for many developing
countries is clearly not favorable. Investments for water resource development
can account for up to 10 percent or more of all public investments, and debt
service burdens are often severe. The present climate of uncertainty regarding
a number of factors, including the future growth of the world economy and
export earnings to provide foreign exchange, interest rates, access to foreign
capital, and so on, have placed greater emphasis on a more systematic and
flexible approach to analysis and decisionmaking in all sectors of the economy.

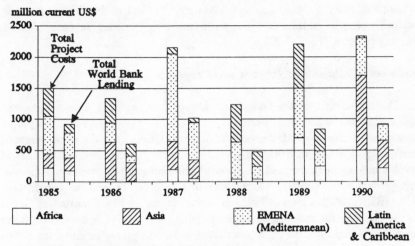

Source: World Bank, FY90 Water Sector Review.

Figure 1.2 Project Costs and World Bank Lending for Water Supply and Sanitation

Book Outline and Summary

The Overall Objective

In the light of the need for decisionmakers in developing countries to adopt a systematic and rational approach to water supply planning, this volume assesses the wide range of questions and issues facing the water sector today and in the future. The objective is to provide a comprehensive and balanced treatment of water policy analysis and planning in the context of environmentally sustainable development. The principal focus is pipeborne water supply, including key aspects of sewerage services.

Integrated Water Resource Planning

Chapter 2 clearly states the need for an integrated water resource planning (IWRP) approach and sets the hydrological, infrastructure, and policy context into which an efficient sector development plan must be woven. The role of water supply in the broader context of sustainable development is explicitly incorporated within the IWRP conceptual framework. IWRP involves four hierarchical levels of analysis (global-transnational, multi-sector macroeconomic, water resources sector, and water subsector-project), as well as the coordinated use of various policy tools for practical water management. A central theme in this publication is the systematic integration of environmental and social considerations into a sound, economic approach, without sacrificing sector financial viability. Critical to this approach is the adoption of efficient least-cost investment and long-run marginal cost (LRMC) pricing policies.

Economic Evaluation of Projects and Programs

The application of the framework begins in Chapter 3 with a thorough discussion of the economic evaluation of water supply projects and programs using the various tools of cost-benefit analysis (CBA). The use of cost-benefit analysis for project justification and to maximize the expected net benefits is explained. Commonly used cost-benefit criteria that are summarized include net present value (NPV), internal rate of return (IRR), and the benefit-cost ratio (BCR). Although no single test is the best under all circumstances, NPV is presented as the most versatile and reliable. Under certain conditions (i.e., equality of benefits), the least-cost criterion for comparing supply alternatives is equivalent to ranking on the basis of NPV.

The use of shadow prices to correct for economic distortions, is also described in Chapter 3, since without them, the true economic value of investment decisions, costs, and benefits cannot be judged. Efficiency shadow prices are used to ensure the efficient allocation of scarce economic resources, while social shadow prices may be used when income distributional considerations are particularly important. A convenient numeraire, and conversion factors that transform domestic market prices into border efficiency prices, are defined. The practical application of shadow prices is explained using simple physical analogies. A broad analysis of benefits is made including economic, social and intangible benefits. The willingness-to-pay of consumers, represented by the area under the demand curve, is presented as the correct measure of economic benefits. Discussions show how the incremental revenues from water consumption provide a minimum measure of benefits. The consumer surplus benefits may be estimated in terms of cost savings and increases in net output, while social gains and intangible benefits also may be included in economic evaluations on a judgmental basis. Adverse impacts on the environment that are quantifiable in monetary terms, should be included in the conventional CBA. However, unquantifiable environmental costs and benefits also should be considered through the use of other techniques involving multi-criteria decisionmaking.

Water Supply System Optimization

Water system optimization is the subject of Chapter 4, which contains a full breakdown of the components of an effective supply system and presents a broad approach involving net benefit optimization that implicitly includes social and environmental issues in the form of quantifiable service quality characteristics. Least-cost system supply planning receives specific attention with a detailed discussion of the planning of bulk production facilities, main pipelines, and the distribution network. The importance of reducing unaccounted for water as the single biggest source of efficiency improvements is stressed through a rigorous theoretical and practical discussion on loss management. Losses often comprise over half the bulk water supplied in developing countries. Technical losses are particularly high because of the relative neglect of distribution networks. Theft and inadequate metering and billing issues also need to be dealt with. A loss optimization model is developed based on the principle of increasing investments in the water system as long as these incremental costs are exceeded by the corresponding benefits achieved through savings in losses. The various practicalities and consequences of loss management are explained.

Environmental Considerations

A key theme in this volume is the role of environmental considerations in determining long-term economic and coverage sustainability of water supply improvements. This is the subject of Chapters 5 and 6, which orient planners to consider environmental management as being both a long and short-term cost-effective component of IWRP. The major environmental issues and their impact on surface and groundwater supplies are clearly and concisely described in a format accessible to decisionmakers. For groundwater, these include depletion through over-pumping, pollution from point and non-point sources, salinization of aquifers and withdrawal-induced land-subsidence. For surface water, the major issues are the negative impacts from river, dam and channel works, irrigation and agriculture, and industrial production. Chapter 5 concludes with a discussion of the major gains that could be made through improved attention to sanitation and health issues, especially among the poor.

The World Bank's approach to environmental impact assessment is presented as a general model in Chapter 6. Concepts and techniques for placing a value on environmental assets and impacts are assessed. Decisionmakers need a rationale for incorporating environmental externalities into their planning framework and project assessment. Chapter 6 provides this rationale by defining an environmental-analytical framework. Wider-scale global and transnational issues also receive attention to the extent that they influence or are influenced by the actions of decisionmakers in developing countries. This Chapter concludes with a description of policy instruments to address environmental issues, and an illustrative case study.

The Demand for Water

Chapter 7 focuses on demand-side issues. It gives demand analysis and forecasting full attention both in theoretical and practical terms. Evidence clearly indicates that many developing country projects are based on significant overestimates of demand growth, resulting in fiscal crises for many water agencies and an uneconomic use of scarce capital. A rigorous state-of-the-art assessment of demand is presented, and in particular its relationship to service and supply quality is explored. The critical role of demand analysis and forecasting is explained, in anticipating water needs for growth and development, and for improving the efficiency of long-lived and capital intensive investments. The most important practical approaches to demand forecasting, including time-trend extrapolation, econometric multiple regression, and field survey methods are described. Practical demand forecasting requires the use of different techniques to suit various circumstances, where necessary supplemented by judgement based on experience. The principal explanatory variables that affect water consumption are listed, followed by a review of recent demand analyses and projections in the developing countries. The model of water demand is explored for both residential and industrial/commercial consumers, and the key role played by service quality is identified. The case study of demand for water connections in rural Brazil and the effects of supply quality provides an illustration of these concepts.

Water Pricing

Since demand and price are closely related, the discussion of pricing in Chapter 8 picks up the main themes of the demand discussions and puts them into the context of tariff setting. The role of water pricing in demand management is fundamental. A basic static model is developed that establishes the optimal price equal to marginal cost. This model can account for long versus short-run marginal costs, peak load pricing, price feedback effects, and the environmental costs of sewerage services. These are all critical factors in effective tariff determination. The definition and calculation of the strict LRMC of water, and cost of consumer service, are described. Methods of adjusting strict LRMC to meet considerations relating to lifeline rates and subsidized prices, sector financial viability, metering and billing, and other sociopolitical constraints, are discussed. Tariff setting is presented as a multi-objective tool designed to influence demand, satisfy financial goals, and achieve important environmental and social goals. Some specific cost recovery objectives, mechanisms and limitations are presented. In particular the subjects of equity and benefit distribution are raised, and the dangers of a perverse bias in benefit allocation developing in favor of an advantaged minority are identified. A summary of special water supply pricing issues is given, including uniform national pricing, urban to rural or industrial to residential cross-subsidization, and second best adjustments. Two appendices to the chapter contain some detailed discussions of important numerical pricing procedures. Appendix 8.1 contains a detailed dynamic model that clarifies the peak load pricing result. Appendix 8.2 shows how water prices may be adjusted to compensate for both efficiency pricing concerns, and subsidized social prices.

Rural and Low-Cost Urban Water Supplies

Chapter 9 focuses attention on the specifics of rural and low-cost urban water supply development. As discussed previously, the International Water Decade directed considerable attention and financial resources towards redressing the disparities between urban and rural water and sanitation coverage levels over the last ten years. A review of rural water supply issues draws on a number of the discussions presented in Chapters 2 to 8. These earlier chapters mostly contain illustrations from the urban context, generally relating to conventional piped water supply systems. Chapter 9 points out the equal relevance of the various principles and analytical techniques to the planning and implementation of rural and low-cost urban water supply systems using an array of appropriate technologies. Technology selection, both in terms of cost and complexity, is an important issue and receives specific attention. A range of different technology choices for water extraction, storage, treatment and distribution are outlined. The effects of pricing and potential for community financing are considered.

Illustrative Case Studies

The volume culminates in a series of case studies that seek to practically illustrate the application of the analytical material presented in the earlier chapters. Thus Chapters 10 to 13 discuss some of the characteristics of water sector management programs in an African, Latin American, and Asian context as an illustration of the urgent need for an IWRP approach. In particular, these chapters provide an insight into the multi-faceted nature of the issues and constraints facing developing country decisionmakers, as well as the complex tradeoffs involved in making practical investment and planning decisions in the water sector.

References

Abu-Zeid, M. 1988. *Egypt's Policies to Use Low-Quality Water for Irrigation.* Cairo: Water Research Center.

Bandyopadhyay, J. 1989. "Riskful Confusion of Drought and Man-Induced Water Scarcity." *Ambio.* 18, No. 5.

Bhatia, R., and M. Falkenmark. 1992. "Water Resource Policies and the Urban Poor." Paper presented at the International Conference on Water and the Environment. Dublin.

Binnie and Partners. 1986. *Kali Sunter Purification Study.* Jakarta: Government of Indonesia.

Budirahardjo, E., and C. Surjadi. 1990. *Environmental and Health Problems in Jakarta.* Jakarta: Government of Indonesia.

Cesti, R. 1989. "Water Resources: Problems and Issues for the Water Supply and Sanitation Sector." Draft paper, INUWS. Washington DC: The World Bank.

Clarke, G., S. Hadiwinoto, and J. Leitmann. 1991. *Environmental Profile of Jakarta.* UNDP/World Bank/UNCHS. Washington DC: The World Bank.

East-West Center and State Science and Technology Commission. 1988. *Water Resources Policy and Management for the Beijing-Tianjin Region.* Honolulu: East-West Environment and Policy Institute.

Falkenmark, M. 1989. "The Massive Water Scarcity Now Threatening Africa: Why Isn't It Being Addressed?" *Ambio.* 18, No. 2.

Falkenmark, M., M. Garn, and R. Cesti. 1990. "Water Resources: A Call for New Ways of Thinking." Draft paper, INUWS. Washington DC: The World Bank.

Krause, P., and H. Krist. 1986. "Eutrophication in Northern Tunisia." *Aqua.* No. 2. pp. 98-102.

Leitmann, J. 1991. "Tianjin Urban Environmental Profile." Draft paper, UNDP/World Bank/UNCHS. Washington DC: The World Bank.

Leonard, H.J., et al. 1989. *Environment and the Poor: Development Strategies for a Common Agenda.* Washington DC: Overseas Developmental Council.

Los Angeles Department of Water and Power. 1991. *LA's Water Supply Situation and the Need for Mandatory Conservation.* Los Angeles: LADWP.

Lovei, L., and D. Whittington. 1991. *Rent Seeking in Water Supply.* Report INU 85. Washington DC: The World Bank.

Munasinghe, M. 1990. *Managing Water Resources to Avoid Environmental Degradation.* ENV. No. 41. Washington DC: The World Bank.

_____. 1988. "Contemporary Water Supply Efficiency and Pricing Issues in Developing Countries." *Proceedings of the International Conference on Cost and Price of Water in Urban Areas.* Paris.

Perera, J. 1988. "Kremlin Moves to Save the Aral Sea." *New Scientist.*

Postel, S. 1989. *Water for Agriculture: Facing the Limits.* Worldwatch Paper 93. Washington DC: Worldwatch Institute.

United Nations Environment Programme. 1990. *The Blue Plan: Futures of the Mediterranean Basin, Environment - Development 2000-2025.* Athens: UNEP Mediterranean Action Plan.

Whittington, D., D. Lauria, and X. Mu. 1989. *Paying for Urban Services: A Study of Water Vending and Willingness-to-Pay for Water in Onitsha, Nigeria.* Report INU 40. Washington DC: The World Bank.

_____, J. Briscoe, and X. Mu. 1987. *Willingness-to-Pay for Water in Rural Areas: Methodological Approaches and an Application in Haiti.* WASH Project. Field Report No. 213. Washington DC: Water and Sanitation for Health Project.

World Bank. 1992. *World Development Report 1992.* Washington DC: The World Bank.

_____. 1990. *Egypt: Environmental Issues Discussion Paper.* Draft paper, Washington DC: The World Bank.

_____. 1990. *The European Investment Bank, The Environmental Program for the Mediterranean.* Washington DC: The World Bank.

_____. 1990. *Water Supply and Sanitation -- FY90 Sector Review.* Infrastructure Department. Washington DC: The World Bank.

_____. 1988. *Water and Sanitation: Toward Equitable and Sustainable Development: A Strategy for the Remainder of the Decade and Beyond.* Washington DC: The World Bank. p. 16.

_____. 1988. *Industry and the Environment: A Preliminary Assessment.* Draft paper. Washington DC: The World Bank.

_____. 1987. "Global Water Scarcity," in Starr and Stoll, (eds.). *U.S. Foreign Policy on Water Resources in the Middle East.* Washington DC: Center for Strategic and International Studies.

World Health Organization. 1988. *Review of Progress of the International Drinking Water Supply and Sanitation Decade, 1981-1990: Eight Years of Implementation.* Geneva: World Health Organization.

_____. 1987. *The International Drinking Water Supply and Sanitation Decade: Review of Mid-Decade Progress* (as of December 1985). Geneva: World Health Organization.

World Resources Institute. 1990. *World Resources 1990.* Washington DC: World Resources Institute.

_____. 1986. *World Resources 1986.* Washington DC: World Resources Institute.

2

An Integrated Approach to
Water Resource Management

Water Resources Policy from a National Perspective

Water is a fundamental requirement for almost all human activities. It plays a pervasive and critical role in every national economy. Because of the substantial investments required to accelerate the pace of water resource development, government involvement of some type becomes necessary. It is not surprising, therefore, that most developing countries are pursuing water supply programs, as part of their economic development efforts. This in turn implies that there are significant advantages to examining water issues in the context of overall national policy objectives, and therefore a multitude of other problems and constraints also have to be taken into consideration. In other words, it is important to recognize that water supply problems cannot be considered in isolation, but must be analyzed in relation to the general socioeconomic matrix within which they are imbedded, and the resources available.

In view of the foregoing, water supply policy and planning should be developed within a framework that is:

- *Holistic* -- viewing water resources as an integral part of the national economy and natural resource base;
- *Realistic* -- based on the actual implementing capacity of the government, especially the managerial, skilled manpower, financial and physical resources available; and
- *Participative* -- with particular attention being paid to the design, implementation and monitoring of programs and projects, to ensure maximum involvement of beneficiaries and equitable distribution of benefits especially to low-income areas.

In most developing countries, it is clear that to achieve the greatest benefits, an integrated approach is required. More specifically, because of the many interactions and non-market forces that shape and affect the water resource sector in any economy, decisionmakers in an increasing number of countries have realized that water sector investment planning, pricing and management should be carried out using an integrated water resource planning (IWRP) framework which helps analyze the whole range of water resource policy options over a long period of time. In most developing countries today, spending in the water sector (all freshwater uses) constitutes 10% of all public sector investments as shown in Table 2.1. This comprises around 0.5% of total GDP. Yet, many face severe water problems and have achieved relatively low water and sanitation coverage, particularly for their rural populations (as shown by Tables 1.1 and 1.2 in Chapter 1). Even small improvements in the efficiency of supply development and resource utilization, therefore, would provide major benefits. This is especially true given the shortages in financial resources forecast for the water sector in the 1990s. How such improvements may be achieved is a main theme of this publication.

Water resources planning, broadly interpreted, denotes a series of steps or procedures by which the myriad of interactions involved in the production and use of water may be studied and understood within an explicit analytical framework. Planning techniques range from simple manual methods to sophisticated computer modelling. The complexity of water problems has forced increasing reliance on the latter approach. Water resource policy analysis is the systematic investigation of the impact of specific water policies or policy packages on the economy and society, at all levels. Water resource management, which includes both supply and demand management, involves the use of a selected set of policies and policy instruments, to achieve desirable patterns of water supply consumption and satisfy national objectives.

An important objective of many countries must be to upgrade the quality of water resource planning, policy analysis and management, especially in the potable water supply sector. However, the word planning, whether applied to the national economy or the water supply sector in particular, need not imply some rigid framework along the lines of centralized and fully planned economies. Planning, whether by design or deliberate default, takes place in every economy, even in those where market forces are dominant. Therefore, it is important to stress the distinction (as well as complementarity) between:

- the IWRP conceptual-analytic framework, which facilitates the process of coordinating water resource planning, policy analysis and formulation; and
- policy implementation, which is most effectively carried out using market forces and decentralized mechanisms (as discussed later in this chapter).

TABLE 2.1   Domestic Investment Profiles of Selected Developing Countries (Total and Water Sector Public Investment)

Country	Years	Total Public Investment as % of GDP	Water Sector as % of Public Investment	Water Sector as % of GDP
Algeria	1985-89	40.0	1.7	0.7
Bangladesh	1985-89	16.6	1.1	0.2
Brazil	1989	6.1	4.1	0.3
Colombia	1990	6.7	12.7	0.8
Dominican Rep	1989-91	9.2	4.8	0.4
Ecuador	1988	8.4	3.3	0.3
Egypt	1981-82	29.0	5.7	1.6
Guatemala	1990	4.9	5.6	0.3
Haiti	1986-89	7.0	9.3	0.6
Indonesia	1984-89	9.8	1.7	0.2
Jamaica	1989-90	11.9	5.8	0.7
Jordan	1986-90	21.9	8.6	1.9
Lesotho	1986-90	56.4	7.0	1.4
Peru	1986-90	8.2	7.5	0.6
Senegal	1987-90	8.7	13.5	0.9
Sri Lanka	1987-91	12.0	3.2	0.4
Syria	1986-90	21.2	5.5	1.2
Tanzania	1985-89	6.4	5.7	0.4
Uruguay	1987-89	5.0	3.6	0.2

Source: World Bank reports.

In water resource planning and policy analysis, the principal emphasis is on the detailed and disaggregated analysis of the water sector, its interactions with the rest of the economy, and the main interactions within the various water subsectors themselves. In particular, such efforts must also focus on methods of enhancing the effectiveness of water supply policy implementation. In order to better understand the role of planning, we begin by identifying below, some of the broad goals of water resource policy as seen from the national perspective.

Integrated Water Resource Planning

National Objectives

The broad rationale underlying national level planning and policymaking of all kinds is the need to ensure the best use of scarce resources, in order to further socioeconomic development efforts and improve the quality of life of citizens. Water resource planning and management, including water supply planning in particular, is a component of national economic planning. Therefore, water resource planning also must be closely integrated with overall economic planning and policy analysis, to meet many more inter-related and frequently conflicting national objectives, to the maximum extent possible.

The major goals of national water resources policy generally include most of the following objectives:

- determining and meeting the detailed water needs of the economy to achieve growth and development targets;
- choosing the mix of water sources to meet future water requirements at lowest costs;
- maximizing employment;
- conserving water resources and eliminating wasteful use;
- diversifying supply and reducing dependence on foreign sources;
- meeting national security requirements;
- supplying the basic water needs of the poor, many of whom are rural;
- saving scarce foreign exchange;
- identifying specific water demand/supply measures to contribute to possible priority development of special regions (particularly rural or remote areas), and priority sectors of the economy;
- raising sufficient revenues from water sales to finance water sector development;
- maintaining water price stability; and
- preserving the environment.

The Scope of IWRP

Management of the water sector to achieve desired national objectives must be accomplished through an integrated framework because of the many economic and environmental interactions between the water supply sector and other elements of the economy. Such an integrated approach will help decisionmakers in formulating policies, and providing market signals and information to economic agents that encourage more efficient development and use of water resources. Summarized in Figure 2.1 is a comprehensive approach to decisionmaking which emphasizes a hierarchical conceptual framework for integrated water resource planning and policymaking IWRP) that could be implemented through a set of water supply and demand management policies (Munasinghe 1990). Thus, this IWRP concept includes the three elements of planning, policy analysis and management, described earlier.

The first two columns of Figure 2.1 underline the complications facing decisionmakers in a modern economy due to multiple actors (with conflicting

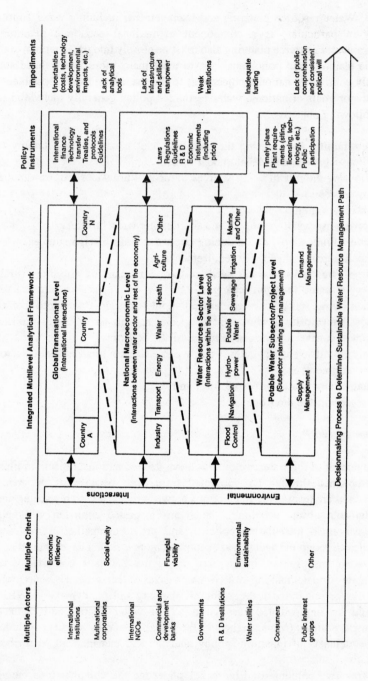

Figure 2.1 Integrated Water Resource Planning (IWRP) Conceptual and Analytical Framework

interests), and multiple criteria (or goals). However, the core of IWRP is the integrated multilevel analytical framework shown in the middle column of the figure. Although IWRP is primarily country focused, we begin by recognizing that many water resource issues have global linkages. Individual countries are embedded in an international economic and environmental matrix. Thus, both the world economy (through trade and financial linkages), and the natural resource base (through linkages via transnational water resources or global climate patterns) will impose an exogenous set of constraints and inputs on decisionmakers. The next hierarchical level in Figure 2.1 treats the water sector as a part of the whole economy. Therefore, water resource planning requires analysis of the links between the water sector and the rest of the economy. These links include the input requirements of the water sector such as capital, labor, raw materials and environmental resources. The linkages also include water sector outputs, and the impact on the economy of policies concerning water availability, prices, and taxes, in relation to the national objectives.

Some of these relationships are at the macro-level, such as foreign exchange requirements for water sector imports, or investment capital requirements for the water supply facilities. Others are more directly linked with and limited to specific user sectors. For example, policies specifically affecting the agricultural sector such as subsidies on farm inputs, guaranteed prices for farm products, or access to credit, may have as profound an impact on the demand for water as more overall and broad-based policies affecting water pricing, allocation, or supply management.

The next level of IWRP treats the water resources sector as a separate entity composed of subsectors such as potable water, sewerage, irrigation and drainage, hydropower, flood and drought control, navigation, recreation, fisheries and so on. This permits detailed analysis of the water sector with special emphasis on interactions among the different subsectors, possibilities for substitution, and the resolution of any resulting policy conflicts. One example of such interaction would be the tradeoffs involved in meeting the needs for irrigation, power production or navigation, from a single multipurpose reservoir. Furthermore, some of the water subsectors may interact directly with other major sectors, like sewerage with the health sector, or hydropower with the energy sector. Intimate knowledge of the hydrological cycle and its sub-cycles are important at this level in determining resource use strategies and the nature of important environmental externalities.

The final and most disaggregated level pertains to planning within each of the water subsectors. Thus, for example, the potable water supply subsector must determine its own demand forecast and long-term investment programs; the irrigation subsector, its supply sources, distribution canals, and likely agricultural demands; and so on. Again, knowledge of the hydrological cycle, the impact of human modifications and any resultant impacts is important. It is at this lowest hierarchical level that most of the detailed formulation, planning, and implementation of water supply projects and schemes are carried out.

In practice, the various levels merge and overlap considerably in the formulation and implementation of integrated water resource plans. Water-environment interactions (represented by the vertical bar) also tend to cut across all levels and need to be incorporated into the analysis systematically (see Chapters 5 and 6). Finally, spatial disaggregation may be required, especially in large and regionally diverse countries.

IWRP facilitates policymaking and does not imply rigid centralized planning. Thus, such a process should result in the development of a flexible, constantly updated water resource strategy designed to meet national goals. This national water strategy (of which the investment program and pricing policy are important elements), may be implemented through water supply and demand policies and programs that make effective use of decentralized market forces and incentives. Consequently, IWRP will lead to improvements in overall economic efficiency through better water resource management. As shown in Figure 2.1, a variety of policy instruments are available to decisionmakers, for instituting sound water management. The figure also summarizes the most important impediments that limit effective policy formulation and implementation.

Because of the importance of understanding the nature of the physical consequences of human interventions in the water cycle, we briefly examine this topic below, before returning to the problems of implementing IWRP.

The Hydrological Cycle and Human Interventions

In order to make informed decisions concerning the development of different water resources in a national context, integrated water resource planners require a sound understanding of the hydrological cycle, which is the driving force determining how water is distributed throughout the natural landscape. The size, nature and location of sources play a significant role in determining which resources can be exploited in an economically, socially and technically efficient manner. The interaction of the water sector with activities in other sectors can be determined only from a systematic assessment of the hydrological cycle.

In supplying water to consumers, modifications are necessarily made to the hydrological cycle. Water is taken from one point in the cycle by man-made mechanisms and used by consumers at another, with waste or surplus water being returned to the natural system. This can result in both upstream and downstream repercussions. From a water resources management point of view, these can be either positive or negative, depending on whether they make hydrological conditions more or less favorable for the purpose the water source was intended for. Thus, building a dam across a river will have a positive effect on the capacity of the river to supply peak daily, seasonal and annual water demands for users downstream. However, it may have a negative effect on the use of the river by other sectors for navigation, fish-breeding, or downstream irrigation. Waste returned to the river downstream may seriously pollute the waterway since the amount of flow let into the river from the dam is reduced compared to natural levels. An understanding of how the hydrological cycle functions and the impact that various human modifications can have is clearly important for planners. A comprehensive analysis of the cycle, therefore can help to provide a solid basis for making rational tradeoffs and water allocation decisions among different uses, and from different sources. Those tradeoffs and the environmental impacts that cause them are discussed in detail in Chapters 5 and 6.

The Hydrological Cycle

In his standard reference volume on applied hydrology, Chow (1964) defines the hydrological cycle as "by no means a simple link but a group of arcs which represent the different paths through which the water in nature circulates and is transformed." Figure 2.2 schematically represents the main elements of the hydrological cycle and the human management of some of these natural processes by means of hydraulic structures, storage and treatment facilities, and conveyance systems. As is clear from the figure, the hydrological cycle comprises a number of atmospheric, surface, and underground sub-cycles of different magnitude where water moves from and between the air, the vegetation, the soil, the solid rock, and the rivers, lakes and seas. Its interactive nature is described below.

Precipitation occurs where water vapor in the clouds condenses on suitable hygroscopic nuclei such as windblown dust, sea salt particles or products of combustion such as ash, exhaust fumes, and smoke (Pettersen 1964, Mason 1975, Shaw 1983). Many of the combustion products contain sulfurous and nitrous compounds resulting in the phenomenon of acid rain. Clouds are blown by the wind, transporting water vapor and nuclei from one location to another. As moist air rises and cools, clouds form more frequently. Precipitation falling on the land surface can enter a number of reservoirs and/or take a number of pathways through the landscape. It may remain as snow or ice in the form of a glacier or a temporary snow pack, or may fall directly into a water body such as a river, lake or the oceans, from which evaporation will occur. For example, Debski (1966) estimated that a combined 45 million cubic kilometers of water per year evaporate from all oceans. Evaporated water remains mainly unseen in atmospheric storage for

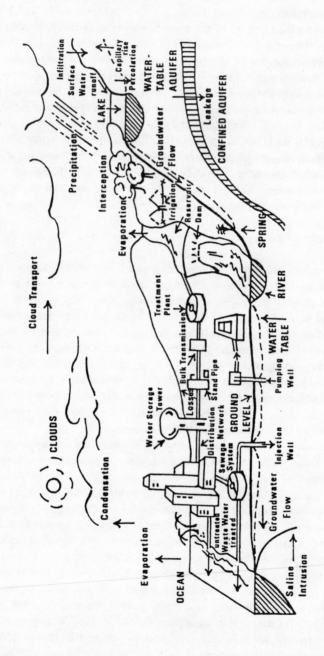

Figure 2.2 Typical Water Supply and Sewerage System and Its Role in the Hydrological Cycle

an average of about ten days before it condenses back to the liquid state in the form of clouds (Shaw 1983).

Rain may do one of four things: it may evaporate back into the atmosphere; it may be intercepted by vegetation; it may infiltrate into the soil; or it may runoff into rivulets, streams, rivers, lakes and eventually, perhaps, into the oceans. Rain intercepted by vegetation will either evaporate or trickle slowly down to the ground. Precipitation that infiltrates into the ground, does so because the soil has the capacity to absorb water and transmit it through the interconnecting air spaces between soil particles. In some cases, rain or snowmelt will occur at a greater rate than the capacity of the soil to infiltrate. In this case, surface runoff will occur. Alternatively, all water will be infiltrated and may percolate down to the unweathered bedrock below the soil layer. Some may return up to the surface by capillary action as the soil dries and water evaporates back into the atmosphere. Some water may be taken up by plants and transpired through their leaves back into the air. This is all part of the evapotranspiration process from the soil. When an impermeable layer is encountered by percolating water, the rock or soil layer above may saturate and a water table will form, rising up towards the surface as more water percolates down. Some water may slowly move to bedrock below the impermeable layer wherever leakage occurs.

Where a bedrock layer is very porous and holds a lot of water, an aquifer is created. Water will flow through an aquifer in a downward direction along the hydraulic gradient of the water table. This is groundwater flow. The volume and rate of flow will depend on the permeability of the rock or soil which is determined by the size and connectivity of pore spaces. Where the water table intersects the land surface, water will flow back out on the surface to form springs, rivers, or lakes. In some cases, where water flows in a bedrock layer which dips below an impermeable confining layer, water can flow up to the surface under considerable pressure through cracks in the rock as artesian springs, or else through boreholes drilled down through the confining layer.

As described above, water can flow across the surface either due to surface runoff from precipitation, or else from re-emerging groundwater. What form this flow takes, how far it travels, and how it is finally stored depend on the size, shape, and slope of the land surface and the kind of vegetation and surface material covering the land. Surface water flow also depends on the length and intensity of precipitation and the antecedent weather conditions. On steep, converging hills with little vegetation, water will form fast-flowing streams and rivers and may cause surface erosion, and on shallow undulating ground, water will form slow-moving rivers, ponds and lakes. Where these surfaces are already wet due to previous precipitation, runoff will be more instantaneous and long-lasting. The longer, larger, and more intense the rainstorm, the more likely it is that surface runoff will occur.

Human Modifications and Their Impacts

As indicated earlier, humans interfere in the hydrological cycle in many ways and for a variety of purposes. The two main are to provide inhabitants of a region with a controlled water supply for domestic, industrial and agricultural uses, and thereby, to control the energy of water: reducing erosion of the land surface; preventing flooding; generating electric power; facilitating transport; and so forth.

For water supply purposes, engineers must modify the natural patterns of surface flow to improve the amount, timing and geographic distribution of water available to the population. Access is an important factor, and engineers may build large storage and transfer structures such as aqueducts, canals, bulk transmission pipelines, distribution networks (to house connections and standpipes) and boreholes, through which water can flow by gravity or be pumped up to population centers from a distant source. Of particular significance to the design of these systems are the daily, seasonal and annual variations in demand for water. Engineers must often construct large storage reservoirs that are capable of fulfilling these variable needs. For example, the total river flow over a given year may be more than sufficient to supply the total needs of a population. However, the rate of flow may be too small to supply peak demand during the day, or summer flow may be less than the summer demand, because the bulk of water flows through the river in the winter months. The answer to this problem in engineering terms is to build a dam at some point upstream to capture river flow and build up a stored volume sufficient to supply daily or seasonal demand. If the total river flow varies greatly from year to year, for instance in a drought-prone region, the extra flow in wetter years can be stored in the reservoir for use in drier years.

Dams and reservoirs, and smaller storage tanks such as water towers are therefore necessary for a controlled release of water over time in a manner that facilitates a reliable supply of water. However, there are often conflicting needs. River flow is needed for more than just potable water supply. It may also be used by wildlife, for recreation, for transport, for power generation and so forth, and such needs may be in conflict with water supply purposes. Consequently, it may be possible to get only a fraction of the water needs of a population from river dams. Other water must be extracted from the ground using pumping wells bored into water-bearing aquifers, or piped from remote mountain or artesian springs. The management of groundwater reservoirs is more difficult because the physical characteristics of aquifers are difficult to measure, compared to surface sources, and may vary substantially over short distances. To reduce water intakes from sources, water can be conserved by reducing demand or by re-using wastewater either through treatment or by substituting it for fresh water where quality is less important (e.g. for cooling). However, water can also be lost unproductively from the man-made water infrastructure by uncontrolled leakage out of pipes or reservoirs. In some cases, water may be purposely leaked back into the source at key locations for its protection, for instance, to keep aquifers from turning salty where saline intrusion occurs due to over-pumping or reduced groundwater flow to the coast. This artificial recharge takes place through injection wells that pump water into the ground or more usually by seepage from recharge basins.

Because most water is taken from natural sources, the quality of the water is not usually appropriate for drinking directly from the source. Treatment at treatment plants is required before use. Runoff over the surface can pick up a range of harmful or distasteful materials including silt, agricultural chemicals, oil residues or human faecal waste, depending on the route it takes, the characteristics of the catchment area and how the water is used upstream of the water supply intake point. If the source is not protected, pollutants may be discharged directly into it by other users such as factories, power stations or sewerage works. Similar problems result from irrigation, which is necessary when the evapotranspiration demands of a crop cannot be met satisfactorily by naturally occurring precipitation. In addition to meeting crop water demands, good irrigation practice provides for extra water to leach out any salts accumulated by agrochemical inputs. Drainage water containing the leachates will enter back into the hydrological cycle and may affect downstream water sources.

Good environmental practice requires treating wastewater before dumping it into water sources or the ocean. Unfortunately, wastewater treatment remains the exception rather than the rule in many developing countries. This is especially true in cases where the incremental costs of exploiting new water sources appear to be less than the corresponding costs of treating and reusing wastewater.

Groundwater may pick up a number of harmful substances during its passage through the soil and rocks. Whilst rocks and soil may sometimes filter all impurities out of the water making it perfect for drinking, in other cases, water may pick up ions that require removal in treatment plants. Some chemicals that are taken up close to the surface, such as radioactive substances, fertilizers and pesticides, toxic hydrocarbons or bacteria, may reach harmful levels in the water, depending on the distance and time travelled from the point of pollution. Impurities may be introduced directly into the aquifer also from pit-latrines or by leachate from underground storage tanks used for industrial chemicals, petroleum products, or hazardous waste.

The amount and timing of runoff production and the amount of groundwater can be affected by major changes in the landscape characteristics exerted outside the water sector, for example by construction or agriculture. Deforestation, urbanization, and landscape modification can all change the pattern and timing of runoff and percolation in a way that significantly alters the size and yield of water sources. Where evapotranspiration or the amount and type of condensation nuclei are also changed in a particular region, micro-climatic modifications can occur resulting in reduced or acidic rainfall. Due to urbanization, the increased impermeability of a significant proportion of the land surface will increase the total and peak runoff and the velocity of runoff flow. This in turn will change the regime of surface water courses (Lazaro 1979, Hall 1984). Also, urbanization could lead to a net increase in groundwater recharge relative to pre-existing land use. An exception may be the case where irrigated agriculture is displaced by urbanization (Foster 1988).

Water-Related Environmental Issues

Human interference in the hydrological cycle is becoming increasingly important and must be considered as part of the overall picture facing the water supply planner. As illustrated, many such interactions are an integral part of the water supply infrastructure, but others may be designed to satisfy needs of related sectors of the national economy that make use of the water sources. Regardless of origin, each use of water has a cost significance that either reduces or increases the net costs of performing the economic functions of each. The costs that one user can impose on another, without payment of compensation can be termed environmental externalities. What may have a positive cost impact (a net benefit) for one sector (e.g., the cheap and convenient disposal of industrial waste into a river that reduces the production costs of a major export factory), may have a negative impact (a net cost) for another sector (e.g., the cost of treating river water at the intake to remove toxic chemicals before providing water to consumers). The benefits and costs of such impacts can be both short and long-term. For the water supply sector, the costs of human intervention are those actions that result in deterioration in the quality, quantity and reliability of water in a given source. The benefits come from interventions that make sources larger, higher yielding, more reliable and cleaner. These impacts, both short and long-term, must be taken into account as part of any water resource planning, policy analysis and management program.

Since the subjects of environmental management and the need to account for quantitative and qualitative externalities of economic and social significance are playing an increasingly important part in water supply economics and IWRP, they are discussed extensively in Chapter 5.

IWRP Implementation

The concept of economic efficiency should play a key role in formulating and implementing a water resource strategy. The basic principles of water economics and the concept of the economic value of scarce resources ties the entire analysis together. Efficient matching of the many alternative sources with multiple uses of freshwater requires ranking of sources by cost of supply, and prioritization of uses by value added in each water activity. The specific prerequisites for economic efficiency include both:

- efficient production of water, by ensuring supply at the least-cost through the optimization of investment planning and water system operation; and
- efficient consumption of water, by providing efficient price signals that ensure optimal water use and resource allocation.

This approach permits the decisionmaker to focus on policy alternatives, and assess tradeoffs arising from the deployment and use of otherwise non-comparable sets of resource inputs and outputs (including water) to meet conflicting policy goals. As far as the water sector is concerned, tradeoffs are reflected in the relative impacts of policies on supply, demand, water quality and prices in the short and long-term.

Sound economic planning is helpful in formulating policies that permit the economy to produce and consume water more efficiently, thereby maximizing net output and growth. Policy analysis provides an assessment of the real economic effects of adopting a given investment schedule or pricing strategy. Coordinated water resource planning and pricing require detailed analyses of the interrelationships between the various economic sectors and their potential water requirements, as well as the advantages and disadvantages of using the various sources of accessible water (such as rivers, lakes, reservoirs, deep and shallow aquifers) to satisfy these requirements on the other. Knowledge of the hydrological cycle and the impacts on it of human modifications is critical here.

Environmental externalities resulting from water and external sector policies must be taken into account to the degree that they affect the supply, demand, water quality and pricing aspects of policy implementation. The discussion applies both to the industrial world and developing countries. In the former, the complex and intricate relationships between the various economic sectors, and the prevalence of private market decisions both on the water demand and supply sides, make analysis and forecasting of policy consequences a difficult task. In the latter, substantial levels of market distortions, shortages of foreign exchange and human and financial resources for development, larger numbers of poor households whose basic needs somehow have to be met, greater emphasis on water problems, and relative paucity and poor quality of data, add to the already complicated problems faced by water planners everywhere.

Policy Instruments for Water Management

Water resources management comprises the practical steps that are taken to implement a given policy, through both supply and demand management, to achieve the stated national objectives of water resource development. Specific decisions concern service levels, coverage, quality control, prices, etc. Clearly, management involves continuous assessment of the impact of policies, and the modification of original plans as required, to achieve the stated national objectives. Since both internal and external conditions change with time, the planning process must clearly be flexible and subject to constant updates if goals are to be achieved or maintained. Five basic public policy instruments are available to manage the use of water. These policy instruments which should be used in a coordinated manner, are described below.

Physical Controls

Physical controls can be used as either a supply-side or a demand-side tool. As a demand-side tool aimed at physically limiting consumption, they are most useful in the short-run when there are unforeseen shortages of water. All methods of limiting consumption by physical means such as complete or rotating water cuts in the water supply subsector, and reducing or rationing the supply of irrigation water during specified periods, are included in this category. Demand-side physical controls are also used as long-run policy tools in some developing countries, but this is generally undesirable because water shortages often cause severe economic losses, for example, when farm output is curtailed by water failures, or public health is threatened by the poor quality of water supply.

On the supply-side, one long-run physical control policy tool is multi-year (or multi-season) reservoir operation. Modifying a flow regime using dams serves as insurance against unpredictable droughts or floods, depending on the geographical area and climatic conditions. Integrated long-run planning becomes indispensable when the reservoir has to meet the conflicting demands of a variety of user groups, e.g., providing a safe margin of empty storage to attenuate floods versus maintaining sufficient hydraulic head to meet peak hydropower requirements. The role of reservoirs in different sectors needs to be reconciled to use this tool effectively.

In order to offset negative environmental externalities and provide sustainable supply, another useful long-term physical control is the imposing of restrictions on the rate of withdrawal from deteriorating aquifers. Aquifers can be viewed as underground reservoirs of water (of relatively large size but low cost), with a much slower response time than the surface reservoirs mentioned above. In addition, the physical characteristics of the (invisible) aquifers, and therefore the repercussions of a certain management policy, are in most cases known with only a rough degree of certainty. Therefore, the operation of aquifers requires thoughtful planning over a long time span, if the policymaker wants to avoid irreversible depletion, saline water intrusion, groundwater contamination, land subsidence, or other undesirable effects. Recovery of aquifers generally takes decades and is prohibitively expensive, even in industrialized countries. Therefore, controls designed to ensure sustainable exploitation are important, in order to avoid significant increases in long-term supply costs (see Box 5.1 in Chapter 5, for an example of US Groundwater Protection). The types of externalities related to surface and groundwater source management are discussed in greater detail in Chapter 5.

Technical Methods

Technical means used to manage the supply of water include selection of the most efficient means of making water available, typically by choosing the least-cost or cheapest source for supplying water. Technology may be used also to influence water demand, for example, by introducing and promoting better water management techniques or water conservation equipment. Furthermore, technology can be more effectively employed in improving the planning and management process (e.g., use of microcomputer-based water system planning models). It is important that technologies selected for developing countries are appropriate for the social, economic, technical and environmental setting in which they are expected to function.

Direct Investments or Investment-Inducing Policies

Investment policies have a major effect on both water supply and consumption patterns in the long run. The supplying of new areas, extension of distribution networks, and building of new water purification plants, are some examples of such policies. It should be noted that since many investment decisions may well be undertaken by sectors other than water (such as the systematic installation of deep-well pumps for irrigation by the agriculture authorities), close cooperation between the water administration and planning authorities of these other sectors is obviously called for. Possible environmental externalities should be identified. One particular area of concern is the impact of private water users on a common water resource, for instance large-scale farmers who access drinking water sources with private equipment such as intakes and pipelines or deep pumping wells. They may make considerable investments in physical plant that might not appear in government statistics. Failure to regulate or manage this type of use may lead to overexploitation and degradation of water sources.

Education and Promotion

The policy tool of education and promotion can help to improve the water supply situation through efforts to make citizens aware of cost-effective ways to reduce water use, of the water use implications of specific appliances, and of the potential for economically beneficial tradeoffs between recurrent water costs and capital expenditures (e.g., to reduce losses through better maintenance of taps, etc.). Water losses and conservation can be significantly influenced by an effective education and promotion policy.

Pricing, Taxes, Subsidies and Other Financial Incentives

Pricing is a politically sensitive but effective means of demand management, including both the magnitude and pattern of water use, especially in the medium and long-run (see Chapter 7 for more details). However, pricing has limitations and must be skillfully combined with other non-price policy instruments for best results. For example, in rural areas that rely on traditional but unsafe sources and where there is no well developed market, pricing policy may not be effective. People who are unaware of the bad effects on their health of such free but polluted sources, may not wish to pay for safe potable water. In the case of very high-income consumers who are willing to pay an extremely high price for their comfort (e.g., lawn sprinkling), high prices might not reduce demand significantly, but could be used instead as a revenue generating mechanism. At the other end of the scale, raising prices to low-income water consumers may simply cause them to spend a greater share of their income for water purchases without affecting water use, because these consumers are already at the "basic needs" level and could not do without a minimum amount of water (e.g., for personal hygiene, drinking and cooking in homes). Such a water pricing policy would cause hardship by limiting the income available to poor households to purchase essential non-water items, whereas making available a lower cost and higher quality pipe-borne water could lead to an improved quality of life and reduced reliance on high-cost water vendors. Pricing may have less effect where significant water is consumed by unaccounted for and unregulated users employing private abstraction facilities.

One central theme in this publication is that pricing should be based, wherever possible, on marginal costs which is the economically most efficient situation. However, a number of constraints exist which make calculating marginal costs difficult. There may be severe market distortions due to taxes, import duties, subsidies, or externalities which cause market (or financial) prices to diverge substantially from the true economic opportunity costs or shadow prices (see Chapter 3 for details). Therefore, on the grounds of economic efficiency alone planners may have to make (second-best) shadow pricing adjustments. Furthermore, there often are severe income disparities and social considerations which call for subsidized water prices or rationing to meet the basic water needs of poor consumers, the majority of whom are rural.

Taxation and subsidies are useful policy instruments that also can profoundly affect water consumption patterns in the long run. For example, the imposition of duties or taxes on the use of certain water resources such as deteriorating aquifers may cause a significant shift to other supply sources, where such a substitution is deemed to be desirable from the national perspective.

Developing a Water Resources Strategy at a National Level

The success or failure of water supply activities in a developing country invariably depends on the extent to which a number of relevant issues have been systematically analyzed and addressed. The following aspects are considered to be essential prerequisites for an effective IWRP effort:

- *Having clear-cut national water sector objectives* -- the main objectives considered by developing countries have been listed previously. They are the starting point for developing a national water supply strategy which should take a longer run perspective (of at least 10 years). These objectives should not be rigid but should be continuously monitored and modified to meet changing priorities and to address new problems as they arise. The objectives may be influenced by factors such as local availability and costs of water and environmental externalities resulting from policies;
- *Consolidating a viable financing plan for water supply investments and recurrent costs* -- the adequacy of initial financing as well as continued flows of funds, must be verified through government and private equity contributions, local and foreign borrowing, and tariff revenues. Cost recovery is increasingly necessary both to ensure sustainability and to achieve greater coverage levels. The chances of obtaining more funds from a given source will be greater if it can be shown that the available funds are effectively used. At the same time, effective use of available funds holds down total costs and improves service quality, thereby increasing the willingness to pay of water users (World Bank 1990);
- *Creating an effective institutional framework for water supply* -- combining the three aspects of policy making, implementation and research and development;
- *Developing and applying suitable engineering and technical standards and design criteria* -- these should clearly be appropriate to local conditions and resource endowment. For example, standards for

handpump technologies have been evaluated by Arlosoroff et al. (1987) whereas Kalbermatten et al. (1981) provide a comprehensive compendium of a full range of appropriate water and sanitation technologies;

- *Devising and establishing procedures for planning, implementation, and follow-up of water supply programs and projects at the field level* -- some of the more important elements to be explicitly treated include, market surveys and water-use promotion activities, demand forecasting, least-cost system design and investment planning, project evaluation and cost-benefit analysis, environmental impact analysis, procurement and construction, pricing and connections policy, and supervision and evaluation of schemes; and

- *Maintaining an adequate level of supply quality, and ensuring satisfactory operation and maintenance* -- this clearly requires effective monitoring and greater responsiveness to customer complaints and needs. Community participation and management in system selection, development and operation is important in most rural and low-income urban situations.

One method of developing a national strategy for potable water supply strategy would be to start with the set of national objectives mentioned earlier in this chapter. For convenience, three broad strategic options or approaches that will influence and shape water supply policy, may be identified.

The first option is centered around the objective of economic efficiency, which implies optimal use of scarce economic resources to maximize output and growth, and therefore, places emphasis on the productive uses of water in activities. According to this strategic approach, areas that showed the greatest promise in terms of industrial, commercial and agricultural growth would be favored. Water prices would tend towards efficient levels based on the long-run marginal costs of supply, with subsidies (if any) being carefully targeted to poverty or other groups (sometimes on an interim basis). Cost recovery would be easier under this regime.

A second approach focuses on the satisfaction of the basic needs of citizens, providing water services to the poor, and improving the distribution of income and welfare. In this strategy, the more economically depressed regions and consumer groups would receive greater attention. Pricing policy would rely more on subsidies, and be based more on the ability-to-pay of low-income groups rather than supply costs or cost recovery.

The third major option is to reach as many consumers as possible, in the shortest possible time, using the least resources. This option is particularly relevant when investment funds are limited. With this strategy, it would be prudent to pursue water supply schemes in areas closest to existing sources and facilities, thus keeping extension costs to a minimum. Encouragement of private participation and investment in water supply would also be more desirable.

In practice, a single strategic approach is unlikely to dominate to the exclusion of all others. However, the relative weights attached to these different objectives are likely to vary significantly from country to country, thus giving rise to quite different or "mixed" strategies for water supply in each case.

As explained in subsequent chapters, specific decisions concerning the pace and timing of water supply, selection of areas to be supplied, investments, and pricing and connections policy, require detailed, systematic analysis. For example, projected national water supply targets over the planning period will depend on the current extent of water supply, the resources and implementation capability available, and the sociopolitical pressures for water supply in different areas. However, ad hoc, politically motivated interventions in water supply policy, especially in priority area selection, should be avoided, since they frequently have disastrous consequences. One of the most important reasons for establishing a systematic IWRP supply strategy is to minimize undesirable arbitrary interventions. Instead, quantitative criteria for ranking areas to be supplied with water may be developed and used in conjunction with other judgmental factors (see later chapters and case studies).

Sector Organization and Enterprise Issues

Institutional Framework

An adequate institutional framework for water resource policy formulation and implementation should have at least three well defined and balanced elements: policymaking, implementation, and research and development (R&D). Most often, all three aspects are muddled together, to the detriment of all. For example, senior water sector decisionmakers, who should be devoting a significant part of their time to major policy issues, are invariably embroiled in day-to-day crisis management. The academic and research communities frequently focus their interest on water problems that are neither significant nor relevant enough, from the national policy viewpoint. Finally, even when separate organizations exist for policy, operations and R&D, their efforts are uncoordinated.

Studies of institutional frameworks that have been successful elsewhere should be of considerable value to many developing countries that are seeking to restructure their water organizations. Usually, the existing line agencies such as water utilities are well able to attend to daily operational needs, while universities and research centers exist for R&D work. The weakest area is policy analysis and formulation. It needs considerable strengthening, especially since the heart of IWRP lies here. The special problems of water supply institutions are discussed further in the next section.

Clearly, one of the important determinants of the success or failure of water supply efforts in any country is the adequacy of the sector institutional framework to carry out this work. In developing countries, a wide range of organizational approaches for implementing water supply schemes may be found. They include:

- single national water supply authority with regional and local branches;
- different water utilities by regions, municipalities etc.;
- local bodies, such as municipal agencies or independent cooperatives; and
- combinations of the above.

Institutional structures vary from country to country, in the extent to which they are centralized, the level of involvement they offer to interested parties, and the methods by which they regulate use and finance their operation. France provides an interesting example of a fairly well specified water management structure in a market economy, as summarized in Box 2.1.

The types of organizational structures and ownership (public or private) that exist in the water sector today tend to depend more on historical accident rather than on deliberate design. For example, strong central water supply institutions were set up in countries where an individual ministry had a dominant influence in the earliest phases of water supply. In other cases, individual cities and towns set up their own institutions. Access to funds is a major problem whatever the organizational structure, especially for upgrading or maintaining existing systems. Excessive demand, subsidized pricing and the inability of customers to generate sufficient revenues all strain the financial resources of organizations. In developing countries, this is aggravated by limited government funds and limited access to capital markets. Revenue raised by the water sector may be returned to a central public investment pool rather than directly allocated for expansion or maintenance needs.

With many organizational structures, a clear picture of investment efficiency cannot be obtained. Difficulties in accounting may occur if water supply is heavily subsidized. Excessive cross-subsidies from urban to rural consumers via water tariffs, or deliberate neglect of urban networks to support water supply efforts, may occur and must be avoided. If the same utility is handling both urban and rural water systems, then at least the finances of the water supply schemes should be separated out, in order to determine their viability, pinpoint internal cross-subsidies and so on. Where municipal water supply agencies or cooperatives are created, they may require major and continuing inputs from the central water supply authorities for policy guidance, technical and financial support, and monitoring of performance.

Some typical water supply institutional structures found in a cross-section of developing countries, their responsibilities, and principal difficulties are summarized in Table 2.2. The selected countries illustrate the situation in the water supply and sanitation sector. As shown, these water supply institutions function within a varied spectrum of ministries. The responsibilities of the water authorities are in most cases well defined. Institutional problems, however, hinder the actual implementation of described tasks in all of the countries observed. Most of the water boards wrestle with a chronic lack of funds. In addition, organizations often lack experienced and well trained managers, planners, technical and operation and maintenance personnel, resulting in substantial delays in the execution of projects and sub-optimal system performances.

Although it is difficult to quantitatively evaluate the relative performance of different frameworks, one critical attribute that might be studied is the degree of centralization or decentralization. A separate central water supply agency will provide more drive and leadership, but may be more insensitive to and less able to adapt policies to local conditions in branches or subsidiaries in various cities and towns. Centralized agencies could have better access to outside funds, but decentralized water supply institutions (e.g., separate water utilities in different cities and towns) may perform better because of greater financial pressures. For example, they might be more in touch with local conditions and consumers at the grass roots level, thus enabling them to achieve higher connection rates, collect revenues more effectively, and minimize losses and theft.

Clearly, no single approach is suitable for all countries, given the wide socioeconomic, political, cultural, historical, geographic, and other differences that exist among them. However, in all cases, the chosen organizational design should provide the motivation, leadership and drive necessary to meet the challenge of satisfying water supply needs for the country's development.

In addition to the broad national requirements that are essential to ensure the success of water supply efforts (listed in the previous section), the institutions responsible for water supply must perform the more specific functions summarized in Table 2.3. In the initial stages of building up a water supply program, greater emphasis is desirable on centralized management, planning and financial activities. In particular, if the national strategy is entrusted to an agency which also has other responsibilities, then the centralized functions associated with the management, policy and programming, planning and design, operation and maintenance, and financial aspects of water supply, must be clearly identified and assigned to the staff implementing the water supply program. As water supply efforts develop and experience is gained, the focus may be shifted gradually towards more decentralized, localized operations and maintenance type functions.

TABLE 2.2 Typical Characteristics of Institutional Frameworks in the Water Supply and Sanitation Sector in Selected Countries

Country	Institutions	Affiliation and (Mode of Operation)	Responsibilities of Institution	Institutional Problems
Cyprus	(i) Department of Water Development	Ministry of Agriculture and Natural Resources (Centralized)	(i) - Planning, design, construction and maintenance of physical works - Delivering water to municipalities and irrigation user groups	- Inadequate planning
	(ii) Ministry of the Interior		(ii) - Exercizing legal authority	
Egypt	(i) National Organization for Potable Water and Sanitary Drainage	Ministry of Construction, New Communities and Public Utilities (Intention to decentralize)	(i) - Formulating policies for potable water supply and sanitation - Providing guidance to provincial governorates	- Fund raising
	(ii) Urban and Provincial Governorates		(ii) - Operating urban and regional water supply systems	
Ghana	Ghana Water and Sewerage Corporation	Ministry of Works and Housing (Decentralized)	- Provision, distribution and conservation of water - Provision and operation of waterborne sewerage systems	- Delegating tasks of managing director
Haiti	(i) Centrale Autonome Metro-politaine d'Eau Potable	Ministry of Public Works (Centralized)	(i) - Operation and maintenance of water supply in Port-au-Prince	- Financial resources - Lack of management
	(ii) Service Nationale d'Eau Potable		(ii) - Operation and maintenance of water supply for the rest of the country	- No operational autonomy - Lack of trained personnel

TABLE 2.2 (continued)

Country	Institutions	Affiliation and (Mode of Operation)	Responsibilities of Institution	Institutional Problems
Uruguay	Administracion de las Obras Sanitarias del Estado	Ministry of Transport and Public Works (Decentralized)	Water supply and sanitation for the entire country except for sewerage services for Montevideo	- Lack of technical staff - Personnel regulations
Yemen	(i) Public Water Corporation	Ministry of Planning and the Public Water Corporation (Centralized)	(i) Planning and construction, operation and maintenance of urban water supply	- Inadequate coordination between involved authorities - Inadequate planning
	(ii) Directorate of Local Government		(ii) Planning sewer systems	
	(iii) Local People's Councils		(iii) Operation and maintenance of sewer systems	
Zaire	(i) Regie de Distribution d'Eau	Ministries of Mining & Energy, and Portfolio (Decentralized)	(i) - Water supply in urban areas - Piped rural water supply	- Financial resources - Lack of trained personnel
	(ii) Service National d'Hydraulique Rural	Ministry of Rural Development	(ii) Non-piped rural water supply	
	(iii) Programme National d'Assainissement	Ministry of Environment	(iii) Planning and implementation of sanitation programs	

Sources: World Bank 1988a, 1988b, 1988c, 1988d, 1989a, 1989b.

TABLE 2.3   Essential Functions of a Water Supply Agency

1. Policy and Programming
   (a) Integration with National Plan and Budget
   (b) Program Formulation and Reviews and Management Information Flow
   (c) Establishment of Tight Appraisal Norms, Realistic Demand and Cost Estimates and Scheduling

2. Planning and Design
   (a) Load forecasting
   (b) Budgeting and Financial Planning
   (c) Market Identification
   (d) Inter- and Intra-Sectoral Coordination
   (e) Engineering Planning
   (f) Project Design
   (g) Monitoring and Evaluation

3. Operation and Maintenance
   (a) Maintenance Identification and Repairs
   (b) Reliability
   (c) Maintenance Feedback and Design Improvements
   (d) Inventory Control

4. Financial
   (a) Accounting
   (b) Record Keeping
   (c) Billing
   (d) Connection/Disconnection
   (e) Consumer Relations and Load Promotion

5. Construction
   (a) Right-of-way Clearance
   (b) Construction
   (c) Procurement
   (d) Project Cost Control
   (e) Quality Control

6. Staffing
   (a) Supervision and Staff Functions
   (b) Personnel Planning
   (c) Benefits, Salaries and Promotion Policy
   (d) Training
   (e) Consultants and Contractors

Coordination of water supply policy and implementation should be maintained on a continuous basis. Very often, a lax attitude in the initial stages of water supply, which encourages many diverse activities and programs (often supported by different foreign donors), may result in duplication or conflicts that will be much more difficult to resolve later, once these separate programs have matured to a significant extent. Project implementation, supervision, and follow-up, especially with regard to the quality of maintenance, is another area where the agency in charge of water supply must maintain vigilance at the field level. Finally, information feedback, including management information systems (MIS), and the continuous training, upgrading and retention of staff, including incentives and attractive working conditions, ought to be ensured within an effective institutional framework.

France: An Example of a Well-Defined Management Framework

The 1963 Law on Water established a water management system in France based on three principles. The first, that water management must take place within an appropriate physical framework, states that administrative units responsible for water should be delineated by watersheds and river basins, rather than by regional or local jurisdiction. In France there are six such basins. Second, within each basin, user dialogue must be efficient, organized and representative of commercial, private and state interests. The third principle is that both consumers and polluters of water should be taxed.

In pursuing these principles of watershed delineation, user dialogue and financial accountability, water management in France has become highly institutionalized. In order to coordinate the involvement of 36,500 municipalities, 95 Departments, and 22 regions, as well as countless private interests, each of France's six water basins is served by a basin commission to provide a forum for user dialogue. The commissions are also responsible for collecting data, studying issues affecting local water supply, setting guidelines for water management and development, and resolving user conflicts. Dialogue on a national scale takes place within the National Water Management Committee, which makes recommendations for national policy on water management issues.

The actual implementation of water management and development policies is directed by basin Agencies in each of the six basins. These financially autonomous organizations use economic incentives to encourage efficient consumption of water and lower levels of pollution. Each agency is operated by a board of directors representing the national government, water users, locally elected officials and a representative from the corresponding commission. Fees collected enable the agency to allocate aid for priorities it outlines in a Five-Year Plan. The amount and type of such aid varies. It can consist of subsidies or loans to local authorities, farmers, industry, associations, or to any party undertaking a project in the private or public sector. Projects range from building and improving equipment to conducting research. Examples include wastewater treatment plants, water supply and sewerage networks, diminution of industrial waste, dams, irrigation wells, etc.

Dividing the country into watershed areas means that local authorities retain most financial, operational, and planning powers. Nevertheless, the national government plays a significant role in the direction of water resources policy on a country-wide scale. The Ministry of the Environment is in charge of the 'Water Police' which collects country-wide data on water and water-related taxes, and uses this information to enforce standards. Basin agencies are under the authority of the Ministry of the Environment, who names the director of each, while the chairman of each agency is picked by the prime minister. The state also has a representative in each department responsible for technical services of national ministries.

An understanding of how the basin agencies work toward pollution abatement can be gained from the example of a factory built a number of years ago. As the plant is not equipped with appropriate anti-pollution devices required by today's laws, it must regularly pay a heavy tax to the basin agency (note that in addition to pollution, users can be taxed for river flow modification and abstraction). After negotiations between the company and the state over measures necessary for a lower tax, an authorization decree is submitted for public hearings. Once the decree is approved, the company must design a plan to solve its problem within a given period of time. The costs of such measures are submitted to the basin agency which may then agree to pay a portion as an incentive to solve the problem. When the company succeeds in reducing effluents, it will qualify for a cut in the tax paid to the basin agency. If the problem is not solved within the time limit, however, the company will be taxed more heavily or may even be shut down.

In the case of a municipality, the process is similar. However, the terms of compliance often include a far longer grace period, and more flexibility in regulations. This is because municipal problems are on a far larger scale than industry problems. In addition, municipalities are uniquely qualified for subsidies from departmental, regional and state sources, to complement funding from the basin agencies.

Although municipalities are free to set up their own services to deal with water supply and sanitation, they often obtain such services from a company which specializes in the field. In France there are several such firms which have a great deal of experience (e.g. Generale des Eaux, Lyonnaise des Eaux, Societe d'Amenagement Urbain et Rural). Private companies provide water management services to more than 17,000 cities and towns, and in 1989 over 70% of the population was served by the private water suppliers.

Efficient Operation of Enterprises

Unfortunately, the performance of water supply institutions in many developing countries has deteriorated in the past few years. Problems (often interlinked) that have plagued these institutions include: the inability to raise prices to meet revenue requirements, weak planning, inefficient operation and inadequate maintenance, high losses, low supply quality and frequent shortages, poor management, excessive staffing and low salaries, poor staff morale and performance, and excessive government interference, etc. Concurrently, there has been a shift towards large monolithic state-owned water enterprises in the developing countries. This trend has been based on reasons such as: scale economies, improved coordination, reduced reserve margins, nationalization and elimination of foreign ownership. Although some of this rationale is still valid, new options for improving enterprise efficiency are being increasingly explored. Many groups have an interest in water management, including consumers, polluters, special interest groups, legislators, and bureaucrats. Together with social customs and historical precedent, these groups influence water management, and in many countries have an institutionalized role.

Of the difficulties plaguing developing country water enterprises, undue government interference in organizational and operational matters may be the most pervasive. Such interference has resulted in loss of management autonomy, and is at least partly responsible for the other problems mentioned above. In order to address these difficulties, an important principle must be recognized, that given the complexity of water problems and the scarcity of resources and managerial talent in developing countries, each set of issues should be dealt with by that level of decisionmaking and management best suited to analyzing the difficulty and implementing the solution.

This hierarchical approach corresponds closely to the analytical framework developed earlier. Thus, political decision makers, senior government officials and ministry level staff would do better if they focused on critical macroeconomic and water sector strategy and policy, in order to determine the global expectations of water sector performance. The senior management of the enterprise, appropriately buffered by an independent board of directors, could then conduct their daily operations free from government interference, to meet the overall national policy objectives and targets within regulatory guidelines. As far as possible, the enterprise management should be assured of continuity at the top, even in the face of political changes. Decisionmakers should discuss any relevant national goals with the management, especially the extent to which government finds it necessary to trade off efficient pricing and investment policies against broader sociopolitical objectives. While the enterprise is provided wider autonomy, it would concurrently become more accountable in terms of performance measured against an agreed set of specific objectives and monitored indicators.

Major changes in enterprise management may be required to mirror changes in the external environment discussed above. The enterprise's organizational structure may be inadequate. Administrative and financial controls might be loose. Management can be timid and lacking in objectives. There should be sufficiently comprehensive management reporting and information systems which address each level of management and ensure accountability. Long range planning and economic analysis responsibilities need to be clearly defined and assigned. Commercial forms of accounting must be instituted to help in assessing performance and making decisions. Billing and collection of receivables often need to be improved. Finally, decentralization of administration, and technical, operational, and commercial activity must keep pace with the increasing size of the enterprise.

The lack of skilled manpower for policy analysis and development, as well as hydrological analysis, water management and project implementation, are severe handicaps. Education and training programs have a vital role. Furthermore, specialists with skills in newer and complex areas of water supply and water resource planning and policymaking are likely to be more scarce, and therefore more valuable, than those having expertise in more conventional topics such as potable water production or sewerage treatment. Teams devoted to multi-disciplinary analysis of water supply problems (e.g., including technologists, economists, financial analysts, and other social scientists), should be built up. Adequate remuneration, job satisfaction, and funding for research and the associated infrastructure, must be provided, to ensure that those trained in these new skills, usually at great cost, are available to the government for reasonable periods of time, and not subject to brain-drain.

To maximize the potential of skilled manpower, a fundamental principle that will help to address some of the problems described above is delegation of authority. Very often, in developing country water enterprises, the senior management attempts to deal with all problems, and trivial issues often get more attention than critical ones. Provided that middle-level managers could be adequately trained and made accountable, senior managers could (by appropriate delegation of tasks) free themselves to deal with higher-level policy. This process would then be repeated down to the lowest working levels. Obviously, staff training and education, and performance incentives at all levels and stages of career would play a critical role in ensuring the success of such an approach.

Finally, the availability of modern analytical tools can significantly enhance enterprise efficiency. One example is the use of computer models. Work done during the last decade has led to the conclusion that a hierarchical modelling framework employing microcomputers might be well suited to more effective policy analysis and application, especially in developing countries. It is important to note that much insightful analysis may first be carried out manually, at a relatively simple level to derive useful first-order results. Later, as understanding of the system, data and local analytical skills are improved, more sophisticated computer modelling could be pursued.

Furthermore, while the computer models are being developed, water resource policy formulation should not be neglected. Key options may be examined using more conventional techniques, and appropriate decisions taken and implemented (e.g., on specific water supply schemes in priority areas, efficient water pricing, demand management and conservation, as well as choice of newer technologies). These early decisions will facilitate timely action on important issues, and they may be coherently incorporated into the longer-term national water strategy subsequently, when the more comprehensive computer runs are carried out. Great care must be taken to ensure that the models represent the real world as accurately as possible, and that they are designed to provide answers to typical questions that senior decisionmakers might ask.

Ownership and Financing

The natural monopoly characteristics of water enterprise functions, as well as the perceived national interest to use these companies as a general policy tool, are in many countries accepted as sufficient reasons for maintaining large public sector monopoly organizations. Nevertheless, the observed problems inherent in stimulating management of developing country monopoly enterprises to be cost conscious, innovative, and responsive to consumer needs, indicates a need for more fundamental change. It could be worthwhile to consider trading off some of the perceived economies of scale in some water enterprises, for new organizational and regulatory structures which would provide greater inherent incentives for management efficiency and consumer responsiveness.

Decentralization Options

The options for decentralization, variations in ownership and corresponding regulatory changes, are numerous. Options for private and cooperative ownership of water enterprises could include both local and foreign participation as well as joint ventures. As long as a given regulatory framework prevails, it can be argued that the form of ownership alone (private or public) may not necessarily affect operating efficiency. The main point is that, to the extent possible, the introduction of competitive market forces should be encouraged by full or partial divestiture of some government-owned enterprises. A first step could be for government-owned water enterprises to competitively contract out activities or functions better handled by others.

There are also opportunities for geographic decentralization. For example, larger countries can, and sometimes do, choose to have independent regional water companies. For example, water companies could be separated by municipality. If private participation were allowed, one advantage might be that at least the large water consumers could also be legitimate shareholders who would be concerned not only with service efficiency but also with the financial viability of the company (the case of France discussed earlier, provides a useful illustration). The next section examines the recent implementation of regional private monopolistic water agencies in England and Wales.

England and Wales: Protecting Water Customers
Under Private Monopoly Conditions

The Water Act of 1989 established a new regulatory framework to manage the recently privatized water sector in England and Wales. A Director General of Water Services was created along with ten regional Customer Service Committees to safeguard the interests of the consumer from monopolistic practices by the various water companies. These water companies operate regional monopolies facing few market pressures which would normally protect consumers from high prices or poor service (Byatt 1991).

The Office of the Director General seeks to 'secure reasonable returns on [the Company's] capital' whilst protecting the interests of customers. These interests implicitly include attention to environmental management issues, particularly the quality of drinking water, the health of the rivers and the status of beaches, all of which are significantly affected by the activities of the ten water and sewerage companies, and 29 water companies that make up the sector. The stated objective is to ensure that the water industry in England and Wales is the best and most efficient in the world.

The Office of Water Services (or OFWAT) run by the director general limits prices which the companies can charge consumers. Annual increases are linked to the retail price index (the index signifying changes in the cost of living based on the changes in price of a hypothetical basket of goods and services purchased by an 'average' consumer) and a factor 'K' allocated to each company on the basis of the investment schedules it must adopt to achieve the necessary standards of service. The water companies have existing ten year investment programs to ensure improved quality of service.

The K factor is judged on the basis of the investment required to achieve pre-selected values for three supply standards: water pressure, interruptions to supply and flooding from sewers. The indices used are:

- the population experiencing head pressures less than 10 m;
- the population experiencing interruptions longer than 12 hours; and
- the number of properties flooded by sewers more than twice every 10 years.

The average value of K will be roughly +5% for the next five years. The value of K is periodically reviewed and companies can appeal to have it increased when they adjust their investment schedule to install new plants, etc. The mechanisms of tariff collection have not yet been worked out effectively. Previously, they were generally linked to the rateable value of residential properties on a flat-fee basis. Since the rateable value has been abolished as a means of taxation, a number of options are considered possible including metering, a flat rate charge and a banded charge based on some characteristic of the property being served.

Effectively, the privately owned water companies are subjected to a multi-tier regulatory network. The three core regulators are the Secretary of State for the Environment (who regulates water quality), the National Rivers Authority (which regulates environmental management) and OFWAT (which regulates economic issues). However, companies are made responsible for monitoring their own performance and for submitting data to OFWAT. One mechanism for regulating companies is through comparative competition which is used as a substitute for free market forces. Companies are compared by OFWAT in terms of operating and capital costs and customer care, and are regulated accordingly. A longer-term perspective is adopted to allow for variations in the relative starting conditions of the various companies such as inherited capital equipment. Making comparisons is complex, since 15 of the water companies are owned by four holding companies, requiring careful selection of peer groups.

OFWAT also has a hand in monopoly and merger supervision linking with other government bodies including the Director General of Fair Trading and the Monopoly and Mergers Commission, to assess the affects on consumers of changes in corporate ownership. The Customer Services Committees appointed by OFWAT champion the interests of consumers by identifying the main concerns of customers, ensuring that complaints are dealt with, and advising OFWAT on appropriate charge levels for their respective companies. The committees help to ensure that companies refund individual customers £5 as a penalty if standards of service are not maintained such as keeping inspection appointments, answering complaints and issuing prior notice of interruptions.

Private Participation in Water Supply

Although efficient public enterprises do exist, recent research indicates that private firms tend to be more efficient, where markets and regulatory frameworks are effective. In a competitive market, the revenues accruing to the private enterprise are linked with costs through the price mechanism. By improving efficiency, the producer can reduce prices, outbid competitors and increase sales and revenues. This link between revenues and cost control, and hence efficiency, is often weak or absent altogether in public enterprises that do not operate in competitive markets. The public sector's area of competitive advantage lies in its capacity to correct for economic externalities, to protect common pool resources, to take an environmental management perspective and to organize or regulate natural monopolies (which may be privately owned). Since water supply has the characteristics of a natural monopoly, some government involvement is often justified to allocate monopoly rights, regulate prices, and monitor performance, and in some situations, to make the most costly capital investments (Triche 1990).

A water utility must have one key characteristic of any viable commercial enterprise - it must be feasible, in the context of appropriate legal, institutional and technical conditions, to specifically charge users of the service and to exclude non-payers. On the other hand, water supply also involves significant externalities in the form of health and productivity benefits for the economy as a whole (costs and benefits are discussed in detail in Chapter 3). Since some individuals may not be aware of the benefits or may not be willing (or able) to pay, an optimal level of water supply might not be produced or consumed without some public sector intervention in the form of subsidization.

Coyaud (1988) describes four types of institutional arrangements for private participation in the water supply sector:

* service contracts;
* management contracts;
* lease contracts; and
* concessions.

Under service and management contracts, a public entity contracts with a private firm for the provision of specific services. The public authority bears the full commercial risk under both contracts, and the compensation of the contractor is usually not directly linked to operational efficiency or cost control. In contrast, under lease contracts and concessions, commercial risks are shifted to the contractor. Under a lease contract, a private firm rents facilities from the public authority. The latter remains responsible for investments, while the lessee finances only working capital for operation and maintenance. The lessee has therefore an incentive to improve efficiency, but is not burdened with capital expenditures. A concessionaire must finance investments as well as working capital. Private provision of public services is discussed in detail in E. Berg Associates (1989).

As discussed earlier, France provides an interesting example of a tight water management framework in a market economy. Lease contract arrangements are widely used in France for water supply, sanitation and solid waste management services. The experience of French companies put them in an advantageous position to bid for lease contracts in some Western African countries under the institutional framework of joint foreign local enterprises. Examples are the urban water sector in Côte d'Ivoire, which has been operated during the last 25 years by a private company, SODECI, under a mix of concessions and lease contracts. Ownership of SODECI is divided between French interests (48 per cent) and Ivorian stockholders (52 per cent). One broad measure of SODECI's effectiveness is the unusually low level of losses (12% of water produced) relative to other developing and developed country water utilities (see Table 4.2. in Chapter 4). In the Republic of Guinea, a state enterprise, SONEG, owns the urban water supply facilities and has entered into a lease contract agreement with a water management company, SEEG, which is a mixed enterprise. In this case, 48 percent of SEEG is owned by the Republic of Guinea, and 52 percent by a consortium of French firms (Triche 1990).

Financial Options

Developing countries are turning increasingly to more innovative financing options, many of which have been used in the industrialized countries (Fano and Brewster 1982, Garn et al. 1990, Goldman and McKenzie 1989, Rao 1988, Roth 1985). Some of the financial instruments that are now being studied in third world nations include:

- non-recourse and limited recourse financing (or project specific financing);
- leasing of individual pieces of equipment or whole plants, by local or foreign investors;
- private ownership or operation of water facilities;
- counter trade, involving barter type exchange of specific export goods for water-related imports;
- novel financial instruments to finance local costs, often involving the creation of new financial intermediaries;
- revenue bonds, with yields tied to enterprise profitability;
- tax-exempt bonds;
- sale of water futures, that encourage large users to seek more stable longer term price contracts; and

- tradeable permits for water sources, especially groundwater.

Developing countries could also reduce the risk to private foreign investors by turning to the Multilateral Investment Guarantee Agency (MIGA) created in 1988 by the World Bank with an authorized initial capital of over US$1 billion (MIGA 1991). MIGA seeks to promote the flow of private foreign investment to developing countries, by providing guarantees (on a fee basis), against the following non-commercial forms of investment risk for external financiers:

- current transfer risk, arising from host government restrictions on the convertibility of local currency earnings and transfer of foreign exchange;
- expropriation risk, resulting from legislative or administrative action (or omission) of the host government that leads to loss of ownership and control of, or rights over insured investment;
- contract repudiation risk, when the outside investor has no recourse to an adequate forum, faces undue delays, or is unable to enforce a favorable judgement; and
- war and civil disturbance risk, when events like revolutions, armed conflict and sabotage result in damage to or destruction of project assets, and business interruptions that affect financial viability.

To conclude, the trend in the 1990s will be for developing countries to explore and implement increasingly decentralized and incentive-based organizational and regulatory frameworks, as well as innovative financing measures, in the water supply sector.

References

Arlosoroff, S., G. Tschannerl, D. Grey, W. Journey, A. Karp, O. Langenegger, and R. Roche. 1987. *Community Water Supply: The Hand Pump Option.* Washington DC: The World Bank.

E. Berg Associates. 1989. *Private Provision of Public Services, A Literature Review.* Country Economics Department. Washington DC: The World Bank.

Bower, T., et al. 1981. *Incentives in Water Quality Management: France and the Ruhr Area.* Resources for the Future, Washington DC. Baltimore, MD: Johns Hopkins University Press.

Byatt, I.C.R. 1991. "UK Office of Water Services: Structure and Policy." *Utilities Policy.* pp. 164-171.

Chow, V.T. 1964. "Hydrology and its Development," in: *Handbook of Applied Hydrology: A Compendium of Water-resources Technology.* V.T. Chow (ed.). New York: McGraw Hill. pp. 1-1 to 1-22.

Coyaud, D.P. 1988. *Private and Public Alternatives for Providing Water Supply and Sewerage Services.* World Bank Infrastructure and Urban Development Papers, Report INU 31. Washington DC: The World Bank.

Debski, K. 1966. *Continental Hydrology, Vol. 2: Physics of Water, Atmospheric Precipitation, and Evaporation.*

The Economist. 1989. "Storming the Barricade." *The Economist.* Oct. 14, pp. 69-70.

Fano, E., and M. Brewster. 1982. "Financing the Planning and Development of Water Resources." *Natural Resources Forum.* 6, pp. 289-305.

Foster, S.S.D. 1988. "Impacts of Urbanization on Groundwater." Unesco-IHP Proc. *Intl Symp Urban Water 88.* Duisberg, Germany.

Garn, H.A., P. Boerma and R. Cesti. 1990. *Financing Water Supply and Sanitation Services.* Infrastructure and Urban Development Department. Washington DC: The World Bank.

Goldman, H.J., and D. McKenzie. 1989. "Infrastructure Financing." *J. Water Pollution Control Federation.* 61, pp. 176-9.

Hall, M.J. 1984. *Urban Hydrology.* London: Elsevier Applied Science Publishers Ltd.

Kalbermatten, J.M., D.S. Julius, C.G. Gunnerson et al. 1981. *Appropriate Technology for Water and Sanitation.* 12 volumes. Washington DC: The World Bank.

Lazaro, T.R. 1979. *Urban Hydrology.* Michigan: Ann Arbor Science Publishers.

Mason, B.J. 1975. *Clouds, Rain and Rainmaking.* Cambridge University Press, 2nd ed.

MIGA. 1991. *Investment Guarantee Guide.* Washington DC.

Ministry of the Environment. 1990. *Water Management in France.* Mimeo. France.

Munasinghe, M. 1990. "Water Supply Policies and Issues in Developing Countries." *Natural Resources Forum.* pp. 33-48.

Oliver, J.L. 1990. *The Economics of Water Pollution Control in France.* Mimeo. France: Ministry of the Environment.

Pettersen, S. 1964. "Meteorology," in *Handbook of Applied Hydrology: A Compendium of Water-resources Technology.* V.T. Chow (ed.). McGraw Hill, pp. 3-1 to 3-39.

Rao, P.K. 1988. "Planning and Financing Water Resource Development in the United States: A Review and Policy Perspective," *American Journal of Economics and Sociology.* 47, pp. 81-96.

Roth, G. 1985. "Role of the Private Sector in Providing Water in Developing Countries," *Natural Resources Forum.* United Nations, 9, pp. 167-77.

Shaw, E.M. 1983. *Hydrology in Practice.* Berkshire, England: Van Nostrand Reinhold (UK) Co. Ltd.

Triche, T.A. 1990. *Private Participation in The Delivery of Water Supply Services: The Case of Guinea.* INUWS. Washington DC: The World Bank.

World Health Organization. 1987. *The International Drinking Water Supply and Sanitation Decade: Review of Mid-Decade Progress* (as of December 1985). Geneva: World Health Organization.

World Bank. 1990. *Water Supply and Sanitation - FY90 Sector Review.* Infrastructure Department. Washington DC: The World Bank.

_____. 1989a. *Republic of Ghana: Water Sector Rehabilitation Project.* Staff Appraisal Report No. 7598-GH. Washington DC: The World Bank.

_____. 1989b. *Haiti: Centrale Autonome Metropolitaine d'eau potable (CAMEP). Port-au-Prince Water Supply Project.* Staff Appraisal Report No. 7613-HA. Washington DC: The World Bank.

_____. 1988a. *Cyprus: Southern Conveyor Project for Water Resources Development (Phase II)*. Staff Appraisal Report No. 6649-CY. Washington DC: The World Bank.

_____. 1988b. *Arab Republic of Egypt: Second Alexandria Water Supply Project*. Staff Appraisal Report No. 7124-EGT. Washington DC: The World Bank.

_____. 1988c. *Uruguay: Water Supply Rehabilitation Project*. Staff Appraisal Report No. 6790-UR. Washington DC: The World Bank.

_____. 1988d. *People's Democratic Republic of Yemen: Al Mukalla Water Supply Project*. Staff Appraisal Report No. 6995-YDR. Washington DC: The World Bank.

_____. 1988e. *Zaire: Third Water Supply Project*. Staff Appraisal Report No. 7204-ZR. Washington DC: The World Bank.

3

Economic Evaluation of
Water Supply Projects and Programs

Background to Project and Program Analysis

As previously introduced, integrated water resources planning (IWRP) and policy analysis provides the essential framework for coordinating decisionmaking and policy throughout the continuous chain represented by the water subsectors, the water sector, and the macro-economy. The outcome of IWRP is a national water supply strategy which may be broken down into regional programs that are composed of individual water supply projects and schemes. Such a project or scheme is a basic element that is convenient to analyze. The techniques described below may be applied to discrete projects as well as to investment programs (or series of projects).

Projects must be evaluated because economic resources are not unlimited, especially in the developing country context. The decision to finance a water supply scheme implies that the scarce resources used for this purpose will not be available for some other project, such as a school or hospital. Moreover, even within a given water supply master plan, it will be necessary to rank individual schemes according to some accepted criteria and select the best ones, because the resources available are generally quite inadequate to undertake all possible projects. These criteria are usually closely related to the national policy objectives mentioned in Chapter 2. One of the chief tools for ranking development projects is cost-benefit analysis, described later.

Whilst some rough choices can be made when regional water supply priorities are being established at the national level, the final investment decision on a particular development project is usually made on the basis of a much more detailed, micro-level analysis. Project analysis from a national viewpoint is the preferred method of rationally allocating scarce productive resources among different sectors of the economy, and among individual projects within a given sector. Comparative analysis is required because every project that is accepted results in an economic opportunity cost represented by the value of output foregone when some alternative project is given up. In order to place water supply project decisions and economic cost-benefit analysis in its proper perspective, the next section briefly summarizes the general approach used by national governments, aid donors, and project financiers, within the context of the project analysis cycle.

The Project Cycle

The successful implementation of any development project usually involves a project cycle consisting of several well defined steps which include: identification, preparation, appraisal, negotiations and financing, implementation and supervision, and auditing (Baum 1978).

- *Project identification* - involves the preliminary selection of potential water supply projects that appear to be feasible and conform to national and sectoral development goals;
- *Project preparation* - may last one year or more. In this phase, the engineering-technical, institutional, economic, financial and environmental aspects of a proposed water supply project are systematically studied. At this stage, a potential external financier may provide staff guidance and financial assistance or help the national water supply authorities obtain other assistance to carry out the studies;
- *Project appraisal* - consists of a detailed review of all aspects of the project to confirm the investment decision. An appraisal report is prepared that comprehensively evaluates the project, in the context of the national and sectoral strategies, as well as the engineering-technical, institutional, economic and financial issues. Environmental impact assessment is also a key element which may affect the design of the project and even alter the investment decision (see Chapter 5). The economic evaluation itself involves several well-defined stages, including the demand forecast, least-cost alternative, benefit measurement and cost-benefit analysis;
- *Project negotiations and financing* - if foreign financial assistance is involved, the appraisal report may be used as the basis for negotiations during which the country and financier discuss the measures required to ensure the success of the project, and the conditions for funding which are usually included in loan agreements;
- *Project implementation and supervision* - implementation involves putting into effect in the field all finalized project plans. Supervision of the implementation process should be carried out through periodic field inspections and progress reports. Reviews of ongoing water supply projects help to continually update and improve implementation procedures; and

- *Project audit* - is the final stage of the project cycle, usually following full disbursement of funds. Project performance audits should be carried out by an independent group involving review of previous project documents and field visits, where appropriate. This analysis can yield valuable information to help improve the processing of future projects.

Economic Justification

In view of its importance, that part of project appraisal which covers economic justification of a water supply project is described below. As mentioned earlier, the first stage of economic analysis involves the preparation of a demand (or market) forecast, which is presented in Chapter 6. Subsequent stages which involve the least-cost alternative, benefit measurement and cost-benefit analysis, are inter-related and depend on the economic criteria described below. When project impacts cannot be economically quantified, multiobjective (or multi-criteria) approaches may be required, as explained in the final section of this chapter.

The two criteria most often used in the economic evaluation of investment projects (often side-by-side in a complementary analysis) are:

- *Maximization of net benefits* - this is the more general criterion, used in the cost-benefit analysis stage, to justify the use of scarce resources in a water supply project, rather than elsewhere in the economy. To make optimal inter- sectoral allocation decisions in such situations requires the explicit determination of all benefits and costs over the lifetime of the investment; and
- *Cost minimization* - this approach is used in deciding on the least-cost solution and eliminates the need to measure the value of the benefits provided. It assumes that a given level of demand must be provided in similar quantities and qualities, whatever the supply source. The question then becomes simply one of selecting the lowest-cost method of supplying water to consumers.

The basic objective function to be maximized here is developed in terms of net benefits or income, following usual cost-benefit practices. Maximizing net benefits leads to maximum economic efficiency in resource allocation. It is equivalent to minimization of economic costs, under the restricting assumptions mentioned earlier. Making efficiency, at least initially, the sole criterion for the choice among alternatives has obvious technical advantages. Thus the choice of efficiency as the goal provides us with an unambiguous ranking order among alternative water supply schemes. A project that yields more net income will be preferable to another that yields less, provided that we ignore the problems that are common to all objective functions, including the evaluation of uncertainty and risk, of unpredictable changes in technology and relative price levels, of the valuation of intangibles and non-marketed outputs, of positive or negative externalities or spillovers, and the troublesome issue of individual and collective time preferences.

However, from the viewpoint of consumers, it is not really income that we ought to maximize, but rather human well-being or satisfaction. The last two are represented in economic theory by the concepts of welfare or total utility of consumers. An analysis which tells us how to maximize income does not necessarily tell us whether or not we are also maximizing welfare. Because of the disproportionate number of low-income households and the existence of a significant non-monetarized sector in many developing countries, the analysis of efficiency may fail to focus on the critical issues of more equitable distribution of benefits. Nevertheless, the income maximization criterion could be defended if the government would be willing to achieve more equitable distribution patterns by redistributing income from the original beneficiaries to those whom the authorities feel to be more deserving. Another alternative is to use appropriate shadow prices as a weighting device, as discussed later in this chapter.

Despite the prevalence of such non-efficiency considerations, it still makes sense to begin by analyzing the efficiency solution. The reasons for this are two-fold:

- it is useful to know which of the various alternatives will yield the largest increase in total net income to the national economy; and
- an assessment of the costs of achieving various distributional or non-quantifiable objectives can be made only if we know how much additional income is guaranteed by the project.

As a basis for evaluating wider considerations, such as social or political issues, the theoretical maximum revenue attainable from the sector must first be calculated on purely economic efficiency terms. Following this, the impact of non-income oriented objectives can be judged since many of these impose an economic efficiency cost.

Ideally, the unweighted income maximization function should tell us which of the various alternative water supply strategies will result in the greatest net increase in real per capita or, perhaps per family income for the entire relevant population. The relevant population consists of those living within the decisionmaker's jurisdiction. If they are represented by a national government, then the analysis should provide an estimate of the net increase in real national income. If the decision is made by a regional government, then the income to be maximized should be the regional one.

Despite its shortcomings, one may conclude that an income maximization function is useful for the evaluation of alternative water supply investments. However, finding the most efficient solution by itself does not indicate which of the various policies are preferable in terms of overall community welfare. It only provides a tool that can be used to calculate how much total income must be sacrificed in order to include other and possibly broader social objectives. The efficiency measure provides a yardstick that may be used to measure the consequences of non-efficiency goals, even if it cannot indicate what their real cost is. It is useful to evaluate potential trade-offs between the multi-dimensional objectives that usually form part and parcel of any comprehensive national development program (for example, providing potable piped water to rural villages at high cost), and associated water supply strategy (for example, reaching the largest number of consumers at the lowest cost to the sector). Such an assessment would be facilitated, if the economic losses associated with the realization of non-efficiency goals were known.

As indicated, a more appropriate objective function may be formulated in terms of total net benefits, where net benefits represent the present-value excess of all social benefits over all social costs, and all required inputs have been treated as costs without further disaggregation. Such an objective function has as its goal the maximization of net social benefits resulting from a series of interdependent public and private activities. A crucial aspect is that it has to account for the opportunity costs or the value of foregone alternative outputs elsewhere in the economy. It also has to account for the fact that water supply users will try to maximize net income (or well-being) from water-derived outputs. This requires explicit evaluation of the total costs and benefits of water-use, i.e., from initial supply to final end-use.

Evaluation Criteria for Cost-Benefit Analysis

Economic cost-benefit analysis of projects is an important step in the appraisal of projects, and is critical when making a final decision regarding the acceptance or rejection of a water supply project. The following section summarizes some of the criteria commonly used in the cost-benefit test of a project, with the emphasis on economic evaluation. However, the economic criterion is not the only arbiter, since a number of other aspects including technical, institutional, environmental and financial criteria also need to be considered in project appraisal. The theoretical framework for economic evaluation described in this chapter is applied in the actual case studies described in Chapters 9 and 10.

Net Present Value

The most basic economic criterion for accepting a project is that the net present value (NPV) of benefits is positive:

$$NPV = \sum_{t=0}^{T} \frac{B_t - C_t}{(1+r)^t} \tag{3.1}$$

where B_t is the benefits in year t, C_t is the costs in year t, r is the discount rate, and T is the planning time horizon. Both benefits and costs are defined as the difference between what would occur *with* and *without* the project being implemented. The discount rate (usually in the range 6-12%) indicates that in the computation of NPV, costs and benefits incurred in the future have a lower weight or value than those in the present. If projects are to be compared or ranked, the one with the highest (and positive) NPV would be the preferred choice, i.e., if NPV_I is greater than NPV_{II} (where NPV_i is the net present value for project i), then project I is preferred to project II. For the comparison to be meaningful, the scale and objectives of the two project options should be roughly the same. The scale and scope of each of the projects under review must be altered so that, at the margin, the last increment of investment in any project yields net benefits that are equal (and greater than zero). Complexities may arise in the analysis of interdependent projects, because the implementation of one will affect the costs and benefits associated with the other and vice-versa.

Internal Rate of Return

The internal rate of return (IRR) may also be used as a project evaluation criterion. The value of IRR is determined by solving the following equation.

$$\sum_{t=0}^{T} \frac{B_t - C_t}{(1+IRR)^t} = 0 \tag{3.2}$$

Thus, the IRR is the discount rate which reduces the NPV to zero. The project is acceptable for financing if IRR is greater than the annual rate of interest (ARI), which in most normal cases implies that the NPV is greater than zero (i.e., ignoring abnormal cases in which multiple roots could occur). Problems of interpretation occur if alternative projects have widely differing lifetimes, so that the discount rate plays a critical role. Multiple roots of equation 3.2 may occur if the annual stream of net benefits change signs several times during the project lifetime.

Benefit to Cost Ratio

Another frequently used criterion is the benefit-cost ratio (BCR):

$$BCR = \frac{\displaystyle\sum_{t=0}^{T} \frac{B_t}{(1+r)^t}}{\displaystyle\sum_{t=0}^{T} \frac{C_t}{(1+r)^t}} \tag{3.3}$$

If BCR is greater than 1, then the NPV is greater than zero and the project is acceptable.

Selecting a Criterion

Each of the above criteria -- net present value, internal rate of return, and benefit-cost ratio -- has its strengths and weaknesses, but NPV is probably the most useful of the three. The use of IRR could be misleading for ranking purposes since $IRR_I > IRR_{II}$ does not guarantee that $NPV_I > NPV_{II}$, and similarly for BCR. On the other hand, a comparison of the IRR versus the discount rate is helpful in making judgements on pricing policy, if the average tariff is used as a proxy for incremental benefits, as shown in the Africa case study in Chapter 9. Also, the IRR and BCR provide some measure of the yield per unit of investment, which may be useful in ranking projects when there is an overall budget constraint. In practice, since they use the same basic data, all the different project criteria should be estimated in order to obtain a balanced project decision.

The Least-Cost Rule

The NPV test could be used to derive the least-cost rule. In the case of water projects, the benefits of two alternative supply systems are often equal (i.e., they both serve the same need or demand). Therefore, the comparison of alternatives is simplified to:

$$NPV_I - NPV_{II} = \sum_{t=0}^{T} \frac{C_{II,t} - C_{I,t}}{(1+r)^t} \tag{3.4}$$

Here, the two benefit streams $B_{I,t}$ and $B_{II,t}$ have been canceled out. Therefore, $NPV_I > NPV_{II}$, provided that:

$$\sum_{t=0}^{T} \frac{C_{II,t}}{(1+r)^t} \; > \; \sum_{t=0}^{T} \frac{C_{I,t}}{(1+r)^t} \tag{3.5}$$

In other words, the project which has the lower present value of costs is preferred. This is called the least-cost alternative (when benefits are equal). However, even after selecting the least-cost supply, it would still be necessary to ensure that the project would provide a positive NPV greater than for any other project, in order to justify any investment.

Introduction to Shadow Pricing

When making a purely financial analysis of water supply projects, the benefits, costs, and discount rates may be defined in simple financial terms. However, for economic testing, B, C, and r must be defined in economic terms and appropriately shadow priced using efficiency border prices. The shadow price represents the true economic value of a given resource. The border price is the equivalent local price determined in units of foreign exchange converted at the official exchange rate. Effective shadow pricing is a complex process.

In this section, we review the chief concepts and applications of shadow pricing used in economic cost-benefit analysis. Shadow pricing is an important element in the evaluation of water supply projects because it allows a more realistic valuation of the various costs and benefits associated with project implementation. Further details are available in the various publications on shadow pricing that are referred to in the text including Ray (1984), Little and Mirlees (1974), and Squire and Van der Tak (1975).

In the idealized, theoretical world of perfect competition, the interaction of atomistic profit-maximizing producers and utility-maximizing consumers give rise to a situation that is called pareto-optimal. In this state, prices reflect the true marginal social costs, scarce resources are efficiently allocated and no one person can be made better off without making someone else worse off. However, conditions are usually far from ideal in the real world. Distortions due to monopoly practices, external economies and diseconomies (which are not internalized in the private market), interventions in the market process through taxes, import duties, and subsidies all result in market (or financial) prices for goods and services, which may diverge substantially from their shadow prices or true economic values.

In the developing countries, market distortions are more prevalent than in the industrialized countries and so shadow pricing is especially useful. The goal of shadow pricing can be either efficiency- or socially-oriented. Efficiency shadow prices try to establish the actual economic values of inputs and outputs, while socially- oriented shadow prices take account of the fact that the income distribution between different social groups or regions may be distorted in terms of overall national objectives. Social policy calls for special adjustments, usually by giving greater weight to benefits and costs accruing to the poor (relative to the rich). The passive acceptance of the existing income distribution, implied by the reliance on strict efficiency criteria for determining economic welfare, may be politically and socially unacceptable if there are large income disparities. Bearing this in mind, in our analysis, we will place primary emphasis on efficiency shadow pricing, but will also make use of social shadow prices and social weights, mainly for determining subsidized water prices and lifeline rates (a full account of pricing theory and practice is presented in Chapter 7).

Besides marketed goods and services, nonpriced inputs and outputs also must be shadow-priced to reflect their economic opportunity costs. Major categories of such nonpriced inputs and outputs are public goods and externalities. Public goods are defined as those goods and services that are freely available to all without payment once they have been made available, such as a public road or police protection. Externalities are defined as beneficial or adverse effects imposed on one individual due to the activity of another. Often the originator of these effects cannot charge or be charged for their consequences (e.g., like air and water pollution). The valuation of environmental externalities provide an economic basis for environmental management in the context of long-term water sector policy implementation, as discussed in Chapter 2. Unfortunately, many externalities are not only difficult to measure in physical terms, but even more difficult to convert into monetary equivalents (e.g., to measure the "willingness to pay" of the parties affected by the externalities). Quite often, therefore, the approach taken is to bypass the externality evaluation process and impose regulations and standards, expressed in physical measurements only, that try to eliminate the perceived external damages (e.g., upper limits on effluent discharge levels). However, this approach may not be effective, because no attempt is made to compare the costs of compliance with the real benefits provided (i.e., damages avoided). Available techniques for valuing the economic impact of environmental effects are discussed further in Chapter 5.

Numeraire

To derive a consistent set of economic shadow prices for goods and services, as a means of valuing benefits and costs, a common yardstick or numeraire to measure value is necessary. This can be illustrated by a simple example.

If one wishes to compare bananas with grapefruit, the equivalent units might be either one banana for one grapefruit, or one kilo of bananas for one kilo of grapefruit. In the first instance, the common yardstick is one fruit; in the second, it is the unit of weight. Clearly, if the weights of the two types of fruit are different, the result of the comparison will depend on the numeraire used.

With a numeraire of economic value the situation is more complicated because the same nominal unit of currency may have a different value depending on the economic circumstances in which it is used. For example, a peso worth of a certain good purchased in a duty-free shop at the border is likely to be more than the physical quantity of the same good obtained for one peso from a retail store, after import duties and taxes have been levied. Therefore, it is possible to distinguish intuitively between the border priced peso, which is used in international markets free of import tariffs, and a domestic-priced peso, which is used in the domestic market subject to various distortions. A more sophisticated example of the value differences of a currency unit in various uses arises in countries where the current investment level is considered inadequate. In these instances, a peso-worth of savings that could be invested now to increase the level of future consumption may be considered more valuable than a peso devoted to current consumption.

The choice of the numeraire, like the choice of a currency unit, should not influence the economic criteria for decisionmaking except in relation to magnitude, provided the same consistent framework and assumptions are used in the analysis. For example, only one difference exists between a study using centavos as units and one using pesos (where the peso is defined as one hundred centavos). In the study using centavos all monetary quantities will be numerically one hundred times as large as in the one using pesos. Therefore, the numeraire may be selected purely on the basis of convenience of application.

Perhaps the most appropriate numeraire to use in a comparative analysis is a unit of uncommitted public income at border shadow prices. Essentially, this unit is the same as freely disposable foreign exchange available to the government, but expressed in terms of units of local currency converted at the official exchange rate. The border-priced numeraire is particularly relevant for the foreign exchange scarce developing countries (See Appendix 3.1 for details). It represents the set of opportunities available to a country to purchase goods and services on the international market.

Using Shadow Prices in Project Evaluation

The estimation and use of shadow prices is facilitated by dividing economic resources into tradeable and nontradeable items. Tradeables and nontradeables are treated differently. To effectively analyze the costs and benefits of a given project in economic terms, the inputs and outputs used in the productive process, along with the opportunity costs incurred in utilizing resources for that process must be calculated. As explained earlier, this is done by tallying all tradeable and non-tradeable items, as well as social and environmental costs and benefits, in standardized (border-priced) economic terms. The most important tradeable inputs used in water supply projects are capital goods while the most important nontradeable primary factor inputs are labor and land.

Tradeable Goods

The values of directly imported or exported goods and services are already known in border prices, that is, their foreign exchange costs converted at the official exchange rate. Locally purchased items whose values are known only in terms of domestic market prices, however, must be converted to border prices, by multiplying the former prices by appropriate conversion factors (CF). The determination of appropriate conversion factors to use for tradeables is discussed in Appendix 3.2.

Border(Shadow) Price = Conversion Factor x Domestic (Market) Price

$$BP = CF \times DP$$

For those tradeables with infinite elasticities (i.e. of world supply for imports and of world demand for exports) the cost, insurance, and freight (C.I.F.) border price for imports and the free-on-board (F.O.B.) border price for exports may be used with a suitable adjustment for the marketing margin. If the relevant elasticities are finite, then the change in import costs or export revenues, as well as any shifts in other domestic consumption or production levels or in income transfers, should be considered (see Appendix 3.2 on conversion factors). The free trade assumption is not required to justify the use of border prices since domestic price distortions are, in effect, adjusted by netting out all taxes, duties, and subsidies.

To clarify this point, consider the household shown in Figure 3.1, where a child is given an allowance of twenty pesos a month as pocket money. The youngster may purchase a bag of sweets from the grocery store at a price of two pesos. Since the parents want to discourage consumption of sweets, however, they impose a fine of one peso on each bag. The fine is exactly like an import duty, and the child must surrender three pesos for every bag of candy (valued at its domestic price, inside the household). From the family's perspective however, the total external payment for the item is only two pesos, because the one peso fine is a net transfer within the household. Therefore,

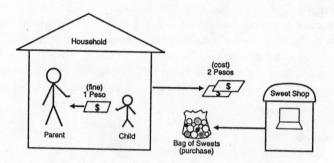

Figure 3.1 Household Analogy to Shadow Pricing of a Traded Good

the true economic cost, or shadow price, of the bag of lollipops to the household is two pesos (i.e., like the border price paid by the national economy), when the impact of the fine on the distribution of income between parent and child is ignored.

Nontradeable Goods

A nontradeable is conventionally defined as a commodity whose domestic supply price lies between the F.O.B. and C.I.F. prices for export and import, respectively. The domestic production costs of these commodities are therefore too high to export them abroad, but still lower than the relevant prices of competing imported goods in the domestic market. Items that are not traded at the margin because of prohibitive trade barriers, such as bans or rigid quotas, are also included within this category. If the increased demand for a given nontradeable good or service is met by the expansion of domestic supply or imports, the associated border-priced marginal social cost (MSC) of this increased supply is the relevant resource cost. If decreased consumption by other domestic or foreign users results, the border-priced marginal social benefit (MSB) of this foregone domestic consumption or of reduced export earnings would be a more appropriate measure of social costs.

The socially optimal level of total consumption for the given input (Q_{opt}) would lie at the point where the curves of MSC and MSB intersect. Price and other distortions lead to non-optimal levels of consumption $Q \neq Q_{opt}$ characterized by differences between MSB and MSC. More generally, if both effects are present, a weighted average of MSC and MSB should be used.

The MSB would tend to dominate in a short-run, supply constrained situation and the MSC would be more important in the longer run, when expansion of output is possible.

The MSC of nontradeable goods and services from many sectors can be determined through the appropriate breaking down of costs into their constituent factors. For example, suppose one peso's worth, of the output of the construction sector, in domestic prices, may be broken down successively into its components (e.g., capital, labor, and materials), which are valued at pesos C_1, C_2, to C_n in border prices. The determination of appropriate conversion factors to use for non-tradeables is discussed in Appendix 3.1. Since the conversion factor of any good is defined as the ratio of the border price to the domestic price, the construction conversion factor is given by:

$$CCF = \sum_{i=1}^{N} C_i \qquad (3.6)$$

The standard conversion factor (SCF) may be used with nontradeables that are not important enough to merit individual attention or lack sufficient data. The SCF is equal to the official exchange rate (OER) divided by the more familiar shadow exchange rate (SER), appropriately defined. Converting domestic priced values into border price equivalents by applying the SCF to the value is conceptually the inverse of the traditional practice of multiplying foreign currency costs by the SER (instead of the OER), to convert to the domestic price equivalent. The standard conversion factor may be approximated by the ratio of the official exchange rate to the free trade exchange rate (FTER), when the country is moving toward a freer trade regime:

$$SCF = \frac{OER}{FTER} = \frac{(eX + nM)}{eX(1-t_x) + nM(1+t_m)} \qquad (3.7)$$

where X = F.O.B. value of exports, M = C.I.F. value of imports, e = elasticity of export supply, n = elasticity of import demand, t_x = average tax rate on exports (negative for subsidy), and t_m = average tax rate on imports.

Labor and Land

The most important non-tradeables are labor and land. Taking labor first, consider a typical case of unskilled labor in a labor surplus country, for example, workers employed in dam construction. The foregone output of workers used in the water sector is the dominant component of the shadow wage rate (SWR). In a labor-surplus developing country, this will commonly be the opportunity costs of labor foregone in agricultural production.

Complications arise because the actual income earned may not reflect the marginal product of agricultural labor. Furthermore, for every new job created in the water sector, more than one worker may give up agricultural work (in the expectation of getting a job in the water sector). Allowance must also be made for seasonal activities such as harvesting, and overhead costs like transport expenses. The foregoing may be represented by the following equation for the efficiency shadow wage rate (ESWR):

$$ESWR = a \cdot m + c \cdot u \tag{3.8}$$

where m and u are the foregone marginal output and overhead costs of labor in domestic prices, and a and c are corresponding conversion factors to convert these values into border prices. A more detailed discussion of the use of social pricing to derive a social shadow wage rate (SSWR) is described in Appendix 3.3.

For land, the appropriate shadow value placed upon it depends on its location. Usually, the market price of urban land is a good indicator of its economic value in domestic prices, and the application of an appropriate conversion factor, such as the SCF, to this domestic price will yield the border-priced cost of urban land inputs. Land that can be used in agriculture may be valued at its opportunity costs, the net benefit of foregone agricultural output. The marginal social cost of other types of land cannot be assumed to be negligible, although historically, this has been the case (see also Chapters 5 and 6). A prime example is the flooding of virgin jungle due to the construction of a large storage dam -- the costs would include, amongst others:

- the destruction of valuable timber;
- the spoilage of a recreational area that has commercial potential;
- the loss of biodiversity (which may be difficult to value economically); and
- the costs of resettling local populations and the loss of cultural heritage associated with traditional native lands.

The Shadow Price of Capital Services

The shadow price of capital services is usually reflected in the discount rate or accounting rate of interest (ARI), which is defined as the rate of decline in the value of the numeraire over time. Although there has been much discussion concerning the choice of an appropriate discount rate, in practice the opportunity cost of capital (OCC) may be used as a proxy for the ARI, in the pure efficiency price regime. The OCC is defined as the expected value of the annual stream of consumption, in border prices net of replacement, which is yielded by the investment of one unit of public income at the margin.

Practical Considerations in Shadow Pricing

The estimation of shadow prices on a rigorous basis is usually a long and complex task (Munasinghe 1979). Therefore, the water sector analyst is best advised to use whatever shadow prices have already been calculated. It is also possible to use some form of sensitivity analysis to highlight those parameters which need closer scrutiny or more refined estimation.

Alternatively, the analyst could estimate a few important items such as the standard conversion factor, opportunity cost of capital, and shadow wage rate. When the data are not precise enough, sensitivity studies may again be made for a range of values of these key national parameters.

Multiobjective Decisionmaking

Traditional economic cost-benefit analysis (CBA) seeks to measure all consequences of a given project in monetary terms and evaluate the result according to some single criterion such as net present value (NPV) or internal rate of return (IRR). When projects and their impacts are to be embedded in a system of broader (national) objectives which cannot be easily quantified in monetary terms, the theory of multiobjective decisionmaking offers an alternative approach which may facilitate the optimal choice among investment options available. More recently, the shortcomings of the conventional approaches, both CBA and multiobjective decisionmaking, have been criticized.

Comparing Evaluation Approaches

In a recent study, MacRae and Whittington (1988), question both the cost-benefit and multiobjective approaches for evaluating alternatives in rural water supply projects. They argue that neither criterion explicitly addresses the moral and ethical issues that complex policy questions entail. The method they proffer involves the use of philosophical arguments as to why particular preferences should be included and others ignored.

In a case study from Haiti, these authors focus on four preferences, normally discarded in cost-benefit or multiobjective analyses:

- preferences for conspicuous consumption (for instance, among those who wish to buy private water taps in rural Haiti);
- the resentment or moral disapproval of husbands if projected changes in water supply will permit their wives to use their time more efficiently and independently;

- individuals' preferences aimed at furthering the general welfare, even when they do not further the chooser's welfare; and
- preferences among people whose attitudes may change as a result of programs not yet begun.

Table 3.1. summarizes how different evaluation procedures might react to each of the four problems. The responses of the conventional procedure are chosen because of their convenience or consistency with the theoretical assumptions of cost-benefit analysis. Counting social externalities is more in accord with the cost-benefit theory but involves difficult problems of estimation. The procedures in the third row involve omission of certain sums that people are willing to pay on the grounds that these aspects of preference satisfaction are unworthy of being counted. The estimation techniques used in these procedures are again non-trivial, and require in addition careful clarification of the principles used in excluding certain preferences. The last row of Table 3.1. includes the proposal to deal with changing preferences by examining ex-post preferences from a similar community. Although feasible in practice, this latter procedure requires additional work in order to translate the results of the estimation into terms meaningful for the observed community.

Which procedure to use depends on the type of problem. For the case shown in Table 3.1., the simplest consistent principle is to try to monetize all preferences that are satisfied or thwarted by the project in question. For conspicuous consumption and husband's preferences the suitable procedure is to include negative social externalities, and for general welfare judgments and preference change the conventional type of procedure is the more appropriate one. MacRae and Whittington argue that the decision on which type of procedure to use should not stem from the convenience of a measurement procedure, but rather should be based on principles thoroughly debated by professionals in the field. Even in the water supply field, where the volumes of water supplied can be readily determined and costs can be well-defined, we face a conflict between formal and substantive (or actual) rationality. The price of formal rationality is that some wrong decisions will be made. The price of seeking substantive rationality may be that no expert advice at all will be available on how some of these decisions are made.

Structure of the Decisionmaking Process

Once the necessity for analysis of a system has been recognized, the desired objectives are specified. Such a set of objectives often exhibits a hierarchical structure, as illustrated in Figure 3.2. The highest level represents the broad overall objectives, often stated in general terms and hence not very operational. However, it can be broken down into lower-level objectives and

TABLE 3.1 Summary of Procedures to Assess Particular Problems in Rural Water Supply

Type of Procedure	PROBLEMS			
	Conspicuous Consumption	Husband's Preferences	General Welfare Judgments	Preference Change
Conventional	Count all of tap owners gain, nothing else	Count all of wives' gains, nothing else	Count preferences fully	Do not attempt analysis
Include Negative Social Externalities	Include losers' losses	Include husbands' losses		
Omit Benefits Due to Unworthy Preferences	Omit "conspicuous" part of gainers' gain		Omit part that does not further chooser's welfare	
Use External Criteria to Estimate				Estimate benefits from ex-post preferences of a similar community

Source: MacRae, D., Jr., and D. Whittington, 1988.

Figure 3.2 Hierarchical Structure of Some Objectives and Attributes of a Water Resources Planning Model

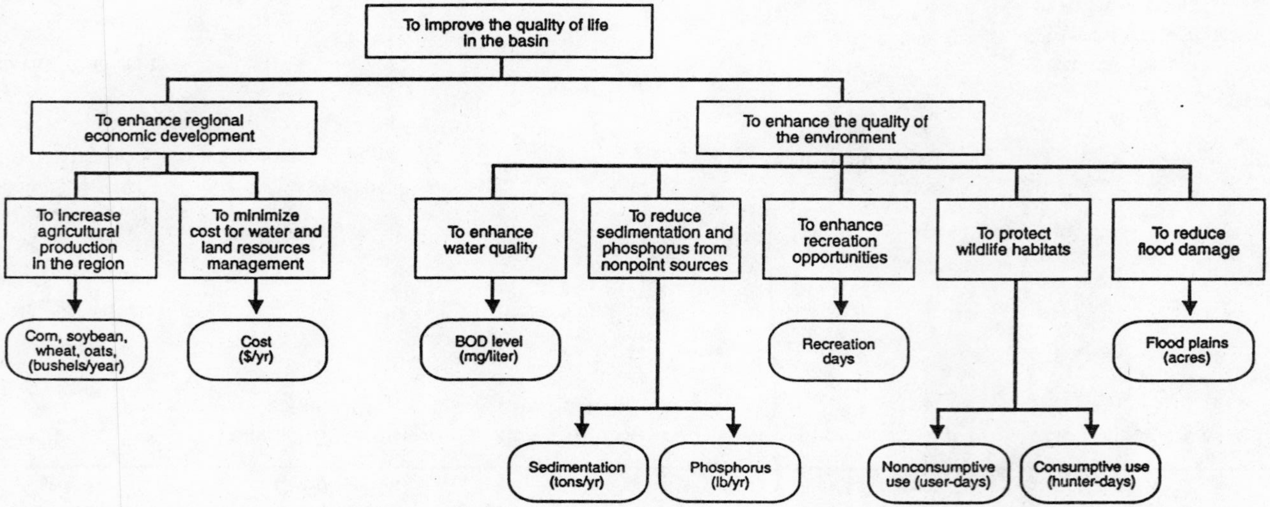

Source: Chankong, V. and Y. Y. Haimes, 1983.

the extent to which these are met may be practically assessed. For this purpose, one or more comprehensive and measurable attributes have to be assigned to each objective. The relationship between objective (e.g., minimizing costs) and attribute (e.g., $ expenditures per year) should be as direct as possible. Sometimes only proxies are available (e.g. if the objective is "to enhance recreation opportunities," the attribute "number of recreation days" can be used).

The General Multiobjective Model

Although some value judgement is required to choose the proper attribute (especially if proxies are involved), with multiobjective decisionmaking the measurement does not have to be in monetary terms, in contrast to the single-criterion methodologies. More explicit recognition is given to the fact that a variety of concerns may be associated with planning decisions. In particular, the general multiobjective model can be expressed as:

$$Maximize \quad \underline{Z}(\underline{x}) = [Z_1(\underline{x}), Z_2(\underline{x}), ... Z_p(\underline{x})],$$

such that

$$g_i(\underline{x}) \leq 0 \quad for \quad i=1,2,...m \qquad (3.9a)$$

$$x_j \geq 0 \quad for \quad j=1,2,...n \qquad (3.9b)$$

where $\underline{Z}(\underline{x})$ is an objective function comprised of p objectives (e.g., the nine lowest-level-objectives given in Figure 3.2); $\underline{x}$ is an n-dimensional vector of decision variables; and $g_i(\underline{x})$ is a set of m constraints (containing, for instance, a maximum budget for the alternatives in the decision).

In its simplest form the vector x is one-dimensional and specifies the various independent alternatives (e.g., n=1 for alternative 1, etc.). It follows from this characterization that the effects of a given project on each objective have to be estimated separately. Thus a broad range of impacts of the project is revealed explicitly, enhancing the appropriateness of the final decision.

Assessing Alternative Options

An intuitive understanding of the fundamentals of multiobjective decisionmaking might be best provided by a two-dimensional graphical exposition. Assume that a project has two non-commensurate and conflicting objectives, Z_1 and Z_2. For a large river basin plan, such objectives could be irrigation and power production. Assume further that six alternative projects

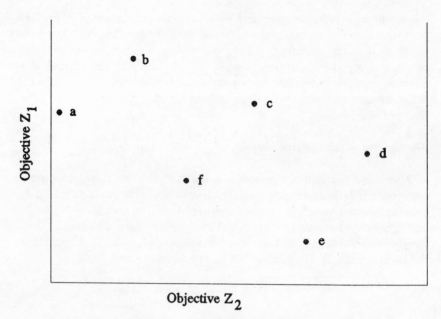

Figure 3.3   Alternative Solutions to Hypothetical Multiobjective Problem

or solutions to the problem have been identified as points a to f, all of which are feasible. As depicted in Figure 3.3, the distance from the origin along each axis represents the extent to which the relevant objective is met (e.g., hectares irrigated or energy generated). In terms of the decision variable, the alternatives can be represented by $x = 1$ for project a, $x = 2$ for project b, etc. It can be seen that alternative b is preferred to alternative f in terms of objective Z_1, but that the reverse is true relative to objective Z_2. Therefore it is not possible, at this stage to make a statement concerning the relative superiority of alternatives b and f with respect to *both* objectives. However, it can be seen that alternative d is preferred to alternative f in terms of both objectives Z_1 and Z_2, and therefore f can be excluded from further consideration (if only one alternative is to be chosen then d dominates f). In general the set of all non-dominated feasible solution points forms a Pareto optimal curve (or curve of best options), also called a transformation curve or efficient frontier.

For an unconstrained problem, further ordering cannot be conducted without the introduction of value judgements. Specific information has to be elicited from the decisionmaker to determine the most-preferred solution. In its most complete form such information may be summarized by a family of isopreference curves as illustrated in Figure 3.4, with the preference level increasing upwards as shown. Each point on a given isopreference curve

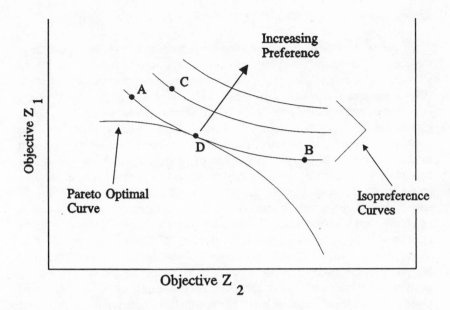

Figure 3.4 Pareto Optimal Curve and Isopreference Curves

indicates a level of achievement of objectives Z_1 and Z_2 which provides the same level of utility or "satisfaction." In other words, the decisionmaker will be indifferent between alternatives A and B, but would prefer alternative C to either A or B. The preferred alternative is that which results in the greatest utility, which occurs (for continuous decision variables as shown here) at the point of tangency D of the highest isopreference curve with the Pareto optimal curve. In this case, the point C is not attainable.

Practical Considerations

Which practical method in particular is suitable to determine the "best" alternative available, depends on the nature of the decision situation. For instance, interactive involvement of the decisionmaker has proved useful in the case of problems characterized by a large number of decision variables and complex causal interrelationships. Some objectives can be dealt with through direct optimization, while others require the satisfaction of a certain standard (e.g. level of biological oxygen demand (BOD) not below 5 milligrams/liter).

The final steps of the decision process involve implementation of the chosen project and its ex-post evaluation.

Theory and Methods of Multiobjective Decisionmaking

Of the existing theoretical developments in multiobjective decisionmaking, the most common fall roughly into two categories. First, utility theory attempts to directly formalize the decisionmaker's preference structure (Chankong and Haimes 1983). Methodologies that originate from utility theory are most suitable when a set of well-defined alternatives is explicitly given, and the problem structure does not involve interdependence between decision variables. For instance, planning of a sewerage treatment plant will include the choice of pumps. A number of producers will be considered as possible suppliers, each of whom may offer various pumps. The alternative solutions are therefore limited, the characteristics of each machine are well-specified, and one type of pump will be chosen. In this example, as only a single decision has to be made, the decision vector x is one-dimensional. Each solution will satisfy the decisionmaker's multiple objectives to different degrees (e.g. production capacity, cost, maintenance-characteristics, service offered by the supplier, etc.). If the analyst succeeds in computing the satisfaction the decisionmaker receives from the achievement-levels of these individual objectives and their combinations, this will help to determine the preferred pump. The task can be best accomplished when the nature of the problem results in a set of well-defined and limited alternatives.

Second, when the problem structure is more complex, vector optimization theory is applicable. Numerous planning situations will ask for simultaneous interdependent decisions. For instance, the boundaries of the above example can be expanded: the decisionmaker may be free to determine project-location, scale, or even institutional structure of the water supply sector in addition to just questions of the technical equipment such as pumps. The system's responses to alternative actions (e.g., a set of simultaneous decisions) may be complex and not easily determined. The preference structure can no longer be based on hypothetical responses of the system. Instead, information about the actual behavior of the system should be presented to the decisionmaker whenever this is possible, without overwhelming the individual with technical data. Then preferences can be judged more accurately.

Methodologies based on vector optimization theory have two goals. First, the non-inferior solutions have to be generated (Pareto curve). Second, within this group the best-compromise solution is identified using some kind of assessment procedure. Chankong and Haimes (1983) provide a summary of theoretical developments with regard to both aspects.

(a) Methods Based on Utility Theory

Direct Assessment Approach: The most prominent method in this class is based on the premise that the decisionmaker's preference can be quantified, measured, and represented in the form of a real-valued function called a multiattribute utility function. In particular, its existence has to be verified (Bell 1981), a suitable form selected (e.g., whether attributes are to be combined by addition or multiplication), preference functions for each component constructed and, finally, appropriate scaling determined. One methodology (see Chankong and Haimes 1983) to accomplish the latter two tasks may involve simply asking the decisionmaker to rank the alternatives on a nominal scale (this is called the direct rating method). An integer value within a given range is assigned to each alternative with respect to each objective. Edwards (1977) extends this method for the continuous case. Further methodologies are discussed in Kirkwood and Sarin (1980), Fishburn (1967) and Keeney and Raiffa (1976).

Lexicographic Method: In this method, the decisionmaker is first asked to rank the criteria (attributes) in terms of their importance. The most important attribute is then used in the first screening step, in which alternatives yielding the most preferred value of this attribute are kept, the others discarded. From this modified set of alternatives, only those yielding the most preferred value of the second most important attribute are selected. The process continues either until the modified set of alternatives contains only a unique element, which is then used as the best alternative, or until every attribute is screened once. In the latter case, if the final set of alternatives contains more than one element, some other means of selecting the final alternative (e.g., introducing additional attributes) may have to be devised. This method first received significant attention from Debreu (1954) and Geogescu-Roegen (1954).

Two further major methods are the ELECTRE-Method (Roy 1971), which is another kind of sequential elimination method, and the Indifference Curves Method (MacCrimmon and Wehrung 1977). Subject to particular conditions it may be preferable to concentrate on determining indifference curves rather than actually constructing a utility function.

(b) Methods Based on Vector Optimization

As mentioned above, the complexity of the problem structure may require active interplay between the processes of systems analysis and preference assessment. Most techniques in this category are therefore process-oriented.

Procedurally there are two possible strategies to follow. The first involves the generation of all (or representative subsets of) non-inferior solutions. This complete set is then presented to the decisionmaker who chooses his preferred solution. A variety of techniques are available to generate the non-inferior solutions, as described below.

The second strategy involves an "integrative" methodology in which the two tasks of determining non-inferior and preferred solutions are pursued simultaneously. Integrative methodologies use the preferences as a basis for generating only needed non-inferior solutions to determine the best-compromise solution.

Generating Non-Inferior Solutions: A common method to solve a vector optimization problem is to convert it into a scaling problem using weights for each attribute:

$$Maximize \ \sum_{k=1}^{P} w_k Z_k(x) \quad with \quad \sum_{k=1}^{P} w_k = 1 \qquad (3.10)$$

If we assume convexity of the objective function, the non-inferior solutions can be generated by varying the weights over their whole range. If particular constraints $g_i(\underline{x}) \leq 0$ are specified the weight-combinations necessary to derive the non-inferior solutions can be constrained analytically (Chankong and Haimes 1983, ch.6). As explained previously, $\underline{x}$ is an n-dimensional vector of decision variables and $g_i(\underline{x})$ is a set of m constraints.

For linear problems, which constitute an important subset of multiobjective decisionmaking problems, simplex-based methods can be used. The multi-dimensional surface of all non-inferior solutions is constructed (Gal 1976; Ecker et al. 1980). Alternatively, the Interval Weights Method (Steuer 1976) creates only a representative subset of non-inferior solutions.

Another methodology is epsilon-constraint characterizations. Most commonly, one primary objective is selected to be maximized and the other objectives are required to meet minimum levels of satisfaction (level epsilon). Computational iteration of this process will give the set of non-inferior solutions (Haimes and Hall 1974).

"Integrative" Solutions: A large variety of integrative methodologies has been developed. This section categorizes some of the major techniques in terms of the information they elicit from the decisionmaker. A more detailed exposition can be found elsewhere (e.g., Chankong and Haimes (1983) provide an extensive overview and further references).

- *methods based on global preference*: For instance, the modified PROTRADE-method uses complete knowledge of the decisionmaker's multiattribute utility function to evaluate trade-offs between risk levels and goal attainment levels (Goicoechea et al. 1979);
- *methods based on weights, priorities, goals and ideals*: These methods seek a best-compromise solution as one that minimizes the combined deviation from goals or ideals. Examples are goal programming (Sfeir-Younis and Bromley 1977), compromise programming (Zeleny 1982), STEP (Benayoun et al. 1971) and sequential multiobjective problem solving (SEMOPS), developed by Monarchi (1973). Most of these methods are interactive; and

- *methods that focus on trade-offs*: For instance, the surrogate worth trade-off method (Haimes and Hall 1974) asks the decisionmaker to compare two objectives at a time (partial trade-off) and elicits from this and previous information the best-compromise solution out of the generated non-inferior solutions.

Accomplishments and Limitations of Multiobjective Decisionmaking

As explained above, the major accomplishment of multiobjective decision models is that they allow for more accurate representation of decision problems, in the sense that several objectives can be accounted for. However, the question of whose preferences are to be considered has not been addressed so far. The model aids only a single decisionmaker (or a homogenous group). It assumes that the decisionmaker is able to consider appropriately the preferences of all affected people. This difficult task will not always be accomplished in reality. Various interested groups will often assign different priorities to the respective objectives, and normally it may not be possible to determine a single "best" solution via the multiobjective model. Also, the mathematical framework imposes constraints upon the ability to represent the planning problem effectively. Non-linear, stochastic and dynamic formulations can assist in better defining the problem, but impose costs in terms of complexity in formulation and solving the model (Cocklin 1989).

Nevertheless, in constructing the model the analyst communicates information about the nature of the problem. He specifies what factors are important and how they interact. Liebman (1976) observes that "modelling is thinking made public," and considers this transfer of knowledge to represent perhaps the most important contribution of modelling. With respect to the second point of criticism, diverse preferences, Liebman suggests that there is value to be gained in constructing models from differing perspectives and comparing the results.

Case Study: An Interactive Multiobjective Decision-Aiding Model

This section exemplifies one algorithm and the way the interaction between the decisionmaker and the analysis-system may be shaped. In particular, a model to identify the optimal water resources investment portfolios for American Indian reservations is used (Deason 1984). The model focuses on three objectives:

1) to maximize the number of acres of land irrigated;
2) to maximize the number of people who benefit; and
3) to maximize the number of acre-feet of water conserved annually.

Five feasible projects have been identified, a combination of which has to be selected subject to a given budget constraint. The algorithm proceeds in four steps:

Step One: The maximum attainable values for all objectives are determined. As this maximization is done for each objective without consideration of the levels of other objectives the solution is referred to as the "ideal unattainable solution."

Step Two: An initial solution (combination of project-realizations under budget constraints) is determined. The decisionmaker is confronted with an achievement rating of each objective using a percentage-scale based on the "ideal unattainable solution."

Step Three: An interactive process is started where the decisionmaker can introduce particular minimum-requirements for certain objectives. A solution that meets these objectives is computed and presented, and the decisionmaker then decides whether the trade-off-price in terms of decreased remaining performance is appropriate or not, corresponding to his preferences. For instance, an initial solution (alternative A) might supply irrigation for 7000 acres (which, in the current example is the maximum area attainable by any solution, and therefore rated 100%), provide benefits to 4000 people (80% of ideal unattainable solution) and conserve 5000 acre-feet of water annually (83% of the ideal unattainable solution). The decisionmaker then may prefer to increase the number of beneficiaries to the maximum level (100% in terms of objective 2). The algorithm computes that this requirement can only be satisfied by a simultaneous reduction of the achievement-levels of the other two objectives to 71% and 17%, respectively. The information presented to the decisionmaker after this step is depicted in Figure 3.5. The decisionmaker may already consider one of these solutions as most preferred, or, alternatively may ask for further iterations with changed minimum requirements.

Step Four: The process is repeated until the best compromise solution is found.

Cost and Benefit Measurement

If costs and benefits are to be measured accurately, it is important to identify the types of water end-use and patterns of demand over the duration of the water supply project. Therefore, before describing methods of estimating the benefits of water supply schemes, it is helpful to begin by

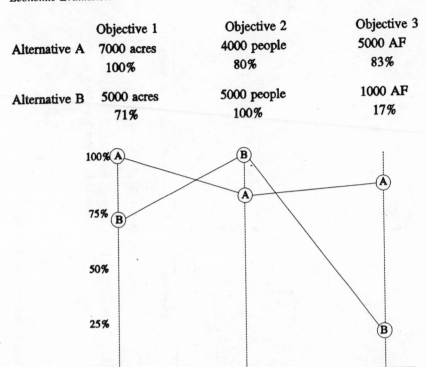

	Objective 1	Objective 2	Objective 3
Alternative A	7000 acres 100%	4000 people 80%	5000 AF 83%
Alternative B	5000 acres 71%	5000 people 100%	1000 AF 17%

Figure 3.5 Indian Reservation Example: Information Presented to the Decisionmaker After Two Solutions Have Been Calculated

analyzing the likely evolution of productive activities and lifestyles in a region, with and without the project.

Patterns of Water Use

Figure 3.6 illustrates, as an example, the likely effects of introducing piped water supply to an area that had no such service previously available. To simplify the exposition, the analysis is presented in comparative static terms. The effects of introducing piped water are likely to be felt over a number of years, as potential users make the necessary investments in water-using appliances over a period of time to take full advantage of the new water system.

There are three main reasons why demand for water will shift because of the development of a water supply system:

- due to cost differentials between the new and old supply (a price shift);

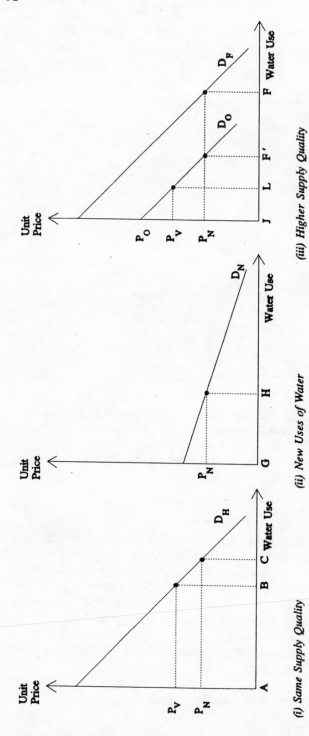

(i) Same Supply Quality

(ii) New Uses of Water

(iii) Higher Supply Quality

D_H = Demand for Household Water
P_V = Cost of Water from Old Source
P_N = Cost of Water from New Supply

D_N = Demand for New Uses of Water

D_O = Demand for Water from Old Source
D_F = Demand for Water from New Supply

Figure 3.6   Effects of Water Supply on Water Use Patterns

- due to consumers finding new uses for water, unrelated to any shift in price (improved availability); and
- due to consumers switching preferences from a less acceptable source (improved quality).

The first demand effect due to a supply change is illustrated in Figure 3.6 (i). It indicates the demand for household water where the new water supply (e.g., pipeborne supply) can substitute for another source of water that was previously used (e.g., water vendor), with little significant change in quality of the useful output. The horizontal axis represents water consumed per unit time, while the vertical axis shows the effective total cost per unit to the customer. Since the price of piped water is usually much lower than the price of water purchased from a vendor, consumers will shift to the new supply, while their demand will also increase from AB to AC, due to the reduction in effective costs.

The second demand effect shown in Figure 3.6 (ii) arises from new uses of water (e.g., watering a vegetable garden) that were previously not thought of, or considered infeasible, because of technical problems or prohibitively high costs. The consumption, GH, therefore, represents an entirely new or induced market for water.

The third demand effect is shown in Figure 3.6 (iii). Here, new pipeborne water also displaces an old source such as contaminated surface water and so there is a significant improvement in quality which results in the demand curve shifting out from D_0 to D_F. If there was no such shift, demand would have increased from JL to JF' because of the lower price of water, but with the displacement of the demand curve, the overall consumption would be JF. Chapter 6 on demand forecasting gives a more detailed account of quality induced shifts in the demand curve.

Basic Economics of Cost and Benefit Measurement

Consider Figure 3.7, which is a static picture of the likely water use by a typical consumer in the water supply project area, both with and without the project being implemented. This case is similar to the one shown in Figure 3.6 (iii), and the symbols indicated in the figure are:

Without Project Condition

D_A = demand curve for an alternative source of water;
Q_A = quantity of alternative water consumed, in liters per month of water required to produce the equivalent output;
MC_A = marginal cost of supplying alternative water;
p_A = price of alternative water (subsidized below MC).

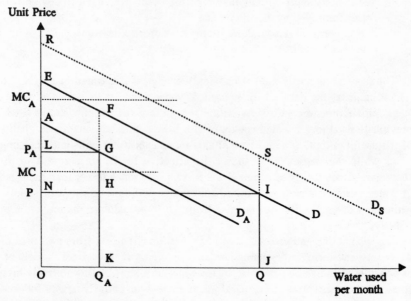

Figure 3.7 Measuring the Net Benefits of Water Supply

With Project Condition

D   = demand curve for water, shifted outward due to higher quality of piped water provided;

Q   = quantity of piped water consumed, in liters per month;

MC = marginal cost of supplying piped water;

p   = price of piped water (subsidized below MC).

In conventional microeconomic consumer theory, the benefit derived from consuming a good or service may be measured by the area under the demand curve. Therefore, in the 'without project' situation, [OAGK] is the user benefit of consuming an amount of water Q_A, where the string of capitals in parentheses indicates the boundary of the area. The corresponding cost of supplying this water is $MC_A \cdot Q_A$. In the same way, the benefit and cost in the 'with project' condition are [OEIJ] and $MC \cdot Q$, respectively.

The incremental benefit, defined as the change in benefits brought about by the project, is:

$$IB = [OEIJ] - [OAGK] = [AEFG] + [FHI] + p(Q-Q_A) \qquad (3.11)$$

Similarly, the incremental cost is:

$$IC = MC \cdot Q - MC_A \cdot Q_A \qquad (3.12)$$

Finally, the net benefit due to the water supply project is:

$$NB = IB-IC = \{p(Q-Q_A) + MC_A \cdot Q_A + [FHI] + [AEFG]\} - [MC \cdot Q] \quad (3.13)$$

In the above expression, the last term indicates the project costs, and we may write:

$$C = [MC \cdot Q] \qquad (3.14)$$

The remaining part of the expression represents what is usually called the project benefit:

$$B = \{p(Q-Q_A) + MC_A \cdot Q_A + [FHI] + [AEFG]\} \qquad (3.15)$$

If we consider the expression for C, the marginal cost element MC is the long-run marginal cost (LRMC) per unit of water supplied. Whilst this is discussed in more detail in Chapter 7, the LRMC may be broadly defined here as the incremental system cost of supplying one unit of sustained future water consumption with the supply system operating at optimal capacity. Q is the total quantity of new water supplied.

The expression for B is somewhat more complicated to interpret. The first term in B is the sales revenue corresponding to the additional water used, while the second is the cost saving due to alternative water not used. The final two terms are areas representing consumer surplus. In general, these demand curves will shift and consumption levels (as well as LRMC) will change over time. The present value of the stream of (shadow priced) net benefits must be evaluated, year by year, over the lifetime of the project, to yield the NPV described earlier in this chapter. The other cost-benefit criteria may also be calculated, once the annual stream of net benefits are estimated.

Estimation of Water Supply Costs and Benefits

Since the least-cost solution has been identified already, the total cost of the new water supply system is available. Alternatively, we may use equation (3.14), where:

MC = (LRMC per unit of water supplied).
Q = (Total quantity of new water supplied).

The First Benefit Term: $p (Q - Q_A)$

Based on the demand forecasts that have been already made, and the corresponding price of water, the component of benefits involving revenues from incremental consumption may be evaluated quite simply. Since the demand projections are usually made with the explicit (or sometimes implicit) assumption that the current price will prevail into the future, in real terms, this is the appropriate price to use when estimating benefits. It would be theoretically possible to assume that the future value of p will increase or decrease in real terms, but in this case the demand forecast should also be based on the same projected evolution of price. Given the quality of data available, it may be rather difficult to make such forecasts of price and consumption with any degree of accuracy. If there is uncertainty concerning future price trends, the "neutral" assumption of constant real future price of water could be used. If this water supply price is well below the level of LRMC, then the consumer surplus portion of benefits [FHI] will be relatively large and its estimation becomes more important, as discussed below. On the other hand, in the event that price is not very different from LRMC, then the incremental revenues will approximate the full benefits more closely. Since these revenues are evaluated in domestic market prices, they must be multiplied by the appropriate conversion factor (usually the standard conversion factor -- SCF, or consumption conversion factor -- CCF), to convert them into border shadow priced values, as explained earlier.

The Second Benefit Term: $MC_A \cdot Q_A$

The second term in the expression for B represents cost savings. Usually, it is reasonably safe to assume that water derived previously from alternative sources will be replaced, and therefore, equivalent border priced cost savings may be estimated. The rate at which this substitution takes place has to be predicted, and also reflected consistently in the demand forecast. However, there is also the issue of new types of water usage that might have come into use, in the 'without project' situation (i.e., even though pipeborne water had not been made available). For example, if the water supply scheme had not been implemented, a more costly alternative private water producing facility might have emerged. In theory, cost saving benefits may be claimed for all these possibilities, but in practice, such predictions are risky to make. Therefore, the usual approach is to evaluate savings on existing water sources and levels of usage, as a base. Additional cost saving benefits due to substitution of hypothetical new water sources that might have emerged in the absence of the water supply project, must be carefully justified on a case-by-case basis.

The Third and Fourth Benefit Terms: [FHI and AEFG]

The third term in the benefit expression, [FHI], is the consumer surplus associated with incremental water consumed. Additional output due to increased productivity in new activities may be used to approximate some of this willingness-to-pay for water. For example, the availability of more water for irrigation might increase farm yields significantly. The border priced economic value of additional output, net of all input costs including expenditures on water, is the appropriate measure of consumer surplus to be used. Similarly, higher net output derived by replacing an existing water source with water, may be used to estimate the consumer surplus area [AEFG] for the alternative water. The benefit [FHI] is over and above the cost saving benefit arising from the replacement of alternative water described earlier.

Some typical examples of potentially quantifiable benefits and costs of water supply, that may be used to estimate both cost savings and net increases in output, are summarized in Tables 3.2.(a) and 3.2.(b).

Benefits that are Difficult to Quantify

Promoters of water supply often claim that there are significant non-quantifiable gains. Because it is very difficult to quantify these benefits in practice, great care and discipline must be exercised to avoid the temptation of using such supposed benefits to justify a water supply project that otherwise would not have been viable. These benefits may be conveniently examined in five categories as discussed below, and summarized in Table 3.2.(a).

Categories of Benefits

First, it is argued that improved water supply supports and stimulates modernization and growth. Most of the productivity gains by households, agriculture and industry, may be quantified as explained earlier. However, if water supply acts as a catalyst, there may be further unrecognized benefits, for example, due to changes in attitudes of the entire community.

Second, social benefits could accrue due to overall improvements in the quality of life. For example, local participation in developing a community water supply scheme might help to improve cooperation and the community spirit. Similar gains could occur in other areas affecting social welfare, such as improved health and sanitation derived from safe drinking water, and the freeing up of people's time due to easier access to water. Other intangible benefits might include, increased personal satisfaction and family welfare, as well as reduced social discontent and unrest (which are not explicitly internalized within the conventional consumer surplus).

Third, water supply may be viewed by some governments as an instrument for improving social equity and income distribution (Munasinghe 1988). As described earlier in the section on shadow pricing, social shadow prices may be used to weight benefits and cost to the poor, in order to quantify some of the welfare gains due to income redistribution. However, this is rather difficult in most cases, for several reasons. Data on incomes are usually very weak, and therefore it is difficult to identify poverty groups and determine the correct social weights. At the same time, the benefits of water supply may in fact accrue mainly to the better off sections of the community, such as local officials, wealthy landowners, and entrepreneurs. Therefore, targeting the benefits of water supply, especially through connections policy and price subsidies (see Chapter 7 for more details), is frequently a much more important practical goal rather than fruitlessly attempting to quantify distributional benefits.

Fourth, there may be significant employment and other gains as a result of the water project. The direct employment effects due to greater productive uses of water will be captured by analyzing incremental output, as described earlier. In the case of rural water supply, another important benefit may arise from reduced rural to urban migration. This may be caused by the perception of greater employment and other opportunities for advancement in hitherto stagnant villages, or because of general improvements in the quality of life.

Fifth, it is sometimes argued that better water supply may provide a number of other general benefits, viewed from the national viewpoint, such as improving political stability and reducing discontent, improving national cohesion, and reducing urban-rural and inter-regional tensions and inequalities.

Sixth, there may be general environmental benefits (and costs), as discussed in Chapters 5 and 6.

The economic basis for claiming additional essentially unrecognized social benefits is analyzed in Figure 3.7. Consider the "social" demand curve for water D_S, which includes surplus benefits represented by the area [ERSI], due to the factors indicated above. While some of the unquantifiable benefits are included conceptually within the users demand curve D, the social surplus benefits are usually not internalized directly within the consumers demand curves, because they are not perceived as benefits by individual users. However, such benefits may be included under the curve D_S which indicates the willingness-to-pay of society as a whole, if they yield identifiable gains to the community.

The successful design and implementation of a water supply scheme depends on the coordinated efforts of environmentalists, health officers, engineers, economists, financial analysts, sociologists, administrators and politicians, as well as local beneficiaries, all of whom have their own viewpoints. They all have different interpretations of the nature of costs and benefits to be identified and included. Furthermore, there will be conflicts of interest among the different project beneficiaries themselves. Given the diversity of sociocultural and ecological conditions in most regions, a tradeoff will be required in different objectives.

Specific Environmental Costs and Benefits

A comparison of Tables 3.2.(a) and 3.2.(b) reveals that certain impacts related to environmental change resulting from water projects and related sector activities appear in both. Thus, one water supply project may favorably affect certain activities, while another scheme at a different site may be harmful to those same activities. For example, increased industrial and agricultural productivity may become possible due to the development of a reliable water supply system (See Table 3.2.(a)). At the same time, however, new developing industries and expanding agriculture are likely to modify the temperature, and the oxygen and nutrient content of the downstream river waters, thereby damaging aquatic life. In other situations, the creation of reservoirs and the thoughtful regulation of river flows might improve fish breeding conditions. For example, shifting the ecological state of a lake from eutro-hypertrophic to oligo-mesotrophic, would improve the environment for successful fish-breeding.

Another example is the effect of a water supply system on the health status of the involved populations. By providing the right breeding conditions for certain parasites or disease carrying organisms, reservoirs and canals often result in outbreaks of endemic diseases like malaria, schistosomiasis, onchocerciasis and filariasis (see Chapter 5). On the other hand, proper regulation of river and canal flows, by controlling the water velocity and/or managing the growth of aquatic plants, may reduce or eliminate conditions for the development of existing parasites. Moreover, the implementation of a water supply and sanitation network substantially enhances general health standards and plays the major role in the prevention of waterborne human diseases.

Some of the adverse impacts of water supply schemes (or more generally, multipurpose projects including a potable water component) can be readily quantified such as the costs involved in vaccinating or relocating people, decrease in fish production, estimated flood damage, or increased salinization of the soil and aquifers (see Table 3.2.(b)). Other observed adverse impacts are harder to include explicitly in the economic assessment of a project, like the encroachment on tribal territories, or the damage inflicted on areas of ecological importance for the sustenance of wild animals or plants. Nevertheless, quantification problems should not be an excuse to leave such impacts out of the project evaluation. An approach that seeks to account for environmental and social impacts in water resources projects has been described by Olivares (1988). A summary of the chief methods used to value

TABLE 3.2 (a) Typical Examples of Water Supply Project Benefits

User Category	Potentially Quantifiable Benefits	
	Cost Savings	*Increased Productivity*
Public Sector	• Reduced water losses • Reduced water contamination due to adequate pressure in supply system • Reduced risk of life and property losses due to better flood control • Reduced damage to aquifers	• Added water production capacity • Improved billing and metering • Increased labour productivity

Industrial & Commercial	• Lower price for alternative means of water supply
	• Decrease in sick-leave hours due to health improvements
		• Potential to develop or extend new productive enterprises which rely on adequate water supply e.g.
		  - industries requiring cooling water
		  - beverage industries
		• Impetus for tourism and watersports

Household	• Lower price for vendor supplied water • Decrease in labour costs for water hauling	
Agriculture	• Lower costs of alternative means of water supply • Reduced aquifer depletion and/or salinisation	• Extension of arable land due to increase in irrigation and drainage potential • Improvement of land quality by leaching of salt-affected soils • Improvement of fish breeding

Benefits that are Difficult to Quantify

• Modernisation, growth, and attitude changes - catalytic effects
• Quality of life and community services
• Income redistribution and social equity
• Employment creation
• Other socio-political effects
• General environmental benefits

TABLE 3.2 (b)   Typical Examples of Adverse Impacts of Water Supply Projects

Category	*Potentially Quantifiable Adverse Impacts*
Health	• Costs of preventing waterborne diseases • Days lost due to ill health • Increased risk of flood damage and family deprivation • Increased amount of waste water produced
Social	• Relocation of certain populations • Demarcation of tribal lands • Employment destroyed by the project
Agricultural	• Increase in salinization of soil and aquifer • Decrease in fish production

Adverse Impacts that are Difficult to Quantify
• Irreversible destruction of existing fauna and flora • Infringements on mankind's aesthetic and cultural heritage • Encroachment on tribal territory • Increase in water related diseases • Human suffering and social disruption • Site specific effects

environmental assets and impacts is provided in Chapter 5.

Parker (1989) provides an overview of the cost-benefit analysis of water pollution abatement policies. For national governments to adopt water pollution abatement policies requires that they reallocate resources from other investment programs as part of a rational decisionmaking framework. Parker indicates that only a few western industrialized countries have made any realistic assessments of the costs and benefits associated with tackling a range of polluting processes. The four major categories used are recreational benefits, non-use benefits (mainly aesthetic), commercial fishery benefits, and diversionary uses (health improvements, reduced treatment costs, improved industrial performance, etc.). Results of studies in the US, Germany and the Netherlands give rise to possible cost savings (benefits) ranging from US$ 0.1 to 1.5 billion for different categories of deterioration that have already taken place.

Recent Experiences With Economic Analysis of Projects and Treatment of Externalities

In this section, we briefly examine how the analytical framework described earlier has been applied in World Bank projects. A more detailed estimation of the externality costs of groundwater depletion is provided in the case study in Chapter 12.

Tables 3.3.(a) and 3.3.(b) present a summary of objectives, quantifiable benefits and costs, as well as the non-quantified benefits and adverse effects, actually identified in several recent water supply projects (World Bank 1988a, 1988b, 1988c, 1988d, 1988e, 1989a, and 1989b). The case studies presented in Chapters 9 to 12 offer a more detailed description of the application of economic analysis to water supply systems.

In Table 3.3.(a) all costs and benefits are converted to and expressed in border prices. In three out of the seven studies the benefits of water projects are estimated using the conventional approach of equating project benefits with the (estimated) revenues from increased water sales as collected by the water utility. As shown earlier, this analysis only assesses partially the quantifiable net project benefits, since consumer surplus is neglected. Consequently, the internal rate of return for those projects is likely to be underestimated.

Without analyzing details, it is illuminating to review how the project benefits were quantified for the water supply schemes located in the People's Democratic Republic of Yemen, Nigeria, Ghana, and Cyprus.

(Former) People's Democratic Republic of Yemen: The benefits of the water project were calculated using the incremental water sales at current tariffs, i.e., the first term in the benefit expression (3.15), plus the estimated reduction in pumping costs for a 50-year period. The latter corresponds to the second term in the benefit expression, i.e., cost savings due to not using alternate water resources.

Nigeria: The economic benefits are based on two aspects:

- The expected incremental revenues arising from added production capacity, improved billing and the avoided system deterioration that would have occurred without the project; and
- The consumer surpluses, reflecting the general benefits to consumers of having an increased volume of lower cost water, the last two terms in equation (3.15). In the estimation of the consumer surpluses, a distinction was made between the willingness-to-pay of households and of industries. A weighted average, reflecting the ratio of water consumption between the two groups, was then used in the analysis.

TABLE 3.3 (a) Results of Economic Analyses of Recent Water Supply Schemes

Country	Project	Key-objective	Proxy for Economic Benefit	Total Cost (million us$)	Internal Rate of Return (%)
Cyprus	Southern Conveyor Project For Water Resources Development (Phase II)	Adequate water supply to 0.6 million domestic water consumers and 4,000 farmers by 1991	• Net economic value of irrigated crop versus rainfed crop • Consumer surplus	164.0	14.0
Egypt	Second Alexandria Water Supply Project	Improving water distribution by reducing unaccounted-for water	• Incremental volume of water sold	36.0	12.0
Ghana	Water Sector Rehabilitation Project	Improving water services throughout the country	• Cost savings • Consumer surplus	125.0	15.0
Haiti	Port-Au-Prince Water Supply Project	Supplying additional 20,000 m3 of water per day	• Incremental volume of water sold	31.2	10.1
Nigeria	Lagos Water Supply Project	Increasing supply to 3.6 million people by 1995	• Incremental volume of water sold	461.8	13.0
Uruguay	Water Supply Rehabilitation Project	Increasing supply to 233,000 people by 2000	• Incremental volume of water sold • Consumer surplus	30.7	25.0
Yemen	Al Mukalla Water Supply Project	Providing piped water supply to 90,000 people by 2002	• Incremental volume of water sold • Estimated reduction	34.7	6.5

Sources: World Bank reports.

TABLE 3.3 (b) Non-Quantified Benefits and Adverse Effects of Selected Recent Water Supply Schemes

Country	Project	Non-quantified Benefits	Non-quantified Adverse Impacts
Cyprus	Southern Conveyor Project For Water Resources Development (Phase II)	• Induce (ground-)water conservation practices	• Detrimental effects on flamingos' feeding grounds • Unanticipated geological effects in the construction of a diversion tunnel
Egypt	Second Alexandria Water Supply Project	• Prevent polluted groundwater to seep into the water distribution system • Facilitate city's economic activity	• None foreseen
Ghana	Water Sector Rehabilitation Project	• Decrease health risks to the poor • Boost economic development	• None foreseen
Haiti	Port-Au-Prince Water Supply Project	• Avoid collapse of current critical water services (with consequent civil unrest) • Abate drinking water contamination	• Minor environmental deterioration
Nigeria	Lagos Water Supply Project	• Increase supplies to the poor • Decrease labor costs involved with fetching water over long distances	• Increase in waste water flows
Uruguay	Water Supply Rehabilitation Project	• Improve sanitary conditions	• None foreseen
Yemen	Al Mukalla Water Supply Project	• Reduce risks of diseases • Boost economic development	• None foreseen

Sources: World Bank reports.

Ghana: The project benefits were estimated from the following:

- The prices currently paid for vendor supplied water, on which many households depend (in the without project case). This corresponds to the cost savings term related to alternative water not used in the project benefits equation (equation 3.15); and
- The area under the water demand curves for existing and new consumers. Both demand curves were empirically identified, each one based on an estimated minimum and a maximum water demand. Next, an exponential curve was regressed with a price-elasticity of 0.2 at the low demand level and an elasticity of 0.8 at the high demand level, based on the general findings of Garn (1987) on the price-elasticity of water consumption. The computed area under this estimated demand curve represents the sum of consumer surpluses relating to both incremental water consumption and the replacement of existing water sources.

Cyprus: The benefits accruing to the farmers were derived from the predicted opportunity costs. Uncontrolled pumping of groundwater from existing boreholes at the current rate would result in severe seawater intrusion and a rapid deterioration from irrigated to rain-fed agriculture. The economic benefits attributable to the farmers were therefore set equal to the net economic value of the irrigated crop less the value of the rain-fed crop.

The benefits from domestic and industrial water were quantified by the consumers' future willingness-to-pay. The latter was estimated by assessing:

- the benefits of the next alternative use which would be irrigation in this case; and
- the costs of developing the next alternative source of supply, which would be desalinization.

The estimate of the second item serves as an upper limit for the value of domestic and industrial water use, while the first item provides the lower limit. The actual judgement on where the willingness-to-pay actually lies within this range is fine-tuned by observing peoples' current demand behavior.

We note that all of the above mentioned projects lack the social component (mentioned earlier) in the evaluation of the estimated benefit. Also no attempt was made to explicitly consider positive or negative impacts on health or the environment, employment opportunities, resettlement or other hard-to-quantify effects in estimating the rate of return. However, for each one of the projects a number of non-quantifiable benefits were reported during appraisal. Those benefits are listed for reference in Table 3.3.(b). Even if they were not formally embedded in the economic analysis, they were considered relevant in the overall project justification.

References

Baum, W. 1978. "The Project Cycle." *Finance and Development*. 15, pp. 2-9.

Bell, D.E. 1981. "Decision Regret: A Component of Risk Aversion?" in J.N. Morse (ed.). *Proceedings: The Multiple Criteria Decisionmaking Conference*. Berlin: Springer.

Benayoun, R., J. de Montgolfier, J. Tergny, and O.I. Larichev. 1971. "Linear Programming With Multiple Objective Functions: STEP method (STEM)." *Mathematical Programming*. 1, pp. 366-375.

Chankong, V., and Y.Y. Haimes. 1983. *Multiobjective Decisionmaking*. North-Holland Series in *System Science and Engineering*. 8. New York: North Holland.

Cocklin, C. 1989. "Mathematical Programming and Resources Planning I: The Limitations of Traditional Optimization." *Journal of Environmental Management*. 28, pp. 127-141.

Cohon, J. 1978. *Multiobjective Programming and Planning*. New York: Academic Press.

Cohon, J., and D. Marks. 1975. "A Review and Evaluation of Multiobjective Programming Techniques." *Water Resources Research*. 11, pp. 208-220.

Deason, J.P. 1984. *A Multiobjective Decision Support System For Water Project Portfolio Selections*. Ph.D. Dissertation. University of Virginia.

Debreu, G. 1954. "Representation of a Preference Ordering by a Numerical Function," in R.M. Thrall et al. (eds.). *Decision Process*. New York: John Wiley.

Ecker, J.G., N.S. Hegner, and I.A. Kouada. 1980. "Generating All Maximal Efficient Faces for Multiple Objective Linear Programs." *Journal of Optimization Theory and Application*. 30, pp. 353-381.

Edwards, W. 1977. "How to Use Multiattribute Utility Measurement for Social Decisionmaking" in D.E. Bell et al. (eds.). *Conflicting Objectives in Decisions*. London: John Wiley.

Fishburn, P.C. 1967. "Methods of Estimating Additive Utilities." *Management Science*. 13, pp. 435-453.

Gal, T. 1976. "A General Method for Determining the Set of All Efficient Solutions to a Linear Vector Maximum Problem." *Report No. 76/12*. Aachen, Germany: Institut fur Wirtschaftswissenschaften.

Garn, H. 1987. "Water Supply Investments in Developing Countries: Some Technical, Economic, and Financial Implications of Experience" in *Resource Mobilization for Drinking Water and Sanitation in Developing Nations*. San Juan, Puerto Rico: Management Dev. & Environmental Div./ASCE.

Geogescu-Roegen, N. 1954. "Choice, Expectations, and Measurability." *Quarterly Journal of Economics*. 68, pp. 503-534.

Goicoechea, A., L. Duckstein, and M.M. Fagel. 1979. "Multiple Objectives Under Uncertainty: An Illustrative Application of PROTRADE." *Water Resources Research*. 15, pp. 203-210.

Haimes, Y.Y., and W.A. Hall. 1974. "Multiobjectives in Water Resources Systems Analysis: The Surrogate Worth Trade-Off (SWT) Method." *Water Resources Research.* 10, pp. 615-624.

Keeney, R.L., and H. Raiffa. 1976. *Decision with Multiple Objectives.* New York: John Wiley.

Kirkwood, C.W., and R.K. Sarin. 1980. "Preference Conditions For Multiattribute Value Functions." *Operations Research.* 28, pp. 225-231.

Liebman, J. 1976. "Some Simple-Minded Observations on the Role of Optimization in Public Systems Decisionmaking." *Interfaces.* 6, pp. 102-108.

Little, I.M.D., and J. Mirlees. 1974. *Project Appraisal and Planning for Developing Countries.* New York: Basic Books.

MacCrimmon, K.R., and D.A. Wehrung. 1977. "Trade-Off Analysis: The Indifference and Preferred Proportions Approaches" in D.E. Bell et al. (eds.). *Conflicting Objectives in Decisions.* London: John Wiley.

MacRae, D. Jr., and D. Whittington. 1988. "Assessing Preferences in Cost-Benefit Analysis: Reflections on Rural Water Supply Evaluation in Haiti." *Journal of Policy Analysis and Management.* 7, No. 2, pp. 246-263.

Monarchi, D.E., C.C. Kisiel, and L. Duckstein. 1973. "Interactive Multiobjective Programming in Water Resources: A Case Study." *Water Resources Research.* 9, pp. 837-850.

Munasinghe, M. 1988. *Contemporary Water Supply Efficiency and Pricing Issues in Developing Countries.* Paper presented at the International Conference on Cost and Price of Water in Urban Areas. Paris, December 6-8.

_____. 1979. *The Economics of Power System Reliability and Planning.* Baltimore, MD: John Hopkins Univ. Press.

Olivares, J. 1988. "The Assessment of Water Resources Projects Involving Economic, Social and Environmental Costs and Benefits: The World Bank's View" in *Assessment of Multiple Objective Water Resources Projects: Approaches for Developing Countries.* New York: United Nations/UNEP.

Parker, A.N. 1989. *Environmental Policy: Case Study of Freshwater Pollution.* Consultant Report. Washington DC: The World Bank.

Ray, A. 1984. *Cost-Benefit Analysis.* Baltimore, MD: Johns Hopkins University Press.

Roy, B. 1971. "Problems and Methods with Multiple Objective Functions." *Mathematical Programming.* 1.

Sfeir-Younis, A., and D.W. Bromley. 1977. *Decisionmaking in Developing Countries.* New York: Praeger Publishers.

Squire, L., and H. Van der Tak. 1975. *Economic Analysis of Projects.* Baltimore, MD: Johns Hopkins University Press.

Steuer, R.E. 1976. "Multiple Objective Linear Programming with Interval Criterion Weights." *Management Science.* 23, pp. 305-316.

World Bank. 1989a. *Republic of Ghana: Water Sector Rehabilitation Project.* Staff Appraisal Report No. 7598-GH. Washington DC: The World Bank.

_____. 1989b. *Haiti: Centrale Autonome Metropolitaine d'eau Potable (CAMEP). Port-au-Prince Water Supply Project.* Staff Appraisal Report No. 7613-HA. Washington DC: The World Bank.

_____. 1988a. *Cyprus: Southern Conveyor Project for Water Resources Development (Phase II).* Staff Appraisal Report No. 6649-CY. Washington DC: The World Bank.

_____. 1988b. *Arab Republic of Egypt: Second Alexandria Water Supply Project.* Staff Appraisal Report No. 7124-EGT. Washington DC: The World Bank.

_____. 1988c. *Uruguay: Water Supply Rehabilitation Project.* Staff Appraisal Report No. 6790-UR. Washington DC: The World Bank.

_____. 1988d. *Nigeria: Lagos Water Supply Project.* Staff Appraisal Report No. 6375-UNI. Washington DC: The World Bank.

_____. 1988e. *Uruguay: Water Supply Rehabilitation Project.* Staff Appraisal Report No. 6790-UR. Washington DC: The World Bank.

_____. 1988f. *People's Democratic Republic of Yemen: Al Mukalla Water Supply Project.* Staff Appraisal Report No. 6995-YDR. Washington DC: The World Bank.

Zeleny, M. 1982. *Multiple Criteria Decisionmaking.* New York: McGraw- Hill.

Appendix 3.1
Border Pricing

The basic rationale underlying the system of efficiency prices (using border prices as the numeraire), may be understood at a more intuitive level if we make use of the following simplified physical analogy.

In Figure A3.1, the sea level, which is a universal reference level, may be compared to the undistorted baseline for efficiency pricing. Thus all heights in meters measured with respect to the sea level, denoted by the abbreviation mS, are like border prices. By contrast, heights of objects measured from the local ground level and represented by the symbol mL, are like domestic market prices evaluated relative to the distorted local economy. It is interesting to compare the strengths and weaknesses of the two sets of prices, by pursuing the pictorial analogy further.

With the respective heights as indicated in the figure, consider an aircraft approaching the landing field, located on a high plateau. As he approaches land, the aircraft pilot has the following conversation (by radio), with observer A on the ground:

Pilot: It's fine and clear up here, except for some clouds coming up ahead. How is it down there?

Observer A: It's sunny down here too, but unfortunately I am standing in the shade of a 500 meter tall building.

Pilot: I see the tower well below me. It is a nice looking building. Thanks for the information.

The pilot now continues on and enters the cloud. He then records the following exchange with observer B, standing on the plateau.

Observer B: How is it up there? You are covered by clouds, but you might want to know that the tallest building in town is only 200 meters high.

Pilot: Fine thanks. I just overflew a 500 meter high tower with a lot of room to spare, so I should clear your town quite easily, although I can't see a thing.

It is not difficult to imagine the unfortunate consequences if the pilot fails to gain altitude, and therefore does not clear building B.

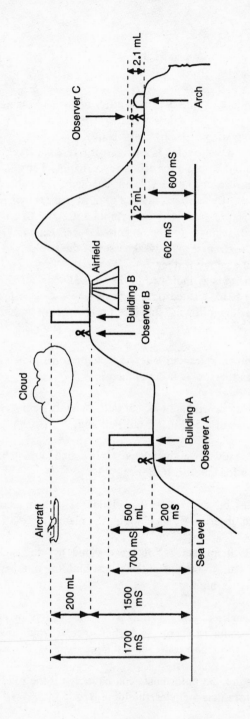

Figure A3.1 A Physical Analogy to Border Pricing

Fortunately, professional pilots are not so naive. They use a much more scientific basis for exchanging information on altitude. Thus if both observers A and B indicated the respective heights of their buildings as 1500 and 1700 meters, with respect to sea level, the pilot would be able to avert the potential tragedy. In a similar vein, the use of border prices provides a measure of economic value relative to a standard reference (like sea level) that is independent of the local observer. On the other hand, domestic market prices are distorted by local constraints (such as import duties and taxes), and these usually vary quite arbitrarily depending on the good or service under consideration. Therefore, the latter set of prices (like heights above some local reference level) may be a rather misleading basis on which to make rational economic decisions.

However, market prices are the prices that the average consumer perceives and deals with every day. To him, the shadow border pricing framework that the national planner uses for his investment decisionmaking is a theoretical construct which is very "shadowy" indeed. Therefore, when it comes to implementing practical pricing policies, domestic market prices play a key role. A further extension of the physical analogy illustrated in Figure A3.1 will clarify this point.

Consider individual C (a blind man) who lives on the other side of the mountain, and has never seen the ocean. Suppose a well-meaning but impractical friend is advising him about potential obstacles in his path. The following conversation ensues:

Individual C: Is there anything ahead of me?

Friend: Yes, you have to walk under an arch that is 602 meters above sea level.

Individual C does not understand the concept of sea level, but only knows that he is 2.1 meters tall. If he proceeds on this basis, he is likely to bump his head. What is relevant for his decisionmaking is the height of the arch above the local ground level. If his friend advised him correctly that the arch was only 2 meters high, he could duck his head and pass safely under it.

As will become clear from the more detailed explanations of pricing theory and practice presented in Chapter 8, border prices are important when considering national tariff setting for water supply services. Throughout this publication, we stress the need for water sector planners to base their pricing strategy around the long-run marginal costs (LRMC) of supply. This requires first calculating the strict LRMC of water supply in border prices and then converting it into its equivalent market price (by dividing the LRMC by the appropriate consumer-specific conversion factor). It is this reconverted market price that the rational consumer will understand. This is the local price he or she will have to pay. The consumers' willingness-to-pay for water clearly depends on the distorted local prices of other competing goods and services. In other words, the reconversion automatically adjusts for distortions relative to local market conditions (like the local ground level).

Appendix 3.2
Conversion Factors (CF)

For a given commodity, the conversion factor may be defined as the ratio of its border price (in terms of the chosen foreign exchange numeraire) to its domestic market price. As an example, we analyze the general case of an input into the water sector that is also consumed by non-water sector users. The input is supplied through imports as well as domestic production.

TS is the total supply curve consisting of the sum of WS and DS which are the world and domestic supply curves (see Figure A3.2). DD is the domestic demand curve of non-water sector users, while TD is the total domestic demand when the requirements of the water sector PD are included. The domestic market price of the input is driven up from P to P + dP due to the effect of the increased demand PD. The corresponding world market C.I.F. (import) prices are smaller by a factor $1/(1 + t_m)$, where t_m is the rate of import duty on the input. The level of consumption due to non-water sector users only (i.e., without the water sector demand), would be Q = D, of which M would be supplied through imports and S from domestic production. The total domestic consumption with PD included is Q + dQ, which is composed of non-water sector demand D - dD and water sector demand (dQ + dD). In this situation, the respective quantities M + dM and S + dS are imported and domestically supplied.

Let us consider the marginal social cost (MSC) of meeting the water sector demand. Firstly, there is the increased expenditure of foreign exchange (i.e., already in border prices) for extra imports:

$$d(FX) = \frac{M \cdot dP \cdot (1 - e_w)}{(1 + t_m)} \qquad (A3.2.1)$$

where $e_w = P \cdot dM/M \cdot dP$ is the price elasticity of world supply.

Secondly, we consider the increased resource cost of additional domestic supply:

$$d(RC) = f \cdot (S \cdot dP \cdot e_d) \qquad (A3.2.2)$$

where $e_d = P \cdot dS/S \cdot dP$ is the price elasticity of domestic supply, and f is the factor which converts the cost of supply from domestic to border prices.

Next, the decrease in the benefit of consumption of non-water sector consumers should be considered as a cost:

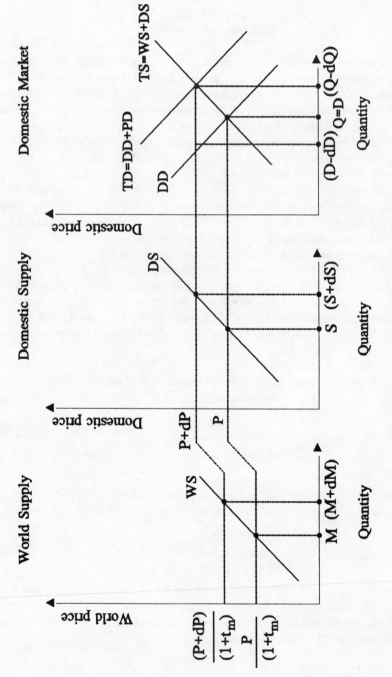

Figure A3.2 Supply and Demand for Water Sector Input

$$d(BD) = w_c \cdot (D \cdot dP \cdot n_d) \qquad \text{(A3.2.3)}$$

where $n_d = P \cdot dP/D \cdot dP$ is the relevant price elasticity of demand (absolute value), and w_c is the social weight attached to domestic consumption at the relevant consumption level.

Fourthly, there is the effect due to the increase in income of non-water sector consumers:

$$dI_c = (b_c - w_c) \cdot (S \cdot dP) \qquad \text{(A3.2.4)}$$

where b_c is the border priced resource cost of increasing domestic consumption (of other goods) by one unit.

Finally, the effect of increased income accruing to domestic producers is:

$$dI_p = (b_p - w_p) \cdot (S \cdot dP) \qquad \text{(A3.2.5)}$$

where b_p and w_p represent the shadow priced resource cost and marginal social benefit (MSB) respectively of a one-unit increase in the income of the producers.

The total cost of the input to the water sector in shadow prices is:

$$d(BP) = d(FX) + d(RC) + d(BD) + dI_c + dI_p \qquad \text{(A3.2.6)}$$

The corresponding cost of the input in domestic prices is:

$$d(DP) = P \cdot (dD + dQ) = dP \cdot (D \cdot n_d + S \cdot e_d + M \cdot e_w) \qquad \text{(A3.2.7)}$$

Therefore, the expression for the conversion factor may be written:

$$CF_m = \frac{d(BP)}{d(DP)} = \frac{M\left[\dfrac{(1+e_w)}{(1+t_m)}\right] + W(fe_d + b_p - w_p) + D(b_c n_d + w_c - b_c)}{Me_w + Se_d + Dn_d} \qquad \text{(A3.2.8)}$$

Often, this expression could be considerably simplified as illustrated below.

Tradeable Input Conversion Factor

Case I: Small country assumption (i.e., where e_w is very large), therefore:

$$CF_m = \frac{1}{1+t_m} \qquad\qquad\text{(A3.2.8)}$$

Nontradeable Input Conversion Factor

<u>Case IIa</u>: No imports and perfectly elastic supply (i.e., where M = 0, and e_d is very large)

<u>Case IIb</u>: No imports, perfectly inelastic demand and no income effects (i.e. where M = 0, n_d = 0, w_p = b_p, and w_c = b_c).

In both of these cases, therefore:

$$CF_2 = f$$

<u>Case IIIa</u>: No imports and perfectly elastic demand (i.e., where M = 0, and n_d is very large).

<u>Case IIIb</u>: No imports and perfectly inelastic supply and no income effects (i.e., where M = 0, e_d = O, w_p = b_p, and w_c = b_c).

In both these case, therefore:

$$CF_3 = b_c$$

We note that the corresponding conversion factor (CF_x) for a water sector input which is domestically produced for export as well as non-water sector domestic consumption may be derived analogously:

$$CF_x = \frac{X\left[\dfrac{(n_w-1)}{(1-t_x)}\right] + S(fe_d+b_p-w_p) + d(b_c n_d+w_c-b_c)}{Xn_w+Se_d+Dn_d} \qquad\text{(A3.2.9)}$$

where X represents exports, t_x is the tax rate on exports, n_w is the price elasticity of world demand, and the other symbols are as defined earlier.

Appendix 3.3
Social Pricing

If analysts are interested in valuing project components such as labor, and project costs and benefits in terms of efficiency pricing only, then they may stop here. However, if social pricing is important, consider the effect of these changes on consumption patterns. Suppose a worker receives a wage W_n in a new job, and that the income foregone is W_o, both in domestic prices; note that W_n may not necessarily be equal to the marginal product foregone m. It could be assumed, quite plausibly, that low-income workers consume the entire increase in income $(W_n - W_o)$. Then this increase in consumption will result in a resource cost to the economy of $b(W_n - W_o)$. The increase in consumption also provides a benefit given by $w(W_n - W_o)$, where w represents the marginal social benefit (MSB in border prices) of increasing domestic-priced private sector consumption by one unit. Therefore, the social shadow wage rate (SSWR) is given by:

$$SSWR = a \cdot m + c \cdot u + (b-w)(W_n - W_0) \qquad (A3.3.1)$$

The symbol b represents the marginal social cost (MSC) to the economy, resulting from the use of the increased income. For example, if all the new income is consumed, then b is the relevant consumption conversion factor or resource cost (in units of the numeraire) of making available to consumers one unit worth (in domestic prices) of the marginal basket of n goods they would purchase. In this case:

$$b = \sum_{i=1}^{n} g_i \cdot CF_i \qquad (A3.3.2)$$

where g_i is the proportion or share of good i in the marginal consumption basket, and CF_i is the corresponding conversion factor.

The MSB of increased consumption may be broken down further: $w = d/v$, where $1/v$ is the value (in units of the numeraire) of a one-unit increase in domestic-priced consumption accruing to someone at the average level of consumption $\hat{c}$. Therefore, v may be roughly thought of as the premium attached to public savings, compared to "average" private consumption. Under certain simplifying assumptions, $b = 1/v$. If MU(c) denotes the marginal utility of consumption at some level c, then:

$$d = \frac{MU(c)}{MU(\hat{c})} \qquad (A3.3.3)$$

Assuming that the marginal utility of consumption is diminishing, d would be greater than unity for "poor" consumers with $c < \hat{c}$, and vice versa.

A simple form of marginal utility function which could be assumed is:

$$MU(c) = c^{-n} \tag{A3.3.4}$$

Thus:

$$d = \frac{MU(c)}{MU(\hat{c})} = \left[\frac{\hat{c}}{c}\right]^{n} \tag{A3.3.5}$$

Making the further assumption that the distribution parameter $n = 1$, gives:

$$d = \frac{\hat{c}}{c} = \frac{\hat{i}}{i} \tag{A3.3.6}$$

where $(\hat{i}/i)$ is the ratio of net incomes, which may be used as a proxy for the corresponding consumption ratio.

The consumption term (b-w) in the expression for SWR disappears if at the margin, the following are true:

(a) society is indifferent to the distribution for income (or consumption), so that everyone's consumption has equivalent value; and

(b) private consumption is considered to be as socially valuable as uncommitted public savings, that is, the numeraire.

With regard to the discount rate, a simple formula for the social-priced ARI, which also includes consumption effects, is given by:

$$ARI = OCC\left[s + (1-s)\frac{w}{b}\right] \tag{A3.3.7}$$

where OCC is the opportunity cost of capital, and s is the fraction of the yield from the original investment that will be saved and reinvested.

4

Water Supply Systems and
Their Optimization

Introduction to Water Systems

The physical aspects of water supply are firmly rooted in traditional water systems engineering and technology. Therefore, it is useful at this stage to briefly review the basic principles underlying water systems.

A water system must supply water to consumers in sufficient volume and at the time and place of their choosing, while maintaining an acceptable quality of service; that is, attributes such as pressure, purity, taste, smell and color levels must lie within specified limits. The limits are usually set by national governments, and most are based on World Health Organization guidelines as defined in WHO (1984a, 1984b, 1985). The different components of a typical. water system are described briefly, next.

The basic constituent elements of a water system may be analyzed in terms of their functions: production, bulk transmission, distribution, sewerage collection and treatment. The concept of a water source or production facility is relatively unambiguous. Next in the chain are bulk transmission mains and distribution networks that carry the water from the source to the consumer. Finally there are conduits which carry wastewater away from the immediate environment of the consumer. Wastewater systems, depend on the level of socioeconomic development of a given country or locality, varying from a simple open sewer through which waste gradually drains off to a river or lake, to a sophisticated network of subterranean pipes, connecting each household with a downstream treatment plant. In such a plant, all harmful components are removed and wastewater is returned to the environment with minimal adverse effects on recipient water bodies.

These ideas are further clarified in Figure 4.1, a schematic diagram of an idealized simple water system. Water is produced in bulk (Q_i) at the headworks (Level 1) which may consist of dams and reservoirs for surface water, or wells and boreholes for ground water. After the dam, the water is

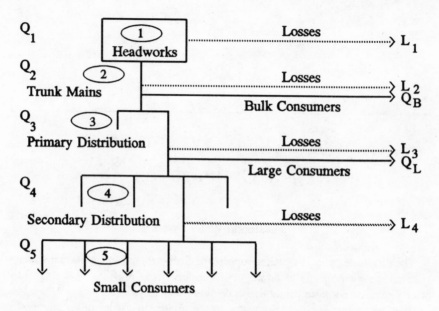

Figure 4.1 Schematic Diagram of a Simple Water Supply System

conveyed via the intake and a raw water pipeline, to the treatment installation (although many developing country supplies, particularly smaller-scale systems in rural area such as spring-fed, gravity-supplied, stand-pipe distribution systems, or hand-pumped boreholes, supply water without any treatment).

Depending on the particular treatment plant, the following stages may be a part of the treatment process:

- removal of floating objects, weeds and sand from the raw water;
- water aeration to control tastes and odors and to activate the bacterial breakdown of organic components;
- addition of coagulants to flocculate sludge; and
- sludge and waste removal from the settling tanks;
- filtering the water and correcting for its pH (acidity level); and
- addition of disinfectants to the water, such as chlorine or fluorine.

Effective treatment plant operation also involves monitoring of the water quality coming in and leaving the plant, to determine the nature and magnitude of the treatment required, and to control the quality of the water supply relative to the designated standards. More details, regarding treatment, can be found in reference manuals such as Barnes (1981) or IWES (1983).

After treatment, the water is stored in a clean water reservoir from which it is subsequently transmitted (Q_2) through bulk transmission mains (Level 2 onwards). Some bulk water consumers may obtain their supplies (Q_B) from the transmission mains, sometimes even before the treatment plant. However such use of untreated water is usually discouraged. At Level 3, the water (Q_3) flows into the primary distribution system. Some of the larger consumers may receive their supply (Q_L) at this stage. Finally, the remaining water (Q_4) is piped (Level 4) through the secondary distribution systems to reach retail consumers (Q_5) such as households (Level 5).

In transporting water the general principle is that the size of pipe used and pressure depends on distance and volume of water flow. Transmission mains are used to carry large amounts of water over long distances, while distribution pipes (primary mains and secondaries) involve smaller water flows over shorter distances. Depending on the water pressure, different pipe materials are considered for the transmission mains, and the primary and secondary distribution systems:

- at high water pressure (above 250m) the only appropriate pipe material is galvanized steel;
- at medium pressures (between 100 and 250 m) the suitable material is ductile iron and some grades of polyvinyl chloride (PVC), for instance the 10 kg/cm^2 class;
- for lower pressures suitable pipes are those made of asbestos cement, PVC, polyethylene, and concrete; and
- for the service pipes connecting the consumer's plumbing to the secondary distribution system, copper, galvanized mild steel and PVC are the materials commonly used.

Storage tanks, pumping stations and other facilities may also be involved at various points in the delivery system. The role of service reservoirs and water towers is to store water at suitable elevations so that the supply can be properly maintained when the demand exceeds the inflow from the trunk main. The storage volume should be large enough to accommodate the cumulative differences between water supply and demand over a period of time (IRC 1987).

There are two categories of pumping stations. The first type are relift stations for lifting water to zones which are higher then the area commanded by the trunk main. The second form of pumping units are so called booster plants. They are used to increase the water pressure in a transmission or distribution main to increase the overall network pressure, especially in large distribution systems. Boosters are useful in meeting peak period conditions where large flow rates are required for only a few hours each day.

Water losses are incurred throughout the system, and they are represented by L_1. They can be divided into two main groups: water losses at the headworks; and water losses in transmission and distribution.

Water losses at the headworks (L_1) consist of:

- spillway flow at the dam;
- leakage and overflow of untreated water from storage reservoirs and tanks;
- losses from inadequately controlled bypasses;
- leakage from untreated water transmission lines; and
- excessive use of water due to inefficient operation of the treatment process.

Losses occurring after water enters the transmission and distribution system (L_2, L_3, L_4 and L_5) are commonly referred to as "unaccounted-for-losses" (Jeffcoate 1987). They include:

- "physical losses" such as leakage from broken and cracked pipes, ill-fitting pipe-joints, dripping or gushing tap fittings, broken valves and stopcocks; and
- "non-physical losses" like under-registration or misreading of meters and supplies through illegal connections.

Non-physical losses represent revenue losses but not necessarily economic losses (since the user willingness-to-pay and benefits are unknown). We note that the physical water balance requires the following condition at the headworks:

$$Q_1 = Q_2 + L_1 \tag{4.1}$$

At level 2, the consumption of bulk consumers also must be considered, yielding:

$$Q_2 = Q_3 + L_2 + Q_B \tag{4.2}$$

Similar identities apply at levels 3 and 4.

Figure 4.2 depicts a simple sewerage system. In this case leakage of outside effluents into the network at each level increases the volume of sewerage that has to be treated and disposed of ultimately. Of course, all this water may not flow into the sewerage system. Some water infiltrates into the soil system or evaporating away into the atmosphere. Thus if the discharge from homes is Q_6, the proportion of net leakages L_6 add to the flow volume in the collection network so that the inflow to the trunk is given by:

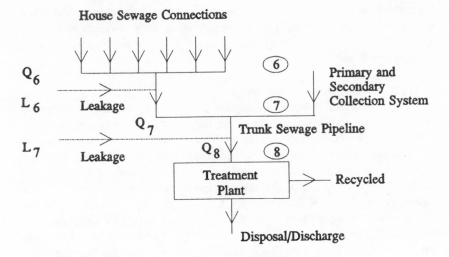

Figure 4.2 Schematic Diagram of a Simple Sewage System

$$Q_7 = Q_6 + L_6 \tag{4.3}$$

Similarly net leakage L_7 into the trunk line results in an inflow to the treatment plant:

$$Q_8 = Q_7 + L_7 \tag{4.4}$$

The treated water is either recycled or discharged as wastewater.

General Water System Optimizing Framework

As discussed in Chapter 3, the economic criterion underlying the evaluation of various water supply projects is the maximization of net economic benefits. In the conventional approach to water system design and planning, costs are minimized subject to supplying the demand at some (arbitrarily) given standard or quality of supply. Both the forecast demand and service quality are assumed to be fixed in this case, and consumption benefits are also constant. Therefore, cost minimization (or the least-cost criterion) is equivalent to maximization of net benefits. Since the traditional least-cost rule will continue to be the most practical one for water supply system design and planning, most of the following discussions are based on this approach. However, we begin by first discussing a more general system optimizing model that subsumes the traditional methodology and concentrates on optimizing service benefits.

Maximizing Benefits

Until recently, the idea of investigating the demand side effects relating to the economic worth of service quality had received little attention, principally because of the difficulties of measuring the benefits of improved quality of service. Data constraints are considerable and have prevented routine incorporation of such a model in water supply planning. The new approach to service quality presented here attempts to redress the above mentioned weakness, by considering the service quality level as a variable to be optimized, rather than an arbitrarily imposed standard derived from past practice and vague notions as to the standard of service which would be acceptable to the water consuming public. A typical example of ad-hoc target minimum standards relating to the quality of water supply has been provided by the WHO as outlined below. In order to achieve this goal a social cost-benefit approach must be adopted to evaluate the inherent trade-off between the increase in water system supply costs required to achieve a higher level of service quality, vis-a-vis a decline in service quality, defined as the economic costs incurred by consumers due to water shortages, poor water quality and other changes in consumption benefits.

WHO Guidelines for Drinking Water Quality Standards

In 1984, the WHO published its "Guidelines for Drinking Water Quality - Volume 1" for use by countries as a basis for the development of standards which, if properly implemented, will ensure the safety of drinking-water supplies. The guidelines are not standards in themselves, and may be modified on the basis of prevailing environmental, social, economic and cultural conditions as to which are appropriate. However, the WHO would like to see all supplies (i.e., not only community piped supplies but also water obtained from standpipes, wells, etc.), conform to these guidelines. The primary aim of the guidelines, published in three volumes, is the protection of public health and thus the elimination, or reduction to a minimum, of constituents of water that are known to be hazardous to the health and wellbeing of the community (WHO 1984a).

The guidelines for the contaminating substances and their significance for health are discussed, along with monitoring and remedial measures. Volume 2 provides criteria detailing the basis on which each guideline is set (WHO 1984b). Volume 3 focuses on the specific issues related to drinking water supply in small communities with emphasis on microbiology. The practical aspects of measurement and contamination prevention are prime concerns of

Volume 3 and are particularly useful for developing country situations, such as rural villages, where no treated, communal supply is provided (WHO 1985).

Volume 1 and 2 are under review by a WHO task group with completion of revised versions scheduled for 1992. Volume 3 guidelines are currently under revision by the WHO (WHO 1989) and are scheduled for publication in 1993. The updated Volume 3 guidelines will expand on the concepts of minimum treatment source selection and drinking water quality surveillance (sanitary surveys), to identify and control source contamination problems and disease transmission.

The following lists provide a basic summary of the recommended maximum limits or required status for each of the five categories:

- *Microbiological and biological constituents* -- no microorganisms known to be pathogenic, no faecal coliforms detectable (particularly Escherichia coli), no pathogenic intestinal protozoa (E. histolytica, Giardia, Balantidium coli), preferably no helminths present (Dracunculus 'Guineaworm' larvae and cyclops, Schistosome larvae and snails, Ascaris), preferably no free-living organisms (fungae, algae, macro-invertebrates, etc.).

- *Inorganic constituents* -- 9 constituents of direct concern are listed for which guidelines are set (in mg/l -- arsenic 0.05, cadmium 0.005, chromium 0.05, cyanide 0.1, fluoride 1.5, lead 0.05, mercury 0.001, nitrate 10.0, selenium 0.01) and 7 constituents of possible health significance are discussed (asbestos, barium, beryllium, hardness, nickel, silver, sodium).

- *Organic constituents* -- more than 600 organic substances have been found in drinking water of which many are pharmacologically active, several are known carcinogens and carcinogenic promoters and some are mutagenic. Important constituents are listed and the most significant are given guidelines (in μg/l -- aldrin and dieldrin 0.03, benzene 10.0, benzo[a]pyrene 0.01, chlordane 0.3, chloroform 30.0, 2,4-D 100.0, DDT 1.0, 1,2-dichloroethane 10.0, 1,1-dichloroethane 0.3, heptachlor 0.1, hexachlorobenzene 0.01, lindane 3.0, methoxychlor 30.0, pentachlorophenol 10.0, 2,4,6-trichlorophenol 10.0).

- *Aesthetic quality* -- 20 constituents were considered particularly important for aesthetic acceptability of water, 15 receiving guideline status, and 5 detailed according to conditions where they are problematic (aluminium 0.2 mg/l, chloride 250.0 mg/l, color 15 units, copper 1.0 mg/l, hardness 500 mg/l, hydrogen sulfide should not be detectable, iron 0.3 mg/l, manganese 0.1 mg/l, pH 6.5-8.5, sodium 200.0 mg/l, solids TDS 1000.0 mg/l, sulfate 400 mg/l, taste and odour should not be offensive, turbidity 5 NTU, zinc 5.0 mg/l. Although no specific values have been set, dissolved oxygen should be close to saturation, induced temperature changes should be low, chlorophenols should be low, monochlorobenzenes and dichlorobenzenes should be low).

- *Radioactive constituents* -- various body tissues have different sensitivities to radiation exposure and the guidelines assume a daily intake of drinking water of 2 liters when calculating guideline concentrations (gross alpha activity 0.1 Bq/l, gross beta activity 1.0 Bq/l).

Effects of Varying Water Quality

We recognize that providing consumers with water at different standards of supply implies that the service quality will vary and that both costs and benefits will change. When the quality of supply or service quality is varied there are two principal ways in which consumption benefits could be affected:

- the total demand changes; and
- the costs incurred by consumers due to poor quality of service changes.

The total demand met, and therefore the benefits, may depend critically on the supply quality. For example, service pressure and volume levels originally intended for households may generally be inappropriate for commercial consumers or industries. Therefore, some commercial or industrial water users may have to rely fully or partially on their own private production rather than the public water supply system. This, in turn, may have a negative feedback on future service quality, if private producers use common water sources such as aquifers in an uncontrolled, and unsustainable fashion (thereby imposing environmental externalities on other water users as discussed in more detail in Chapters 5 and 6). Even in cases where no significant water using industries exist initially, their future growth may be retarded or hindered by the adoption of low water supply standards, or further system costs may have to be incurred later on to meet these heavier demands.

Poor service including inadequate water quality, low pressure, water cuts (or service interruptions), and so on, will impose service quality costs on the consumer, thus reducing the consumption benefits. In general, these costs of poor service quality will vary by type of consumer, according to service interruption characteristics (e.g., frequency, duration, time of occurrence, and so on), extent of pressure fluctuations (especially during peak hours), and water purity (bacterial content, hardness, etc.), color, taste and odor.

A mathematical model is developed in the following sections that shows for a given price structure, how an optimal long-run water system expansion plan and a corresponding range of service quality levels may be determined which maximize net social benefits of water consumption, and thus reflects the national viewpoint. This planning rule effectively subsumes the traditional criterion of minimizing only the system cost (which is more consistent with the viewpoint of a private water utility). Such a balanced treatment of both the supply and demand side effects of service quality requires accurate estimates of both system costs and service quality costs. The former category of costs may be determined from straightforward engineering-economic considerations normally associated with water supply system design and planning. However, the determination of service quality costs is more difficult and methods of estimating such costs are also discussed in the following sections.

Analytical Model for Optimizing Water Service Quality

Basic Concepts

The two principal concerns of water sector policymakers are the investment and pricing decisions, as introduced in Chapter 2 in the context of economic efficiency.

The investment decision has traditionally been treated within the framework of the least-cost system expansion plan. In recent times sophisticated system planning models and techniques have been developed, based on the criterion of minimizing the cost of supplying a given long-range demand forecast, at some acceptable service quality level. The optimal size, mix and timing of new capacity additions are determined in this way, and related models also provide for optimal (least-cost) operation of the system.

On the other hand, the theoretical foundations of optimal water prices based on marginal costs date back to the path-breaking efforts of Dupuit and Hotelling. Their work has been developed further by other authors as discussed in Chapter 8.

While the close relationship between optimal investment and pricing policies have been generally recognized for some time, recent work has emphasized that the optimal conditions for price and investment levels must be simultaneously satisfied to maximize the net social benefits of water consumption. In this context, determining the optimal investment level is usually considered equivalent to establishing the optimal level of service quality, since capacity additions do improve the service quality level. However, in our model we will focus specifically on optimal service quality. This viewpoint is more general because, although excess capacity is an important determinant of the supply quality, other factors such as improved operation and maintenance procedures could also achieve the same result, and none of these wider possibilities should be excluded from the analysis.

Summarizing the complex analysis underlying the joint optimality condition, we can simply state that the optimal service quality level (and hence the level of investment to achieve it) is defined as the point at which the marginal cost of increasing service quality is exactly equal to the corresponding increase in marginal benefits e.g., due to the reduction in costs incurred by consumers due to poor service quality (i.e., the service quality costs). Simultaneously, the optimal price is the marginal cost of supply (see Chapter 8 for details).

For purposes of clarity, we must distinguish between the short-run and long-run marginal costs (SRMC and LRMC). SRMC is the cost of meeting additional water consumption with fixed production and supply capacity, while LRMC is the incremental cost of providing an increase in consumption sustained indefinitely into the future with capacity adjustments permitted. When the system is optimally planned and operated (i.e., investment and service quality levels are optimal), SRMC and LRMC coincide. However, if the system plan is sub-optimal, significant deviations between SRMC and LRMC will have to be resolved within the pricing policy framework (see Chapter 8).

For practical purposes, however, the joint optimal price and service quality conditions are used in an essentially uncoupled form. The optimal service quality rule is more difficult to apply, especially because supply quality costs are not easy to estimate. A simplified framework for using this criterion for water system expansion planning is summarized below. Application of the marginal cost pricing rule is discussed in Chapter 8.

The essence of the optimizing methodology is that supply quality, R, should be treated as a generalized variable that is to be optimized. As indicated earlier, the quality of supply affecting various customers may be defined in terms of a set of measures including frequency and duration of interruptions, water pressure, purity, color, smell, etc. Since many of these attributes are influenced by a range of environmental externalities, as briefly explained in Chapter 2, and more widely discussed in Chapter 5, the following analysis provides a tool with which the planner can judge, in economic terms, the impact of a range of actual or potential environmental problems on consumer benefits, and or supply costs. The total benefit of water consumption is a function of the total quantity of water consumed D, and the quality of service, R. If the service quality were perfect, i.e., $R = RP$, total benefits may be written as TB (D, RP). In practice, water supply is not of perfect quality. To account for this, we define a function QC to represent the costs and inconveniences suffered by consumers due to disruptions in supply including service interruptions, low pressure, and impure water. As R rises QC will decrease. An improvement in supply quality will also raise the consumers' expectation regarding the future level of service quality (R^*) and is also likely to induce increased water demand which provides additional net benefits of consumption. Changes in R^* may also affect QC as consumers adapt their behavior patterns to reduce these service quality costs. On the other hand, as supply quality increases, the cost of building, operating, and maintaining the system (SC) also increases. Thus by increasing R, it would be possible to trade off the higher system costs against the decrease in QC and increased net benefits of induced demand. Environmental externalities clearly can influence the costs and inconveniences suffered by consumers (QC) reducing the quality of service (R and especially R* as the impact of externalities persist). If externalities affect the water bearing capacity of sources, or preclude the use of certain sources, then clearly the supply costs (SC) will increase accordingly. Provided that systematic estimates are made concerning the range of externalities that may be experienced for a given water system, under a number of supply scenarios (for instance using a form of environmental impact assessment), then the model becomes a tool for the meaningful evaluation of alternative measures to manage various environmental problems.

Model Formulation

Let the demand for water in the service area of a water system be given by:

$$D = D(P, R^*, Y, \underline{Z})$$

where P is the price per unit, R* is the service quality or service quality consumers expect to receive, Y is a variable which captures the level of economic activity (e.g., income), and $\underline{Z}$ is a vector of other relevant explanatory variables. For purposes of optimization, we assume Y and $\underline{Z}$ are exogenously given.

The net benefits of water consumption may be written:

$$NB(D,R) = TB(D,RP) - SC(D,R) - QC(D,R,R^*) \tag{4.5}$$

Total benefits TB, as well as supply costs SC and service quality costs QC are functions of D, while the functional dependence of SC and QC on R and R* has been explained earlier. We note that TB is also a function of the perfect service quality RP which does not change with R.

Before proceeding further, it should be recognized that water tariffs are relatively static and inflexible (as explained in Chapter 7), and simultaneous optimization of price and capacity is, therefore, a theoretical ideal. Thus from a practical point of view, it is often necessary to uncouple the joint price and service quality optimization conditions by attempting to "optimize" service quality in the presence of fixed or given tariffs, at least on the first round. Once optimal service quality (subject to given prices as defined above) is determined, tariffs can be revised to reflect any changes in the marginal cost of supplying water implied by the new service quality level. Using this new level of tariffs and resulting demand, service quality can be reoptimized iteratively.

Allowing only R to vary, the first order (necessary) condition for maximization of net benefits is given by:

$$\frac{dNB}{dR} = \frac{\partial D}{\partial R^*} \cdot \frac{\partial R^*}{\partial R} \cdot \frac{\partial(TB-SC-QC)}{\partial D} - \frac{\partial(SC+QC)}{\partial R^*} - \frac{\partial R^*}{\partial R} \cdot \frac{\partial QC}{\partial R^*} = 0 \quad (4.6)$$

We may rewrite the above as:

$$\frac{dSC}{dR} = -\frac{\partial QC}{\partial R} + \frac{\partial TB}{\partial R} \quad (4.7)$$

where:

$$\frac{dSC}{dR} = \frac{\partial SC}{\partial R^*} + \left[\frac{\partial R^*}{\partial R} \cdot \frac{\partial D}{\partial R^*} \cdot \frac{\partial SC}{\partial D} \right]$$

$$\frac{dQC}{dR} = \frac{\partial QC}{\partial R^*} + \frac{\partial R^*}{\partial R} \left[\frac{\partial D}{\partial R^*} \cdot \frac{\partial QC}{\partial D} + \frac{\partial QC}{\partial R} \right]$$

$$\frac{dTB}{dR} = \frac{\partial R^*}{\partial R} \cdot \frac{\partial D}{\partial R^*} \cdot \frac{\partial TB}{\partial D}$$

It should be understood that (dTB/dR) is to be evaluated at R = RP, because changes in TB occur only through changes in D.

The term (dSC/dR) on the left hand side of equation (4.7) represents the total changes in supply costs due to variations in the actual supply quality, and consists of two components. The first part ($\partial SC/\partial R$) is the direct effect of R on SC, while the second component ($\partial R^*/\partial R$)·($\partial D/\partial R^*$)·($\partial SC/\partial D$) captures the indirect effect via the chain of interactions in which R affects R*, which in turn affects the demand, which finally causes a change in supply costs.

The term (dQC/dR) is the total change in service quality costs with respect to service quality, and has three components, among which the first two may be interpreted analogously to the corresponding components of (dSC/dR). The last part ($\partial R^*/\partial R$)·($\partial QC/\partial R^*$), represents the change in QC due to changes in service quality expectation R*, themselves caused by variations in R.

Finally, the term (dTB/dR) denotes the change in total benefits caused by the induced demand changes arising from variations in R*, themselves caused by changes in R. We will refer to this term as the change in total benefits due to induced demand. Thus, equation (4.7) implies that to maximize the net benefits of water consumption, the quality of service should be increased up to the point where the marginal increase in system costs is equal to the marginal decrease in the costs of poor supply quality plus increase in the benefits of induced demand. These marginal costs and benefits include both the direct effects of changes in R, and the indirect effects due to induced variations in R* and D.

We note that (dSC/dR) > 0, since all the components such as $\partial SC/\partial R$, $\partial R/\partial R$, $\partial D/\partial R$ and $\partial SC/\partial D$ would be positive.

Similarly (dTB/dR) > 0, because all its components are also positive. Finally, we might expect (dQC/dR) < 0, since the dominant component ($\partial QC/\partial R$) is always negative (although some of the other components may be positive or indeterminate).

These results may be interpreted more clearly using Figure 4.3, where SC and QC are shown (by solid lines) as monotonically increasing and decreasing functions of quality of supply (R), respectively. The total costs curve is defined by TC = SC + QC. TB is also an increasing function of R due to the effects of induced demand. As shown in the figure, the optimal value of quality of supply (Rm) where the marginality conditions in equation (4.6) are satisfied occurs when the slopes of the TC and TB curves are exactly equal, i.e., dTB/dR = ∂(SC + QC)/∂R = $\partial TC/\partial R$, or equivalently $S_1 = S_2$. At this point, net benefits NB = TB - TC, are maximized. This new economic criterion for water system optimization is general enough to be applicable to all levels of water system planning, that is, for production, transmission and distribution.

It is useful to analyze the way in which the above approach relates to and subsumes traditional economic criteria used in water system planning. First, suppose the effects due to changes in expected service quality are ignored, i.e., $\partial D/\partial R^* = 0$ and $\partial QC/\partial R^* = 0$. Then equation (4.7) may be written:

$$\frac{\partial SC}{\partial R} = -\frac{\partial QC}{\partial R} \tag{4.8}$$

This more restricted marginality condition may be interpreted also using Figure 4.3, in which the broken curves SC_1 and QC_1 are both shown slightly displaced to the right because the ignored components in ($\partial SC/\partial R$) and ($\partial QC/\partial R$) are both assumed to be positive and would tend to increase the slopes of SC and QC respectively. In other words, equation (4.8) implies that the optimal service quality level Rm_1 occurs when the slope S_3 of SC_1 is equal to the negative slope S_4 of QC_1. This point is also the minimum of the (broken) total costs curve: $TC_1 = SC_1 + QC_1$. Equivalently, since TB_1 is now independent of R, from equation (4.5), minimizing TC_1 is equivalent to maximizing net benefits. In general Rm_1 and Rm would not coincide. Although Figure 4.3 shows Rm_1 being higher level of service quality than Rm, this is not necessarily so in all cases.

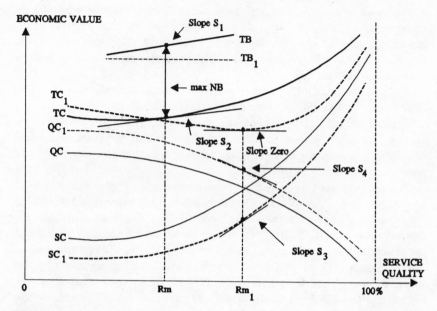

Figure 4.3 Optimal Service Quality Levels

Next, suppose that both the demand D and the target service quality level
R are assumed to be fixed. Then maximizing NB reduces to simply
minimizing the costs of supply SC for exogenously given D and R, which is
the conventional and most commonly encountered planning criterion, i.e.,
least-cost system expansion. This approach and its implications for water
system design are discussed at greater length in subsequent chapters.

Clearly, the least-cost rule is most appropriate for a private utility which is
concerned only with its own costs. In contrast, both equations (4.7) and (4.8)
imply that not only SC but also the costs and benefits of consumption should
be included in the planning criterion. This is more comprehensive and
represents the viewpoint of society as a whole. However, equation (4.7) is
more general than equation (4.8), because the effects of induced demand have
been included.

Environmental Impacts and Service Quality

The differential terms that indicate the changes in total benefits, service
quality costs and supply costs due to a variation in service quality allows the
incorporation of the effects of environmental impacts. This is because service
quality is itself affected by environmental problems. Service quality will

clearly decrease because the onset of negative environmental effects such as pollution, saline intrusion into groundwater, or aquifer depletion will result in:

- increased costs of supply just to maintain a given level of service quality, or offset a decrease in quality, due to the need for more water treatment, deeper pumping, artificial recharge, etc.;
- increased service quality costs for the consumer due to the increased incidence of contamination, the falling yield of supplies or supply interruptions; and
- decreased total (and hence net) benefits due to impact of service quality deterioration manifesting itself in falling demand as consumers switch to traditional sources, and/or consume less due to higher costs or, reduced water quality considerations.

Clearly, the opposite effects also can occur where effective environmental management policies improve the water supply performance of a particular source in terms of the quality, quantity, availability and reliability of service.

Procedure for Implementing the Model

Before discussing the procedure for practical application of the theoretical model, it is useful to explain the concept of a service quality path. Ideally, the service quality or quality of supply R should be represented by a multidimensional vector reflecting the many relevant attributes of water supply that affect consumers, such as frequency, duration, time of occurrence and extent of service interruptions, pressure variations, color, smell, odor and impurities. Although the use of this methodology does not depend on the actual measure of R used, it is convenient for clear graphical exposition of the results, to define one relatively simple measure of quality of supply to any group of customers in year t, i.e., service interruptions.

One measure that reflects service interruptions may be defined by:

$$R_t = 1 - \frac{IW_t}{TW_t} \tag{4.9}$$

where:

IW_t =   volume of water not supplied because of service interruptions in year t.

TW_t =   total volume of water that would have been supplied in year t if there were no service interruptions.

SERVICE QUALITY

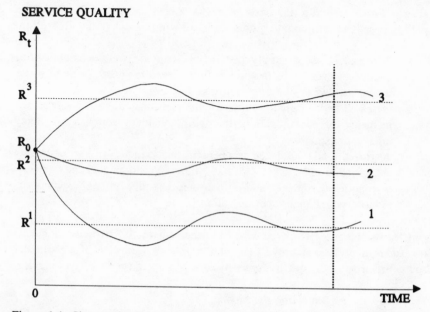

Figure 4.4 Characterization of Alternative Expansion Paths According to the Service Quality Level

Because of the lumpiness of water system investments and their long lifetimes, system planning is usually carried out for a fairly long period, e.g., 10-15 years. Consider Figure 4.4 which shows three possible evolutionary paths of system service quality starting from the initial level R_0 and extending over some planning time horizon; i.e., 0 to T. Path 2 represents the case in which expenditures on the water system are sufficient to maintain the medium level of service quality R_2. In paths 1 and 3 the service quality is adjusted to two different target levels, i.e., R_1 and R_3. The paths vary about the trend line because of the lumpy nature of the investments corresponding to each system expansion plan.

Now, for $t = 0,\ldots,T$, and for expansion path i, let:

$SC_t^i =$ the annual stream of future system supply costs (i.e., investment, maintenance, etc.) net of marginal production costs of water not supplied due to service interruptions;

$QC_t^i =$ the corresponding costs of poor supply quality.

Next we define the present discounted values:

$$SC^i = \sum_{t=0}^{T} \frac{SC_i^t}{(1+r)^t} \qquad (4.10)$$

and:

$$QC^i = \sum_{t=0}^{T} \frac{QC_i^t}{(1+r)^t} \qquad (4.11)$$

where r is the appropriate economic discount rate (as explained in detail in Chapter 3).

An aggregate service quality index may also be defined based on water supply:

$$R_i = 1 - \frac{\displaystyle\sum_{t=0}^{T} \frac{IW_t^i}{(1+r)^t}}{\displaystyle\sum_{t=0}^{T} \frac{TW_t^i}{(1+r)^t}} \qquad (4.12)$$

If we also define:

$$TB^i = \sum_{t=0}^{T} \frac{TB_t^i}{(1+r)^t} \qquad (4.13)$$

where TB^i are the total benefits of water consumption associated with system design i, in the absence of costs due to poor supply quality (i.e., where R = RP), then choosing the system plan m which maximizes net benefits:

$$NB^m = TB^m - SC^m - QC^m \qquad (4.14)$$

also yields the optimum service quality level R_m. Note that we are interested only in relative changes, and therefore TB^i need not be estimated completely. Instead only the change in total benefits (due to induced demand) between a given system design i and some baseline system plan b needs to be evaluated, i.e.,

$$dTB^{ib} = TB^i - TB^b \qquad (4.15)$$

A method for practical application of the theoretical model is summarized in Figure 4.5 First, a set of n likely future paths of expected service quality $(R^{1*},...,R^{n*})$ are chosen, where R^{i*} characterizes the service quality of path i during the planning time horizon as discussed earlier. For example, if we wished to explore different environmentally-oriented scenarios, several of the paths R^i could be chosen to represent options in which environmental variations caused changes in service quality. This information is combined with a given price forecast and other socioeconomic and demographic data to prepare alternative disaggregate demand forecasts $(D^i,...,D^n)$ corresponding to each expected service quality path. We may normally expect that in any given future year, the demand would be greater for higher levels of expected quality of supply.

Second, water system models and data are used to design n alternative long-range system plans to meet the n demand forecasts at the n alternative service quality levels $(R^1,...,R^n)$ which conform as closely as possible to the original target set $(R^{1*},...,R^n)$. Each system plan is least-cost for the given demand and service quality path, and has an associated supply cost SC.

Third, service quality cost models, the demand forecasts, and the service quality information are combined to make estimates of future shortage costs QC corresponding to each system plan. The total benefits of consumption TB are also estimated for each demand forecast.

Finally, the values of TB^i, SC^i and QC^i corresponding to each alternative path i are compared and the path m which maximizes the present discounted value of net benefits:

$$NB^m = TB^m - SC^n - QC^m \qquad (4.16)$$

over the long-range time horizon is chosen as the optimal one. In practice, because the system design process involves discrete jumps in R rather than continuous variations, it is better to consider a band of optimum service quality levels around R^m rather than a unique value. In this formulation, the measure R^i is an aggregate scalar quantity used for convenience to simply characterize a given system path i. The process of choosing the optimum system design is carried out on the basis of an economic cost benefit analysis, and is quite independent of the actual measure of service quality. Furthermore, by specifically introducing various environmental changes into the picture, the impact of environmental externalities can be implicitly included in the optimal planning procedure, via the effects on service quality.

We conclude by examining several iterative feedback loops. First, if a designed system has a significantly different service quality path than the

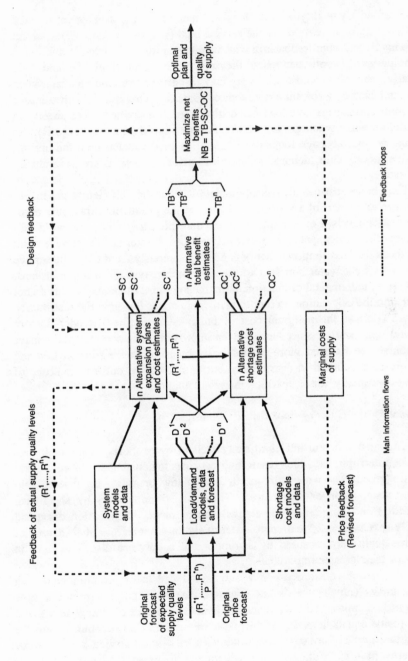

Figure 4.5 Optimal System Planning Framework

expected supply quality assumed for the demand forecast, then for consistency the latter must be revised via the service quality feedback loop. The second loop involves design feedback in which a given system plan may be fine-tuned to improve the optimum using the information concerning TB and QC. Finally, the marginal costs of supply may be derived from the optimal system plan and used to revise the original price forecast. This allows us to recouple the joint optimal price and service quality conditions (which were uncoupled for convenience when the model was first optimized with respect to R). In summary, the feedback loops permit iteration of the model until the optimal service quality path, demand forecast and price projections are all mutually consistent.

The above cost-benefit based simulation model is sufficiently general to optimize all or part of a water system, ie., at the production, transmission or distribution levels. For example, only the distribution system could be varied, whereas the service quality of water delivered to an intermediate storage point that feeds this distribution network is held exogenously fixed (i.e., the service quality of bulk water supplied to the distribution system is held constant). Therefore, incremental production, bulk transmission, and storage costs do not enter into the calculation, except to help value water losses in the distribution system (i.e., at the marginal cost of bulk water supplied). Under a more general optimization procedure, a given improvement in service quality may, of course, be realized more economically by strengthening production and transmission rather than distribution, but this would be outside the scope of normal secondary water distribution system analysis.

Estimating the Costs of Poor Service Quality

The most dramatic and significant effects of water shortages are unplanned service interruptions, which result in direct costs to consumers. More general service quality costs may also occur due to low pressure, or unacceptable color, taste, odor or impurities. These are often caused by short-term (episodic) and long-term (cumulative) environmental degradation discussed briefly in Chapter 2, and more extensively in Chapter 5. The nature of service quality costs caused by disruptions of supply are discussed first, in view of their greater importance.

Production is a process in which capital and labor are combined with other inputs (raw materials and intermediate products) to produce a time stream of outputs. The net economic benefit of a unit of output in a given time period equals the value of the output minus the value of inputs. Thus the opportunity cost of not supplying water with the desired service quality can be measured in terms of the resulting reduction in the present value of the stream of net benefits. If market distortions are present in the economy, appropriate shadow prices have to be used to value inputs and outputs (see Chapter 3 for details).

When a water supply interruption, for instance the temporary drying up of an intake or the failure of a poorly-maintained pump, curtails production of goods and services, the net benefits derived from such activities are reduced, i.e., direct service quality costs are incurred, since the costs of inputs may be increased, and the value of outputs reduced. Thus, a service interruption can result in productive factors being made idle, and also cause raw materials, intermediate products, or final outputs to be lost. The loss is represented by an opportunity cost equal to the value of the final product made unavailable by the supply failure, minus the net value of additional inputs not now needed.

In particular, industrial consumers suffer service quality costs because materials and products are spoiled, and normal production cannot take place, which results in an opportunity cost in the form of idle capital and labor, both during the service interruption and any restart period following it. If there is slack capacity, some of the lost value added may be recovered by using this productive capacity more intensively during normal working hours. In addition, the firm may operate overtime to make up lost production. The cost of providing backup or alternative (private) water supply facilities (storage tanks, wells, and so on) could provide an upper bound on the estimate of service interruption costs.

In the case of domestic water consumers, the costs of measures to mitigate supply interruptions (such as storage tanks or private wells), can provide a helpful guideline for service quality costs. Alternatively, since households produce outputs that are not sold directly in the market, a different approach could be used to estimate the costs of supply interruptions. Using the microeconomic theory of the household labor-leisure choice, it is possible to relate incremental wage rates to the value of leisure time foregone due to service interruptions. Survey techniques may also be used to provide additional information on the residential users willingness-to-pay to avoid service interruptions, or the willingness-to-accept compensation for interruption costs incurred.

Commercial and domestic use sometimes come into conflict. Examples exist from the developing world of economically productive concerns such as intensive plantations or industrial estates creating service interruptions for domestic users by consuming all the locally available water (for specific examples see Chapter 5). From a planning point of view, it is necessary to compare the opportunity cost of the reduced productivity caused by rationing commercial water use, to the increase in net benefits to household consumers from a more reliable supply. For the latter, social costs and benefits are an important consideration. This raises the questions of equity in relation to shared resources, and which category of users have priority when there are such conflicts of interest. This is a difficult decision for planners in many developing countries, where the need for industrial and agricultural output, particularly for export, must be reconciled against the desire to improve water supply coverage to urban and rural populations from only limited potable water resources.

Next we deal with the other characteristic of the multidimensional supply quality vector R, due to pollution. We will use the terms pollution and pollutants in a general sense to include aspects such as color, undesirable taste or smell, the presence of hazardous chemicals or diseases carriers, and even thermal pollution from upstream industrial cooling processes. Again, many of these problems develop from environmental mismanagement in the water and related sectors, and show the need for an environment-oriented approach to integrated water resources planning. However, estimating the costs (or foregone benefits) of poor water quality as a result of these attributes is not as straightforward as the analysis of the repercussions of supply interruptions. Given the wide range of potential pollutants, it becomes clear that all "impurities" cannot be captured under one single denominator for the sake of economic evaluation. Some generic techniques for economic valuation of environmental effects are summarized in Chapter 5. Different cost estimation techniques are warranted to analyze the economic costs of distinct pollution sources. Although it is not within the scope of this volume to make an in depth analysis for each type of pollutant, some methods proposed by natural resource economists are outlined briefly below.

Smith and Krutilla (1982) suggest that all approaches for measuring the benefits of a change in an environmental resource (such as polluted water) can be classified as involving either physical or behavioral assumptions. The first category identifies technical relationships between water quality and a number of economic activities. These relationships are sometimes referred to as damage functions. One example is the evaluation of health risks associated with a given type and degree of water pollution (see, e.g., Page et al. 1981). Another example is the decrease in a commercial fish population due to unfavorable changes in the water temperature.

Smith and Desvousges (1986) argue that, although damage functions might sometimes provide a good measure of certain pollution impacts, they fall short in cases where behavioral changes of the consumer become important. Following the taxonomy of Smith and Krutilla, the behavioral responses of the consumer can be analyzed in terms of the indirect and direct links between water quality change and observed effects. One widely employed method in the indirect links approach is the travel cost approach. Smith and Desvousges apply the method to measure households' valuation of water quality changes in relation to the recreational value of water. An example more closely related to water supply is the reduced costs in collecting and transporting water. Okun and Ernst (1987) mention the case of villages in Kenya, where female heads of households devote a third of their total worktime collecting water.

Easier access to safe water would not only provide women with more time for income producing work, but also for child care and attending educational programs. Children obliged to carry water can spend their time in school instead.

The state of the art method in the direct link approach is the contingent valuation technique. Detailed descriptions of the methodology in water resource applications are presented by Cummings et al. (1986) and Mitchell and Carson (1989). This technique also has a long history in other sectors like electric power (Energy Journal 1988, Munasinghe 1979). The contingent valuation approach is based on the design and analysis of surveys in which individuals are asked their willingness-to-pay for a non-market commodity. One illustrative example would be a household survey designed to determine the monetary value users attach to improving one or more of the impurity components of potable water. A practical application of the use of the methodology is presented in a recent report (WASH 1989). The study tries to determine the willingness-to-pay of villagers in the Kitangari Water Scheme, Tanzania, for the costs of the diesel fuel to run a pumping station and a water treatment plant. Although the contingent valuation method is enjoying increasing popularity amongst resource economists, Cummings et al., point out that the method might be least accurate when most needed. For example, in the case of environmental amenities that are not easy to understand or that the respondent cannot readily relate to market-based experiences (e.g., color or odor of drinking water), the potential of the methodology is greatest but the results of a survey might be least precise. Mitchell and Carson (1984), therefore stress the need for the economists to pay more attention to questionnaire design and survey-related issues.

A practical application of the contingent valuation method where the amenities of the choice are well-understood by the respondents is described in a case-study from Brazil in Chapter 7. In it, the willingness-to-pay of Brazilian rural households for new sources of water supply is surveyed. The study shows the crucial dependence of households' satisfaction on the quality supplied (in that particular case public taps vs. private yard taps), which in turn is used for appropriate demand forecasting.

Least-Cost System Planning

While the general optimization model just summarized subsumes traditional least-cost planning, it is still very important from a practical viewpoint to design specific supply systems to deliver water to consumers in the cheapest possible way. The link between the least-cost alternative and water supply project evaluation (especially cost-benefit analysis), has already been described in Chapter 3.

The first major step in least-cost planning is the choice of one or more water sources. These might typically include surface water (from rivers, dams, lakes, etc.), or ground water (from wells and boreholes). The various technical and economic issues underlying this selection are described below, starting with the principles of water system planning. Second, the water supply network must be optimized. The basics of bulk transmission and distribution planning are also summarized later in this Chapter.

Ideally, the planning of the whole water system should be integrated. To make the practical problems of system design workable, however, it is convenient to break the procedure down into parts associated with the main subsystems: production (and storage), transmission, distribution (see e.g., Brandon 1984). This type of hierarchical reduction is logical from several points of view.

Evolution of Modeling Approaches

As mentioned earlier, various completion times are associated with the discrete projects in a long-range plan for system expansion. These range from up to ten years for the design and construction of a large production/treatment facility to one or two years for distribution schemes. Also, the problems and design philosophies associated with the different parts of the total water system are inherently dissimilar. For example, water supply distribution system planners require detailed knowledge of localized geographic areas and must deal with many small components such as distribution pipes, valves and taps. At the other extreme, production planning is carried out at a more global level and is concerned with large components such as dams and treatment plants, and these generally have interaction modes that are more complex to analyze. Consequently, the models and criteria used to design the various subsystems are also different. The following non-mathematical discussion is cast in the context of traditional system expansion planning, that is, choosing the design that minimizes system cost while meeting given requirements for demand and service quality. The basic ideas involved, however, may be readily adapted to the new approach outlined earlier, in which the service quality level is treated as a variable, and the total cost to society, or sum of system and service quality costs, is minimized.

Early approaches to system design and planning were rather intuitive and relied heavily on the designers' past experience. In contrast, the mathematical methods currently used rely on optimization models. The goal is to minimize an objective function, usually the present discounted value of system cost subject to various constraints, such as meeting targets for demand and service quality (these constraints are in fact the optimization variables in the previous approach), and maintaining technical and operating requirements.

In the search for the techno-economic optimum, engineers and scientists have relied on two major techniques: the trial-and-error simulation models and the operations research optimization models. Simulation models are mathematical models, based on the hydraulics and design parameters of a water supply system. They typically allow the engineer to assess the repercussions of alternative design schemes and are indispensable for a safe and good design. However, to attempt to employ the simulation model in a number of trial-and-error runs (in combination with heuristic rules) is a time consuming task, given the enormous number of possible technical combinations. Even then, the designer does not have the guarantee that the resulting solution is a low-cost one, let alone the least-cost solution. Operations research optimization models on the other hand, often make use of overly simplified hydraulics and design details, for the mere sake of being able to solve the optimization algorithm. Although in such a case a true mathematical solution can be found, which in itself is not always guaranteed as in the case of nonlinear programming, one might wonder to what extent the physical simplifications of the system under optimization still mirror the realities of the system being modeled. This casts doubt on the validity of the "optimal" solution. Recently, however, the number of efforts to embed technically comprehensive simulation models into optimization models is increasing. This tendency seems to be attuned to the availability of faster and more powerful computers.

Details about the hydraulics and design requirements from which water supply design simulation models are constructed can be found in Babbitt et al. (1962), AWWA (1986) and Brandon (1984). Loucks et al. (1981) give an excellent overview of the operations research techniques and models, commonly used in water resources planning. These models include:

- deterministic and stochastic linear and dynamic programming;
- chance constrained models; and
- multiobjective models.

It should be noted that, like the result of any model, even combined simulation-optimization models are not free of flaws under all circumstances. Many researchers stress that the model outcome has to be used mainly for guidance in the design and planning process, and not as the final design solution, in which results are adopted without practical judgement (see e.g., Loucks et al. 1985, Lansey and Mays 1989).

Past Use of Reliability as a System Performance Criterion

While the model presented earlier seeks to integrate the quality of water supply directly into the planning process, in the past the reliability of supply has been used mainly as a separate criterion to judge the performance of a water supply system. This criterion was used to assess the ability of existing or proposed water systems to operate satisfactorily under a wide range of possible future demands and hydrologic conditions. A system was considered more or less reliable depending on the frequency of water shortages occurring in the system (e.g., see Equation 4.9). Reliability could also be related to the water quality of the system. Water shortages or quality problems are the results of naturally occurring or human influenced events as summarized by Kersnar (1985):

(a) Hydrologic events:

• Flood; and
• Drought.

(b) Mechanical failures:

• Pump equipment breakdown;
• Water main break;
• Failure of treatment plant; and
• Dam failure.

(c) Contamination events:

• Hazardous material spill;
• Saltwater intrusion; and
• Back siphoning.

Examples of design models that incorporate the shortage risk factor explicitly in the optimization procedure are: Goulter and Bouchart (1990) for the planning of the water transmission; and Duan et al. (1990) for the distribution system.

Besides reliability, two other criteria define the performance of water resource systems (Hashimoto et al. 1982), namely resiliency and vulnerability. Resiliency describes how quickly the water supply system is likely to recover or bounce back from failure. In this context Fiering and Holling (1974), and Fiering (1977) question the wisdom of strategies enforcing stability in the structure of managed water resource and ecosystems. They argue that striving for stability can backfire and greatly reduce the resiliency of a system. Vulnerability refers to the likely magnitude of a failure, if one occurs. Few studies have been undertaken that incorporate resiliency and vulnerability in the techno-economic optimal design of a water supply system. Hashimoto et al. (1982) applied the reliability, resiliency and vulnerability concepts in the operation of a water supply reservoir.

Planning of Bulk Production Facilities

The basic questions encountered in the planning of bulk water production and treatment facilities concern:

- the volume of production;
- the timing of production and consumption;
- the type of water source (or mix of sources); and
- the location of plants.

The economic aspects of the choices involved are clarified below by using a simple approach. Figure 4.6 depicts the problem of size and timing resulting from the growth of demand over time in a typical system with limited capacity. The installed capacity of existing bulk water production plant (QM) will not be sufficient to meet the baseline demand in two years, allowing for a suitable reserve margin. Two expansion alternatives are available that meet all the constraints. In the first, two medium-size groundwater sources (e.g., wells) would come on stream in the second and fourth years. In the second option, a small borehole would be commissioned in the second year, followed by a large surface water plant (e.g., a dam on a river) in the sixth year. The system planner must choose the cheaper alternative. In a real system, the water system expansion paths over a longer period of time might have to be compared. In this example, the two alternative plans have been made roughly equivalent after the sixth year, to highlight the nature of the choice of size, timing and source type of the next two increments of production capacity. The case study presented in Chapter 10 numerically illustrates some of the more detailed aspects of least-cost production planning and project evaluation.

The broken curve in Figure 4.6 represents reduced demand that will meet the same human needs, but with less need for water. The latter could be achieved by reducing water losses in the system (as explained in Section 4.4 that follows) and through better demand management (e.g., raising the price of water or increasing the water end-use efficiency). In certain cases, reducing demand and thereby deferring capacity expansion may be more cost-effective (i.e., least-cost) than building new plant.

Planning of Bulk Main Pipelines

Usually, the problem of locating production facilities is closely linked with the design of the bulk transmission system; therefore, they should be discussed

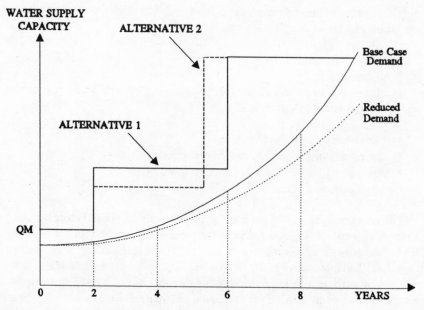

Figure 4.6 Capacity Additions to a Water System

in the same context. Transmission main pipeline planning typically involves solving a dynamic network-type problem. The basic objective is to select the type, timing, and location of primary and secondary distribution pipelines that would connect the various production, treatment and storage facilities to the different demand centers in the least expensive way. In addition, requirements involving the demand, service quality level, and other constraints must be satisfied. As indicated, these may be treated as variables to be maximized relative to pre-defined target levels.

A commonly used type of network model for planning bulk main systems is the volumetric flow model, which may be used in either a linear or nonlinear framework. In single-step, static approaches, the design optimization is repeated at various points in time. When production and demand levels are specified, for example in the first and last year of the planning horizon, the repetition provides instantaneous snapshots of the system's evolution. In dynamic approaches, long computing times are required to handle bulk transmission line variations in both space and time, as in the analysis of a large multiple-connected area during each year of the planning period. This problem may be simplified by preselecting several expansion alternatives according to certain performance criteria. None of these techniques can guarantee a definitive solution, however, given the size of the problem and limits on calculating times.

There are two general types of criteria for main pipeline system performance:

1) Steady state performance criteria consist basically of verifying that system design limits are not exceeded under normal flow and operating conditions or with single contingencies, such as loss of a major pipeline, production plant or storage facility.

2) Transient performance criteria are used to test the model for stability in various situations. One group of tests involves examining how well a complex system would maintain steady state stability under both normal and contingency conditions, when perturbed by a small disturbance such as sudden demand imposed on it by a new consumer. Verifying the system's dynamic stability is also important. This involves the degree of damping of high amplitude oscillations or pressure surges induced by a major breakdown, such as failure of a large pipeline.

A return to the question of production plant location is appropriate at this point. The analysis of combined production and pipeline system models raises formidable problems. Therefore, although the production and bulk main sub-systems are intimately related, separate models are generally used for the design of each sub-system. A typical large computerized production planning model would predict the appropriate plant mix, size, and timing. It might include a limited representation of the bulk mains network in its calculations, but this is usually inaccurate for detailed network planning d. The optimal pipeline locations to supply the specified demand centers would be chosen from among several potential sites within the context of a more detailed pipeline planning model. In practice, it would be necessary to iterate between the models to derive the best mutually consistent solution.

A recent example of a trial-and-error simulation approach for the integral optimal design of a water treatment plant was presented by Vigneswaran and Rudeleert (1988). Clark and Males (1985) developed a model that studies the hydraulic and economic aspects of the acquisition-treatment and the bulk main and distribution pipeline components both in isolation and in combination. This model is currently used by the Environmental Protection Agency of the USA (EPA). These references provide useful practical material to help understand and implement such planning models.

Examples of operations research optimization models include those of Sathaye and Hall (1976) and Martin (1980) who focus on the pipeline or aqueduct optimization. References for models of capacity expansion in bulk production include Jacoby and Loucks (1972), Bogle and O'Sullivan (1979) and Braga et al. (1985). A comprehensive bulk production-main pipeline optimization model was developed by Fleming et al. (1983). These authors employ dynamic programming to integrate the optimal design of the reservoir, the water treatment plant and the pipeline system. The model takes into account the time variability of demands along with the stochasticity of inflow to the reservoir. Nakashima et al. (1985) use a two-phase heuristic optimization technique to arrive at the economical optimum water supply system lay-out and size of water production and bulk main facilities, assuming increasing water demands during the planning horizon.

Water systems analysts wishing to adopt a planning model for production system design should refer to the texts indicated in the previous discussions in order to select the model most appropriate for their local circumstances and objectives.

Distribution Planning

Although planning production and bulk main systems is an interrelated process, the distribution network serving a localized geographic area or demand center can be designed independently of the production system that supplies the water. Recently, computerized methods have been developed to determine the optimal size, timing, and location of distribution pipes and intermediate storage facilities. Sophisticated models and computerized algorithms, however, are not as widely used in the design of distribution systems as in production and transmission work.

In the more conventional approach, forecast demands are imposed on the existing distribution system at various times in the future, and the network is systematically strengthened to meet these flows adequately. The location of new storage points and primary pipelines and the upgrading of existing ones would be determined to meet consumer demand within acceptable service quality standards under both normal and emergency conditions, as well as during periods of peak and off-peak flow. Flexibility in the design to facilitate isolating faulty sections of pipes and to permit customers to be switched from faulty to functioning pipelines would be an important consideration.

Operations research optimization models that can be aptly used in the practical design of water distribution systems were developed by Alperovits and Shamir (1977), Quindry et al. (1981), and Morgan and Goultzer (1985). The challenge remains to create a model that optimizes the water supply system and at the same time does not over-simplify the complex hydraulics and the sizing of pipe networks, pump stations, control and pressure-reducing valves, and tanks. A recent model that does not avoid these challenges is presented by Lansey and Mays (1989). Their model combines nonlinear optimization techniques with detailed hydraulic simulation modeling. At the same time, however, the authors admit that even their model cannot fully solve the water distribution problem as it does not guarantee global optimality (in the mathematical sense). Also, when multiple demands are analyzed, the problem exceeds the problem dimensions that can be solved by existing nonlinear programming codes.

Often, because of the large numbers of customers and components such as pipeline sections, intermediate storage points or pumping stations, and so on, only certain representative distribution pipelines would be analyzed in detail to establish general criteria such as maximum water flow rates and pressures in a circuit. Such criteria could then be applied to other pipelines without further detailed study. In general, the larger and more complex the service area, the greater would be the advantage of using even simple computerized techniques for pipeline-by-pipeline analysis.

Management of Water Losses

The world-wide scarcity of water resources and the high costs of water supply have highlighted the importance of water conservation and elimination of waste by both producers and users of water. Water system loss reduction is one of the principal ways for achieving this objective. A major failure of past and current projects has been the lack of attention to reduction of waste of water and resource conservation, and the limited implementation of unaccounted-for-water reduction programs (World Bank 1990). One of the first stages of any integrated water resources plan in a developing country, should be the development of a non-revenue water reduction program using some of the planning tools described in this section. Water losses must be minimized in order to reduce unnecessary production costs, delay the need for supply expansion and to increase revenue.

Water Losses in the Developing World

As explained earlier, in the process of delivering water to consumers, losses are incurred at the production, transmission and distribution stages of a water system (see Figure 4.1). Leaving production aside (where acceptable norms for losses vary according to the type of water source and treatment facilities required), recent work indicates that average water losses in the water delivery system, i.e., bulk transmission and distribution, should normally be below 20% of gross production, while economically optimal loss levels may be as low as 10%. However, the corresponding technical losses in many developing country networks range from 25-50% even after allowing for substantial amounts of theft. The highest losses (around 50%) may be found in systems with faulty pipelines and high pressure such as Buenos Aires, Managua, Mexico City and Montevideo (Echeverri 1983). It should be recognized that these figures themselves have a significant margin of error because of non-technical losses such as metering errors, poor record keeping, etc.

As an example of the make-up of non-revenue water in a developing country supply system, Price (1988) presented a summary of conditions in Petaling Jaya town, Malaysia. Out of a total water production of around 140,000 m³/day for 250,000 people, the non-revenue water was estimated as:

Distribution leakage	23,670	m³/day
Transmission main losses	2,392	m³/day
Firefighting	475	m³/day
Squatters and illegal use	3,327	m³/day
Meter under-registration	20,520	m³/day
Total	50,384	m³/day (36% of production)

Whilst clearly there is a need for continued improvements in the efficiency of water production facilities, it is the technical losses in water transmission and distribution networks that account for the bulk of total system losses. Two principal reasons account for the high levels of water supply distribution losses in developing countries. First, the selling price of water has failed to keep pace with the rapid increase in the costs of supply in recent decades. The consequent decline in the financial position of many LDC water companies has led to reduced investment and system maintenance, while low water prices have tended to over-stimulate demand. In general, most utilities have preferred to cut back expenditures on distribution systems (especially relating to maintenance costs), rather than reduce their water production and bulk transmission investments. This is because the results of capacity shortages in bulk supply plant lead to global or system-wide shortcomings in water supply that are highly visible, whereas distribution level weaknesses only manifest themselves locally and less spectacularly in terms of low pressure, high losses, poor water quality, and so on. Investments in impressive new production facilities are also more attractive as a visible sign of "progress," whereas loss reducing network improvements are considerably less glamorous.

The second reason for high distribution system loss levels also stems from the recent rapid rise in water production costs. As the existing (and cheapest) freshwater sources become fully exploited, water authorities have to develop remoter and less pure water resources, which are also more expensive. Therefore, the ratio of production costs to distribution costs is higher for many systems today than it was some decades ago. The optimized design of a water system should seek to economically trade off the increased investment costs of system improvement versus the resultant benefits of reduced water losses (valued at the cost of bulk production). Unfortunately, the guidelines and rules of thumb for system engineering and design, still used by many LDC utilities, implicitly embody relative production to distribution costs more appropriate to the 1960s than the 1990s. In other words, additional expenditures on transmission and distribution system hardware can bring about water loss reductions that have a higher economic value than the increased investments costs. Therefore, a water supply engineer today should be willing to spend more on network improvements to achieve a lower level of system losses, than he would have, two or three decades ago. However, this logic is frequently ignored.

Generally, the need for more effective management of water production and transmission facilities has been accepted as a basic component of most projects in LDCs, as shown by a recent study by Garn (1987). This has not been translated into action however. In a review of the performance of 54 World Bank water supply projects in developing countries, completed during the period 1966 to 1980, Garn showed that in the planning stage, substantial reductions in unaccounted-for-water were anticipated from both:

- better detection and repair of leaks; and
- improvements in billing and collection.

On average, a decrease in unaccounted-for-water from 30% to 24% was forecast, over the six years after project startup. However, in actuality, the starting value of average losses was 34%, and remained at this level thereafter, implying no overall improvement (see Table 4.1). Only 13% of the reviewed projects met or exceeded the loss reductions expected at the time of appraisal.

Some planners may neglect to tackle water leakages, particularly in urban areas, because they see the significant urban groundwater recharge originating from leaks in the water supply system, and therefore the potential to recoup the water through borehole pumping. For example, Lerner (1987) demonstrated that leakage into the soil from the water supply system in Lima, Peru ranged from 300 to 2800 mm per year, with a mean of 830 mm per year. The relative importance of this figure can be weighed against the estimated mean of 950 mm per year for total recharge of groundwater in Lima (Geake et al. 1986). Although the leakage from pipes could be perceived as being beneficial to restoring the groundwater reservoir, Foster (1986) argues that this benefit is insufficient to compensate for the loss of revenue to the water supply company. This conclusion is valid because even if the planner is right, and most of the recharged groundwater is recuperated by local production boreholes, it is rendered uneconomic due to the considerable additional energy costs for pumping. At the same time the quality of the groundwater extracted from urban areas tends to be very poor, compared to the original piped water, and is costly to treat.

Techno-Economic Loss Optimizing Model

The economic outcome of reducing technical losses in the distribution system can be analyzed by applying the principles of cost benefit analysis

TABLE 4.1   Discrepancies Between Expected and Actual Unaccounted-for Water for
54 Water Supply Projects, Completed Before 1980

	Unaccounted-for Water (average yearly percentage of total production)	
Year after loan effectiveness	Expected	Actual
1	30	34
2	29	35
3	27	36
4	26	35
5	24	35
6	24	35

Source : Garn 1987.

explained in Chapter 3.

Consider Figure 4.7, where the rectangle symbolically represents the physical boundaries of an entire water supply system, or any one of its component subsystems, i.e., production, bulk transmission or distribution facilities. This water system, designated by the letter i, is planned with a time horizon of T periods, each of duration 1 year. Equation (4.5) can be rewritten to indicate the present discounted value of net benefits to society (NB) for the planning period:

$$NB_i = \sum_{t=0}^{T} \frac{(TB_{it} - SC_{it} - QC_{it})}{(1+r)^t} \qquad (4.17)$$

We note that the total benefit (TB) derived from water supplied by system design i in any time period (t) is a function of the total quantity of water delivered assuming that the quality of supply is perfect.

The quality optimizing model of Section 4.2 sought to maximize net benefit by optimizing service quality through the trade-off between supply costs (SC_i) and service quality costs (QC_i). Here we attempt to maximize net benefits by optimizing the level of technical losses in the system (or subsystem) under consideration.

In Figure 4.7, let a_{it} be the units of water entering the system i in the time period t; b_{it} the corresponding units of water exiting the system; and L_{it} the level of losses. Then the physical water balance condition yields:

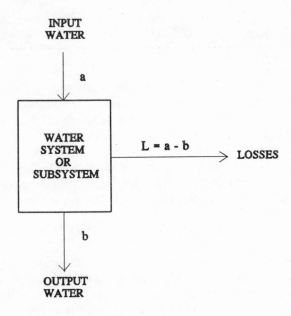

Figure 4.7 Schematic Representation of Water Losses

$$a_{it} = b_{it} + L_{it} \qquad (4.18)$$

Before we apply the expression (4.17) for net benefits to this system (or subsystem), it is convenient to disaggregate the total supply cost term SC, as follows:

$$SC_{it} = UC_{it} + SPC_{it} \qquad (4.19)$$

where UC_{it} is the upstream cost of supplying a_{it} units of input water, and SPC_{it} is the investment, operating and maintenance cost associated with all the plant within the rectangle in Figure 4.7.

Now let us compare two systems (or subsystems) that are designed to provide the same water output (b_{it}), but have slightly different loss levels (L_{it}) and supply costs (SC_{it}). We might imagine that System 1 is an upgraded and costlier version of System 2, but having correspondingly lower losses. The difference in net benefits between the two systems (or subsystems) may be derived by using equations (4.17) and (4.19).

$$NB_1 - NB_2 = \sum_{t=0}^{T} \frac{\left[(TB_{1t} - TB_{2t}) - (UC_{1t} - UC_{2t}) - (SPC_{1t} - SPC_{2t}) - (QC_{1t} - QC_{2t})\right]}{(1+r)^t} \quad (4.20)$$

Considering the first term in equation (4.20), we find that since total benefits derived from the system (or subsystem) are a function of the volume of water delivered, and $b_{1t} = b_{2t}$, we may conclude that $TB_{1t} - TB_{2t} = 0$. At the same time, using equation (4.18), we get: $(a_{1t} - a_{2t}) = (L_{1t} - L_{2t})$.

Next, we observe that the term $(UC_{1t} - UC_{2t})$ represents the differential cost of providing $(a_{1t} - a_{2t})$ incremental units of water, which should be valued at their long-run marginal cost of supply, denoted by MC (this point is explained in more detail at the end of this section). Therefore, we may conclude that:

$$(UC_{1t} - UC_{2t}) = (L_{1t} \cdot MC_{1t} - L_{2t} \cdot MC_{2t}) \quad (4.21)$$

Since we are dealing with two systems (or subsystems) that are design variants of each other, drawing slightly different levels of water input from the same upstream source, we might safely assume that: $MC_{1t} = MC_{2t} = MC_t$, and thus:

$$(UC_{1t} - UC_{2t}) = (L_{1t} - L_{2t})MC_t \quad (4.22)$$

Furthermore, we assume for the time being that the term involving changes in service quality costs QC is negligible. For example, we could consider improvements and loss reduction in systems where the supply quality is quite good to begin with. In general, it is assumed that QC would be a small correctional term in the analysis.

Equation (4.20) now may be simplified to yield:

$$NB_1 - NB_2 = \sum_{t=0}^{T} \frac{\left[(L_{1t} - L_{2t})MC_t - (SPC_{1t} - SPC_{2t})\right]}{(1+r)^t} \quad (4.23)$$

Let us now define the net supply cost for the system (or subsystem) as follows:

$$NSC_{it} = SPC_{it} + VL_{it} \quad (4.24)$$

where $VL_{it} = L_{it} \cdot MC_t$ = Value of Losses.

Rewriting equation (4.23) in the difference form yields:

$$\Delta NB = -\Delta NSC \quad (4.25)$$

where:

$$\Delta NB = (NB_1 - NB_2) \qquad\qquad (4.25a)$$

$$\Delta NSC = (NSC_1 - NSC_2) \qquad\qquad (4.25b)$$

$$NSC_i = \sum_{t=0}^{T} \frac{NSC_{it}}{(1+r)^t} \qquad\qquad (4.25c)$$

Equation (4.25) indicates that $NB_1 > NB_2$, and system 1 provides better net benefits than system 2, if the former has a lower value of net supply costs, i.e., $NSC_1 < NSC_2$. Alternatively, we can argue that NB will be maximized when NSC is minimized.

Thus writing NSC = VL + SPC and taking derivatives with respect to physical losses L:

$$\frac{\partial NSC}{\partial L} = \frac{\partial VL}{\partial L} + \frac{\partial SPC}{\partial L} \qquad\qquad (4.26)$$

The net supply costs in the system is at a minimum with respect to losses when: $(\partial NSC/\partial L) = 0$. Therefore:

$$\frac{\partial SPC}{\partial L} = -\frac{\partial VL}{\partial L} \qquad\qquad (4.27)$$

This indicates that optimal losses in the system (or subsystem), which maximizes the net benefits, occur when the marginal increase in supply costs are exactly offset by the marginal decrease in the value of losses. The same result is graphically depicted in Figure 4.8 by plotting costs on the vertical axis, and losses measured in physical units on the horizontal axis. SPC is a downward sloping curve since, as costs or investments decrease, the losses incurred in the system increase. VL (value of losses) is an upward sloping curve since as losses increase, more units of input water will have to be supplied to feed the same volume of output water. The sum of SPC and VL gives the net supply costs (NSC). The minimum point of the NSC curve occurs at the level of physical losses $L = L_M$, where the slope (f) of the VL curve equals the negative slope (g) of the SPC curve (assuming negligible differences in service quality costs). The curve VL_0 depicts the situation which might have existed some time ago, when the marginal cost of supply (and therefore, the value of losses) was lower than today. In this case, both the curve NSC_0 and the optimal loss level L_{MO} would be shifted to the right. Therefore, the engineering criteria for system design should aim for lower target loss levels today than was the practice earlier.

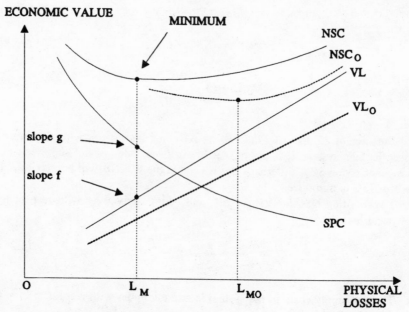

Figure 4.8   Optimal Economic Loss Level (L$^\cdot$)

As mentioned, the above result may be applied to the entire water system or any of its subsystems. For example, if the model is applied to the distribution network, the input water (a_i) will be supplied from the bulk supply system and MC should reflect the long-run marginal costs of production and bulk transmission facilities that are upstream of the distribution system. In this case, the term involving SPC in equation (4.27) includes the investment and operating and maintenance costs of the distribution system only (i.e., plant located inside the rectangle in Figure 4.8).

We conclude this section by discussing further the rationale for using the long-run marginal cost of water input into the system from upstream, as a measure of the value of water losses in the system. Consider the specific example of a distribution network, which draws water (a_i) from a bulk supply system and delivers water (b_i) to consumers. The key point is that as far as water supplied by, and costs incurred due to production and bulk transmission facilities upstream of the distribution are concerned, losses L_i and legitimate consumption b_i are indistinguishable. Thus, when losses are reduced, it is equivalent to a reduction in demand, and bulk system capacity additions may be deferred yielding cost savings represented by the LRMC of bulk supply.

Sometimes, it is incorrectly argued that a small decrease in losses will not result in a reduction in the large and lumpy future investment stream of a water system (although operating costs that are proportional to water produced will decline). To demonstrate this conclusion, we recall that in an optimally planned water supply system, there are two conditions that must be satisfied:

- the optimal price equals the LRMC of supply; and
- the optimal incremental cost of system improvements equals the costs avoided due to improved service quality.

Therefore, after a loss reduction, even if the production and transmission expansion investments continue relatively unchanged (e.g., due to lumpiness), then the increased reserve capacity margin in bulk supply facilities will yield marginal service quality improvements and resultant cost saving benefits to water users. These are equivalent to the marginal savings that could have been realized from deferred production and transmission investments. Even in an extreme situation where there is significant existing upstream overcapacity, the analysis is valid. In this case the value of losses will be relatively small, because the incremental costs of producing more water to either feed losses or new consumers will be negligible.

We note that if plant investments are actually deferred, then the cost savings accrue to the water supplying company whereas in the other case where the quality of water service improves, the customers gain. Thus from a social viewpoint both costs savings are equivalent, whereas from the water company's viewpoint the former is more desirable.

Practical Issues and Consequences of Losses

Norms for Technical Loss Reduction Measures

Although the loss optimization approach described above requires detailed data and analysis for application, it is possible to reach some practical conclusions of a more general nature, on the basis of some recent information. Table 4.2 summarizes some typical loss levels in water utilities. Many water systems are currently designed and operated on the basis of traditional engineering criteria. The value (usually implicit) assigned to losses is often rather low, when establishing these criteria. However, losses should be one of the most important considerations in establishing design (and operating) criteria. As well as resulting in reduced revenue for a given operating cost, losses also force the water utility to invest more in chemicals and energy inputs for the same amount of water delivered to the customer. Leakages in the transmission system also directly influence the ability to provide adequate fire protection. In addition they increase the possibility of cross connections and backflow of contaminating fluids and disease carriers into the water system.

158

TABLE 4.2 Estimates of Unaccounted-for Water in Developing and Industrialized Countries

Country	Year	Unaccounted for Water (percent of total water produced)				Reference
		Total	Leakage	Under-metering	Other	
Developing Countries						
Brazil	1982	31	n.a.	n.a.	n.a.	Garn, 1987
Cote d'Ivoire	1989	12	n.a.	n.a.	n.a.	Triche, 1990
Ecuador	1980	47	n.a.	n.a.	n.a.	Garn, 1987
Egypt	1987	50	n.a.	n.a.	n.a.	World Bank, 1988b
Ghana	1981	47	n.a.	n.a.	n.a.	Garn, 1987
Kenya	1977	18	n.a.	n.a.	n.a.	Garn, 1987
Peru	1981	50	n.a.	n.a.	n.a.	Binnie & Partners, 1981
Qatar	1982	18	n.a.	n.a.	n.a.	Pencol et al, 1985
Uruguay	1987	40	n.a.	n.a.	n.a.	World Bank, 1988d
Yemen	1987	30	n.a.	n.a.	n.a.	World Bank, 1988a
Industrialized Countries						
Perth (Australia)	1982	n.a.	n.a.	14	n.a.	Sullivan, 1982
Birmingham (UK)	1984	21	n.a.	n.a.	n.a.	Lerner, 1988
Boston (USA)	1978	45	17	22	6	Boyle, 1982
California (USA)	1982	10	4	4	2	Boyle, 1982
Louisville (USA)	1980	19	13	5	1	Male et al, 1985

One side effect of leakages is intermittent supplies, which in turn cause low or even negative pressures in the distribution system. Backflow results from "back-siphoning," i.e., wastewater being sucked into the system through the defective pipes, joints and fittings. As a first instinctive remedial action to maintain the design pressure, water supply authorities tend to increase the pressure in the system, thereby triggering a vicious circle that subjects defective components to greater internal water pressure, and further amplifying the losses (OECD 1987, Okun and Ernst 1987, AWWA 1986). Together, all these loss effects finally hasten the time when capital expenditures will be necessary to improve the pipeline system, expand filtration plant capacity, construct new pumping stations, and locate new water sources (AWWA 1986).

Within practical limitations, in most developing countries it is much less costly to locate leakages by water audits and reduce distribution losses by strengthening these networks, than it is to build new upstream bulk water supply facilities, to feed the losses. Short-term solutions like increasing pipe pressures to maintain flow rates, have costly long-term implications and a more effective practice would be to correct the defects causing poor supply problems through a systematic program of repair and rehabilitation, and a greater weighting of budgets towards operation and maintenance. Further references on the detection of leaks and repairs can be found in IWES (1984) and AWWA (1986).

Production losses occurring in a surface reservoir are a function of the evaporation and seepage losses. Depending on the climate (i.e., evaporation into the atmosphere) and the porosity of the bed, these losses can vary between 20% and 60%. Losses at the level of the treatment plant can be as high as 5%, especially when sand-bed filters are used in the treatment process. Causes for system losses in the trunk mains and primary distribution systems were enumerated previously. Those losses are seldom less than 5 to 10 percent of the raw water produced, even in a new system (IWES 1983). Finally, in the distribution system, it has been found that most leakage problems are due to innumerable small leaks in the service connections (secondary distribution system). Although generalizations are difficult to make, for somewhat average conditions, ideal loss levels in the primary and secondary distribution systems should be around 5% and 10% respectively.

Non-Technical Losses

We recognize that other types of loss such as theft or unmetered consumption may increase the fraction of unaccounted-for water significantly in some systems and should be reduced. Table 4.2 summarizes losses for both developing and industrialized countries. The comparison of the different figures should be carried out with some caution, since it is not always clear from the references whether the definition of total water losses embraces all of the following major factors:

- leakage (a technical loss);
- meter under-registration;
- unauthorized, unmetered losses; and
- official nonpaying customers (e.g., water used for public activities such as firefighting, water supplied to public buildings, military purposes, irrigation of public parks and roadsides, streetwashing, etc.).

However, it should be noted that, strictly speaking, the last category is not considered as unaccounted-for-water although it has the same effect. On the other hand, distinguishing between any of these four categories is not an easy task since unaccounted-for water is by definition not monitored. In Table 4.2, the category "Undermetering" includes both meter under-registration and lack of meters whereas "Other Unaccounted-for" water includes all water used for authorized unmetered public uses. Unauthorized water use is also included in this category.

Minimizing such unaccounted-for water must involve all or some of the following steps:

- replacing broken meters;
- disconnecting and prosecuting customers who steal water;
- establishing a system of prepayment of bills; and
- using different individuals to do the meter reading and billing (as an anti-corruption measure).

References

Alperovits, E., and U. Shamir. 1977. "Design of Optimal Distribution Systems." *Water Resources Research.* 13, pp. 885-900.

AWWA. 1986. *Introduction to Water Distribution Vol 3.: Principles and Practices of Water Supply Operations.* Denver, Colorado: American Water Works Association.

Babbitt, H.E., J.J. Doland, and J.L. Cleasby. 1962. *Water Supply Engineering.* 6th ed. New York: McGraw-Hill.

Barnes, D., et al. 1981. *Water and Wastewater Engineering Systems.* London: Pitman Books, Ltd.

Binnie & Partners. 1981. *Final Study of the Transfer of Water From the Upper Catchment of the River Mantaro to Lima: Appendix B, Groundwater Studies.* Unpublished report to the Government of Peru.

Bogle, M.G.V., and M.J. O'Sullivan. 1979. "Stochastic Optimization of Water Supply Expansion." *Water Resources Research.* 15, pp. 1229-1237.

Braga, Jr., B.P.F., J.G.L. Conejo, L. Becker, and W.W.G. Yeh. 1985. "Capacity Expansion of São Paulo Water Supply." *Journal of Water Resources Planning and Management.* ASCE, 111, pp. 238-252.

Brandon, T.W. 1984. *Water Distribution Systems, Water Practice Manuals.* London: The Institution of Water Engineers and Scientists.

Clark, R.M., and R.M. Males. 1985. "Simulating Cost and Quality in Water Distribution." *Journal of Water Resources Planning and Management.* ASCE. 111, pp. 454-466.

Cummings, R.G., D.S. Brookshire, and W.D. Schulze. 1986. *Valuing Public Goods: The Contingent Valuation Method.* Totowa, New Jersey: Rowman and Allanheld Publishers.

Echeverri, A.A.E. 1983. "Runaway Water: The Lost Resource." *World Water.* pp. 23-25.

Energy Journal. 1988. Special Issue on Electricity Reliability.

Fleming, D.E., R.K. Hanson, and J.W. Labadie. 1983. "Integrated Sizing of Water Storage and Conveyance." *Journal of Water Resources Planning and Management.* ASCE. 109, pp. 94-111.

Foster, S.S.D. 1986. "Getting to Grips with Groundwater Pollution Protection in Developing Countries." *Natural Resources Forum.* 10, pp. 51-60.

Garn, H.A. 1987. *Patterns in the Data Reported on Completed Water Supply Projects.* Washington DC: The World Bank.

Geake, A.K., S.S.D. Foster, N. Nakamatsu, C.F. Valenzuela, and M.L. Valverde. 1986. "Groundwater Recharge and Pollution Mechanisms in Urban Aquifers of Arid Regions." *BGS Hydrogeology Research Report 86/1.* Wallingford, U.K.

IRC. 1987. *Small Community Water Supplies. Technology of Small Water Supply Systems in Developing Countries. Technical Paper Series 18.* The Hague: IRC.

IWES. 1984. *Water Distribution Systems* T.W. Brandon (ed.). London: Institute of Water Engineers and Scientists.

_____. 1983. *Water Supply and Sanitation in Developing Countries.* J. Dangerfield (ed.). London: Institute of Water Engineers and Scientists.

Jacoby, H.D., and D.P. Loucks. 1972. "Combined Use of Optimization and Simulation Models in River Basin Planning." *Water Resources Research.* 8, pp. 1401-1414.

Jeffcoate, P., and A. Saravanapavan. 1987. *The Reduction and Control of Unaccounted-for Water, Working Guidelines.* World Bank Technical Paper Number 72. Washington DC: The World Bank.

Lansey, K.E., and L.W. Mays. 1989. "Optimization Model for Water Distribution System Design." *Journal of Hydraulic Engineering.* ASCE. 115, pp. 1401-1418.

Lerner, D.N. 1988. "Unaccounted-For Water -- A Groundwater Resource?" *Aqua (JIWSA).* 1, pp. 33-42.

_____. 1987. "Leaking Pipes Recharge Groundwater." *Groundwater.* 26, pp. 654-662.

Loucks, D.P., J.R. Stedinger, and D.A. Haith. 1981. *Water Resources Systems Planning and Analysis.* Englewood Cliffs, N.J.: Prentice Hall, Inc.

Martin, Q. 1980. "Optimal Design of Water Conveyance Systems." *Journal of the Hydraulics Division.* ASCE. 106, pp. 1415-1433.

Mitchell, R.C., and R.T. Carson. 1989. *Using Surveys to Value Public Goods : The Contingent Valuation Method.* Washington DC: Resources for the Future.

_____. 1984. *Willingness to Pay for National Freshwater Quality Improvements.* Washington DC: Resources for the Future.

Morgan. D.R., and I. Goulter. 1985. "Optimal Urban Water Distribution Design." *Water Resources Research.* 21, pp. 642-652.

Munasinghe, M. 1979. *The Economics of Power System Reliability and Planning.* Baltimore, Md.: Johns Hopkins University Press.

Nakashima, M., H.G. Wenzel, Jr., and E.D. Brill, Jr. 1986. "Water Supply System Models with Capacity Expansion." *Journal of Water Resources Planning and Management.* ASCE, 112, pp. 87-103.

OECD. 1987. *Pricing of Water Services.* Paris: Organization for Economic Co-operation and Development.

Okun, D.A., and W.R. Ernst. 1987. *Community Piped Water Supply Systems in Developing Countries. World Bank Technical Paper No 60.* Washington DC: The World Bank.

Page, T., R. Harris, and J. Bruser. 1981. "Waterborne Carcinogens: An Economist's View." R.W. Crandall and L.B. Lave (eds.). *The Scientific Basis of Health and Safety Regulation.* Washington DC: The Brookings Institution. pp. 197-228.

Pencol, John Taylor and Sons. 1985. *Doha Stormwater and Groundwater Management Action Report.* Report to the Ministry of Public Works, State of Qatar.

Price, A.J. 1988. "Assessment of Non-Revenue Water in Malaysia." *Annex V/IV in WHO/CWS, Draft Guidelines on Cost Recovery in Community Water Supply and Sanitation.* Geneva: World Health Organization.

Quindry, G.E., E.D. Brill, and J.C. Liebman. 1981. "Optimization of Looped Water Distribution Systems." *Journal of Environmental Engineering.* ASCE. 107, pp. 665-679.

Satheye, J., and W.A. Hall. 1976. "Optimization of Design Capacity of an Aqueduct." *Journal of Irrigation and Drainage.* ASCE. 102, pp. 295-305.

Smith, V.K., and W.H. Desvousges. 1986. *Measuring Water Quality Benefits.* Boston: Kluwer-Nijhoff Publishing. pp. 327.

Smith, V.K., and J.V. Krutilla. 1982. "Toward Formulating the Role of National Resources in Economic Models." V.K. Smith and J.V. Krutilla (eds.). *Explorations in Natural Resource Economics.* Baltimore, MD: John Hopkins University Press. pp. 1-43.

Vigneswaran, S., and T. Rudeleert. 1988. "Integral Water Treatment Plant Design: Optimization of Design Parameters." *Aqua, Journal of Water Research and Technology.* IWSA/AIDE. 6, pp. 322-327.

WASH. 1989. *Willingness to Pay for Water in Newala District, Tanzania: Strategies for Cost Recovery. WASH Field Report No. 246.* Washington DC: Water and Sanitation for Health Project.

WHO. 1989. *UNEP/WHO Project on Control of Drinking Water Qaulity in Rural Areas.* Report of a review meeting. Robens Institute, UK. WHO/PEP/89.5. Geneva: World Health Organization.

_____. 1985. *Guidelines for Drinking Water Quality - Volume 3. Drinking Water Quality Control in Small Community Supplies.* Geneva: World Health Organization.

_____1984a. *Guidelines for Drinking Water Quality - Volume 1. Recommendations.* Geneva: World Health Organization.

_____. 1984b. *Guidelines for Drinking Water Quality - Volume 2. Criteria.* Geneva: World Health Organization.

World Bank. 1990. *Water Supply and Sanitation - FY90 Sector Review.* Infrastructure Department. Washington DC: The World Bank.

5

Environmental Issues in
Water Management

In the broadest context, water is an environmental resource, and the principles of sound natural resource management may be used to address water related environmental issues. However, since the latter have received the serious consideration they deserve only in recent years, it is useful to specifically identify key environmental problems that arise in water resource management, i.e., both environmental problems that degrade water sources and environmental issues caused by water projects or policies. Then we proceed to explore how this additional information might be incorporated better into the decisionmaking process.

An Environmental Orientation for IWRP

This chapter elaborates on an environmental-economic framework that is very much in the spirit of the IWRP approach. Conceptually, it is of great benefit in terms of long-term sustainability and effectiveness of integrating water and environmental management. By having a better and wider understanding of the nature of environmental impacts that affect water sources, due to both water sector and other sector activities, decisionmakers can integrate the economic and service quality effects of these externalities into their IWRP. Specifically, the important considerations are how these factors affect the long-run marginal costs of supplying water, the service quality level and the investment required to maintain or achieve target service and coverage under a given set of conditions. The causes and impacts of significant environmental changes affecting the water sector can be local, national and even global in origin.

This kind of environment-oriented IWRP recognizes the important and growing role of environmental constraints and requires that a systematic assessment of the order of magnitude, the scale, and the cost implications of a full range of potential environmental effects be made.   Although the techniques and data required to do this are still evolving, there are tools available currently that allow a fairly rigorous review to be made of significant factors and, by extension, the costs and benefits of various environmental management options.   Increasingly, the most common tool used by planners in the project planning cycle is the environmental impact assessment (EIA). EIA is the explicit tool that has been developed for determining the main environmental concerns that may arise as a result of a water resource project or program.   As indicated in Chapter 3, governments and international development agencies have, in recent years, elevated EIA to the same level of importance as other analyses involving the more traditional disciplines (e.g., engineering-technical, economic and financial evaluation of projects).

In the water sector, specific project EIAs have generally been used as a method of determining the impacts of a given project (such as a large dam reservoir) on the environment, the water sector itself and on related sectors. Increasingly, EIAs are placing greater emphasis also on the sociocultural impacts of projects.   At the same time, an EIA can be used as a tool for looking at indirectly generated effects on the water sector and water supply project in question, i.e., factors resulting from other non-project activities, or management of projects in other sectors.   This involves taking a more regional and multisectoral perspective in many instances.   For example, from the point of view of environmental management, it is important to know what the effects of catchment deforestation (caused by agriculture or commercial forestry) will have on future dam reservoir capacity, or on the water inflow regime.   This is not an impact of the dam, per se, but a related impact on the dam from additional effects that may occur in the future.

The example given is clearly an integrated planning issue.   If the effects of allowing increasing rural populations to colonize the catchment area of a major dam and to practice slash-and-burn agriculture would be large-scale sedimentation and increased periodicity of river inflows, it would obviously be necessary to formulate a policy of catchment protection as an implicit component of dam management.   The planning decisions that facilitate such changes might come from the Ministry of Agriculture or the Ministry of Lands, rather than the Ministry of Water, and apply to a complete region (e.g., a drainage basin) rather than an individual project site.   The cost implications of such a strategy for the country as a whole, particularly the opportunity costs of agricultural output foregone, and the social costs to poor land-less peasants would need to be accounted for as part of a full project assessment.   In some cases, the rather narrow outlook of conventional EIA does not lend itself to such a wide-ranging assessment of issues.   A basic problem with most EIAs are that they focus on environmental changes that result from a particular water sector project, rather than look for environmental changes that cause problems affecting water projects.   Since the term EIA clearly has a specific project connotation, we prefer to adopt the more general term of Environmental Assessment (EA) which suggests a more holistic view of the positive (benefits) and negative (costs) impacts of human activities in a range of economic sectors on water projects and vice versa.

Prior to a more detailed discussion of both the environmental impact assessment procedures and the environmental-economic framework that extends the analytical approaches of previous chapters, a discussion of the scale and nature of the main environmental effects of concern to planners developing groundwater and surface water supplies is provided. This sets the environmental context in which the analytical tools must be used. However, recognizing that some planners will already have a good basic grasp of the specific and wider environmental issues, they may choose to familiarize themselves with the analytical framework first, and hence should go directly to Chapter 6. Those readers who would first like to find out more about the range of environmental considerations they must deal with, and then to turn to the tools available to assess and integrate these issues into their planning framework, should follow Chapter 5. Tables 5.1 to 5.4 provide a broad overview of the environmental impacts of concern to decisionmakers, both negative and positive, in relation to water sources themselves, water treatment, water conveyance and water use.

To show that the question of environmental impacts are more than just a local, project-specific problem, this chapter also focuses attention on the transnational and global nature of many water related environmental issues. Although individual decisionmakers in developing countries can often have little direct influence in mitigating the problems causing these issues, they can still be viewed in the context of the environmental-economic analytical framework developed in previous chapters. Indirectly, through supporting international cooperation and by seeking to address the role played by their own country, no matter how small, they can contribute to the worldwide efforts to bring some of these environmental problems under control. We indicate how this can often only be accomplished with the help of external assistance since the costs of environmental management and the short-run benefits foregone by using the environment in a less intensive, environmentally sound manner can be too high for many resource scarce developing countries to bear alone.

Scale of Environmental Impacts

The efficient and optimal use of our global natural resource base, including air, land and water, has emerged as an area of universal concern during recent decades. According to Bowers (1990), dealing with the world's environmental problems will undoubtedly impose substantial costs on current generations. In the water sector, resources are needed to restore degraded environments, to

TABLE 5.1   Environmental Impact of Water Sources

Impact / Activity	Explanation
Dams and Reservoirs	
Land Losses	loss of large tracts of land, involuntary resettlement, inundation of forest, impact on CO_2 balance.
Animal Life	impact on animal habitat, extinction.
Health	water related diseases
Fisheries	reduced fishery productivity due to reduced nutrient supply downstream and in estuaries
Water weeds	proliferation of weeds can impair water quality, increase disease vectors and water loss (through plant transpiration).
Downstream hydrology	changes in downstream flows can impair ecosystems dependant on seasonal flooding, and have an impact on traditional flood-recession agriculture.
Water quality	water quality changes due to loss of flushing, increased nutrients, salinization.
Erosion	increased erosivity on downstream riverbed and structures, i.e., the hungry waters effect.
Water temperature changes	influence on aquatic fauna and flora, reduction of crop yields, especially for rice.
Recreation	value of recreation opportunities gained or lost.
Involuntary resettlement	reservoir creation may involve inundation of villages, farms and infrastructure such as roads and transmission lines.
Cultural and historical sites	inundation of sites of historic, religious, aesthetic value, and sites of archeological and paleontological significance.
Seismicity	seismicity might be induced by large reservoirs.
Local climate	Large reservoirs may modify the local climate, especially in terms of humidity and local fog.
Groundwater	
Pollution	seepage of fertilizers and pesticides due to agricultural practices, industrial spill of chemicals that runoff and infiltrate the soil, contamination by unsewered human and animal wastes, recharge of aquifer with waste water, in the absence of tertiary treatment.
Salinization	saline sea water can intrude as a result of mining the aquifer, reuse of agricultural drainage can cause salinity build up in the aquifer.
Subsidence	some soils are prone to subsidence caused by a drop in the water table.

Sources: World Bank 1990a; Dixon, et al. 1989; Munasinghe 1991.

TABLE 5.2 Environmental Impact of Water Treatment

Impact / Activity	Explanation
Disinfection	widely used chlorine raises some occupational health and safety issues concerns about chloramines as carcinogens.
Algae control	health hazards related to use of copper sulfate in reservoirs to eliminate algal blooms.
Desalinization	is energy intensive, all methods produce highly saline brine which requires disposal.
Municipal waste water treatment	while obviously beneficial in overall terms, sludge disposal, and point discharge to receiving waters are main issues.
Industrial waste water treatment	sludge and ash residuals frequently have high concentrations of toxic materials.
Desalination	hydrology: alteration of flow characteristics of receiving water body; thermal impact: temperature may rise appreciably downstream from desalination plant, producing wide range of biological, chemical and physical changes; pollution: downstream increase in biocide residuals (brine, chlorine, heavy metals).

Sources: World Bank 1990a; Keenan 1991.

clean up water systems and polluted land, to replant forests (to regulate water flows) and to recreate damaged habitats. To create an economic system that is environmentally friendly and non-polluting will require a significant mobilization of resources. In many current social systems that are based on the concept of continuous growth, a shift to a more sustainable development path will involve profound changes in the social structure. Equity questions are critical since sustainable development in the water and other sectors involves, in essence, a shift of resource allocation from current generations to those of the future.

Major issues vary widely, but for purposes of analysis, one useful classification is by scale or magnitude of impact.

In order of decreasing scale, it is possible to identify environmental problems of a global, transnational, national and local impact.

Global problems comprise such issues as the potential worldwide warming due to increasing accumulation of green house gases like carbon dioxide (CO_2), methane (CH_4), and nitrous oxide (N_2O) in the atmosphere, high altitude ozone depletion because of excessive release of chlorofluorocarbons (CFCs), reduction of biodiversity, and progressive pollution of the oceanic and marine environment by oil spills and other wastes.

TABLE 5.3   Environmental Impact of Water Conveyance Systems

Impact / Activity	Explanation
Canals and aqueducts	can favor breeding grounds for disease vectors, impact of construction, especially in remote areas.
Major pipelines	construction impacts, especially in remote areas, in the case of inter-basing transfers, possibility of introducing new pollutants and disease vectors.
Dredging	possible release of toxic materials trapped in sediments, dredge spoil disposal.
Flood control water treatment	channelization projects may impact downstream hydrology.
Storm drainage	water quality impact of discharges containing suspended solids, oils and grease, possible disease vectors.
Water distribution systems	lead is a concern in old pipes and solder in copper joints, leakages may cause backsiphoning of pollutants and disease vectors.

Sources: World Bank 1990a.

Transnational problems are issues that are international in nature, but more specifically act to affect the immediate environment shared by two or more countries over a common border.   An example would be acid rain or radioactive fallout in one european country due to industrial or nuclear emissions in a neighboring nation.   Another example is the excessive downstream siltation of river water in one country due to deforestation of watersheds and soil erosion in another country situated upstream.

Thirdly, there are the national and regional problems and their effects, for example those involving the development of the Amazon basin in Brazil, or the Mahaweli basin in Sri Lanka.

Finally, there are more localized and project specific problems like urban waste disposal and water pollution in a given city, the complex environmental and social impacts of a specific hydroelectric or multipurpose dam, and noxious effluents from an industrial plant, all of which have an impact on the immediate surroundings and their human, plant and animal communities.

While environmental and natural resource problems of any kind are a matter for serious concern, those that fall within the national boundaries of a given country are inherently easier to deal with from the viewpoint of policy implementation.   Nevertheless, driven by strong pressures arising from far-reaching potential consequences of global issues like atmospheric greenhouse gas accumulation, significant efforts are being made to improve not

TABLE 5.4   Environmental Impact of Water Use

Impact / Activity	Explanation
Irrigation	salinization as a result of poorly managed irrigation, impact of reduced downstream flows may be serious.
Drainage	drainage water of agricultural areas carry residuals of agrochemicals.
Water conservation	installation of meters, reduction of leakages, reduction of infiltration into sewers: environmentally beneficial.
Drinking water supply	positive impacts of engineered drinking water supply on human health may outweigh adverse construction phase and implementation impacts.
Industrial use	thermal impacts on receiving water body, water quality deterioration, consumptive use in estuarine areas poses danger of saline intrusions into upper estuaries.
Hydro-power generation	conflicts between optimal releases for power generation and downstream flow needs.

Sources: World Bank 1990a.

only scientific analysis, but also international cooperation mechanisms to implement mitigatory measures.

In the following sections, we seek to examine primarily the subset of issues that arise in the area of water resource management within a single country. This narrowing of the focus permits us to spotlight more direct and tangible issues facing the planner, and to deepen the analysis. We are helped in this by the work of Lee and Bastemeijer (1991), who have reviewed the range of environmental factors affecting the quantity, quality and reliability of water sources and supplies in developing countries. In keeping with their focus on water supplies for low-income urban and rural communities, they split the externalities into two groups -- those affecting small and large water sources respectively. This provides a checklist from which planners could assess which externalities are most prevalent in each context. Here, we summarize the main externalities of importance for planners dealing with the macro-aspects of the water sector (i.e., the complete range of domestic, industrial and agricultural consumers), sub-divided into groundwater and surface water issues. Subsequently, we address the range of external problems using the policy tools available to decisionmakers in a conventional sociopolitical and economic framework, as previously explained. By establishing an economic rationale and an analytical framework for considering various options, the goals of sound water supply economics and environmental management can be more closely achieved.

Environmental Issues in Groundwater Use

Groundwater is widely and increasingly exploited for potable water supply in developing countries. In smaller towns and rural areas groundwater is a major source of potable water, because it may be the cheapest and safest option. In many regions, such utilization involves large numbers of low yielding boreholes (0.5 to 5 liters per second -- l/s), generally drilled on an uncontrolled basis and providing untreated and unmonitored supplies, often through handpumps. Much higher yielding (10 to 100 l/s) boreholes are also quite widely used to provide drinking water supplies to cities, including major urban centers such as Bangkok, Beijing, Cairo, Jakarta, Lima, Manila and Mexico City. In Latin America and the Caribbean, aquifers now provide drinking supplies to an estimated 140 million people in the region. Even though the majority of the users are in the metropolitan areas, raw water surveillance and treatment is limited and/or intermittent for these groundwater supplies (Foster et al. 1987).

The four major externalities associated with groundwater use that affect and are caused by the water supply and related economic sectors are aquifer depletion, pollution, salinization and land subsidence (as summarized in Tables 5.1 to 5.4). Frequently they are experienced concurrently. A subsequent section provides an overview of groundwater problems experienced in the United States and some useful regulatory measures and practical procedures designed by the Environmental Protection Agency to help protect drinking water aquifers.

Depletion of Groundwater

Over-extraction of groundwater is becoming an increasingly common problem in developing countries. Water is abstracted by large-volume users using growing numbers of ever deeper boreholes and more sophisticated and powerful pumps, often at the expense of rural or poor peri-urban communities using hand-dug wells and hand-pumps. According to Lee and Bastemeijer (1991), causes of the problem include one or more of the following:

A. Policy and Planning

- lack of integrated water management policies;
- lack of water reuse and conservation strategies as tools for pollution control and abstraction reduction;

- lack of adequate alternative surface water resources partly due to pollution of these sources by industrial and municipal waste; and
- absence of an effective large-scale artificial recharge program.

B. Enforcement

- ineffective and inadequate enforcement of legislation to curb over-extraction; and
- unregistered, uncontrolled and unsustainable use coupled with a lack of regulations.

C. Data

- lack of yield potential and recharge data from which sustainable extraction levels can be determined and used in planning.

The development and promotion of low-cost technology options for water supply and community-based maintenance systems is negatively affected by a general lowering of the water table (DANIDA 1988). Where developing countries plan to achieve coverage level targets for their rural and peri-urban populations using these technologies, the externalities resulting from unequal access to common aquifers by the industrial and agricultural sectors has serious implications. An example from India illustrates the problem. In Maharashtra, irrigated sugarcane cultivation and water-intensive processing has lead to severe aquifer depletion and in the two years since 1985 has reportedly resulted in over 21,000 villages experiencing seasonal exhaustion of traditional and improved well water supplies (Bandyopadhyay 1987). Another striking example comes from the Yemen where measurement of groundwater on the Sana'a Plain has showed levels to have fallen by 20 meters in ten years (Charalambous 1986). The Sadah Plain has seen an almost equal rate of decline (Gun 1985, 1986). At Sadah, the rate of natural groundwater recharge is roughly 10×10^6 m^3/year whereas by 1983, abstraction by a growing number of bored wells and diesel pumps was already 57×10^6 m^3/year. Public water supply is becoming increasingly difficult, the viability of groundwater-irrigated agriculture is gradually declining and the water sources might finally be exhausted. With little potential for artificial recharge of aquifers due to the lack of surface water resources, planners are faced with the task of reducing and controlling groundwater abstraction rates. In many other cases like these, current lower-cost supply options such as well drilling and hand-pump installation may have to be replaced by higher-cost options including piped-in remote surface supplies or electrically-pumped deeper groundwater. Where applicable, water prices also could be raised to reduce demand and pay for better water conservation measures.

Pollution of Groundwater

Groundwater pollution is already a critical issue in the industrialized countries of the world. So far, however, it has not received much consideration in developing countries. This is a function of a variety of factors including the lack of monitoring and surveillance to identify problems areas, and because problems often take a considerable amount of time to develop, with health-hazard levels being exceeded slowly, and often irreversibly. The latter occurs because often, very slow groundwater movement results in slow pollutant migration from the land surface into the aquifer and slow routing through the aquifer itself, so that it can take decades before the full impact of a pollution incident triggers any reaction. Pollution can arise from a number of causes (Foster 1988 and Lloyd 1987) encompassing both point and non-point sources. For developing countries there are three main sources of groundwater pollution. First is contamination by unsewered and inappropriate sanitation. Although the chemo-physical characteristics of soils are natural purifiers of human and animal wastes, not all soil profiles are 100% effective (an in-depth discussion on the soil-physical characteristics governing groundwater pollution is provided by Geraghty and Miller 1984). Under certain conditions there can be a risk of direct migration of pathogens to underlying aquifers and transmission from there to neighboring groundwater. Some viruses can live for years in the subsurface environment. If contaminated groundwater is consumed without treatment by humans it can cause outbreaks of waterborne diseases. Major sources of seepage result from on-site sanitation such as latrines and septic tanks, and from aeration lagoons or sewerage spreading areas (Lee and Bastemeijer 1991).

A second source of contamination can be related to industrial discharges or urban effluents. In many developing countries, even today, large parts of urban areas are deprived of sewerage systems. In some of these zones, small-scale industries (particularly textiles, metal processing and tanneries) may be located. When those industries generate wastes, such as spent oils and solvents, they often discharge them directly into the soil, where it penetrates over time into the aquifer, usually by seepage from stabilization ponds or drainage ditches.

The third major contaminant source is associated with agricultural activities such as the application of fertilizers and pesticides.

PAHO/CEPIS have recently tried to provide adequate procedures for the identification and evaluation of pollution risk for regional aquifers in Latin America and the Caribbean (Adams 1990). Many of the aquifers, which as indicated serve at least 140 million consumers, are vulnerable to pollution from discharge of liquid effluent, land disposal of solid wastes, transport, storage and handling of toxic chemicals and the intensification of agricultural land management within their catchment areas. As well as being a major source for urban centers, groundwater is also being widely and increasingly exploited for potable water-supply in rural areas, because it is seen as the cheapest and safest source. With these, and other aquifers around the globe, the long-term effects of groundwater pollution can preclude future use, and rehabilitation of the polluted aquifer is generally infeasible due to prohibitive costs, persistence of the contaminants, or the lack of adequate monitoring methods.

Salinization of Aquifers

The third well known consequence of mismanagement of groundwater resources is salinization, and again there are numerous reasons that can cause an aquifer to become saline and unsuitable for irrigation or drinking water supplies. The reuse of agricultural drainage water for irrigation purposes has led to a build-up of salt in shallow aquifers. Well known examples are the Wadi Bisha alluvial aquifer in Saudi Arabia (BRGM 1985) and the aquifers of the Punjab region in Pakistan (Rathur 1987). Deforestation at the end of the 19th century, combined with a high evaporative demand caused salinization of vast aquifers in Australia, resulting in the abandonment of millions of hectares of land in the semi-arid areas of the country (Jenkin 1981).

Mining or over-pumping of aquifers in coastal regions has also led to salinization by seawater intrusion. The dynamics of saline water seepage are presented schematically in Figure 5.1. A feature of this type of pollution is that there are two distinct bodies of water, which differ in density and are relatively immiscible. There is a distinct brackish interface that demarcates the pollution, beyond which there is no migration of salt. Without human interference the intrusion front can move either away from or back towards the sea, depending on the amount of recharge from inland over a particular period, although it will do so within rather narrow spatial limits. When the natural equilibrium is disturbed by human activities such as over-pumping (i.e., more water is taken away from the aquifer than is replenished by precipitation percolating down), the saline water body will move inland, replacing the depleted fresh water. In other words the progress of the pollution is mainly determined by the pumping rate. This scenario contrasts with other types of pollution (e.g., the movement of agro- or industrial chemicals), which are governed by the physical flow characteristics of the "fresh" groundwater itself and the rate of chemical release, rather than depending mainly on the pumping regime. Numerous examples are available, including the Niger delta in Nigeria (Busari and Amadi 1989), the coast of Hermisollo in Mexico (Busch et al. 1966) and Peninsular Malaysia (Peng 1987). In the US, the problem has been recognized as particularly serious on the coasts of California, Texas, Florida, New-York and Hawaii since the 1960s (Todd 1967). An illustrative case study of the economic effects of groundwater depletion and deterioration

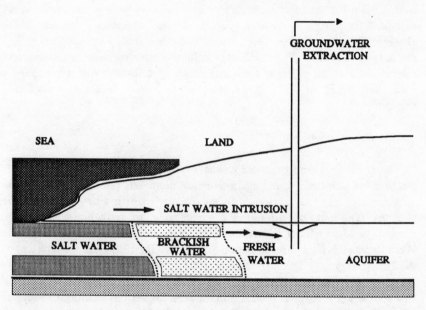

Figure 5.1 Schematic Diagram of Salt Water Intrusion in an Aquifer

of aquifer quality in the Philippines is presented in Chapter 13, and policy options to effectively address the issues are also analyzed.

Land Subsidence

For urban water supply and industry, over-pumping or mining of the aquifer frequently leads to problems of land subsidence, often resulting in the collapse of buildings and other surface structures. Accounts from Japan, Thailand, the United States and many other countries are documented (Chuamthaisong 1989). The city of Bangkok provides a good example of subsidence problems. Water levels dropped 10-12 meters in three years since 1985 (Nair 1988) as unregulated and unregistered pumping facilities proliferated in and around the metropolitan area. Up to 1 million cubic meters were being pumped per day. Land subsided on a large scale resulting in flooding of sewerage and storm drainage systems at high tides. Subsidence and water quantity depletion are not the only problems. Pipelines are breaking and, consequently, industrial and domestic waste is finding its way into the Bangkok aquifer. Another serious threat to aquifer water quality is through saline intrusion, which is penetrating inland at a rate of 100 to 200 m per year. Concentrations of chloride in public wells have risen five times up to a level of 1000-1250 milligrams per liter (mg/l).

Equity and Fairness Issues in Groundwater Use

Optimal exploitation of an aquifer requires that users account for the effects of current pumping on both the level and quality of the groundwater in future periods. This requires that the marginal user cost be accounted for in current pumping decisions. The marginal user cost or externality cost is the present and future cost to other users arising from current extraction by any given well-user. In one study, Cummings (1971) has broken down the user cost into several components, first, the marginal value of water in storage, second, the marginal cost of water use in terms of capital consumption, and third the marginal cost of salt intrusion. One could also include the marginal costs of groundwater pollution, land subsidence, and other effects.

The burden of environmental impacts are often unevenly allocated. The optimum output of the good (e.g., water or untreated waste) for society differs from that for the sub-group taking the decisions (Bowers 1990). Decisionmakers often take little account of the effects of their decisions on the welfare of third parties. The example of groundwater abstraction is a prime one. Abstractors usually have no incentive to conserve an aquifer since they have no guarantee that their sacrifices will not be nullified by the continued abstraction of non-conservers. Groundwater has the characteristics of a commonly owned property. When water is pumped by many individuals who act independently rather than collectively, there are strong incentives to ignore the marginal user cost. This normally results in economic inefficiencies since too much water is pumped too soon (Vaux 1985). Therefore the establishment of a regulatory framework that imposes rules on all users so as to implicitly account for the externality costs, is to the long-term advantage of all (see Philippine case study in Chapter 12).

An Example: Groundwater Protection in the United States

Institutional Framework

In the United States today, 95% of rural populations and 50% of the population as a whole rely on groundwater for their drinking water supply. Since 1984, the United States Environmental Protection Agency (EPA) has implemented a groundwater protection strategy through its national and regional Office of Groundwater Protection. The Office of Groundwater Protection works in tandem with other key EPA offices including: Solid Waste and Emergency Response; Pesticides and Toxic Substances; Air and Radiation; Research and Development; and Policy, Planning and Evaluation (EPA, 1990), to set standards for groundwater management in order to ensure safe drinking water supply. Individual State and Local Governments have primary responsibility for actual protection and management of their groundwater sources.   The EPA regulates specific contaminants and sources of contamination and provides technical and financial support to States to implement these regulations.

Groundwater Pollution

The major sources of groundwater pollution include:

- 92,000 hazardous and potentially hazardous waste landfills;
- 200,000 surface impoundments for storage of liquid wastes built without consideration of groundwater impacts;
- 3 to 10 million storage tanks for toxic liquids (of which between 3 and 25% could be leaking at this time);
- 23 million septic tanks;
- roughly 50 m tons of fertilizers, pesticides and animal waste applied to the land annually;
- 12 million tons of salt applied to highways annually;
- chemicals and residues in abandoned mineworkings; and
- salt-water intrusion due to overpumping of coastal aquifers (EPA, 1987a).

The costs of ameliorating contamination of drinking water aquifers is very high.   One example was the 1977 leak of 2000-3000 gallons (9000-13500 liters) of unleaded petrol from a storage tank in Massachusetts located 600 feet (200 meters) from a well in the middle of a municipal well field.   The clean-up operation which took 13 years to complete, involved pumping out groundwater, treating it, and recharging the aquifer, at a cost of US$ 3.3 million (EPA, 1987b).

The Wellhead Protection Program

Wellhead Protection measures were incorporated into the Safe Drinking Water Act of 1986. The Amendment called for the protection of groundwater supplying wells and wellfields that contribute drinking water to public water supply systems.   The EPA has since mounted a nationwide program to encourage States to develop systematic and comprehensive programs to protect public water supply wells and wellfields from contamination from a variety of sources (see Table 5.5). The EPA has no authority to actually implement the protection measures.   However, they have a budget of around $8 million annually to encourage States to meet the broad federal guidelines set down in the act.

As decreed by the 1986 Amendments to the Safe Drinking Water Act, each State's Wellhead Protection Program must (EPA 1989):

TABLE 5.5   Sources of Groundwater Contamination

Sources Designed to Discharge Substances
  1.   Subsurface percolation
  2.   Injection wells
  3.   Land application

Sources Designed to Store, Treat, and/or Dispose of Substances
  1.   Landfills
  2.   Open dumps
  3.   Residential disposal
  4.   Surface impoundments
  5.   Waste tailings
  6.   Waste piles
  7.   Graveyards
  8.   Animal burial
  9.   Aboveground storage tanks
  10.   Underground storage tanks
  11.   Containers
  12.   Open burning and detonation sites
  13.   Radioactive disposal sites

Sources Designed to Retain Substances During Transport
  1.   Pipelines
  2.   Materials transport and transfer operations

Sources Discharging Substances as a Consequence of Other Activities
  1.   Irrigation practices
  2.   Pesticide applications
  3.   Fertilizer applications
  4.   Animal feeding operations
  5.   De-icing salts operations
  6.   Urban runoff
  7.   Percolation of atmospheric pollutants
  8.   Mining and mine drainage

Sources Providing Conduit or Inducing Discharge Through Altered Flow Patterns
  1.   Production wells
  2.   Other wells (non-waste)
  3.   Construction excavation

Naturally Occurring Sources Whose Discharge is Created and/or Exacerbated by Human Activity
  1.   Groundwater-surface water interactions
  2.   Natural leaching
  3.   Salt-water intrusion/brackish upconing

Source: EPA 1987d.

- specify roles and duties of State agencies, local government, and public water suppliers;
- delineate wellhead protection areas (WHPA) for each wellhead;
- identify sources of contaminants;
- develop management approaches to protect water supply from within WHPA from such contaminants;
- develop contingency plans to respond to well or wellfield contamination;
- site new wells to maximize yield but minimize contamination risks; and
- ensure public participation in wellhead protection.

Protection Management

The EPA has produced a clear set of supporting and instructional documents concerning groundwater protection efforts and the Wellhead Protection Program (1985, 1987a, 1987b, 1987c, 1987d, 1989, 1990). The EPA guidelines of 1989 detail a series of well-defined management approaches to be used by local governments in the US to protect their groundwater. The broad strategy includes:

- assessing the local needs (the contamination and control context);
- choosing appropriate management tools for protection including zoning, subdivision, plan review, design standards, operating standards, contamination source prohibitions, property purchase, public education, monitoring, waste collection and water conservation; and
- implementing a local program -- staff requirements, communication methods, enforcement.

The US example may be useful for decisionmakers elsewhere to get some insight into planning a more effective groundwater protection methodology.

Environmental Issues in Surface Water Use

As with groundwater, a number of externalities are of major concern to planners in the water sector and related sectors (see Tables 5.1 to 5.4). Since surface water is a more visible entity, the impacts of different sector activities, and the conflicts that these sometimes cause are more transparent. In many cases, externalities affecting surface water sources will have a corresponding impact on groundwater depending on the nature of the modification of their links in the hydrological cycle (as discussed previously in Chapter 2). In most situations, larger surface water sources are more than just a source of drinking water. As explained, they are used for recreation, for navigation and in the production of energy, and wildlife is dependent on them. They are also used as receptacles, processors and purifiers of waste.

Rivers, Dams and Channels

Dams and reservoirs are essential human modifications used to capture surface water in order to exploit it in a manageable way over a period of time, and to meet multiple sector uses including drinking, irrigation, electricity generation, transport, flood control, fishing and so forth. The benefits of dam construction are self-evident. However, they also have environmental impacts (Goodland 1990). The building of dams may severely affect the environmental equilibrium in the project region and even beyond. Depending on the shape of the landscape, and the height of the dam, large areas of land may become flooded. This will have impacts on human settlements, wildlife habitats and agricultural lands. From an aesthetic-environmental viewpoint, the loss depends on the uniqueness of the flooded land and on the value placed on it by society (OECD 1985). With many dams built in pristine locations, cultural heritage issues are raised since ancient, indigenous populations may be forced to abandon traditional land. Another basic environmental question to be asked is what irreversible changes might occur in eradicating certain plant or animal species (Maler and Wyzga 1976). The answer to this question may raise biodiversity related concerns of local, national, or even global scope. Some of the involved species may contain genetic features which could be of medicinal or agricultural importance for future generations. Comprehensive overviews and case studies of the environmental effects and economic consequences of reservoirs and dams, in World Bank projects, are presented by Dixon et al. (1989) and Le Moigne et al. (1990). In addition to the above mentioned impacts, these references encompass a broad spectrum of environmental issues dealing with diverse topics such as the preservation of religious and archeological sites, the inundation of potentially valuable mineral resources, and the risk of induced seismicity and water-related human diseases. These are all environmental issues raised by the construction of dams which must be considered and reconciled as part of an IWRP.

Dams, once built are also the focus of a number of other externality issues. Because of increasing turbidity of runoff water, many reservoirs have lifetimes which are considerably shortened by the accumulation of silt originating from soil erosion in deforested upstream water catchment areas. The deforestation involved may occur as a direct result of planning decisions made by another government sector, for instance forestry, power or land management. The conflicts of interest, both in economic and in social terms must be reconciled as part of an integrated planning process.

Other waterway modifications also may have positive and negative effects. In the case of flood control canals or storm sewers, the engineering project can actually become a synergistic component in environmental resource management or else aggravate the problems of flooding. Maintenance works in flood canals are chronically under-funded and unglamorous. The results of neglect are accumulation of silt and uncontrolled vegetation in the channel beds, thereby increasing the risk of floods. The negative impacts of the latter on the environment are readily understood. Well maintained canals, however, with provision for an artificial flood-plain may, on the other hand, contribute by enhancing the environmental value of a flood plain. For example, Williams (1990) argues that the terrace provides space for a walking trail. Planting riparian trees on the banks shades out the channel, which prevents vegetation encroachment, minimizes maintenance, improves water quality and creates a continuous corridor for wildlife. Riparian vegetation can also slow bank erosion.

Irrigation and Agriculture

The use of increasingly scarce surface water for irrigation competes with potable water supply (see Chapter 1). Furthermore, such agricultural use can have significant adverse environmental impacts. Each year, some 3300 km^3 of water are removed from the earth's rivers and aquifers to water crops. Practiced on such a scale, irrigation has had a profound impact (both good and bad) on the cropland receiving it, as well as on water bodies. The agricultural and drinking water supply sectors are inherently linked on two issues: firstly, the competition for limited water resources, and secondly, the quality reduction due to the washing off of evaporated salts, fertilizers and pesticides from irrigated fields. As the use of organic fertilizers, pesticides and herbicides increase in developing countries, the concentration of phosphates and nitrates in groundwater sources grows. Problems related to poor irrigation management, such as waterlogging and salinity build up, which adversely affect agricultural productivity may actually be caused by water sector planning decisions. Both problems threaten the longer term sustainability of an irrigation project. Excessive irrigation in the absence of adequate provision of drainage, and seepage losses in the water conveyance systems (which may amount to 25%) can both contribute to mobilizing salts and raising water tables. Some researchers (e.g., Repetto 1986) argue that the main cause is underpriced irrigation water, as it gives irrigators little incentive to economize on the amount of water used and results in mismanagement of water. It is estimated that irrigation-related soil salinity alone is the cause of damage to over 60 million hectares or about a quarter of all irrigated land in the world. Not only does irrigation cause tremendous salinity problems in the soil and drainage water, it is also responsible for the uneconomic waste of vast quantities of water. Falkenmark (1987) indicates that irrigation consumes over 80% of all fresh water used today, but the efficiency of irrigation systems (defined as the ratio of water delivered to water produced) is seldom more than 50% and often as low as 30%. Therefore, the potential for conserving water by increasing irrigation efficiency is tremendous. On a related note, significant trade-offs will need to be made in the water sector of developing countries in the 1990s. Whereas currently, water consumption is comprised overall in the ratios 85% agriculture, 10% industry and 5% domestic, development is creating a divergence in water uses toward the pattern in developed countries where industry and domestic uses take a much larger share. Estimates indicate that by the year 2000, domestic and industrial demand will have risen to over 22% of the total. Consequently, agriculture will be allocated a smaller share of available resources and at a much higher cost making water efficiency an even higher priority.

Drainage water from agricultural activities spawns yet another set of ecological problems as it contains large concentrations of hazardous chemicals, originating from fertilizer and pesticide applications. This type of pollution has a multisector externality effect, not only influencing water supply, but also long-term agricultural productivity, health, and the natural ecology. The results can be death, grotesque deformities, and reproductive failure in fish, birds and other wildlife (Postel 1989). In addition, accumulation of fertilizer in reservoirs boosts algal growth (eutrophication), kills aquatic life, and destroys the recreational value of reservoirs (OECD 1985). There are two types of polluting effects from pesticides and fertilizers: point pollution; and non-point pollution. Point pollution refers to the concentrated input of chemicals into the water source, and non-point pollution occurs due to the gradual influx of low-concentrations of chemicals into the water source over a wide area of land. Both take place in areas of extensive agricultural activity. The WHO is seriously concerned with the growing threat from pesticides and has shown that increasing pesticides in the environment can result in DDT appearing in the milk of lactating women (WHO 1985). As pesticide use increases, the concentration of carcinogenic substances in the water supply and food chain will also increase (de Koning 1987) affecting human and wildlife populations due to their toxicity. Increases in alkalinity from fertilizer residues can lead to long-term falls in plant yields. Related effects on water supply include eutrophication of lakes, affecting recreation, ecology, and transport (due to accelerated water weed growth).

Industrial Production

Most industrial production processes result in some form of liquid waste which is often discharged into waterways. Some clear examples of the problems of industrial pollution of surface sources can be taken from Indian and Latin American rivers. In India, rapid growth of industrial capacity has resulted in considerable increases in stream and river water pollution by industrial waste. One example is the Neeva River in Andhra Pradesh. There, the effect of inflowing distillery wastewater on the color, odor, taste and chemical constituents of river water makes it unfit for domestic use (Reddy 1987). According to CEPIS (1989), many of Latin America's rivers receive serious levels of toxic industrial pollution due to untreated factory discharge. They include the Reconquista, Matanza-Riachuelo, Choqueyapu-Reni, Tiete, Magdalena, Bio-Bio, Maipo, Guayas, Rimac and Tuy rivers. A majority of these provide significant proportions of water supplies for major metropolitan areas.

According to the review of Lee and Bastemeijer (1991), unchecked waste discharge from the industrial sector has a number of underlying causes:

- industries do not see an economic benefit from waste treatment because their waste contains no recyclable products which they could use again in their industrial process or sell to a second party;
- industries have insufficient access to cheap treatment technologies, either due to a lack of technical knowledge or awareness of the existence of treatment processes, because treatment technologies are too expensive, or else because they have not yet been developed for their particular scale and type of industrial operation; and
- industries have no incentives to treat their waste because government regulations do not penalize discharge of wastes, government monitoring facilities are ineffective and cannot identify the nature and source of pollution from discharge, or enforcement arrangements are too weak or inadequate to implement regulations. Most developing countries currently have no toxic chemical control laws, nor the technical or institutional capability for implementing such laws (UNEP 1989).

Health and Sanitation Issues

Although water supply and sanitation are usually not thought of primarily as environmental issues, for low-income households in the developing world these are high priority environmental concerns -- since they define the environment in which the poor live and also directly affect their health and welfare. Inadequate sanitation and clean water provision remain, in terms of the scale of human suffering, the most serious of all environmental problems. As indicated in Chapter 1, poor sanitation results in millions of deaths and billions of episodes of illness each year. In addition, it severely degrades surface and groundwater quality.

In developing countries, many urban areas have no sewerage treatment facilities or ones that are poorly maintained or antiquated. In Central and South America, CEPIS (1989) estimates that 50% of the urban population has no access to sewerage systems, and over 90% of the sewerage water collected from those that do is discharged into rivers without any treatment. Figures on sanitation coverage presented earlier show this is similar for other geographic regions too. For example, sewerage from Bogota, Colombia is discharged into the Rio Bogota creating enormous concentrations of faecal coliforms downstream. Some of this water is used to irrigate market crops which often results in sickness amongst consumers (Okun 1990). Data collected by the World Bank for the Eastern Mediterranean and north Africa region indicates the serious pollution load on the aquatic environment due to the failure to treat wastewater flows (Table 5.6).

Water supply and sanitation affect health in several distinct ways. Fecal-oral diseases all depend on pathogens being present in the environment as a result of poor sanitation. Some of these diseases such as typhoid and cholera are often water-borne and are thus affected mainly by the bacteriological quality of the drinking water. The incidence of other fecal-oral diseases, like dysentery, may be reduced by making available larger quantities of water for personal hygiene. Another group of diseases like schistosomiasis or bilharzia is water-based and depend on direct contact between people and infected water. Finally, some diseases, such as sleeping sickness and river blindness, are transmitted by water-related insect vectors which breed in or near water sources.

The direct impact of these diseases related to water supply and sanitation in huge, especially for the poor who are most at risk. Diarrheal diseases alone account for over 5 million deaths, mainly children under five years of age, and for about 900 million episodes of illness each year. In addition, many of these diseases have large indirect effects -- for instance, frequent diarrhea can deplete children's nutritional reserves, leaving them vulnerable to illness and death from other causes. On the other hand, the health impact of improving water and sanitation conditions in developing countries are large. Table 5.7 illustrates the reduction in sickness due to sanitation improvements, compiled recently from a review of about 100 studies. The Table shows that the effects are substantial, with median reductions ranging from 22% for diarrhea morbidity to 76% for guinea worm prevalence. The same review also showed that the impact of sanitation improvements on avoided deaths is even more dramatic than the positive impact on sickness reduction. For example, it was found that median reductions in mortality from diarrheal diseases amounted to 60%.

Information from the International Water Decade previously presented in Chapter 1 shows that for many millions of people in the developing world, water supply systems are developed for consumers without corresponding improvements in sanitation facilities. In such cases, the potential is very high for the onset of serious environmental externalities that may affect the costs and quality of supply. Simply providing more water, but no mechanisms to

TABLE 5.6 Wastewater Production and Treatment in the EMENA Region (in millions of m^3 per year)

Country	Year of Data	Production	Treatment
Cyprus	1989	22	4
Egypt	1985	986	0
Jordan	1986	53	23
Kuwait	1985	93	78
Morocco	1985	244	6
Saudi Arabia	1989	480	380
Syria	1985	189	0
Tunisia	1986	124	60
Turkey	1987	1086	139
Yemen AR	1986	21	6

Source: World Bank reports.

deal with wastewater disposal, can create the opportunity for diseases to spread wider and faster, thereby nullifying the improvements in health and welfare expected from upgrading water supply. The economic costs of wastewater are significant. Wastewater collection and disposal costs are particularly difficult to come by and are seldom hard data. However, economies of scale realized from expansion of water supply facilities and customer service levels may be reversed quickly by diseconomies due to the collection, treatment, disposal and environmental costs associated with the increased volume of wastewater (Gunnerson 1989).

Examples of negative externalities are the recent major outbreak of hepatitis A in Shanghai, China, which was ascribed to sewerage contamination. The same cause was identified in the cholera epidemic in Peru and other Latin American countries. Other environmental and health impacts arise from releases of untreated sewerage in coastal areas. For example, pollution of coastal waters in northern China has been blamed for a sharp drop in prawn and shellfish harvests. In a sample of fish and shellfish caught in Jakarta Bay, 44% exceeded WHO standards for lead, and 76% for cadmium. The consumption of such contaminated items could obviously lead to both short or long-term food poisoning. In addition to the health hazard, pools of odorous sewerage and wastewater in the street and in low-lying areas, create aesthetic problems. In many urban settings in developing countries, the demand for adequate sanitation services may be determined primarily by aesthetic rather than health concerns. These included a wish for privacy, convenience, status, and concern with removing polluted water from the vicinity, because of odors and the mosquitos which breed in these waters. One undesirable environmental externality arising from the foregoing, was the dumping of untreated wastewater from affluent neighborhoods into poorer areas. Other

TABLE 5.7   Effects of Improved Water and Sanitation on Occurrence of Sickness in Developing Countries

Disease	Incidence cases per year (millions)	Prevalence number infected (millions)	Median Reduction due to Sanitation Improvement (%)
Diarrhea	900		22
Ascariasis		900	28
Guinea worm		4	76
Schistosomiasis		200	73
Trachoma		500	50

Source: Esrey et al. 1990.

serious environmental impacts of non-sewered sanitation systems include the degradation of groundwater quality. In Buenos Aires, for example, nitrate levels in aquifers are well above WHO guideline values and are continuing to rise rapidly. These problems are even more serious in arid areas without significant aquifer flow.

In developing countries the major technological challenges in the sanitation sector have to do with the collection, rather than the disposal of excreta and wastewater. The underlying problem is that conventional water-borne sewerage, even without treatment, is much too expensive for the majority of the population, as initial costs are usually well over US$ 1000 per household. The bulk of efforts at developing sanitation technologies has been on solutions for the on-site disposal of excreta, with pour-flush latrines and ventilated improved pit (VIP) latrines. The advantages of these technologies are that they provide good service at more reasonable costs, which are typically US$ 100 to US$ 200 per unit. At the same time, their installation, operation and maintenance, does not depend on the performance of the local government or other organizations. At even lower cost, are the simpler improvements which will remain important for the considerable segment of the population which cannot afford a pour-flush or VIP latrines. An example is the successful latrine slab program in Mozambique.

Sanitation systems for the collection, treatment and disposal of wastewater will have significant positive environmental impacts if planned, sited, designed, constructed, operated and maintained properly. In general, the benefits include:

- abatement of nuisances and public health hazards
- improvement in received water quality;
- increases in beneficial use of receiving waters;
- opportunities for more effective control of industrial wastewater;
- opportunities for beneficial use of treated effluent and sludge;

- provision of serviced sites for development;
- increase in property values, following installation of sewers;
- increased fishery productivity and revenues;
- increased tourist and recreational activity;
- increased agricultural productivity;
- decreased chemical fertilizer requirements; and
- reduced demand on other water sources if effluent water is reused.

One method of assigning a value to each of these impacts is generally in terms of costs avoided, for instance, the reduced costs of health care and lost workdays due to lower illness rates amongst workers and their families resulting from better excreta disposal.

However, if sanitation systems are inappropriate or inadequate, they are likely to have a negative overall environmental impact for the opposite reasons (see Listorti 1990, for a summary of environment health aspects related to water supply and sanitation projects).

There is a growing literature that covers the design and assessment of large and small-scale collection, treatment and disposal facilities for developing countries (Feacham et al. 1977, Kalbermatten et al. 1980, Grover et al. 1983).

Transnational and Global Issues

Scale of Interaction

It is important to note here that environmental externalities are not limited to national boundaries, individual water sources or supply systems. Just as the activities of different sectors within a national economy have impacts that affect the quantity, quality and price of water supplied by authorities, the activities of different nations create important externalities too. The following scenarios are important:

- where two countries share a common source, such as a river, lake or aquifer;
- where one or more countries have an upstream influence on the water sources of others (i.e., they constitute part of the catchment area); and
- where another country can affect the climatic conditions, particularly the precipitation, experienced by another.

The first two tend to be transnational in character, i.e., interactions between only a few adjacent nations, whereas the last can be both transnational or global depending on the scale of influence.

Global Warming and Water Resources Management

Global externalities tend to be indirect and have a more collective origin. The prime example affecting the water sector is the case of long-term global warming. Due to the accumulation of carbon dioxide, methane, nitrous oxide, chlorofluorocarbons and other greenhouse gases in the atmosphere, the average temperature of the earth's climate is increasing. This phenomenon is expected to have a direct and substantial impact on the global water budget. Climate scientists project that the major hydrological cycle (cloud formation-precipitation-runoff-evaporation) will accelerate. Because of the complexity involved, there is considerable uncertainty in currently available global climate models (see, e.g., Mintzer 1987). Nevertheless, one estimate suggests that both precipitation and evaporation are expected to increase globally by 7 to 15 percent if the heat-trapping effect doubles over preindustrial levels (Postel 1989). However, the distribution of these increases will not necessarily be identical, resulting in areas with markedly different hydrological regimes. Particularly affected will be peak flows, groundwater recharge and surface storage levels. The increase in temperatures, evapotranspiration and CO_2 levels will also affect vegetation growth differently around the world (Falkenmark 1990).

Global warming, due to the greenhouse effect, is likely to have significant impact, both positive and negative, on the worlds water resources. Williams (1989) summarizes the likely impacts on water resources for a worst-case scenario for semi-arid and humid areas in relation to major water resources management considerations. His results, although of a preliminary nature, provide an indication of possible future consequences. The hydrologic response to global warming will be changes in the average annual runoff amount and changes in the runoff variability both annually and seasonally. In the area of water supply, storage reservoirs could be affected by changes in the amount and distribution of runoff throughout the year. In particular, in arid areas a reduction in total runoff and increases in drought frequency may reduce the effectiveness of storage reservoirs. Consequently a modest 25 % reduction in precipitation may require a disproportionately large increase in size of reservoir to maintain a given yield and reliability (Nemec and Schaake 1982). Sediment delivery will increase through erosion from less evenly distributed, larger rainstorms so reducing reservoir lifespans. Reduced frequency of wet years will significantly limit aquifer recharge.

High-value low-lying land will be more frequently inundated as the flow-regime alters. Higher peak discharges and greater seasonal variation will over-load structural flood control measures. Dams used for hydropower will experience drops in firm-load power generation due to lower reservoir storage resulting from increased flow periodicity and greater over-spill of excess water during flood flows. Base river-flow regimes will alter to significantly affect fish and riparian ecosystems and in semi-arid areas, rivers may become intermittent and ephemeral rather than perennial.

The likely water management responses under the global warming scenario are also summarized by Williams. As they apply to developing countries, they are:

- significant water reallocation will be needed as competition increases for scarcer water resources. Priority will likely be given to urban and industrial use, reducing the amount and reliability of supply for irrigation;
- water will increase in value and become even more highly politicized. Subsidies for water will be curtailed and only urban and industrial users may be able to afford the true costs of supply;
- there will be an incentive and comparative advantage to maximize crop production in areas where rainfall is plentiful (and hence away from many tropical developing countries depriving them of major revenue sources);
- there will be an increased need for expensive flood controls due to increased frequency and magnitude, especially for low-lying areas (for example Bangladesh);
- there will be a need for better watershed management to control runoff and erosion as the value of dry season flows and consequences of hillside soil loss and downstream sedimentation increase; and
- large-scale investments will be required in hydraulic engineering structures to handle larger peak and smaller base flows (diversions, intakes, dam spillways, etc.).

As an example of local impacts of global warming on the water sector, Schaake (1990) has analyzed changes in runoff for the Animas River at Durango, Colorado. His model projects that a 2-degree Celsius increase would hardly affect the annual average flow but would drastically change the seasonal runoff patterns. The risk of winter flooding would increase, requiring costly trade-offs between hydropower and water supply needs. Water scarcities would occur over summer, when water demands for crops and urban areas are greatest. The effects of global warming on developing countries have not been studied as closely. However, the possible impact scenarios give rise to serious concern. For example, even if the conservative estimates prove true that only 5% of currently rainfed crops will need irrigation to cope with increased evaporation demands due to higher temperatures, some 60 million more hectares of irrigation could become necessary to maintain productivity. Building the necessary dams, canals and other infrastructure might require investments of about US$ 150-300 billion

(Gleick 1988), which are well beyond the means available to developing countries.

Developing Countries and the Mitigation Effort

Ameliorating transnational and global externalities requires collective actions. Developed countries have made a number of important strides forward in domestic environmental management, some of which, such as controls on pollution emissions, will have transnational impacts. Whilst costly in the short-run, in the long-term, these are seen to be generally economically beneficial. On a local scale, developing countries also have considerable scope for environment-improving activities that are economically attractive for them, e.g., water conservation and ameliorating the domestic environmental consequences of water use. Some of these actions have significant positive transnational environmental benefits also:

- negative impacts on downstream or estuarine flow regimes can be reduced by water conservation and catchment management in upstream nations; and
- pollution of collectively used water bodies such as border rivers or lakes could be reduced by control of untreated waste discharge, particularly of sewerage and stormwater runoff.

However, on a larger scale, developing countries are less able to afford actions to protect the global environment. This is also an equity issue, since much of the responsibility for cumulative damage to the global environment lies firmly with the developed countries. They should take an active role in partnering the developing countries in environmental management issues. A key question here is the extent to which developing countries contribute to and are affected by global environmental problems. This is not a clear-cut issue since some countries may feel themselves highly vulnerable yet virtually non-contributory to global climate changes (e.g., Bangladesh and The Maldives who are susceptible to sea level rises), whilst others clearly do contribute whilst at the same time, experiencing varying degrees of impact (e.g., China and India).

The foregoing discussion sets the context within which the developing countries are capable of participating in environmental mitigation efforts. It is quite obvious that developing countries do not have the ability to contribute financially for global environmental cleanup efforts where the measurable benefits to the national economy are too low to induce the necessary investment. Coincidentally, many developing country projects which do have positive measurable benefits at the more local level are being bypassed on account of capital constraints. However, the picture is not all bleak. The principle of assistance to developing countries to make local and global environmental mitigation efforts, in terms of technology transfer, financial support and other means, is already well established. Bi-lateral donors are already emphasizing environment-oriented development programs designed to achieve greater sustainability of assisted projects. For instance, on May 21st 1987, the Danish Parliament passed a resolution to strengthen efforts on natural resources rehabilitation and conservation in official Danish development cooperation (DANIDA 1988). The Netherlands have adopted similar objectives. Some of the current multilateral initiatives to aid developing country environmental management such as the proposed Global Environmental Fund and Ozone Fund are briefly outlined below, along with their significance for developing countries. Developing countries clearly should take advantage of this available funding and other kinds of technical support offered by developed nations to tackle environmental management issues of both national and international significance.

Global Environmental Initiatives

The Montreal Protocol, which was adopted in 1987 as a framework within which reduction in the consumption and production of certain types of chlorofluorocarbons (CFCs) is to be achieved, recognized the need for global cooperation and assistance to the developing countries. Subsequent Ministerial Conferences on various aspects of global environmental issues have reinforced the idea of protecting the global commons.

Recently, following discussions among world bodies and governments to define effective criteria and mechanisms for both generating and disbursing funds, a pilot global environmental fund facility (GEF) was set up. A larger, more permanent framework is being pursued, once the early results of the GEF can be analyzed in the context of the 1992 UN Conference on Environment and Development in Brazil. More generally, global financing issues might be analyzed and resolved through a tradeoff involving several criteria: *affordability/additionality, fairness/equity and economic efficiency* (Munasinghe 1990).

First, since developing countries cannot afford to finance even their present water supply development, to address global environmental concerns they will need financial assistance on concessionary terms that is additional to existing conventional aid. Second, as noted in the Brundtland Commission report (World Commission on Environment and Development 1987) past growth in the industrialized countries has exhausted a disproportionately high share of global resources, suggesting that the developed countries owe an "environmental debt" to the larger global community. This approach could help to determine how the remaining finite global resources may be shared more fairly and used sustainably. Finally, the economic efficiency criterion indicates that the "polluter pays" principle may be applied to generate revenues, to the extent which global environmental costs of human activity can be quantified. For example, if total emission limits are established (e.g., for CO_2), then trading in emission permits among nations and other market mechanisms could be harnessed to increase efficiency.

The GEF is a core multilateral fund, with initial commitments of about US$ 1.5 billion. Contributions are made, on a voluntary basis, in the form of grants. Set up in November 1990, it is assumed to be operational by mid-1991 and function as a pilot project over the next three years. This fund would finance investment, technical assistance and institutional development activities in four areas:

- Protecting the ozone layer;
- Limiting "greenhouse" gas emissions;
- Protecting biodiversity; and
- Protecting international waters.

Developing countries with a per-capita Gross Domestic Product at or below US$ 4000 in 1989 are eligible for GEF funding for investment projects and the full range of associated support. While most projects will be country-specific, some regional projects covering two or more adjacent countries, will also qualify.

A more narrowly focused Ozone Fund of about US$ 160 to 240 million has been created also to help implement measures to reduce CFC emissions under the Montreal Protocol. Both funds are likely to be managed under a collaborative arrangement between the UNDP, UNEP and the World Bank. In case of the GEF, the three cooperating agencies determine whether a project qualifies for support. They ensure that it protects the global environment in a cost-effective, technologically sound way, while respecting the interests of the country's people. In particular, they have begun to fund those investment activities that would provide cost-effective benefits to the global environment, but would, however, not be undertaken by individual countries without concessions. Training and other human resource development activities are another focus of the Facility. Thus, these funds have been specifically designed to fill the void which is created by the lack of individual national incentives for those activities which would, nonetheless, benefit us all.

To summarize, international pressures to implement environmental mitigatory measures place a severe burden on developing countries. The crucial dilemma this poses to developing countries is how to reconcile development goals and the elimination of poverty -- which will require increased use of water and raw materials -- with responsible stewardship of the environment, and without overburdening economies that are already weak. It can be argued that in view of the severe financial constraints that developing countries already face, the response of these countries in relation to environmental preservation cannot extend beyond the realm of measures that are consistent with near-term economic development goals. More specifically, the environmental policy response of developing countries in the coming decade will be limited to conventional technologies in efficiency improvement, conservation and resource development.

The developed countries are ready to substitute environmental preservation for further economic expansion and should, therefore, be ready to cross the threshold, providing the financial resources that the developing countries need today and developing the technological innovations and knowledge-base to be used in the 21st century by all nations. The Global Environmental Fund and Ozone Fund, presently being established, will facilitate the participation of developing countries in addressing issues at the global level.

References

Adams, B. 1990. *Groundwater Pollution Risk Assessment in Latin America and the Caribbean*. Working Meeting on Drinking Water Source Protection. The Hague: IRC International Water and Sanitation Centre.

Bandyopadhyay, J. 1987. "Political Ecology of Drought and Water Scarcity -- Need for an Ecological Water Resources Policy." *Economic and Political Weekly*. pp. 2159-2169.

Bowers, J. 1990. *Economics of the Environment -- The Conservationists' Response to the Pearce Report*. British Association of Nature Conservationists.

Braden, J.B., and C.D. Kolstad (eds.). 1991. *Measuring the Demand for Environmental Quality*. Amsterdam: North Holland.

BRGM. 1985. *Water, Agriculture and Soil Studies of the Saq and Overlying Aquifers*. Report to the Ministry of Agriculture and Water from the Bureau de Recherches Geologiques et Minieries. Riyadh, Saudi Arabia.

Busari, M.A.O., and U.M.P. Amadi. 1989. "Water Quality of Coastal Aquifers in Southern Nigeria." *International Water Quality Bulletin*. 14, pp. 31-35.

Busch, C.W., W. Matlock, and M. Fogel. 1966. "Utilization of Water Resources in a Coastal Groundwater Basin." *J. Soil Water Conservation*. 21, pp. 163-169.

CEPIS. 1989. *Health Conditions in the Americas*. Lima, Peru.

Charalambous, A.N. 1986. "Problems of Groundwater Development in the Sana'a Basin, Yemen Arab Republic." *Proceedings of the Exeter Symposium*. IAHS Publication 136.

Chuamthaisong, C. 1989. "Economics of Groundwater Development in Thailand." *International Water Quality Bulletin*. 14, pp. 24-30.

Cummings, R.G. 1971. "Optimum Exploitation of Groundwater Reserves with Saltwater Intrusion." *Water Resources Research*. 7, pp. 1415-1424.

DANIDA. 1988. *Environmental Issues in Water Resources Management: A Strategy for Water Resources Management*. Copenhagen, Denmark.

de Koning, H.W. 1987. *Setting Environmental Standards -- Guidelines for Decisionmaking*. Geneva, Switzerland.

Dixon, J.A., L.M. Talbot, and G. Le Moigne. 1989. *Dams and the Environment: Considerations in World Bank Projects*. World Bank Technical Paper No 110. Washington DC: The World Bank.

Duan, N., L.W. Mays, and K.E. Lansey. 1990. "Optimal Reliability-Based Design of Pumping and Distribution Systems." *Journal of Hydraulic Engineering*. ASCE. 116, pp. 249-269.

Esrey, S.A., J.B. Potash, L. Roberts, and C. Shiff. 1990. *Health Benefits from Improvements in Water Supply and Sanitation*. Bureau for Science and Technology. Washington DC: USAID.

EPA. 1990. *Progress in Groundwater Protection and Restoration*. EPA 440/6-90-001. Washington DC: Environmental Protection Agency.

_____. 1989. *Wellhead Protection Programs: Tools for Local Governments*. EPA 440/6-89-002. Washington DC: Environmental Protection Agency.

_____. 1987a. *Improved Protection of Water Resources from Long-term and Cumulative Pollution: Prevention of Groundwater Contamination in the United States*. Report to OECD. EPA 440/6-87-001. Washington DC: Environmental Protection Agency.

_____. 1987b. *Wellhead Protection -- A Decisionmakers Guide*. EPA 440/6-87-009. Washington DC: Environmental Protection Agency.

_____. 1987c. *Guidelines for Delineation of Wellhead Protection Areas*. EPA 440/6-87-010. Washington DC: Environmental Protection Agency.

_____. 1987d. *Guidelines for Applicants for State Wellhead Protection Program Assistance Funds Under the Safe Drinking Water Act*. EPA 440/6-87-011. Washington DC: Environmental Protection Agency.

_____. 1985. *Protecting Our Groundwater*. Washington DC: Environmental Protection Agency.

Falkenmark, M., et al. 1987. "Water Related Limitations to Local Developments." *Ambio*. 16.

Falkenmark, M. 1990. Personal communication.

Feacham, R.G., D.D. Mara, and M.G. McGarry. 1977. *Water, Wastes and Health in Hot Climates*. New York: John Wiley.

Fiering, M.B. 1977. *Preliminary Notions on Resilience*. Draft. Cambridge, Mass.: Harvard University.

_____, and C.S. Holling. 1974. "Management and Standards for Perturbed Ecosystems." *Agro-Ecosystem*. 1, pp. 301-321.

Foster, S.S.D. 1988. "Impacts of Urbanisation on Groundwater." *Urban Water 88*. UNESCO-IHP III Proceedings Intl Symposium. Duisberg, Germany.

_____, M. Ventura, and R. Hirata. 1987. *Groundwater Pollution: an Executive Overview of the Latin America-Caribbean Situation in Relation to Potable Water Supply*. Lima, Peru: WHO/PAHO/CEPIS.

Geraghty and Miller, Inc. 1984. *Protection of Groundwater Quality*. Proceedings *Groundwater Pollution: Environmental and Legal Problems*. Travis, C.C., and E.L. Etnier (eds.). Washington DC: AAAS.

Gleick, P.H. 1988. "Climate Change and California: Past, Present and Future Vulnerabilities." M.H. Glantz (ed.). *Societal Responses to Regional Climate Change: Forecasting by Analogy*. Boulder, Colorado: Westview Press.

Goodland, R. 1990. "The World Bank's New Environmental Policy for Dams and Reservoirs." *Water Resources Development*. 6, pp. 226-239.

Goulter, I.C., and F. Bouchart. 1990. "Reliability-Constrained Pipe Network Model." *Journal of Hydraulic Engineering.* 116, pp. 211-229.

Graham, D.A. 1981. "Cost-Benefit Analysis under Uncertainty." *American Economic Review.* 71, pp. 715-25.

Grover, B., N. Burnett, and M. McGarry. 1983. *Water Supply and Sanitation Project Preparation Handbook.* Washington DC: World Bank.

Gun, J.A.M. van der. 1986. *High Rates of Groundwater Abstraction in the Yemen Highlands. Proceedings of the 19th Congress of the Int. Assoc. Hydrogeologists.* Karlovy Vary 8. Czechoslovakia.

_____. 1985. *Water Resources of the Sadah Area.* Unpublished Main Report WRAY-3. Delft, Netherlands: Sana'a/Delft University.

Gunnerson, C.G. 1989. *Responding to Diseconomies of Scale in Water Supply and Sanitation.* Unpublished extension of paper presented at the Conference on Water and the City. Chicago: APWA.

Hashimoto, T., J.R. Stedinger, and D.P. Loucks. 1982. "Reliability, Resiliency, and Vulnerability Criteria for Water Resource System Performance Evaluation." *Water Resources Research.* 18, pp. 14-20.

Jenkin, J.J. 1981. *Dryland Salting in Australia.* Kew, Victoria: Water Research Foundation Sym., Soil Conservation Authority.

Kalbermatten, J., D. Julius, and C. Gunnerson. 1980. *Appropriate Technology for Water Supply and Sanitation: Technical and Economic Options.* Washington DC: World Bank.

Keenan, J.D. 1991. *Technological Aspects of Water Resources Management.* World Bank International Workshop on Comprehensive Water Resources Management Policies. Washington DC: The World Bank.

Kersnar, J.M. 1985. *Water Shortage Risk Analysis for Municipal Water Supply Districts.* M.S. Thesis. Cornell University: Dept. Civil and Environmental Engineering.

Lee, M.D., and T.F. Bastemeijer. 1991. *Drinking Water Source Protection: An Overview of Problems, Causes, Experiences and Needs.* Occasional Paper 15. The Hague: IRC International Water and Sanitation Centre.

Le Moigne, G., S. Barghouti, and H. Plusquellec (eds.). 1990. *Dam Safety and the Environment.* World Bank Technical Paper No. 115. Washington DC: World Bank.

Listorti, J.A. 1990. *Environmental Health Components for Water Supply, Sanitation, and Urban Projects.* Technical Paper No. 121, Washington DC: World Bank.

Lloyd, J.W. 1987. "Aspects of Interaction between Groundwater and the Environment." S. Awadalla, and I.M. Noor (eds.). *Groundwater and the Environment, Proceedings of the International Groundwater Conference.* Kuala Lumpur, Malaysia. pp. 1 -25.

Maler, K.G., and R.E. Wyzga. 1976. *La Mesure Economique des Dommages Dans le Domaine de l'Environnement.* Paris: OECD.

Mintzer, I.M. 1987. *A Matter of Degrees: The Potential For Controlling the Greenhouse Effect. Research Report #5.* Washington DC: World Resources Institute.

Munasinghe, M. 1991. "Groundwater Resource Management and Environmental Protection." *Natural Resources Forum.* 15, pp. 302-12.

_____. 1990. "The Challenge Facing the Developing World." *EPA Journal.* Vol. 16, pp. 52-53. Washington DC: Environmental Protection Agency.

Nair, C. 1988. *Bangkok's Deteriorating Groundwater - Environmental Issues.* 14th WEDC Conference: Water and Urban Services in Asia and the Pacific. Kuala Lumpur. pp. 67-70.

Nemec, J., and J. Schaake. 1982. "Sensitivity of Water Resource Systems to Climate Variation." *Hydrological Sciences.* 27, pp. 327-343.

OECD. 1985. *Management of Water Projects: Decisionmaking and Investment Appraisal.* Paris: Organization for Economic Co-operation and Development.

Okun, D. 1990. "Water Reuse in Developing Countries." *Water and Wastewater.* 5, pp. 13-21.

Parker, A.N. 1989. *Environmental Policy: Case Study of Freshwater Pollution.* Consultant Report. Washington DC: World Bank.

Peng, S.C. 1987. "Salt Water Intrusion in Groundwater in Peninsular Malaysia - An Overview." S. Awadalla, and I.M. Noor (eds.). *Groundwater and the Environment, Proceedings of the International Groundwater Conference.* Kuala Lumpur, Malaysia. pp. E37-E50.

Postel, S. 1989. *Water for Agriculture: Facing the Limits.* Worldwatch Paper 93. Washington DC: The Worldwatch Institute.

Rathur, A.Q. 1987. "Groundwater Management to Eradicate Waterlogging and Salinity in the Upper Indus Basin, Punjab, Pakistan." S. Awadalla and I.M. Noor (eds.). *Groundwater and the Environment. Proceedings of the International Groundwater Conference.* Kuala Lumpur, Malaysia. pp. G.96-G.107.

Reddy, T.V.K. 1987. "Effects of Distillery Waste Water Discharges on Rivers -- A Case Study of Neeva River, Chittoor District, Andhra Pradesh, India." *Asian Environment.* 9, pp. 20-22.

Repetto, R. 1986. *Skimming the Water: Rent-Seeking and the Performance of Public Irrigation Systems.* Washington DC: World Resources Institute.

Schaake, J.C. 1990. "From Climate to Flow." *Climatic Variability, Climate Change, and the Planning and Management of US Water Resources.* American Association for the Advancement of Science. New York: John Wiley.

Todd, D. 1967. "Seawater Intrusion of Coastal Aquifers." *Paper Presented at 6th lecture on Hydrology.* Beirut, Lebanon: American University of Beirut.

UNEP. 1989. *The State of the World Environment.* Nairobi, Kenya: United Nations Environment Programme.

Vaux, H.J. Jr. 1985. "Economic Aspects of Groundwater Recharge." T. Asano (ed.). *Artificial Recharge of Groundwater.* Butterworth Publishers. pp. 703-718.

WHO. 1985. *Environmental Pollution Control in Relation to Development. Technical Report Series No. 718.* Geneva: World Health Organization.

Williams, P. 1989. "Adapting Water Resources Management to Global Climate Change." *Climatic Change.* 15, pp. 83-93.

Williams, P.B. 1990. "Rethinking Flood-Control Channel Design." *Civil Engineering.* ASCE, 60, pp. 57-59.

World Bank. 1990a. *A Taxonomy of Environmental Issues.* Consultant report prepared by IDEA Inc. Environmental Dept. Washington DC: The World Bank.

_____. 1990b. *Environmental Sourcebook.* Washington DC: The World Bank.

_____ and European Investment Bank. 1990c. *The Environmental Program for the Mediterranean.* Washington DC: The World Bank.

_____. 1989. *Striking a Balance. The Environmental Challenge of Development.* Washington DC: The World Bank.

World Commission on Environment and Development. 1987. *Our Common Future*. Oxford University Press.

Appendix 5
The Role of Computer Models: An Example

Because of the complexities involved and the interaction between surface and sub-surface sources, solutions to water source problems involves an integrated approach. Clearly, protection of sources from pollution and depletion is a better policy than remedial action, both in terms of cost and efficacy (see Lee and Bastemeijer 1991, for a detailed overview of environmental problems affecting the water sector in developing countries). An holistic view is required which examines the interacting links between precipitation, surface runoff, irrigation and other human activities, aquifers, springs, wells, artificial drainage, rivers and oceans. Historically, planners have had to rely on broad assumptions and rules of thumb or, at best, approximate guidelines backed by limited monitoring programs to tell them when a particular management action is having a detrimental effect. This is increasingly being replaced by a growing body of comprehensive mathematical models that simulate the impact of human activities on various hydrological links. Increasingly, EIA is including the use of a growing range of models and types including lumped and distributed hydrological models, pollution transport and dispersion models, eutrophication models, chemical path/fate determination models and risk analysis models. Predictions concerning global warming discussed in the previous section may be made using sophisticated computer techniques.

One model being used by planners in the water sector to assess local and regional scale environmental impacts issues is the European Hydrological System - SHE (Abbott et al. 1978, 1986a, 1986b, DHI 1986, 1988). As a distributed computer simulation model, SHE has been a large-scale attempt to translate scientific hydrology into a practical instrument for water and environmental resources engineering. As such, it provides a useful indication of the principles of action-oriented hydrological modeling. The model has been developed through a joint effort by the Institute of Hydrology (UK), SOGREAH (France) and the Danish Hydraulic Institute. An advantage of the model is its modular structure which encompasses different levels of complexity. The user can opt for simpler or more comprehensive modules in the model and can also choose which modules to retain for the study. A module will typically simulate one component or link in the hydrological cycle. Examples of applications are the simulation of water flow and soil erosion in Thailand, predictions of the effects of irrigation schemes, land-use change and surface-water/groundwater interaction in India, and environmental impacts of fertilizer application in Denmark.

References

Abbott, M.B., R. Clarke, and A. Preismann. 1978. *Logistics and Benefits of the European Hydrologic System. Proceedings, International Symposium on Logistics and Benefits of Using Mathematical Models of Hydrologic and Water Resource Systems.* Pisa, Italy.

Abbott, M.B., J.C. Bathurst, J.A. Cunge, P.E. O'Connell, and J. Rasmussen. 1986a. "An Introduction to the European Hydrological System - Systeme Hydrologique Europeen, 'SHE'. 1: History and Philosophy of a Physically-Based, Distributed Modelling System." *J. Hydrology.* 87, pp. 45-60.

_____, J.C. Bathurst, J.A. Cunge, P.E. O'Connell, and J. Rasmussen. 1986b. "An Introduction to the European Hydrological System - Systeme Hydrologique Europeen, 'SHE'. 2: Structure of a Physically-Based, Distributed Modelling System." *J. Hydrology.* 87, pp. 61-77.

Danish Hydraulic Institute. 1986. *Introduction to the SHE -- Systeme Hydrologique Europeen.* Horsholm, Denmark: Danish Hydraulic Institute.

Danish Hydraulic Institute. 1988. *Note on Status of SHE at DHI.* Horsholm, Denmark: Danish Hydraulic Institute.

Lee, M.D., and T.F. Bastemeijer. 1991. *Drinking Water Source Protection: An Overview of Problems, Causes, Experiences and Needs.* Occasional Paper 15. The Hague: IRC International Water and Sanitation Centre.

6

Incorporating Environmental Concerns into Decisionmaking

In this chapter, we discuss methods of determining the physical (including biological and social) impacts of human activity on the environment, through the environmental assessment process. Then the conceptual basis and practical techniques for economically valuing such impacts, are described. The chapter also contains an environment-economic analytical framework, a discussion of policy instruments, and a brief empirical case study, that illustrate the incorporation of environmental concerns into economic decisionmaking.

Environmental Assessment Techniques

There are a variety of forms of environmental assessment (EA) including:

- project environmental assessment: an attempt to identify the environmental costs and benefits of a particular project;
- regional environmental assessments: a more widespread approach to assessing the range of problems and influences of one or more projects or a development program within a determined region (e.g., a river basin); and
- macro/sector environmental assessment: an analysis of the impact of sectorwide or economywide policies.

This section does not provide an exhaustive review of the theory and practice of any single method since they are all evolving methodologies that are gradually being reformulated and refined by agencies as the various techniques of appraisal, implementation and review are applied under actual project conditions. Instead, the World Bank's own broad-based, flexible approach to EA is described and the main points, applicable for use by developing country planners and decisionmakers under most general circumstances, are outlined. Since the World Bank's approach encompasses project-specific, regional, and micro or sectoral EAs, it provides a useful framework for introducing some of the important multi-level concepts to be adopted by planners. The information is particularly relevant to those planners who might otherwise discount EA as a luxury rather than a fundamental tool of project planning and implementation.

Background

In 1989 the World Bank introduced formal environmental reviews (ERs) as a mandatory part of its project appraisal process, the culmination of a gradual shift during the previous decades towards more comprehensive environmental analysis in the Bank's operations. The World Bank has made a move to "integrate environmental considerations into its work.....The Bank's goal is to blur the lines between environmental activities and the rest of the Bank's work - to make them one" (World Bank 1989). Depending on the outcome of the ER (also known as a screening), an environmental assessment (EA) can be requested from the borrower as a mandatory requirement for the acceptance of a project proposal. EA is becoming a routine component of project preparation and is often part of the engineering feasibility study.

The basic concept behind EA is that during a creative project design phase, cost-effective prevention and mitigation of environmental factors is possible, whereas if a consideration of the environment is left to the implementation phase, changes in the project become increasingly difficult and costly.

EAs usually require as much time as technical feasibility studies, varying between 6 and 18 months and usually take up a small fraction of the total capital costs of a project. ERs and EAs should always emphasize:

- the identification of all important environmental issues early in the project cycle;
- the design of environmental improvements into any basic project objectives; and
- the avoidance, mitigation or compensation for any adverse impacts resulting from a project.

Implementation of an EA in terms of prevention, mitigation and compensation for project impacts usually costs between 0 and 10% of a total project budget, averaging at around 5%. This does not include possible savings resulting from the various measures.

Procedures

The World Bank project EA is normally carried out after a period of Environmental Review (ER) known as screening. The ER decides which of three categories the project falls into based on the extent to which projects are expected to have environmental impacts:

1) environmental assessment required - project may have diverse and significant environmental impacts;
2) limited environmental analysis required - project may have specific environmental impacts; and
3) EA is unnecessary -- project with negligible environmental impacts expected.

EAs are the responsibility of the borrower, who must arrange for funds and appoint a multi-disciplinary team of consultants (preferably with a significant national component of specialists). The Bank can provide financial assistance for EAs through a Project Preparation Facility advance, or from the Technical Assistance Grant Program for the Environment. The Bank expects the borrower to take the views of affected groups and local NGOs fully into account in project design and implementation and in particular in the preparation of EAs. The thrust of the EA, carried out by appointees of the borrower, focuses on issues critical to deciding whether or not to proceed with a given project, in a given format and how to implement it efficiently.

In the context of Bank Operations, EA is undertaken in tandem with pre-feasibility and feasibility studies, incorporated into the loan agreement negotiations with borrowers, and assessed for compliance during supervision of implementation. Evaluation of impacts and effectiveness of mitigatory methods are incorporated in the project completion report.

Prior to implementation, a Bank appraisal mission will review the EA with the borrower, resolve any remaining environmental questions, assess the capacity of country institutions to implement recommendations, and discuss environmental conditionalities to the loan agreements. The borrower is then obliged to implement measures to mitigate anticipated environmental impacts, to monitor programs, to correct unanticipated impacts, and to comply with any environmental agreements.

The project EA has the main components of:

- a baseline data synthesis;
- an assessment of potential environmental impacts (+/-);
- a systematic analysis of alternative options;
- formulation of a prevention, mitigation and compensatory action plan;

- a review of environmental management and training requirements and a plan to meet them;
- formulation of a monitoring plan during and after project implementation; and
- a summary of interagency coordination aspects and needs; and
- a series of consultations with affected communities and local NGOs.

The purpose of Regional EAs is to be used as planning tools to help devise implementation strategies which account for the combined impact of existing projects and to help prepare projects sensitive to the cumulative impacts, synergisms, iterations and competition for natural and sociocultural resources. Regional EAs usually comprise the following main components:

- definition of the regional area in question;
- the selection of sustainable development patterns from available alternatives;
- the identification of cumulative impacts of different activities;
- the identification of environmental interactions or conflicting demands on resources in terms of costs and benefits;
- the formulation of criteria for environmentally sustainable development;
- the identification of regional monitoring and data needs; and
- an examination of policy alternatives for achieving sustainable development.

Clearly, the regional EA fits in comfortably with the IWRP approach to water sector development and is a useful, if not pre-requisite database for more effective planning.

Sector EAs are also very useful to the IWRP process since their purpose is to examine the impacts of multiple projects planned in the same sector, to view alternative investment or technology strategies (e.g., the decision to adopt centralized, or decentralized wastewater treatment), and to evaluate the effects of sector policy changes (e.g., the decision to price water at its true costs rather than at a subsidized rate).

Sector EAs can help define guidelines and criteria for the successful design and implementation of projects in the sector and so preclude the need for multiple project specific EAs. They help identify the major environmental issues in the sector and help develop a database, enabling project-specific EAs to proceed more quickly. Sector EAs also help evaluate the capabilities of agencies to carry our ERs and EAs and hence determine the need for institutional strengthening and support.

Checklist of Environmental Factors for Assessment

The operational directives issued by the Bank request that the appointee implementing the EA consider the following broad checklist of factors when assessing the project, region, or sector environmental impacts and sensitivities (World Bank 1990b):

- agrochemicals -- impact on surface and groundwater by these;
- biological diversity -- conservation of endangered species, critical habitats, protected areas;
- coastal and marine resources -- planning and management of these; impact of activities on these;
- cultural properties -- preservation of archaeological and historic sites;
- dams and reservoirs -- environmental issues in planning, implementation and operation of these;
- hazardous and toxic materials -- safe management, use, transport, storage and disposal of these; impact on surface and groundwater by these;
- induced development and other sociocultural aspects -- impacts of these (i.e., the 'boomtown' effects of secondary growth of settlements and infrastructure);
- industrial hazards -- prevention and management of these;
- international treaties and agreements on the environment and natural resources -- review of status and application of these;
- international waterways -- effects of activities on quality or quantity of water flows in these;
- involuntary resettlement -- issues related to this;
- land settlement -- physical, biological, socioeconomic and cultural impacts of these agreements;
- natural hazards -- effects on project from these;
- occupational health and safety -- dangers from former and promotion of latter;
- tribal peoples -- rights to land and to water of these;
- tropical forests -- issues relating to use and preservation of these;
- watersheds -- protection and management of these;
- wetlands -- conservation and management of these; and
- wildlands -- protection of these from adverse impacts.

Limitations and Implementation Difficulties

One of the main limitations for effective EA is the relatively minor experience in environmental management in developing countries. Also lacking is an inter-agency, inter-sectoral framework for coordinated action in the fields of monitoring and managing various interactive activities (hence the need for an IWRP as proposed in this publication). The World Bank consequently views inter-agency coordination (especially government agencies and NGOs) as crucial to effective EA because environmental issues, in their complexity and variety, are often inter-sectoral, regional, and even international in nature. Training and institutional support is required in environment-related issues and is usually a prime component of any World Bank initiated project ER and EA.

The effectiveness and acceptability of an environmental management program depends on the environmental policies and regulatory structure in the project country. This determines how well the recommendations of the EA can be put into effect and hence the preventive, mitigatory and compensatory actions that can be taken. Major difficulties facing many developing countries are the weak environmental inspection, monitoring and enforcement functions.

According to Bowers (1990), EAs should attempt also to better identify the distributional implications of public investment decisions. Environmental effects tend to be more disadvantageous to the poor, because they usually are less able to influence policy decisions and also are more vulnerable to adverse impacts. As discussed in the next section, one remedy is to adopt a more rigorous approach to cost-benefit analysis, which entails the identification of all impacts of a project on social welfare, including differential environmental impacts. Where items can be meaningfully valued, they should be, and the costs and benefits for different segments of society identified. Items for which monetary values cannot be assigned should be assessed in whatever units are appropriate to them and an informed judgement made about their significance.

Economic Valuation of Environmental
Impacts and Assets

The cost-benefit analysis methodology presented in Chapter 3 was developed in the general context of economic evaluation of development projects, in particular, water supply schemes. In this section, some of the issues arising from the economic valuation of environmental costs and benefits of human activity are summarized (for further details, see Munasinghe 1992).

The environment provides three essential services or functions:

- it is a *source* of renewable and non-renewable resources used for production and consumption;
- it is a *sink* for absorbing and recycling the waste products of human activity; and
- it serves as an essential *life support* mechanism (e.g., high altitude ozone layer that protects us from harmful ultraviolet radiation).

The first step in doing environmentally sound economic analyses is to determine the impacts of the project or policies in question, on the environment. These physical impacts (broadly defined to include also biological and social effects) are determined by comparing the "with project" and the "without project" scenarios (see Chapter 3). For determining such impacts, the economist will have to rely on the expertise of engineers, ecologists, agronomists, social scientists, and other experts.

The second step in considering environmental effects involves valuing the physical impacts and relationships. An environmental impact can result in a measurable change in production and/or change in environmental quality. A number of concepts of value, and practical valuation techniques have been developed to trace the welfare impacts of these changes (Munasinghe 1992).

Basic Concepts of Economic Value and Classification of Valuation Techniques

Conceptually, the *total economic value* (TEV) of a resource consists of its (i) use value (UV) and (ii) non-use value (NUV). *Use values* may be broken down further into the direct use value (DUV), the indirect use value (IUV) and the option value (OV) (potential use value). One needs to be careful not to double-count both the indirect use value of supporting environmental functions *and* the value of the resulting direct use. The categories of *non-use value* are existence value (EV) and bequest value (BV). Therefore, we may write:

$$TEV = UV + NUV$$
$$or \ TEV = (DUV + IUV + OV) + (EV + BV)$$

Figure 6.1 shows this disaggregation of TEV, in schematic form. Below each valuation concept, a short description of its meaning and a few typical examples of the environmental resources underlying the perceived value, are provided.

- *direct use value* is determined by the contribution an environmental asset makes to current production or consumption (e.g., this category spans the range from the direct use of a water source, to the visual satisfaction a tourist might receive from visiting a water-fall;
- *indirect use value* includes the benefits derived basically from functional services that the environment provides to support current production and consumption (e.g., ecological functions like natural filtration of polluted water);
- *option value* is the willingness-to-pay today based on the future benefit to be derived from an unutilized asset when the option to use it will be exercised (for a more detailed discussion, see Graham 1981);

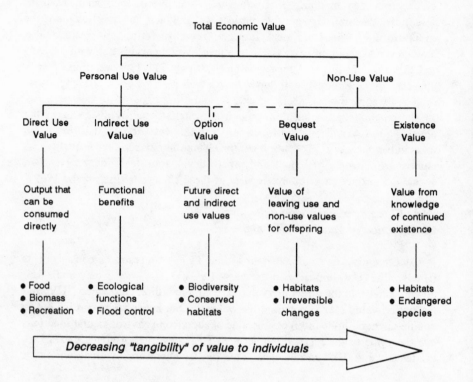

Figure 6.1 Categories of Economic Value Attributed to Environmental Assets (with examples from a primary tropical rain forest)

- *existence value* arises from the satisfaction of merely knowing that the asset exists, although the valuer has no intention of using it (e.g., existence of a famous spring or waterfall that one has no intention of visiting, ever); and
- *bequest value* is determined by the satisfaction of preserving an asset as a legacy for future generations.

Option values, bequest values and existence values are shaded in the figure, to caution the analyst concerning some of the ambiguities associated with defining these concepts -- as shown in the examples, they can spring from similar or identical resources, while their estimation could be interlinked also. However, these concepts of value are generally quite distinct.

Direct and indirect use values and option value tend to be conceptually clearer, whereas existence and bequest values are linked to more altruistic motives. Nevertheless, whatever the conceptual basis of economic value, there are several practical techniques that permit us to estimate a monetary value for environmental assets and impacts. However, there is considerable uncertainty in the results derived from these techniques even in developed market economies, and therefore their use in developing countries should be tempered by caution and sound judgement.

Practical Valuation Techniques

A variety of valuation techniques may be used to quantify the above concepts of value. The basic concept of economic valuation underlying all these techniques is the willingness-to-pay (WTP) of individuals for an environmental service or resource, i.e., the area under the compensated or Hicksian demand curve (Braden and Kolstad 1991). As shown in Table 6.1, valuation methods can be categorized, on the one hand, according to which type of market they rely on, and on the other hand, by considering how they make use of actual or potential behavior.

Next, we group the valuation techniques in Table 6.1 according to analytical method and provide some general comments, before discussing each technique in greater detail.

Under specific conditions, such as when the environmental impact leads to a marginal change in the supply of a good or service that is bought on a competitive market, the WTP can be estimated directly in terms of changes valued at prevailing market prices. If the market is not fully competitive, then the market valuation will be a partial measure, and shadow price corrections may need to be made. The foregoing comments apply to:

• Change of productivity

Often, the result of the impact cannot be directly related to a market activity. In some of these cases, the WTP could be estimated at conventional market value by using a closely related proxy. Care should be exercised on the following points: (1) the relevant attributes affected by the environmental impact might, in the case of the proxy measure, be mixed with other attributes -- thereby affecting the value of proxy; and (2) if the proxy attributes are identical to the ones lost by the impact, then the value given by the proxy is only a lower bound for the true WTP. This approach applies to the following techniques:

- loss of earnings;
- defensive expenditure;
- replacement cost; and
- shadow project.

TABLE 6.1   Taxonomy of Relevant Valuation Techniques

	Conventional market	*Implicit market*	*Constructed market*
Based on actual behavior	• Change of Productivity • Loss of Earnings • Defensive Expenditure	• Travel Cost • Wage Differences • Property values • Marketed Proxies	• Artificial market
Based on potential behavior	• Replacement Cost • Shadow project		• Contingent valuation

In certain cases the WTP can be estimated through derivation of a demand function for the environmental asset through analysis of actual behavior. Examples of this approach (also called surrogate market techniques) include:

- travel cost;
- wage differential; and
- property valuation.

The WTP can also be elicited through a controlled experiment or direct interviews, in the following approaches:

- artificial market; and
- contingent valuation.

Direct Effects Based on Conventional Markets

Change in Productivity: When a change in the environment affects actual production or productive capability, the value of the change in net output may be used to estimate the value of the environmental change. For example, the pollution of a lake by toxic industrial discharges may be valued in terms of the reduced value of fish-catches.

Loss of Earnings: Deteriorating environmental quality may affect human health. Ideally, the monetary value should be determined by the willingness-to-pay by individuals to preserve the environment. In practice, second-best techniques are used to value environmental impacts, such as: i) foregone earnings due to premature death or sickness; and ii) medical expenditure to recover health. Although this "value-of-health" approach is often questioned on ethical grounds (e.g., that it dehumanizes life), it does have a practical rationale. Thus, the underlying assumption of the finite worth of human life is the same one used by governments in various other social and health care decisions.

Actual Defensive or Preventive Expenditures: Individuals, firms, and governments undertake a variety of "defensive expenditures" in order to avoid or reduce unwanted environmental effects. Environmental damages are often difficult to assess, but information on defensive expenditures may be available or can be obtained at lesser cost than direct valuations of the environmental good in question. Such *actual* expenditures indicate that individuals, firms or governments judge the resultant benefits to be greater than the costs. The defensive expenditures can then be interpreted as a minimum valuation of benefits. However, caution is advisable with this approach, especially in cases where defensive expenditures are arbitrarily mandated by governments, having little or no relationship to market forces or free choices by informed economic agents.

Considerable work is going on to identify defensive expenditures. Such expenditures by firms are treated in the current System of National Account (SNA) as intermediate cost and are therefore not part of value added or final output. Defensive expenditures by households and governments, on the other hand, are treated as final expenditures and included in GDP. This practice is being questioned, and proposals are under consideration to change it (Munasinghe 1991).

Potential Expenditure Valued on
Conventional Markets

Replacement Cost: Under this approach, the costs that would have to be incurred in order to replace a damaged asset, are estimated. The estimate is *not* a measure of benefit of avoiding the damage in the first place, since the damage costs may be higher or lower than the replacement cost. However, it *is* an appropriate technique if there is some compelling reason as to why the environmental asset should be replaced or reasonable certainty that this will occur (see Chapter 13 for an example of this approach).

Shadow Project: When evaluating projects that have negative environmental impacts, this approach involves the design and costing of one or more "shadow projects" that provide for substitute environmental services to compensate for the loss of environmental assets under the ongoing projects. This approach is essentially an institutional judgment of the replacement cost, and is increasingly being mentioned as a possible way of operationalizing the concept of sustainability at the project level. It assumes that there is a constraint to maintain environmental capital intact, and therefore could be most relevant when "critical" environmental assets are at risk.

Valuation Using Implicit (or Surrogate) Markets

The methods and techniques described in this section use market information indirectly. The approaches discussed are the travel cost method, the property value approach, the wage differential approach, and uses of marketed goods as surrogates for non-marketed goods. Each technique has its particular advantages and disadvantages, as well as requirements for data and resources. The task of the analyst is to determine which of the techniques might be applicable to a particular situation.

Travel Cost: This approach is most often connected with recreational analysis in industrial countries, where it can serve to measure the benefits produced by recreation sites (parks, lakes, forests, wilderness). Essentially the same approach can also be used to value "travel time" in projects dealing with collecting water or fuelwood (Hanley 1989).

The surrounding area of a site is divided into concentric zones of increasing distance. (Visits from the various zones involves different travel costs). A survey of users, conducted at the site, determines the zone of origin, visitation rates, travel costs, and various socioeconomic characteristics. Users close to the site would be expected to make more use of it, because its implicit price, as measured by travel costs, is lower than for the more distant users. Based on the analysis of the questionnaires, a demand curve can be constructed and the associated consumers' surplus determined. This surplus represents an estimate of the value of the environmental good in question.

Property Value: This valuation method is referred to also as a hedonic price technique, and it is based on the general land value approach. The objective here is to determine the implicit prices of certain characteristics of properties. In the environmental area, the aim of the method is to place a value on the benefits of environmental quality improvements or to estimate the costs of a deterioration.

The property value approach has been used to analyze the effects of water or air pollution in certain areas. Where pollution is localized, the method compares prices of houses in affected areas with houses of equal size and similar neighborhood characteristics elsewhere in the same metropolitan area. The approach is based on the assumption of a competitive real estate market, and its demands on information and statistical analysis are significant; therefore, applicability to developing countries is limited.

Wage Differential: This approach is based on the theory that in a competitive market the demand for labor equals the value of the marginal product, and that the supply of labor varies with working and living conditions in an area. A higher wage is therefore necessary to attract workers to locate in polluted areas or to undertake more risky occupations. Again, as in the case of the property value approach, the wage differential approach can only be followed if the labor market is very competitive. Also, the approach reflects private valuation of health risks, but not necessarily social ones. In this context, the level of information concerning occupational hazards must be high, for private individuals to make meaningful tradeoffs between health-risk and remuneration. Finally, the effects of all factors other than environment (e.g., skill level, job responsibility, etc.) that might influence wages must be eliminated, to isolate the impacts of environment.

Marketed Goods as Proxies for Non-Marketed Goods: There are situations where environmental goods have close substitutes which are marketed, and where therefore the value of the environmental good in question can be approximated by the observed market price. For example, the value of a non-marketed fish variety can be valued at the price of the most similar fish being sold in local markets.

Valuation Using a Constructed Market

Contingent Valuation: In the absence of people's preferences as revealed in markets, the contingent valuation method tries to obtain information on consumers' preferences by posing direct questions about willingness to pay. It basically asks people what they are willing to pay for a benefit, and/or what they are willing to accept by way of compensation to tolerate a cost. This process of "asking" may be either through a direct questionnaire/survey, or by experimental techniques in which subjects respond to various stimuli in "laboratory" conditions. What is sought are personal valuations of the respondent for increases or decreases in the quantity of some good, contingent upon a hypothetical market. Willingness-to-pay is constrained by the income level of the respondent, whereas willingness to accept payment for a loss is not constrained. Estimates of willingness to accept tend to be several times willingness-to-pay estimates.

Pearce and Markandya (1989) compared the contingent valuation method with other, more market-based methods and found that in seven studies done in industrial countries the overlap of estimates is complete, if accuracy is expressed as plus or minus 60 percent of the estimates computed. This result provides some reassurance that a rigorously applied contingent valuation method, while not being very precise, nevertheless can produce valuations that are of the right order of magnitude. This may be sufficient to rule out certain alternative projects or favor others, which can be valuable in decisionmaking.

The contingent valuation method has certain shortcomings, including problems of designing, implementing and interpreting questionnaires (Energy Journal 1988). While its applicability may be limited, there is now considerable experience in applying this survey-based approach in developing countries, e.g., to evaluate the quality of supply of potable water and electricity services (Munasinghe 1990).

In certain circumstances, the contingent valuation method may be the only available technique for benefit estimation, which can and has been applied to common property resources, amenity resources with scenic, ecological or other characteristics, or to other situations where market information is not available (Mitchell and Carson, 1989). Caution should be exercised in seeking to pursue some of the more abstract benefits of environmental assets such as existence value of an asset, which may never be used, but promises psychic satisfaction merely because it exists (Randall and Stoll 1983).

The study on willingness-to-pay for water services in southern Haiti, described in the next section, illustrates how the CVM methodology may be practically applied. In this case study, the valuation technique is tested for different forms of bias, thereby proving its reliability.

Artificial Market: Such markets could be constructed for experimental purposes, to determine consumer willingness-to-pay for a good or service. For example, a home water purification kit might be marketed at various price levels, or access to a game reserve may be offered on the basis of different access fees, thereby facilitating the estimation of values placed by individuals on water purity or use of a recreational facility, respectively.

Contingent Valuation Case Study: The Willingness to Pay for Water Services in Haiti[1]

Background

In rural areas many of those who are "served" by new water supply systems have chosen to continue with their traditional practices. If rural water projects are to be both sustainable and replicable, an improved planning methodology is required that includes a procedure for eliciting information on the value placed on different levels of service, and tariffs must be designed so that at least operation and maintenance costs (and preferably capital costs) can be recovered. A key concept in such an improved planning methodology is that of "Willingness-to-Pay" (WTP).

Two basic theoretical approaches are available for making reliable estimates of households' WTP. The first, "indirect" approach, uses data on observed water use behavior (such as quantities used, travel times to collection points,

---

[1] Summary derived from Whittington et al. 1990.

perceptions of water quality) to assess the response of consumers to different characteristics of an improved water system. The second "direct" approach, is simply to ask an individual how much he or she would be willing to pay for the improved water service. This survey approach is termed "contingent valuation method" and is the focus of the case study.

The Study Area

In August 1986 the research team conducted a contingent valuation survey and source observations in Laurent, a village in southern Haiti. At the time USAID was funding a rural water supply project designed to provide services to about 160,000 individuals in 40 towns and villages. The project was executed by CARE. The affiliation with CARE provided access to villages and justified the presence of the team to the local population.

Haiti, with two-thirds of the population at an annual per capita income of less than US$ 155 in 1980, provides a field setting similar to the situation in much of Africa and some parts of Asia. In such poor areas an accurate understanding of the willingness of the population to pay for rural water services is likely to be particularly important for sound investment decisions.

The population of Laurent is about 1,500, predominantly small farmers with a few people having regular wage employment. Remittances from relatives and friends are common. More than 80% of the population are illiterate and malnourishment among children is widespread.

There are seven sources of fresh water within approximately 2 km of most of the population: one protected well and six springs in dry river beds. The springs provide only modest amounts of water, and individuals often wait more than an hour to draw supplies. The average 3 km round trip to a water source can sometimes take several hours. The preference for clean drinking water is strong, and people sometimes will walk considerable distances past alternative sources to collect drinking water that is considered pure.

Research Design

Economic theory suggests that an individual's demand for a good is a function of the price of the good, prices of substitute and complementary goods, the individual's income, and the individual's tastes. Maximum WTP for a new water system will vary from household to household and should be positively related to income, the cost of obtaining water from existing sources, and the education of household members, and negatively correlated with the individual's perception of the quality of water at the traditional source used before the construction of the improved water supply system. We would hypothesize that the WTP bids of women respondents would be higher than those of men because women carry most of the water, but alternative interpretations are certainly possible.

The research design attempted to test whether WTP bids are systematically related to the variables suggested by economic theory. Different ways of posing the questions were tried. The bidding-game format worked better than direct, open-ended questions. The bidding-game was very familiar and easily understood because it was similar to the ordinary kind of bargaining that goes on in local markets of rural Haiti. Tests were also included for the existence and magnitude of several types of threats to the validity of the survey results, such as strategic bias, starting point bias and hypothetical bias.

Strategic bias may arise when an individual thinks he may influence an investment or policy decision by not answering the interviewer's questions truthfully. Such strategic behavior may influence an individual's answers in either of two ways. Suppose the individual is asked how much he would be willing to pay to have a public standpost near his house. If he thinks the water agency or donor will provide the service if the responses of individuals in the village are positive, but that someone else will ultimately pay for the service, he will have an incentive to overstate his actual WTP. On the other hand, if he believes the water agency has already made the decision to install public standposts in the village, and the purpose of the survey is for the water agency to determine the amount people will pay for the service in order to assess charges, the individual will have an incentive to understate his true WTP.

An attempt to estimate the magnitude of the bias was made by dividing the study population in two groups. One group was read an opening statement that was intended to minimize strategic bias. It was clarified that CARE had already decided to build the new system and that people would neither have to pay CARE for the system, nor to pay money at the public fountains. The second group was read another statement that was accurate but left more questions about the purpose of the study unanswered, especially concerning the role of the interview in designing a water fee.

The hypothesis was that if individuals acted strategically, then bids from those who received the second statement would be lower than bids from those who received the first, because the former would fear that a high bid would result in a higher charge by the community water committee.

Starting-point bias exists if the initial price in a bidding-game affects the individual's final WTP. This could, for example, be the case if the respondent wants to please the interviewer and interprets the initial price as a clue to the "correct" bid. To test for starting-point bias three different versions of the questionnaire was randomly distributed, each with different initial prices in the bidding game.

Hypothetical bias may arise from two kinds of reasons. First, the respondents may not understand or correctly perceive the characteristics of the good being described by the interviewer. This has been a particular problem when the contingent valuation method has been used to measure individuals' WTP for changes in environmental quality, because it may be difficult for people to perceive what a change, for example, in sulfur dioxide of dissolved oxygen means in terms of air or water quality. This bias is not likely in the present case. The respondents were familiar with public water fountains and private water connections and photos of public standposts built in nearby villages were shown as part of the interview.

The second source of hypothetical bias is the possibility that the respondents do not take the questions seriously and will respond by giving whatever answer first comes to mind. The test for this is the same as for the applicability of consumer demand theory: were bids systematically related to the variables suggested by economic theory?

Field Procedure

Fieldwork in the village consisted of two parts: household surveys and source observation. The majority of households in Laurent were interviewed (170 questionnaires completed out of approximately 225 household). The household interview consisted of four sections. The first dealt with basic occupational and demographic data for the family. The second consisted of a number of specific water-related questions. In the third section the enumerator read one of the statements used to test for strategic bias and showed the photographs of public standposts in other villages. The respondent was then asked for (a) a WTP bid per month for public standposts (assuming no private connection) and (b) for a private connection (assuming public standposts were already installed). The fourth section was a series of questions on the health and education of family members and the household's assets (such as radio or kerosene lamp). The latter was used, along with observations about the quality of the house itself, as a substitute for expenditure questions, to form a household wealth index.

The second part of the fieldwork consisted of observing the quantities of water collected by individuals at all the sources used by the population of the village. The objective of these observations was to verify the information individuals provided in household interviews on the sources they used and the quantities of water collected. All sources were observed on the same day from sunrise to sunset. The analysis of the source observation data for Laurent increased the confidence in the quality of the water-use data obtained form the household interviews. Out of 119 observations of trips to water sources, the interview responses were consistent with the source observation for 101 households (85%).

Analysis of Contingent Valuation Bids

Fourteen percent of the households gave an answer of "I don't know" in response to WTP question for public standposts; there was a 25% non-response rate for the WTP question for private connections. The mean for the bids for the standposts, 5.7 gourdes per month (US$ 1.14) seemed realistic.

The *test for strategic bias* showed the anticipated higher bids for those who had received the neutral statement, but the difference was not statistically significant (*t*-statistics of 1.1 and 0.5, respectively, for bids on standposts and private connections). On the basis of this test, the hypothesis that respondents were not acting strategically when they answered the WTP questions cannot be rejected.

The *test for starting-point bias* showed that the bids did not vary systematically with the starting-point. The null hypothesis that the three samples are from the same population cannot be rejected, although the confidence intervals are wide.

On the basis of these results, there was no reason to attempt to adjust the WTP bids for strategic or starting-point bias. The mean of WTP bids for the public standposts was 5.7 gourdes per household per month. Assuming an average annual income in Laurent of 4,000 gourdes (US$ 800), the mean bid is about 1.7% of household income and is significantly lower than the 5% rule of thumb often used in rural water-supply planning for maximum "ability to pay" for public standposts. The mean of WTP bids for private connections, 7.1 gourdes, was not much higher (2.1% of household income), but these bids are based on the assumption that the public standposts are already in place.

The variations in the bids for public standposts and private connections were modeled as a function of the identified explanatory variables. The dependent variable obtained from the bidding game is probably not the maximum amount the household would be willing to pay but, rather, an interval within which the "true" willingness-to-pay falls. Linear regression is not an appropriate procedure for dealing with such an ordinal dependent variable because the assumptions regarding the specification of the error term in the linear model will be violated. An ordered probit model was instead used to explain the variations in WTP bids.

The results of the estimations can be seen in Table 6.2. The coefficients for all the independent variables are in the direction expected. The *t*-statistics indicate that the variables for household wealth, household education, distance of the household from the existing water source, and water quality are all significant at the 0.05 level in both models. The sex of the respondent was statistically significant in the model for public standposts, but not in the model for private connections. The results clearly indicate that the WTP bids are not random numbers but are systematically related to the variables suggested by economic theory.

TABLE 6.2   Willingness-To-Pay Bids for Public Standpost and Private Connections

Dependent variable: Probability that a household's WTP falls within a specified interval

Independent variables:	for a public standpost		for a private connection	
	Coefficient	t-ratio	Coefficient	t-ratio
Intercept	.841	1.350	-.896	-1.344
Household wealth index	.126	2.939	.217	4.166
HH with foreign income (1 if yes)	.064	.232	.046	.194
Occupation index (1 if farmer)	-.209	-.848	-.597	-2.541
Household education level	.157	2.113	.090	1.818
Distance from existing water source	.001	5.716	.000	1.949
Quality index of existing source	-.072	-2.163	-.099	-2.526
Sex of respondent (1 if male)	-.104	-5.410	-.045	-.207
Log-likelihood	-206.01		-173.56	
Restricted log-likelihood	-231.95		-202.48	
Chi-square (df = 7)	51.88		57.83	
Adjusted likelihood ratio	.142		.177	
Degrees of freedom	137		120	

The ordered probit model can be used to predict the number of households in a community which will use a new source if various prices were charged. Such demand schedules are precisely the kind of information needed by planners and engineers to make sound investment decisions.

Conclusion

The results of this study suggest that it is possible to do a contingent valuation survey among a very poor, illiterate population and obtain reasonable, consistent answers. The results strongly suggests that contingent valuation surveys are a feasible method for estimating individuals' willingness to pay for improved water services in rural Haiti. It may also prove to be a viable method for collecting information on individuals' willingness to pay for a wide range of public infrastructure projects and public services in developing countries.

Environmental-Economic Analytical Framework

The above mentioned factors may be clarified further in relation to an environmental-economic framework which considers the principal points concerning water use, environmental impacts and economic efficiency. In many countries today, inappropriate policies have encouraged wasteful and unproductive uses of water. In such cases, better water management could lead to improvements in:

- economic efficiency (higher value of net output produced);
- water use efficiency (higher value of net output per unit of water used);
- water conservation (reduced absolute amount of water used); and
- environmental protection (reduced water-related environmental costs).

While such a result appears to satisfy multiple goals, it is fortuitous because all four objectives are not always mutually consistent. For example, in some developing countries the existing levels of per capita water consumption may be very low, or certain types of high value added water could be uneconomically constrained, in order to protect competing claims by lower value added water users. In such cases, it would be appropriate to increase or re-allocate water consumption in order to raise net output (thereby increasing economic efficiency).

Despite the above complications, the basic approach of maximizing economic efficiency remains valid. In other words, the economic efficiency criterion which helps us maximize the present value of net output from all available scarce resources in the economy (especially water resources and the environment in the present context), should effectively subsume purely water oriented objectives such as water use efficiency and water conservation. Furthermore, the costs arising from water-related adverse environmental impacts may be included (to the extent possible) in the water supply economic analytical framework, to determine how much water use and net output that society should be willing to forego in order to abate or mitigate environmental damage. It must be remembered that the existence of the many other national policy objectives described in Chapter 2, including social goals that are particularly relevant in the case of low-income populations, will complicate the decisionmaking process even further.

The foregoing discussion may be reinforced by the use of a simplified static analysis of the trade-off between water use, environmental costs and net output of an economic activity (see Figure 6.2).

Graphical Representation

Symbol Y represents the usual measurement of the net output of productive economic activity in a country, as a function of some resource input (say water) and considering only the conventional internalized costs, i.e., not accounting for environmental impacts. Due to policy distortions (for example, subsidized prices), the point of operation in many developing countries appears

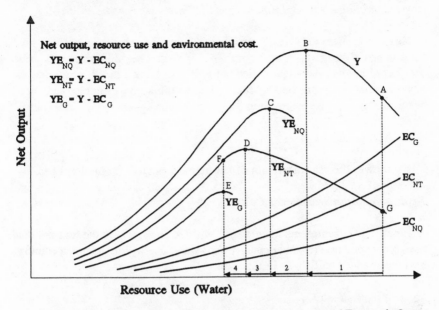

Figure 6.2 Trade-off Between Water Use, Environmental Costs and Economic Output

to be at A, where the resource is being used wastefully. Therefore, without invoking any environmental considerations, but merely by increasing economic and resource use efficiency (i.e., water efficiency), output as usually measured could be maximized by moving from A to B. A typical example might be improving water end-use efficiency or reducing water supply system losses (as explained in detail in Chapter 4).

Quantifiable National Environmental Costs

Now consider the curve EC_{NQ} which represents economically quantifiable national environmental costs associated with water use. Examples might be groundwater depletion and pollution (including costs of avoidance or protection measures like sewerage treatment), or the costs of resettlement at a dam site. The corresponding corrected net output curve is:

$$Y_{NQ} = Y - EC_{NQ}$$

This has a maximum at C that lies to the left of B, implying lower use of (more costly) water.

Non-Quantifiable National Environmental Costs

Next, consider the "real" national output Y_{NT}, which is net of total environmental costs, whether quantifiable or not. The additional costs to be considered include the unquantified yet very real human health and other unmonetarized environmental costs. These total (quantifiable and non-quantifiable) costs are depicted as EC_{NT}, and once again:

$$Y_{NT} = Y - EC_{NT}$$

As shown, the real maximum of net output lies at D, to the left of C.

Transnational Environmental Costs

Finally, EC_G represents the globally adjusted costs, where the transnational environmental costs (to other countries) of water use within the given country, have been added to EC_{NT}. In this case:

$$YE_G = Y - EC_G$$

This is the correspondingly corrected net output which implies an even lower level of optimal water use. For example, consider the costs imposed on other countries (such as transborder impacts of a major dam or excessive use of an aquifer). If it is decided to reduce water use within this country further in order to achieve the internationally adjusted optimum at E, then a purely national analysis will show this up as a drop in net output, i.e., from D to E. As other countries benefit, this drop in net output may justify compensation in the form of a transfer of resources from the beneficiary countries. More generally, the transnational costs imposed by other countries on the nation in question will be a function of regional or global resource use rather than the national resource use shown on the horizontal axis.

The additional curve Y_A shows net output for a technologically advanced future society that has achieved a much lower resource intensity of production.

Policy Issues for Developing Countries

The foregoing analysis illustrates the crucial dilemma for developing countries. In Figure 6.2, all nations (including the poorest) would readily adopt measures that will lead to shift (1) which simultaneously and unambiguously provides both economic efficiency and environmental gains. Most developing countries are indicating increasing willingness to undertake shift (2). However, implementing shift (3) will definitely involve crossing a "pain threshold" for many third world nations, as other pressing socioeconomic needs compete against the costs of mitigating unquantifiable adverse environmental impacts of water use.

We note that real economic output increases with each of the shifts (1),(2) and (3) as shown by the movement upward along the curve YE_{NT} from G to D. However, these shifts are often mistakenly perceived as being upward only from A to B (water use efficiency improvements), followed by downward movements from B through C to D. It is therefore important to correct any misconceptions that environmental protection results in reduced net output. This can be achieved through institutional development, applied research, strengthening of planning capabilities etc. However, it is clear that shift (4) would hardly appeal to resource constrained developing countries unless concessionary external financing was made available, since this movement would imply optimization of a global value function and costs that most often exceed in-country benefits. It must be noted that in the foregoing, we have neglected considerations involving reciprocal benefits to the given country due to water use reductions in other countries.

In other words, the developing countries can be expected to cooperate in transnational and global environmental programs only to the extent that such cooperation is consistent with their national growth objectives. The role of the developed countries, on the other hand, is to incur the risks inherent in developing innovative technological measures which are the prerequisites for the next level in environmental protection and the mitigation of adverse consequences. These risks include the possibility that the more extreme measures may turn out to be unnecessary or inapplicable after all, given the prevailing uncertainty about the future impact of current environmental developments.

We may briefly further conclude that, while the water required for economic development will continue to grow in the developing countries, in the short to medium run there is generally considerable scope for most of them to practice better water management, thereby increasing net output, using their water resources more efficiently, and increasing the global availability of water. In the medium to long run, it should be possible for the developing countries to adopt the newer and more advanced (water efficient) technologies that are now emerging in the industrialized world. Developing countries must mobilize a greater fraction of their accessible water supply to match the rising needs of a growing population, and the demands of newly served rural populations. This can be offset by the reduction in water losses (as discussed in Chapter 4) and the reuse of wastewater. However, as the percentage of accessible water being exploited increases, the need for more effective conservation and recycling will grow. Consequent to a growth in population and water use is a corresponding increase in the amount and potential for pollution and or one of the other environmental externalities discussed earlier to occur. Also consequent to the exploitation of a greater percentage of accessible resources is the reduced ability to cope with major environmental perturbations such as droughts or flood damage, since the reserve capacity is reduced and new sources increasingly difficult to exploit. Protection of existing and future water resources will therefore become even more important in the long-term. The sooner the adoption of environmental management techniques as part of an IWRP, therefore, the better.

Environmental Policy Instruments

When water users seem unwilling to take actions to protect water sources for other users (i.e., downstream or adjacent communities) or to conserve water for future generations, the public sector may necessarily invoke pricing, legal and regulatory measures to achieve these aims.

There are two basic types of policy that have been considered in OECD countries to abate water pollution (Parker 1989):

- regulatory instruments imposing standards through legislation and enforcement; and
- economic instruments including charges, taxes, subsidies, etc.

Regulatory instruments are often criticized as being static, inflexible and suboptimal in terms of environmental and economic efficiency. Instead, Parker suggests the use of optimal pollution taxes to equate the marginal social cost of pollution and the marginal cost of pollution abatement.

Economic instruments are receiving increased attention from many OECD national governments. Charges on pollution are based on the principle that polluter pays in the form of a tax related to the amount of pollutant emissions. Polluters have an incentive to minimize emissions up to the point at which their marginal cost of reducing pollution is equal to their marginal benefit of reducing pollution. The marketable emission permit system that could be traded among polluters, will facilitate the creation of a more efficient pollution reduction process.

There are several different types of environmentally-oriented taxes.

- effluent charges levy costs on the quantity or quality of emissions;
- user charges are based on the cost of treating effluent;
- product charges are levied on products that contain known polluting qualities or characteristics;
- administrative charges are based on the cost of monitoring and enforcing standards and regulations placed on the polluters; and
- tax differentiation is the setting of preferentially lower rates to encourage consumption of less environmentally damaging products.

Different forms of subsidies that could be offered as incentives for pollution abatement include:

- grants to help assist polluters having trouble complying with emission standards and to encourage persistent polluters to modify their behavior;
- subsidized credit offered to polluters willing to make capital investments or take other actions leading to improved pollution control; and
- tax allowances offered on investments made for pollution abatement measures.

However, such subsidies have the general drawback of helping uneconomic firms to continue operating.

Other economic instruments include:

- deposit-refund incentives where refundable surcharges are placed on polluting, especially recyclable products (the cost of administration needs to be carefully taken into account);
- market intervention where national governments offer reduced-rate treatment processes designed to recover pollutants; and
- enforcement incentives including non-compliance fees (paid in arrears due to failure to prevent pollution), forfeitable performance bonds (paid in advance and refunded on successful abatement achievement).

In the specific context of pollution control, Bowers (1990) similarly classifies two main approaches: through the price-mechanism; and by command and control policies. Using the price mechanism to achieve optimal pollution levels (from an economic point of view) involves imposing a tax on pollution equal to the difference between private and social costs. Command and control policies involve fixing a pollution standard at some optimal level and enforcing it by monetary and legal measures. In both cases, pollution must be monitored and measured. The external costs of pollution, however, are not easily identified. Standards must therefore be fixed on the basis of available knowledge of the kinds and magnitude of deterioration in economically tangible concerns such as health, productivity, etc.

Developing country decisionmakers need to adopt a more systematic IWRP approach that includes the following (Falkenmark et al. 1990):

- treat water as a scarce, important resource to be conserved or at least used in a sustainable way;
- assess the severity of water resource problems as a means of prioritizing actions amongst users, regions, and communities;
- assess the impacts of land and water use on quality, quantity and availability;

- accurately consider the cost implications of rapidly growing water demand and increasing deterioration in supply conditions; and
- develop policies for a more rational utilization of existing and future water sources.

Such an approach is being adopted for the Mediterranean -- a region shared by both developed and developing nations. A range of environmental management options are currently being considered to combat water source degradation as part of the Mediterranean Environmental Program, sponsored by the World Bank and other aid donors (World Bank 1990b). One third of the population have inadequate water and sanitation facilities and will need to be provided improved service levels from what are already limited resources. This objective is made harder by population growth at around 4% per annum which exacerbates the rapid depletion in quality and quantity of available water. Demand-side management is clearly as important as supply production in achieving any sustained improvement in coverage for the region.

The environmental program for the region has proposed a number of coordinated measures to improve supply and demand management and protect available water sources:

- establish effective technical standards;
- retrofit and rehabilitate water-using equipment (irrigation, industrial processes and individual households);
- regulate surface water pollution;
- regulate groundwater abstraction;
- enforce regulations;
- introduce consumer awareness schemes;
- enforce recycling of wastewater;
- introduce financial and/or other incentives to ensure all new water users install high efficiency technologies;
- promote better pricing regimes where feasible; and
- reduce water losses and leakages.

These and the regulatory and economic measures discussed above can be considered for other developing regions or countries where current and future water sources are under threat.

Water Pollution Control and Conservation
Case Study: Water Pricing in Jamshedpur, India[2]

We conclude this chapter with an example of various policy options to encourage water treatment, recycling and conservation in Jamshedpur. This city, located in eastern India, is known as a steel city because one of the oldest steel mills (Tata Iron and Steel Company or TISCO) is located here. Over time, a number of associated companies of the Tata group have been established in the city, as well as a number of ancillary units. In the metropolitan area, there are 13 major industrial units, 16 medium industries, and 567 small industrial units.

Current and Future Water Demands

The total annual water withdrawal by these industrial units in 1990 were estimated at 59 MCM (million cubic meters), of which TISCO accounts for 33 MCM. Domestic and institutional sources consumed 65 MCM of treated water, corresponding to a population of around one million. In 1990, about 90% of the water requirements for domestic and commercial use in Jamshedpur and surrounding areas were met by TISCO. The average per capita consumption for water in the area supplied by TISCO was 280 lpd (liters per day). The government, through the Public Health Engineering Department and through the involved municipalities, supplied the remaining 10%. The corresponding levels of water consumption in areas receiving government supply were considerably less than for the TISCO Township, and ranged from 60 lpd in the Mango area to 140 lpd in the Adityapur town.

Currently water is pumped free of charge from the Subernarekha river. There was no allocation for agriculture in 1990. However, a reservoir near Jamshedpur is under construction (as a part of the Subernarekha multipurpose project), and began supplying water in early 1992, to irrigate around 82,000 hectares of land in the region. The estimated water requirements for irrigation in the command area of this reservoir, are 720 MCM annually. Because of the pending competition with irrigation, industries will have to pay for future water supplied by the irrigation department. As a reaction, the industry has started evaluating options of conserving and recycling water.

Water Quality Issues

Surface water in industrial Jamshedpur is contaminated by both organic pollution from human waste and industrial chemical pollution. The latter is

---

[2] Summary derived from Bhatia, Cesti, and Winpenny 1992.

caused by untreated effluents from a steel plant, an automobile unit, and from the engineering industry. Both these contaminants cause (non-documented) health problems and risks to users of water from the river, where the effluents and sewerage are dumped in the absence of effective pollution control mechanisms.

Water quality issues pose all the more concern, since for almost 8 months of the year the natural river discharge is low -- the mean dry season flow being only 75 m³/s. During the dry season, the natural discharge is not capable of flushing the discharged pollutants. Unfortunately, the water quality database is still quite rudimentary in the Jamshedpur area. Nevertheless, the available data strongly suggest that ambient water quality in the greater part of the river Subernarekha is unsuitable for drinking water supply and outdoor bathing. Analysis reports of water quality from four sampling stations revealed high levels of fecal coliform (ranging between 3,300 to 92,000 bacteria per 100 ml) and total coliform (between 54,000 and 240,000 bacteria per 100 ml). Low dissolved oxygen levels indicate that the water quality is detrimental to aquatic life during at least some months. Furthermore, high biological oxygen demand (BOD) values point to heavy organic pollution of the river.

Information on heavy metals and chemical contaminants are not available as yet in the sampling stations on the river. However, reports exist based on physico-chemical water analysis of samples drawn from open drains where the industries discharge their effluents. Those revealed high level of cyanides, phenol, oil and grease, nitrogen, total dissolved and suspended solids, all in concentrations beyond the acceptable limits.

Water and Environmental Management Policies

The following analysis is based on limited information collected from three major industrial units, accounting for about 90% of the total withdrawal of industrial water in Jamshedpur. Even on the basis of preliminary data analyzed below, the water quality situation can be improved considerably with the help of a judicious mix of regulatory and incentive policies, including water tariff structures, effluent charges and investment support for effluent and sewerage treatment plants. The analysis also provides some idea of the economic cost of water supply, and the opportunity cost of water use. Improved water and more detailed analysis would help to determine more specific policies.

Water Conservation and Recycling Options

There will be shortages and increases in the price of water (which is currently free) with the introduction of irrigation in the area. Therefore, industrial managers have studied the potential of water conservation and recycling. Both TISCO and the Tin Plate Company have prepared plans for water conservation through process change, and for reducing withdrawals of freshwater supplies through recycling of water from the effluent and sewerage treatment plants. An estimated 5 MCM could be saved through process change in the Tin Plate Company. In TISCO, these savings are expected to be 10 MCM annually. Moreover, TISCO plans to recycle 50% of the effluent water, further reducing the withdrawal of fresh water by 13 MCM, or about 30% of its total annual intake. In addition, 50% of the household sewerage will be treated and recycled for industrial use, which would reduce the fresh water intake of industry by another 7 MCM.

In summary, a total of 15 MCM could be saved by process change, and another 20 MCM through recycling of treated water. The total forecast savings would equal about 60% of industrial use, or 30% of the total water consumption in the Jamshedpur region. The 35 MCM of water thus saved could not only supply 4 MCM to a new mini steel mill plant under consideration, but also provide additional water for household purposes, such that total domestic supply would increase from the current 9.3 MCM to 40 MCM. This would be enough to supply 220 lpd to another half million people who currently do not have access to piped water.

Water Tariffs to Encourage Conservation,
Recycling and Effluent Treatment

The above numbers show that significant quantities of fresh water can be saved by conservation and recycling, which could subsequently be made available to the urban poor. The data also revealed that this could be done without incurring additional investment costs for water pumping, treatment and distribution pipelines. Additional supplies could enable the municipalities to provide more drinking water, especially since non-availability of investment funds for new water supply projects is a major reason for water shortages experienced by the unserved population in parts of the Jamshedpur metropolitan area.

However, there will be a need to strengthen the necessary institutional framework by which the additional supplies are made available to the poor, such as through the purchase of water by the municipalities from industry. Further, it would be necessary to resolve questions regarding water tariffs for different categories of consumers, as well as prices to be paid by the municipalities to industry. Nevertheless, there are good prospects that innovative institutional arrangements can be set up, since Jamshedpur is a rare example of a city in developing countries where the private sector is providing water supply as well as other infrastructure services for household, commercial and industrial purposes.

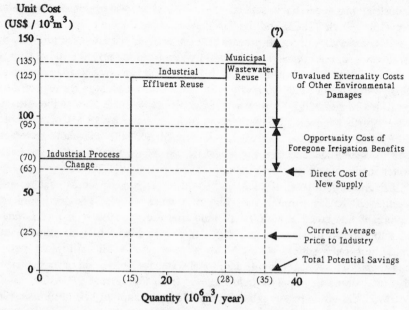

Source: Adapted from Bhatia, Cesti, and Winpenny 1992.

Figure 6.3 Marginal Costs of Water

The estimates of costs of conservation and recycling can be used for exploring the relationship between water tariffs and financial viability of investing in water conservation and recycling. The cost of conserved water is estimated from data obtained from the industrial plants. The results of the analysis are summarized in Figure 6.3. The method used to calculate marginal (or incremental) costs of water are based on the average incremental cost (AIC) approach described in Chapter 8.

The direct cost of new water supply is US$ 0.065 per m³. However, when the opportunity cost of water (i.e., its value in alternative use for irrigation) is considered, the economic cost estimate is US$ 0.095 per m³. On the other hand, the marginal cost of conserved water through process change is estimated at $0.070 per m³. The marginal cost of treated and recycled industrial and municipal wastewater is estimated to be respectively $0.125 and $0.135 per m³.

On the basis of the above mentioned marginal costs, a water tariff can be discussed. If the average tariff for water supply to industrial units is fixed to cover only the direct costs of new supplies, the tariff will be less than the unit cost of water conservation to the Tin Plate Company. This provides little incentive to the industry to invest in process change technology. However, if the price of water charged reflects the opportunity cost of irrigation water then water-saving technologies would pay off.

However, even when the tariff incorporates the opportunity cost of water in irrigated agriculture, it still does not internalize the environmental impacts. The environmental externality cost could be estimated in terms of the damages inflicted by industries and households due to contamination of water sources. Establishing damage functions for deterioration of water quality is rather complicated, since this would require quantifying and valuing the effects of various contaminants from distinct sources on a large number of downstream users. Nevertheless, it is important to recognize the principle that the water tariff should include an estimate of the likely adverse impact of water quality on other members of society. A water tariff reflecting environmental externality costs would provide significant new incentives for industry to recycle its water.

References

Bhatia, R., R. Cesti, and J. Winpenny. 1992. *Policies for Water Conservation and Reallocation*. INUWS draft paper. Washington DC: The World Bank.

Bowers, J. 1990. *Economics of the Environment -- The Conservationists' Response to the Pearce Report*. British Association of Nature Conservationists.

Braden, J.B., and C.D. Kolstad (eds.). 1991. *Measuring the Demand for Environmental Quality*. Amsterdam: North Holland.

Energy Journal. 1988. *Special Issues on Electricity Reliability*. 9.

Falkenmark, M. 1990. Personal communication.

Graham, D.A. 1981. "Cost-Benefit Analysis under Uncertainty." *American Economic Review*. 71, pp. 715-25.

Hanley, N.D. 1989. "Valuing Rural Recreation Benefits: An Empirical Comparison of Two Approaches." *Journal of Agricultural Economics*. 40, pp. 361-374.

Lutz, E., and M. Munasinghe. 1991. "Accounting for the Environment." *Finance and Development*. 28, pp. 19-21.

Mitchell, R.C., and R.T. Carson. 1989. *Using Surveys to Value Public Goods: The Contingent Valuation Method*. Washington DC: Resources for the Future.

Munasinghe, M. 1992. *Environmental Economics and Valuation in Development Decisionmaking*. ENV Working Paper No. 51. Washington DC: The World Bank.

_____. 1990. *Electric Power Economics*. London: Butterworths Press. Chapters 2, 7, 8, and 9.

Parker, A.N. 1989. *Environmental Policy: Case Study of Freshwater Pollution*. Consultant Report. Washington DC: World Bank.

Pearce, D.W., and A. Markandaya. 1989. *Environmental Policy Benefits: Monetary Valuation*. Paris: OECD.

Randall and Stoll. 1983. "Existence Value in a Total Valuation Framework" in *Managing Air Quality and Scenic Resources at National Parks and Wilderness Areas*. Boulder, Colorado: Westview Press.

Whittington, D., J. Briscoe, X. Mu, and W. Barron. 1990. "Estimating the Willingness-to-Pay for Water Services in Developing Countries: A Case Study of the Use of Contingent Valuation Surveys in Southern Haiti." *Economic Development and Cultural Change*. 38.

World Bank. 1991. *Environmental Assessment Sourcebook*. Environment Department. Washington DC: The World Bank.

_____. 1989. *Striking a Balance. The Environmental Challenge of Development*. Washington DC: The World Bank.

7

Demand Analysis and Forecasting

Background

The purpose of this chapter is to provide an introduction to water demand analysis and forecasting, and identify some of the main problems of practical implementation. Accurate demand projections are an important pre-requisite for sound water management, especially for determining future investments in supply capacity. Furthermore, together with the price at which water supplies are set, the level of demand determines the revenue generated by the sale of water to consumers. It is important to look at demand from two perspectives, the first being demand forecasting, and the second being demand management.

Demand Forecasting

Demand forecasting is accomplished by a rational assessment of the range of possible demand schedules of consumers for a new, or improved water supply. These will depend on a wide range of factors including current and future population levels, current consumption levels, characteristics of current source and supply, quality and cost of planned service, levels of economic activity, household income, opportunities for water use, etc. Assessment is carried out through consumer survey, water use data collection, and a variety of demand forecasting models and analytical techniques, some of which are described in the following sections. Market research is important to establish willingness-to-pay and demand agendas for different consumer categories. Many of the assessment techniques are contingent valuations which rely on answers to hypothetical questions concerning consumer actions under a range of future supply conditions. Where forecasts are made on the basis of meter readings from existing consumers and projections of past trends, water utilities usually have a quantitative basis for forecasting consumption based on past and present patterns of use under a given price schedule.

There are several interrelated reasons underlying the importance of accurate demand projection. First, the timely and reasonably reliable anticipation of water needs is vital not only with regard to potable water, but also in the context of overall integrated water resource planning. Second, the expansion of water supply systems usually requires many years to plan and implement. Third, investments in such systems generally are highly capital intensive. If forecasts are too low, shortages may retard development, and the costs of such shortages to consumers are usually a multiple of the value of water not supplied. However, if forecasts are too high, large amounts of capital with high opportunity costs might be uselessly tied up for long periods of time. Either of these consequences is costly to an economy; far more costly than the resources that are needed to undertake detailed and reliable demand studies that could help to avoid such errors. Finally, for the purposes of cost-recovery and liquidity, water agencies need to make accurate assessments of demand under given supply conditions of service and tariff levels in order to establish the likely revenue generation vis-a-vis supply costs. Increasingly, this must account for social issues and the varying abilities of consumer groups to pay for basic services.

A persistent problem has been the heavily over-optimistic assumptions on demand and hence revenue generation used in economic and financial analyses. Consequently, many projects turn out to be premature and over-sized, failing to meet projected targets of critical variables such as unaccounted for water, growth in demand, growth in operating costs, and growth in real tariffs and sales revenue (World Bank 1990). One result has been that in several recent projects, tariffs have had to be raised at a rapid rate and to higher than planned levels to attempt to achieve projected revenue increases in the face of slower than anticipated demand growth and higher than anticipated unaccounted-for-water losses and other production and distribution costs.

Clearly, specific emphasis must be placed on demand forecasting as part of an IWRP to help ensure the optimal use of existing assets, that proposed new investments (often requiring significant foreign currency inputs) are fully justified, and that a given range of user charges are adequate and acceptable to meet revenue targets.

Demand Management

Demand management, is achieved through three main mechanisms: the setting of a tariff regime; the selection of a system coverage and service expansion plan; and the education of consumers on water-use practices.

The price charged for water (and the methods of revenue collection) can have a significant impact on the amount of water used by consumers, the exact nature depending upon the price elasticity of demand of each group. Consequently price can be used as a means of distributing social benefits as well as raising revenue for the sector. According to the WHO (1988a), demand management in the context of most developing countries consists of orienting consumption through appropriate tariff structures.

The selection of a type of supply system and the service level provided can affect demand. If the convenience (in terms of hardware and distribution), quality (as defined in Chapter 4) and continuity of supply (frequency of supply, daily rationing, etc.) are below consumers expectations, the amount of consumption will be low, and will be offset by consumers taking water from alternative traditional, or privately-developed sources. Rather than being a conscious management tool, these affects on demand are often a by-product of a poorly designed or managed system. One of the objectives of an appropriate supply is to provide consumers with the highest possible service levels and to discourage the use of usually unsanitary traditional sources. Normally, one important objective of a new supply system is to increase demand amongst particular consumers up to desired levels that promote the health and economic welfare of those consumers.

The role of education is usually designed to encourage more efficient, less wasteful use of water supplies, cutting down on losses through consumers: reporting or repairing leaks in secondary pipes and connections; conserving their water; and using water more productively, etc. Education may be used also to encourage new uses of water, for instance for commercial enterprises or for domestic food production.

When unforeseen events (such as a severe and prolonged drought) or poor planning lead to water shortages, various water use restrictions may have to be used. Although arbitrary restrictions are an undesirable method of rationing water use, the social and economic losses arising from such drastic demand management measures may be reduced by careful analysis. For example, if the sensitivity of different consumers to water shortages is first studied, and water cuts are then imposed in increasing order of sensitivity, then the socioeconomic impacts of the shortage may be minimized (see Chapter 4 for a discussion of shortage costs).

Planners must add water-loss control to the these instruments of demand management (previously discussed in detail in Chapter 4). The total amount of water produced at the source will be greater than the corresponding values consumed because of losses in the system. Over 50% of available water supply is lost in many developing countries during production and distribution. Reducing physical losses by efficient design, use of better materials, quality control in construction, sound operation and maintenance, better leak detection and repair, and so on, reduces the effective demand on production systems caused by the losses. Another type of loss is theft due to illegal connections, meter tampering or breakage of pipelines, and allowances must be made for it in the demand forecast. Theoretically, since it is also a type of water consumption, the corresponding illegal user benefits and costs should also be

considered in the optimizing process (they represent users who are clearly
unable or unwilling to pay for water but need water nevertheless). In practice
such a cost benefit analysis would be extremely difficult to do, because little
is likely to be known about the illegal consumers, and ethical considerations
may make it difficult for the planning authority to give special considerations
to such unlawfully appropriated benefits.

Demand management is also an important part of the IWRP process since
clearly, many developing countries are faced with an increasingly tight water
supply situation in which coverage and service levels can only be expanded by
a careful control of water use amongst consumers. Water lost, wasted or used
at significantly below-optimum benefit levels by one group of consumers is a
heavy burden on urban and rural supply systems. In many of these, direct
consumption and losses already outstrip production and supply capacities,
leaving large groups of consumers unserved or experiencing considerable
service quality costs. According to mainstream opinion, the price mechanism
is the major management tool and clearly, many cities throughout the
developing world require that tariffs be used as instruments for more effective
demand management (Summerfield 1988). They include Nairobi, Karachi,
Lahore, Hyderabad and Damascus, for example. These and other cities are
faced with the increasing capital costs of conveying water from sources which
are a greater distance away or becoming increasingly depleted (for reasons
discussed previously in Chapter 5). Urban growth requires improved access
to potable water and often, planners see large new capital works as the only
solution. However, as explained previously, the reduction of unaccounted-for-
water, and the reduction of demand and wasteful use through price and other
demand management mechanisms could offset costly capital developments.

The subject of water losses has previously been discussed in Chapter 4 and
the role of pricing is important enough to warrant its own subsequent chapter
(Chapter 8). Therefore, the rest of this chapter will be devoted to the subject
of demand forecasting.

Methods of Forecasting

General Considerations

Demand forecasts are made for time periods of varying duration:

Very Short-Term Demand Projections

- are made on a daily or weekly basis for purposes such as optimizing
  system operation and drawdown;

Short-Run Forecasts

- range between one and three years and are used in water reservoir management, distribution system planning and so on.

Medium-Term Demand Projections

- have a time-frame of about four to eight years, which corresponds to the lead times required for projects involving major transmission and production facilities. Such forecasts, therefore, are especially useful to determine the next steps in building these facilities;

Long-Range Demand Projections

- are usually of a duration of at least 10 years, and are extremely important in long-run water supply system expansion planning. These are of crucial importance in most IWRPs and require analytical methods such as time trend analysis, econometric-multiple correlation techniques, and surveys (as described below).

The recent history of demand forecasting in developing countries has not been encouraging. Garn (1987) evaluated demand forecasts in 54 World Bank water supply projects completed between 1966 and 1980. Although a wide range of developing countries were represented in the study, projects from Latin America, the Caribbean and the Mediterranean regions predominated. In order to assess demand, two main criteria were considered: the number of new connections and the amount of water sold. A comparison of actual and projected values was made for five years following loan effectiveness. The results presented in Table 7.1, show that an average annual number of new connections in excess of 17,000 was anticipated in the first year, rising to 20,000 new connections after five years. In fact, the realized averages were well below the projections, increasing from only 8,700 in year 1 to about 14,000 by year five. More than 80 percent of the projects failed to reach the forecast amount of water sold. Fifty percent reached less than 85% of the targets and twenty percent of the projects did not meet 67% of the volumes expected (at the time of project appraisal) after five years. The second column of Table 7.1. quantifies the discrepancy between expected and realized average increase in the amount of water sold. It can be seen that the numbers fall substantially short of what was predicted.

A more recent World Bank study (INU 1988) using the same 54 projects plus an additional 14, all launched between 1966 and 1981, further confirms the divergence between expected and actual performance in production, sales and unaccounted-for water (UAW). Overestimation of demand for water is

TABLE 7.1   Discrepancy Between Expected and Actual Number of New Connections
and Amount of Water Sold for 54 Water Supply Projects, Completed Before 1980

Year after loan effectiveness	New Connections (average yearly number in thousands)		Water Sold (average annual increase in millions of cubic meters)	
	Expected	Actual	Expected	Actual
1	17.4	8.7	5.9	4.0
2	17.1	10.3	9.8	3.3
3	17.5	12.5	8.1	4.6
4	18.4	13.9	9.2	3.8
5	20.6	13.8	7.4	4.2

Source: Garn 1987.

much too common, as is evidenced by the report's finding that the actual
fraction of projects (11%) able to cover all costs from sales revenues fell far
short of the expected number (56%).   Because of the adverse financial
implications of poor cost recovery for both the implementing country and the
lender, the report sought to reduce the problem of overestimation by
developing benchmarks for determining the probability of projects achieving
their performance targets.   As previously indicated, the success of loss
reduction and control efforts is one factor that can significantly influence
future production needs. For example, a project which begins with a system
losing 40% of water produced, has about a one-in-three probability of reducing
this figure to 36% over six years. A reduction from 40% to 30% in
unaccounted-for water over the same period has only a 5% probability. Such
a review, based on data from the 70 projects, could be useful in the realistic
evaluation of future projects.

Together the observations contained in the two reports of Garn and INU
illustrate clearly the ineffectiveness of recent forecasting of demand and the
need to improve the methods used. The main methods of demand projection
available to planners and recommended for consideration as part of IWRP are:

- Time trend extrapolation;
- Econometric multiple regression; and
- Field surveys (such as Willingness-to-Pay assessments).

Time Trend Extrapolation

Trend analysis is a commonly used approach when relevant historical data
on water consumption (either in the water supply project area or in a region
having similar characteristics), is available. It consists of the extrapolation of

past growth trends assuming that there will be little change in the growth pattern of the determinants of demand such as incomes, prices, consumer tastes, etc. These trends are usually estimated by a least square fit of past consumption data against time or by some similar statistical methodology. Depending on the availability of data, they may be estimated either on a global basis for a given area or they may be broken down by consuming sector (e.g., households, commercial enterprises, industry, etc.). Sometimes, ad hoc adjustments are made to account for substantial changes in expected future demands due to specific reasons. For example, this may take the form of projecting on a case by case basis the expected demands of new agricultural or industrial initiatives or other economic activities. This combination of overall trend projection is frequently used together with specific adjustments based on survey-research type data.

The main advantages of this approach are its simplicity and modest requirements of both data and analytical skills. Forecasts can be based on whatever data are available. The major disadvantage is that no attempt is made to explain why certain water consumption trends were established in the past. The underlying, and usually unstated, assumption is that whatever factors brought about consumption changes in the past will continue unchanged in the future. This is, of course, a rather limiting restrictive assumption, especially in a world in which relative water prices may change rapidly. Another limitation, is that for many developing country rural and peri-urban communities there is often no past consumption data available. In such cases, water has previously been supplied from traditional sources, and there is little basis for comparison between them and the improved new supplies, in terms of quality, availability or quantity. Extrapolating data from poor urban consumers may be ineffective which means that this methodology may require coupling with extensive field survey methods such as contingent valuation.

Econometric Multiple Regression

Econometric forecasting techniques are usually somewhat more sophisticated than time trend extrapolation, and, in theory, hold out the promise of greater forecast accuracy. Past water demand is first correlated with other variables such as prices and incomes, and then future demands are related to the predicted growth of these other variables. However, these methods are frequently nothing more than a special form of trend analysis if the projections of the selected determinants are themselves based on historical trends. The other problem encountered is that of data availability. Usually it is rather difficult to obtain the required time series that are needed to produce quantitatively acceptable (i.e., statistically significant) results. Data series are often short and incomplete especially if the country concerned has only a brief history of water supply. They are also subject to changes in definitions over time and, even more frequently, are in error. Furthermore, the need for "proving" statistically significant results is such that long periods of time have to be covered, periods long enough to have encompassed significant changes in the underlying structure of the economy. Hence, the confidence in the results must be low, even if they pass the test of statistical significance. However, the advantages of econometric studies are that they can take a number of important, demand-determining variables, such as price and income, explicitly into account. A specific type of forecasting approach called end-use analysis is used, especially for household consumption, where the numbers and types of water using devices become important explanatory variables. However, this technique is quite data-intensive and again may need to be coupled with field surveys.

A typical residential demand model can be formulated in economic terms using consumer theory (Nicholson 1978). The direct utility function of a consumer which indicates the intrinsic value he derives from the consumption of various goods may be written:

$$U = U(Q_1, Q_2, ..., Q_n; \underline{Z}) \tag{7.1}$$

where Q_i represents the level of consumption of good i in a given time period (e.g., one year) and $\underline{Z}$ is a set of parameters representing consumer tastes and other factors.

The set of prices P_1, P_2, ..., P_n, for these n consumer goods, and the consumer's income I, define the budget constraint:

$$I \geq \sum_{i=1}^{n} P_i Q_i \tag{7.2}$$

Maximization of the consumer's utility U subject to the budget constraint yields the set of Marshallian demand functions for each of the i goods and services consumed by the household:

$$Q_i = Q_i (P_1, P_2, ..., P_n; I; \underline{Z}) \quad for \ i = 1 \ to \ n \tag{7.3}$$

Consider the demand function for water. Then equation (7.3) may be written in the simplified form:

$$Q_w = Q_w (P_w, P_a, P; I; \underline{Z}) \tag{7.4}$$

where the subscript w denotes potable water from the system, while P_a indicates the price of some other alternative source of water that may be of a different quality (e.g., private well), and P is an average price index representing all other goods and services.

Next, assuming that demand is homogenous of degree one in the money variables (i.e., prices and income), we may write:

$$Q_w = Q_w(\frac{P_w}{P}, \frac{P_a}{P}; \frac{I}{P}; \underline{Z}) \tag{7.5}$$

Thus, starting from consumer preference theory, we may arrive at a demand function for potable water which depends on its own price, the prices of substitutes and income, all in real terms. The effects of other factors, $\underline{Z}$, such as quality of supply, shifts in tastes, and so on can also be explicitly considered. More specific examples of the effects of supply quality on demand are discussed later in this chapter. Examples of other sectors in which the quality of service is a key explanatory variable of demand include telecommunications (Munasinghe and Corbo 1978) and electric power (Munasinghe et al. 1982).

The final specification of an equation such as (7.5) could vary widely. Q_w could be household consumption or per capita consumption; the demand function could be linear or linear in the logarithms of the variables or in the transcendental logarithmic form and could include lagged variables; and $\underline{Z}$ could include supply side constraints such as access to supply, and so on. Furthermore, imposing additional restrictions on the demand functions, such as monotonicity and integrability, will generally improve the significance of parameters estimated using these equations.

Analogously, the industrial demand for water may be derived from production function theory in economics. For example, consider the output (X) of a particular firm of industry over a given time period:

$$X = F(K, L, M, Q_w, Q_a; S) \tag{7.6}$$

where K, L, and M represent the inputs of capital, labor and other materials respectively; Q_w is the input of water supplied from the system; Q_a is the volume of water used from an alternative source; and S is a set of parameters that represents other factors such as shifts in technology, industrial policy, and so on.

The problem posed in production theory is the minimization of the costs of producing a given quantity of output X, given exogenous prices of inputs (Shepard 1953). In principle, the solution yields, as in the household case, the following demand function for water supplied by the system:

$$Q_w = Q_w (P_k, P_l, P_m; P_w, P_a; X; S) \tag{7.7}$$

As before, we may use one of the factor input prices as numeraire, (e.g., price of capital P_k) and rewrite Q_w in normalized form:

$$Q_w = Q_w(\frac{P_l}{P_k}, \frac{P_m}{P_k}, \frac{P_w}{P_k}, \frac{P_a}{P_k}; \frac{X}{P_k}; S) \qquad (7.8)$$

The demand for water at time t is therefore a function of its own price, the prices of other substitutes, the prices of inputs, and other parameters S. Many different choices of variables and specifications of demand function may be used.

A recent developing country example is given by Abu Riziaza (1991). Employing a double-log function he regresses the annual residential water usage (QWTR) of major cities in Saudi Arabia against total family income (INCM), family size of the household (FSIZ), price of water (PRIC), average annual temperature (TEMP), and a dummy variable to account for the presence of a garden (GRDN). A typical result is:

log(QWTR) = .22 GRDN + 0.11 log(INCM) - 0.48 log(PRIC)
        (3.41)   (2.95)   (20.8)

     + 0.47 log(FSIZ) + 1.26 log(TEMP)   (R Square = .8)
       (16.3)   (10.72)

With the values in brackets indicating the t statistic. The estimated coefficients are all significant (at least at the 95% level), and have the expected sign, i.e., except for price, increases in all other explanatory variables (GRDN, INCM, FSIZ and TEMP) have a positive effect on water use.

In this way demand functions could be developed for other end-use sectors such as agriculture, commerce, and so on. The demand function may be estimated by standard econometric techniques. The estimated equations then could form the basis for future demand forecasts.

The main issues with this approach are:

- The mechanistic nature of the econometric equations and their extrapolation into the future, which often fails to capture structural shifts in demand growth. Such structural shifts are particularly important in developing countries as a result of the introduction of new ideas and techniques.
- The difficulties of separating out short-run and long-run effects in the analysis of changes in the structure and level of prices.
- The lack of an adequate data base to make accurate regression estimates. In the areas of developing countries this problem is particularly severe because price and consumption data by consuming sector are usually lacking, income data are unreliable or nonexistent and

do not account for changes in income distribution, and statistical data of output and sales of specific industries are often unobtainable because of their confidentiality if the number of producers is small.

- The inherent limitation of estimating procedures that concentrate on water prices as demand determinants, but do not account for the costs, availability, life expectancies and replaceability of the water-using appliances and equipment that must be utilized with various water sources. The inability of many developing country consumers to afford connection charges also may undermine such demand projection.
- The erratic behavior of water prices, unless the analysis relied on cross-sectional data only (there is usually insufficient data collected at different locations during the same time period, to make this a practical procedure in developing countries).
- The fact that specific water resources are often allocated by governmental fiat, or determined by such factors as availability or reliability of supply, rather than observable market price.
- The fact that actual service levels in terms of quality, reliability, etc. may be less than those used in the demand analysis, thus leading consumers to adopt different demand schedules than forecast. The role of unforeseen environmental externalities can play an important part in this, reinforcing the importance of environmental assessments as part of the IWRP process.
- The problem that demand elasticities, even if they were known (and little data exists for developing countries) or estimated accurately, are likely to change significantly themselves, rather than remain constant, if expected price changes of water are large. This is so because for most activities the ability to substitute other resources for water (including alternative water sources) is limited.

Field Surveys

Given the limitations of the other forecasting methodologies, surveys potentially provide a direct and reliable tool of demand analysis and forecasting. In essence, surveys consist of a list of more or less sophisticated questions that are put to existing and potential water users in order to measure and record their present consumption and future consumption plans. Surveys often take the form of a contingent valuation because the respondent is asked what he or she would do in a hypothetical situation.

The basic types of questions that might be asked are the following:

- How much water (of each type) do you use per month/year?
- What do you use it for?
- How much do you pay per unit of water used (by type of source)?

- What do you grow, produce or sell and what is the value and value added of each major product?
- Can you identify specific water uses with specific outputs?
- What is your net income (for households)?
- What are your future expansion plans, and their timing, and what additional water requirements do they imply?
- What additional water-using appliances or equipment are you planning to acquire in the foreseeable future (identify)?
- What would you be willing to pay for a connection with different options such as a flat user-fee for unlimited consumption of a given volume of water supplied from a particular type of water supply facility?

One of the most common forms of survey being carried out in developing country water supply design is the willingness-to-pay survey, particularly in rural or low-income urban settings. This has a dual purpose in that it is designed to forecast demand for a given type of service, and to establish an appropriate tariff setting and assess the potential for revenue generation and cost-recovery (of both investment and operating costs). Both the WHO (1988a, 1988b, 1988c) and the WASH project (WASH 1988. Whittington et al. 1989) have recently produced several documents discussing willingness-to-pay issues. The guidelines on conducting surveys (WASH 1988) is a particularly useful document for planners considering using this kind of data-gathering method.

As with the previous two methods, field surveys have their drawbacks and limitations:

- they require substantial amounts of time;
- they can be costly;
- they require skilled and conscientious interviewers;
- users may be unable to provide the information asked because they themselves do not know;
- users may be unwilling to provide the information for competitive reasons or because of fear of the consequences of revealing the information, etc.;
- users may wittingly or unknowingly give inaccurate answers; and
- future water use plans may be vague, or too optimistic or pessimistic.

Surveys of actual or future consumption could also be usefully combined with others, such as general population censuses or similar inquiries (such as income studies, etc.). The important factor is to collect a broad data-base of information from which informed estimates can be made of the likely consumption patterns of a given consumer group over the lifetime of the water supply system being developed. This involves the considerations of income, numbers of consumers, types of water use and other data which can only be gained from a variety of sources rather than surveys alone (see Table 7.2).

Practical Application

We may conclude with the following summary. There is no single, universally superior approach to demand forecasting. The more sophisticated techniques tend to obscure the basic methodological assumptions as well as weaknesses in the data, and therefore the simpler techniques may be more appropriate in situations where the available information is known to be unreliable. As a counterbalance, the sum of many disaggregate demand forecasts (by consumer type), estimated using a variety of techniques, can be effectively compared with an independently made global forecast for the entire project area. Table 7.2 lists some of the major factors that are likely to determine the demand for water. Estimates of future changes in these determinants are helpful to projecting demand.

Whenever possible, survey approaches should be used to forecast the demand of large users. This may account for a substantial percentage of the total load. Frequent updating of this information, to account for unexpected changes is an additional important requirement. The determinants of demand for diverse users have to be carefully selected, because they vary from case to case, and the level of disaggregation chosen will depend on the data, as well as on the ultimate purpose of the projection. Demand forecasting is a dynamic process in the sense that the procedure must be repeated often, in light of improved information and techniques of analysis. The building up of a reliable data bank is an invaluable tool in this process of constant revision.

Informed judgement is an invaluable supplement to the various quantitative methods of water supply demand forecasting. An experienced forecaster will be able to make appropriate adjustments based on a number of constraints and complicating factors that essentially cannot be incorporated mechanistically into a numerical algorithm for forecasting water consumption. This means that the process of demand forecasting relies quite heavily on rules of thumb interpretations which include the following caveats:

- there is considerable need to plan on the basis of a range of demand forecasts. For example, the low-demand scenario might be scaled down by a factor equivalent to the overestimates found by Garn (1987) and INU (1988), e.g., around 50%; and
- projects must be evaluated to see if the demand projections are the main justification for implementation, i.e., whether the high estimates are fundamental in tipping a cost-benefit analysis towards acceptance (remembering that Total Benefits are a function of consumption). Extra

TABLE 7.2   Major Demand Determinants of Water Consumption

A. RESIDENTIAL SECTOR

1. Number and size of households (or population)
2. Real family income weighted by income distribution
3. Price of water
4. Connection charges
5. Availability of service
6. Quality of service
7. Cost and availability of water-using devices and appliances
8. Availability and cost of consumer credit
9. Costs of alternative water sources

B. COMMERCIAL SECTOR

1. Sales or value added of nonsubsistence commercial sector
2. Price of water
3. Connection charges
4. Costs of water-using appliances
5. Quality of service
6. Working hours of various types of commercial establishments

C. INDUSTRIAL SECTOR

1. Price of water (demand and water charges by type of service)
2. Type of industry and water use intensity
3. Degree of market water of individual industry
4. Relative price of alternative water sources
5. Quality of supply
6. Availability

D. AGRICULTURAL SECTOR

1. Price of water
2. Availability
3. Quality of service
4. Supply cost of alternative water systems e.g., diesel-driven irrigation pumps

E. PUBLIC SERVICES SECTOR

1. Price of water
2. Per capita revenue of local governments
3. Number and size of public schools, hospitals, etc.

care must be taken with these conditions to be sure of avoiding unrealistic and unnecessary major capital investments. In particular, capacity expansion decisions that are robust (or invariant) over the range of future demand forecasts, would be more desirable and prudent to adopt when the future is more uncertain.

Clearly, in support of these two points, a distinction should be made between the underlying or potential demand, and the consumption level that is actually achievable. Many practical constraints may prevent the realization of over-ambitious demand forecasts, including lack of skilled manpower, apathy of the authorities, delays in supplying equipment or unavailability of critical components, diversion of resources for other purposes due to political interference, and so on. In some cases, institutionally imposed constraints which suppress demand, such as providing only intermittent supply or non-connection of consumers, as well as the presence of alternative water sources, may lead to a substantial gap between the potential and achievable (or realistic) demand. This is exacerbated by poor implementation of physical plant in the form of construction quality control, defective or inappropriate materials, low-capacity connections, poor operation and maintenance capacities, etc. As indicated, unforeseen environmental externalities may also play a role in causing sudden or gradual deterioration in supply capabilities.

The demand forecast for a given consumer category will depend on the growth rates of the number of connections, the average water use per connection, and the user population. Therefore, the evolution of each of these variables needs to be analyzed separately. In particular, connection policy is a factor that must be carefully studied. The role of tariffs in the form of connection charges, flat-fees or volumetric charges is important and is discussed more widely in Chapter 8 which considers water supply pricing policy. Briefly, in view of the low levels of income in many of the rural and urban communities targeted for future water supply coverage, high connection charges could act as a significant barrier and negate the favorable effects of low water prices. The deterrent effects of excessive connection costs may be inadvertently overlooked, especially in the case of quantitative demand forecasts that rely exclusively on the price variable. On the other hand, heavily subsidized connection charges may help to achieve the high connection rates anticipated in the demand projection, while increasing the risk that the actual consumption per connection would fall far short of the target level assumed in the forecast. As yet, the only practical way to closely assess the probable reaction of consumers in this context is to conduct field surveys designed to assess willingness to pay various tariffs, and therefore get an empirical basis for making appropriate planning decisions (see the bidding game descriptions in WASH 1988, and Whittington et al. 1989 for practical examples).

Model of Water Demand and the
Quality of Water Supply

The importance of quality of service in water system planning was described in Chapter 4. Demand for water is affected by the quality of service. When the supply quality changes (i.e., due to service interruptions, low pressure, water contamination, unacceptable odor, taste or color, etc.), consumption benefits are affected in two ways. In the short run, if the quality drops below the expected level, planned consumption is affected and consumers experience inconveniences and costs, e.g., inconvenience to households or loss of output for industries, due to water shortages (see Chapter 4). In the longer run, if consumers anticipate a change in the supply quality, they will adjust their planned demand and behavior patterns. The adjustment will clearly depend on the elasticity of demand of consumers with respect to the variable of quality (as opposed to price). Very little empirical data exists on this subject. One would expect lower income communities, especially those with no access to alternative supplies, to have consumption relatively less affected by a drop in quality. Then again, it depends very much on other factors such as the nature of the deterioration (visible or invisible, smell/taste or chemical contamination, salinity or pesticides, etc.), the ability of different consumers to store, boil or filter water, and the kinds of uses the water is put to. Thus the reaction is somewhat complex.

Recognizing this complexity and the practical difficulties of forecasting quality-induced shifts in demand, we nevertheless proceed with the development and estimation of models to investigate the long-run changes in residential, commercial, and industrial water consumption due to variations in the quality of supply. Although necessarily simplified, the results show that when the output quality is improved, the planned level of consumption should increase at any given price. This induced demand effect will shift the water demand curve outward and increase the consumer surplus, thus providing additional consumption benefits. Such effects of supply quality on the demand for other types of infrastructure services like telecommunications and electricity have been demonstrated in earlier work (Munasinghe and Corbo 1978, Munasinghe et al. 1982).

Modeling Background

The dependence of demand on quality of supply will vary for different types of water consumers. For example, an industrial consumer of water could behave very differently from a residential consumer of water when faced with an identical change in the quality of supply. What is an "adequate" quality for one may be far from adequate for another. This clearly depends on the uses to which the water is put. If this analysis is taken to an extreme, we could say that every single consumer of water behaves differently, and that separate demand functions have to be derived for each of them.

In practice it would be impossible to estimate separate demand functions for each water consumer. Even if extensive data were available for each one (and such data will certainly not be available in practice), there would be insufficient variation in the independent variables to give meaningful results. On the other hand, the fairly extensive literature on aggregation theory demonstrates that only under unrealistic and restrictive assumptions is it possible to aggregate these functions, for the purpose of estimation, into a single, very large assuming function with aggregate variables.

A compromise has to be made between the two extremes of one aggregate demand function and a large number of individual demand functions. Therefore, water consumers are divided into three broad categories: residential, industrial, and commercial. Since there exist similar behavioral characteristics within these classes, we will assume that aggregation is possible within them (although in practical terms, planners may wish to sub-divide these broad categories further). Demand functions will be derived and estimated for "typical" consumers in each of these categories.

The demand functions derived and estimated here have the empirically convenient double-log form also used by others (Sato 1982). They are based on explicit utility-maximizing theory. Furthermore, they are unique in that they explicitly contain the price of substitute water sources as an independent variable. In addition to the above contribution, the methodology used here to derive a water demand function can be used to derive similar double-log functions (which explicitly include the price of substitutes) for other goods and services besides water. This ability to extend the methodology is especially useful because many empirical demand studies simply assume the double-log form and include the price of substitutes, without a theoretical derivation.

Residential Water Demand

Consider a residential consumer of water. Let the consumer's utility function be:

$$U = U(B,N) \tag{7.9}$$

where B = quantity consumed of all goods and services except water and N = total quantity of water consumed, that is, from both potable water supply (W) and substitute water sources (S). In general, $N = N(W,S)$, which says that water services are a function of the public potable water supply and substitute water sources.

The consumer's budget constraint may be written as:

$$Y = p_b B + p_w W + p_s S \qquad (7.10)$$

where:

Y = income
p_w = effective price of potable water supply
p_b = price of all goods and services except water and
p_s = effective price of substitute water sources

The consumer's utility maximizing problem can thus be written as:

$$Optimize \quad L = U[B, N(W,S)] + m(Y - p_b B - p_w W - p_s S) \qquad (7.11)$$

where m is an appropriate Lagrange multiplier. The first-order conditions reduce to:

$$\frac{(\partial U / \partial B)}{p_b} = \frac{\dfrac{(\partial U / \partial N)}{(\partial N / \partial S)}}{p_s} \qquad (7.12a)$$

$$\frac{(\partial N / \partial S)}{(\partial N / \partial W)} = \frac{p_s}{p_w} \qquad (7.12b)$$

Suppose that the consumer utility function may be written in the log-linear form (Munasinghe et al. 1982):

$$U = B^{f1} \cdot N^{f2} \qquad (7.13)$$

and also that:

$$N = \exp(S^{g1} W^{g2}) \qquad (7.14)$$

where f1, f2, g1 and g2 are parameters.

This function has sufficient generality but still allows further mathematical analysis. Substituting for the partial derivatives of N and eliminating S gives:

$$W = H \, p_s^{t1} p_w^{t2} Y^{t3} \qquad (7.15)$$

where H, t1, t2, and t3 depend on f1, f2, g1 and g2.

Note that t1 + t2 + t3 = 0, which is a linear restriction on the coefficients. The parameters t1 and t2 are price elasticities of demand for water supply, while t3 is the income elasticity of demand for water supply.

Assuming no money illusion (i.e., W is homogeneous of degree zero in p_s, p_w, and Y, so that equal percentage changes in all three money variables will leave W unchanged), the condition $t1 + t2 + t3 = 0$ is the familiar elasticity condition derived in consumer theory by a straightforward application of Euler's theorem to a general demand function for W.

W and S have been defined as the quantities of water and substitute water services, respectively. For substitute water we will simply assume that the quantity of service is directly proportional to the volume of such water consumed. The constant of proportionality may be set to 1 without loss of generality. With this assumption, p_s can be reinterpreted as simply the price of substitute water. For potable water supply, however, the notion of quality of supply enters into the argument. Assume that such water services depend on the actual quantity of potable water consumed, X_{wr} (measured in cubic meters), and on the quality of water supply, R. The subscripts w and r refer to potable water and residential consumers, respectively. A relatively simple and reasonable functional form for W is $W = f(R) \cdot X_{wr}$, which says that the services derived from the supply of potable water is proportional to the volume water consumed and that the constant of proportionality depends on the quality of supply.

Variations in R affect the effective price of water services p_w according to the relationship $p_w W = p_x X_{wr} = p_x \cdot [W/f(R)]$, where p_x is the price of water (per cubic meter). Solving for p_w and substituting for p_w and W in equation (7.15), we have

$$X_{wr} = h(R)\ p_s^{t1} p_x^{t2} Y^{t3} \tag{7.16}$$

where:

$$h(R) = Hf(R)^{(-1-t2)} \tag{7.17}$$

This equation relates demand and the quality of supply. As discussed earlier, when demand shifts with changes in quality, consumption benefits will also change. To estimate these consumption benefits, it is necessary to calculate the area under the (compensated or Hicksian) demand curve for water up to the point p_x, the actual price of water. Although (7.16) is not Hicksian, the error resulting from using the area under this demand curve is generally negligible (Willig 1976). In this range p_x will vary up to infinity. This reveals a weakness in the demand function (7.15). If $-1 < t2 < 0$, the area representing total benefits becomes infinite. One possible way to avoid this weakness, while at the same time making the demand function more realistic, is to allow the own-price elasticity of demand (t2) to vary. It is reasonable to assume that t2 does not remain constant over the wide range of price variations that are possible. One simple assumption about this elasticity may be represented by: $t2 = ko + k1 \ lnp_x$. Since we expect $t2 < 0$ and since demand for water is likely to become more elastic as p_x increases, we expect $k0, k1, < 0$.

Substituting for $t2$ in the expression for X_{wr}, we have:

$$X_{wr} = h(R) \ p_s^{t1} \ p_x^{(k0+k1 \ \bullet \ ln px)} \ Y^{t3} \qquad (7.18)$$

If $g(R) = ln[h(R)]$, taking logarithms of both sides we have:

$$lnX_{wr} = g(R) + t1 \bullet lnp_s + k_0 \bullet lnp_x + k1 \bullet (lnp_x)^2 + t3 \bullet lnY \quad (7.19)$$

One difficulty associated with allowing the price elasticity of demand to vary in the double-log formulation is that the demand equation is no longer homogeneous of degree zero. The homogeneity of the equation depends on the condition $t1 + t2 + t3 = 0$ or, in this case, $t1, k0 + k1 \cdot ln \ p_x + t3 = 0$. Since p_x can vary for any estimated values of the coefficients $t1, k0, k1$, and $t3$, the left-hand side of this equation cannot always be zero unless $k1 = 0$. If $k1 = 0$, the price elasticity would not longer be variable. Postulating that some other variable beside p_x causes the variation in price elasticity will not eliminate the inconsistency. The left-hand side of the equation cannot be zero for different values of this variable unless the coefficient associated with this variable is zero and $t1 + k0 + t3 = 0$.

Although a demand function estimated using the functional form (7.19) is not homogeneous of degree zero in income and prices, it is still possible to make this condition hold (at least approximately). This may be done during estimation by placing the linear restriction:

$$t1 + k0 + k1 \bullet lnp_{xav} + t3 = 0 \qquad (7.20)$$

on the coefficients of the model, where p_{xav} is the mean price of water in the sample. This restriction constrains the demand function to be homogeneous of degree zero at the mean price.

Industrial and Commercial Water Demand

Consider an industrial or commercial firm consuming water and other types of water. Let $O = O(J,N)$ be the firm's production function, where N is the total quantity of services derived from water consumed, from both the public water system (W) and substitute water sources (S), and J is the quantity consumed of all other inputs.

As in the case of residential consumers, suppose $N = N(W,S)$. The producer's optimizing problem can be stated as one of minimizing the cost of producing some given quantity of output. It may be written in Lagrangian form as:

$$Optimize \quad L = p_w W + p_s S + p_j J + m[\underline{O} - O\{J, N(W,S)\}] \quad (7.21)$$

where:

p_w = effective price of public water supply
p_s = effective price of substitute water services
p_j = price of other inputs
m = a Lagrange multiplier

The first-order conditions reduce to:

$$\frac{(\partial O / \partial J)}{p_j} = \frac{\dfrac{(\partial O / \partial N)}{(\partial N / \partial S)}}{p_s} \quad (7.22a)$$

and:

$$\frac{(\partial N / \partial S)}{(\partial N / \partial E)} = \frac{p_s}{p_w} \quad (7.22b)$$

Suppose that the production function can be written in Cobb-Douglas form:

$$O = J^{\beta} N^{\gamma 4} \quad (7.23)$$

Define $V_i = P_j J$ as the total returns to all factors except water, and as for the case of residential consumers, suppose $N = \exp (S^{g3} \cdot W^{g4})$. Proceeding exactly as for the case of residential consumers leads to an equation of the form of (7.19) with V_i in place of Y. Therefore:

$$lnX_{wi} = G(R) + r1 \cdot lnp_s + r2 \cdot lnp_x + r3 \cdot (lnp_x)^2 + r4 \cdot lnV_i \quad (7.24)$$

where X_{wi} is the firm's water demand.

Empirical Estimation of Demand Functions

One common characteristic of the demand functions (7.19) and (7.24) is the existence of terms of the form $g(R)$ and $G(R)$, representing the effect of the quality of water supply on demand.

Two problems arise when attempting to estimate a function with such a term. First, the exact functional forms of $g(R)$ and $G(R)$ are unknown. Second, as discussed earlier, the quality of water supply, R, encompasses a variety of different aspects of water, and it will be very difficult to quantify such a concept. Both problems may be mitigated if, rather than a continuous range of values for R, we consider a set of discrete levels R_0, R_1,..., R_p, where R_0 refers to the lowest quality of supply and R_1, R_2,...are successively higher qualities of supply, and we introduce a set of dummy variables D_1, D_2,..., D_p, where

$$D_1 = D_2 = D_3 = ... = D_p \ = O \quad \text{when } R = R_0$$

$$D_1 = 1, D_2 = D_3 = ... = D_p = O \quad \text{when } R = R_1, \text{ and so on.}$$

Introducing an error term u into equation (7.19), we can then write

$$lnX_{wr} = (C + a_1D_1 + a_2D_2 + ... + a_pD_p) + t1 \cdot lnp_s + k0 \cdot lnp_x \\ + k1 \cdot (lnp_x)^2 + t3 \cdot lnY + u \quad (7.25)$$

where:
C is a constant, a_1 represents the difference between $g(R_0)$ and $g(R_1)$, a_2 represents the difference between $g(R_0)$ and $g(R_2)$, and so on.

Using the regression model (7.25), we can estimate C, a_1, a_2, ..., a_p, t_1, k0, k1, and t3. From equation (7.19) the fractional change in quantity demanded when the quality of supply is changed from R_i to R_j is given by [exp $\{g(R_j) - g(R_i)\}$ - 1]. Using equation (7.25), this expression may now be represented by [exp(a_j-a_i)-1]. An equation similar to (7.25) may be derived for industrial and commercial consumers, starting from equation (7.24).

Supply Quality and Demand for Water Connections in Rural Brazil — A Practical Case Study

While the theoretical model in the previous section focused on the effect of quality of supply on the quantity of water consumed, supply quality could also influence the decision to connect to a new pipe-borne system. Furthermore, as discussed earlier, the performance-evaluation of previous water supply projects in rural areas have indicated the crucial importance of adequate anticipation of household connection levels. The direct transfer of techniques used in industrialized countries, emphasizing mainly price-elasticities of demand and income levels, but taking connection rates for granted have often resulted in poor water project demand forecasts. An assessment of the literature shows that few workable examples exist of price elasticities of demand, and particularly how demand is quantitatively related to quality (although, as shown in the previous section, a theoretical model can be developed with which demand shifts could be analyzed). Demand elasticities established from the developed world, for example from the USA, are only of limited use for residential consumers since they represent only the wealthier, higher end of the consumer range. For example, a study by the American Public Works Association (APWA) in 1981 estimated the short-run elasticity of water use to be -0.1 and the long-run elasticity to be -0.4. Hence a 10% increase in price will only yield a fall in demand of 1 to 4% depending on the time available for adjustment of consumption schedules. Comparable studies for developing countries are very limited. One might conjecture that high-end and low-end income groups are likely to have their demand less affected by price changes than middle income groups. In the case of the rich, the cost of water is insignificant relative to income. For the poor, the price elasticity of course depends on the availability of "free" traditional alternative sources. However, many poor communities already consume only the bare minimum volume for basic human needs and would not be able to cut back on consumption to any appreciable extent. Instead, they would be forced to use an ever increasing proportion of their income to maintain their minimum supply requirements. Since the potential for demand elasticity studies per se are limited, a more useful approach may be to focus on measurement of household connection aspirations as a first stage assessment, followed by a related analysis of consumption plans and appropriate pricing policies.

A recent study carried out in three Brazilian regions suggests a relatively simple survey method to help predict the number of potential users who will choose to connect (Briscoe et al. 1989). The accuracy of two different methods is tested based on rather extensive field survey data covering both already supplied areas and new ones. First an econometric model is employed to determine what household characteristics influence the decision to use the new source. The relative importance of parameters like the family head's education, formal sector employment, monthly household income, major appliance ownership, distance to old water source and real price of yard tap are determined and could be used for demand forecasting in areas not yet supplied or where system improvements are being made.

The estimated parameters for this model are summarized in Table 7.3. Analysis of these results first concentrates on the direction of influence, and second on the magnitude. The signs of all parameters are in accordance with the ex-ante hypothesized effects, and in most cases the estimates are highly significant. Household characteristics affect both tastes and the opportunity cost of time (i.e time saved due to having a household connection). A family is more likely to connect if it is:

- relatively well-off;
- if the family-head is relatively well-educated and is employed in the formal sector; and
- if the household owns major electrical appliances.

TABLE 7.3   Rural Brazil: Effects of Independent Variables on the Probability of
Connecting to the Improved System (see text for explanation of results)

Independent Variable	Hypothesized Effect	Marginal Probability (for discrete variables)		Elasticity (for continuous variables)	
Constant		+0.45			
Family Characteristics:					
Head's education, 1-4 years	+	+0.07	**		
Head's education, > 4 years	+	+0.20	**		
Monthly household income	+			+0.015	**
Formal sector employment	+	+0.07	**		
Major appliance ownership	+	+0.17	**		
Characteristics of old source:				+0.03	*
Distance	+				
Characteristics of new source:					
Real price of yard tap	-			-0.68	**

** the estimate is statistically significant at the 95% level (one tailed test).
* the estimate is statistically significant at the 90% level (one tailed test).

Similarly the likelihood of connecting is increased, the lower the price of
the improved source, and the greater the distance to the alternative source.

The magnitude of the effects may be interpreted in the following way: the
intercept can be viewed as the probability of hooking up for a hypothetical
family which has an uneducated head, has no income, owns few appliances,
has a source close to his house, and can have a yard tap for free. From Table
7.3 the probability of such a family connecting to the improved system would
be 45%. Education would have a large effect:

• having less than primary education only would raise this probability by
   7%; and
• the additional effect of completing primary education would raise the
   probability a further 20%.

For the continuous variables elasticities are computed at the sample means.
For the average family, the probability of connecting would: increase by 15%
if income were doubled; decrease by 68% if the tariff were doubled and
increase by 3% if distance to the existing source were doubled.

The study then applies a second method to approach the problem. It shows
that the much less data intensive method of surveying only the households'
willingness-to-pay (WTP) for a new water source gives (basically) equivalent

results and is reliable. In particular, the technique of contingent valuation (see also Chapter 4) was used, as described below. The basic approach was to ask families:

"If you were required to pay X cruzados per month for a connection, would you choose to connect to the system or would you prefer to use the alternative source?"

Each family was asked this question for a range of monthly tariffs. Based on experience in industrialized countries, the sequence of the bids was to start at one of the two extremes (alternating across families) and converge inward. Thus, for instance, for a low starting point and prescribed values of 50, 100, 150 and 200 cruzados, the order would be: 50, 200, 100, 150.

Analysis of this data and comparison with the econometric results mentioned above indicate that the level of WTP stated by households indeed depends in the same way on the same crucial household characteristics that actually determined connection levels in past cases. However, the major problem with this method is that biases may arise, for three related reasons:

1) individuals may not understand or perceive correctly the characteristics of the good being described by the interviewer ("hypothetical bias");
2) the respondent may think that he can influence the provision of the services in his favor by not answering the questions truthfully ("strategic bias"); and
3) the respondent may give answers which are influenced by his desire to please the interviewer ("compliance bias").

These issues are discussed in more detail in the willingness-to-pay study guidelines of WASH (1988). This Brazilian study shows that due to the question-sequence used and the clear understanding of the options by interviewed households (which is not unexpected since water use is familiar), only a strategic bias was actually encountered. But even this bias appeared in a price range where it would have no effect on the actual decision (the government would never have considered charges in this range). However, as about 40% of interviewed persons in areas not yet supplied appeared to have acted strategically (in the belief they could manipulate the governmental price-decision downwards), results have to be considered as a "lower bound" estimate of the average WTP surveyed in those areas.

Another interesting set of results arise from the comparison of two very different qualities of supply: yard tap vs. public tap. The implementation-decision in favor of one or the other system affects ultimate water use (i.e., the demand pattern) enormously. Regional differences in both the absolute

WTP-value and range of WTP-divergence between the two supply qualities occur mainly due to the availability of alternative resources.

It is noteworthy that the price-elasticity of demand depends on the quality of supply (in terms of the convenience). The direct price-elasticity of the private yard tap at the mean is -0.47, whereas it is -0.36 for the public yard tap. The difference in the cross-price-elasticity is even larger. The elasticity of demand for a yard tap with respect to public tap price changes is 0.04 (quite inelastic), compared to a rather large effect on public tap demand following yard tap price changes (elasticity of 0.81). In relation to the model developed earlier (showing the impact of quality of supply on water demand), the results indicate that major changes in quality of supply could not only cause parametric shifts in the demand curve but also change the price elasticities (i.e., change slopes).

In addition the study shows that equity concerns can be partly addressed by providing public taps free of charge, financed by cross-subsidization from yard taps, without running the risk of undercutting yard tap revenues (as households do not see them as close substitutes). Thus the overall-benefits of the project could be increased by adoption of such a policy.

References

Abu Rizaiza, O.S. 1991. "Residential Water Usage: A Case Study of the Major Cities of the Western Region of Saudi Arabia." *Water Resources Research*. 27 (5), pp. 667-671.

APWA. 1981. *Special Report 48 -- Planning and Evaluating Water Conservation Measures.*

Briscoe, J., P.F. de Castro, C. Griffin, J. North, and O. Olsen. 1989. *Towards Equitable and Sustainable Rural Water Supplies: A Contingent Valuation Study in Rural Brazil*. Draft. Washington DC: The World Bank.

Garn, H.A. 1987. *Patterns in the Data Reported on Completed Water Supply Projects.* Washington DC: The World Bank.

INU. 1988. *Evaluation of Water Supply Projects: Demand Forecast. Infrastructure Department.* Washington DC: The World Bank.

Munasinghe, M., and Corbo. 1990. "The Challenge Facing the Developing World." *EPA Journal*. Vol. 16, pp. 52-4. Washington DC: Environmental Protection Agency.

_____, W.G. Scott, and R. Dias-Bandaranaike. 1982. *Optimizing Rural Electricity Supply*. Energy Department. Washington DC: The World Bank.

_____. 1978. "The Demand for CATV Services in Canada." *Canadian J. of Economics*. II, pp. 506-20.

Nicholson, W. 1978. *Microeconomic Theory*. Second Edition. Hinsdale, Illinois: Dryden Press.

Sato, K. 1982. "Additive Utility Function With Double-log Consumer Demand Functions." *Journal of Political Economy*. pp. 102-24.

Saunders, R., and J. Warford. 1977. *Village Water Supply*. Baltimore, MD: Johns Hopkins University Press.

Shepard, R.W. 1953. *Cost and Production Functions*. Princeton, N.J.: Princeton University Press.

Summerfield, M.T. 1988. *Water Demand Management in Cities of Kenya, Pakistan and Syria. Annex V/III in WHO*. Geneva: World Health Organization.

WASH. 1988. *Guidelines for Conducting Willingness-To-Pay Studies for Improved Water Services in Developing Countries. WASH Field Report No. 306*. Arlington: Water and Sanitation for Health Project.

Willig, R.D. 1976. "Consumer Surplus Without Apology." *American Economic Review*. Vol. 66.

WHO. 1988a. *Draft Guidelines on Cost Recovery in Community Water Supply and Sanitation. Preliminary Draft Report of the Third Informal Consultation on Institutional Development*. pp. 11-15. Geneva: World Health Organization.

_____. 1988b. *Managerial and Financial Principles for Water Supply and Sanitation Agencies. WHO/CWS/89.5. Report of the Fourth Consultation on Institutional Development Working Group on Cost Recovery*. I. Geneva: World Health Organization.

_____. 1988c. *Principles and Models to Achieve Sustainable Community Water Supply and to Extend Household Sanitation. WHO/CWS/89.6. Report of the Fourth Consultation on Institutional Development Working Group on Cost Recovery*. II. Geneva: World Health Organization.

Whittington, D., M. Mujwahuzi, G. McMahon, and C. Kyeongae. 1989. *Willingness to Pay for Water in Newala District, Tanzania: Strategies for Cost Recovery. WASH Field Report No. 246*. Arlington: Water and Sanitation for Health Project.

World Bank. 1990. *Water Supply and Sanitation -- FY90 Sector Review*. Infrastructure Department. Washington DC: The World Bank.

_____. 1986. *Improving the Effectiveness of Investment in the Water Sector*. Water and Urban Department. Washington DC: The World Bank.

8

Pricing Policy

The concept of water pricing as an instrument for effective demand management and conservation, has already been discussed in the context of integrated water resource planning. The coordinated use of both price and non-price policy tools was stressed. This chapter provides a more specific review of the general methodology for water pricing (Munasinghe 1990).

Introduction and Overview

Traditionally, water pricing policy in most countries has been determined mainly on the basis of financial or accounting criteria, e.g., raising sufficient sales revenues to meet operating expenses and debt service requirements, while providing a reasonable contribution towards the capital required for future water system expansion.

However, in recent times several new factors have arisen, including the rapid growth of demand, increase in equipment costs, dwindling availability of cheaply exploitable water resources, and expansion of water systems into areas of lower consumer density at higher unit costs. These developments have led to increasing emphasis on the use of economic principles in order to produce and consume water efficiently, while conserving scarce resources, especially in the developing countries. In particular, a great deal of attention has been paid to the use of marginal cost pricing policies in the water sector.

Objectives of Water Pricing

The modern approach to water pricing recognizes the existence of several objectives or criteria, not all of which are mutually consistent:

- national economic resources must be allocated efficiently not only among different sectors of the economy, but within the water sector itself. This implies that cost-reflecting prices must be used to indicate to the water consumers the true economic costs of supplying their specific needs, so that supply and demand can be matched efficiently;

- certain principles relating to fairness and equity must be satisfied, including:
  - (a) fair allocation of costs among consumers according to the burdens they impose on the system;
  - (b) assurance of a reasonable degree of price stability over time; and
  - (c) provision of a minimum level of service to meet the basic water needs of persons who may not be able to afford the full cost;
- the water prices should raise sufficient revenues to meet the financial needs of the sector, as described earlier;
- the water tariff structure must be simple enough to facilitate metering and billing customers; and
- other economic and political requirements must also be considered, such as subsidized water supply to certain sectors to enhance growth or to certain geographic areas for regional development.

Since the above criteria are often in conflict with one another, it is necessary to accept certain tradeoffs between them. The long-run marginal cost (LRMC) approach to price-setting described below has both the analytical rigor and inherent flexibility to provide a tariff structure that is responsive to these basic objectives. The LRMC may be broadly defined as the incremental system cost of supplying one unit of sustained future water consumption, with an adjustment in the optimal capacity. In the following sections we make a case for planners adopting an LRMC policy as a basis for price setting. Methods for estimating LRMC and incorporating it into a practical and equitable revenue generation framework are described.

Since the LRMC calculation (by definition) involves a long-term assessment of costs, it inherently becomes a vehicle for environmental management issues to be taken into account. The longer the time period involved, the greater the likelihood that significant cost-influencing feedback will occur from a range of negative or positive environmental impacts caused by activities within and outside the water sector.

Tariffs Based on Long-Run Marginal Costs (LRMC)

A tariff based on LRMC is consistent with the first objective listed above (i.e., the efficient allocation of resources), because the price charged for water reflects the incremental costs to the community of satisfying marginal demands. If calculated correctly, these incremental costs should include the usual various capital and operating expenses as well as resource depletion and environmental damage costs. The more traditional accounting approach to tariff setting is concerned with the recovery of sunk costs whereas, in the LRMC calculation, it is the economic value of future resources used or saved by consumer decisions that is important. Since prices are the amounts paid for increments of consumption, in general they should reflect the marginal cost thereby incurred. In the absence of excess capacity, water supply costs increase if existing consumers increase their demand or if new consumers are connected to the system. Therefore, prices that act as a signal to consumers should be related to the economic value of resources to be used in the future to meet such consumption changes. The accounting approach, which uses historical assets and embedded costs, implies that future economic resources will be as cheap or as expensive as in the past. This could lead to over-investment and waste, or under-investment and additional costs incurred by consumers due to water supply shortages. Inefficient use of water might also have severe repercussions on the environment. The LRMC tariff should not just include the 'private' direct costs incurred in supplying water to the consumer but also social costs incurred by the wider community as a whole from supplying that water to a specific group of consumers. Socially efficient pricing requires that prices reflect social costs at the margin as well as private costs. If they do not, then demand for goods with significant environmental costs will be too high resulting in inefficient investment for society as a whole.

In order to promote better utilization of capacity and avoid unnecessary investments to meet peak demands (which tend to grow very rapidly), the LRMC approach permits the structuring of prices to vary with the marginal costs of serving demands:

- by different consumer categories;
- by volume of supply (e.g., large versus small users);
- by different times-of-use and consumption patterns;
- by quality of supply provided; and
- in different geographical areas and so on.

The structuring of LRMC-based tariffs also meets sub- categories (a) and (b) of the second (or fairness) objective. The economic resource costs of future consumption are allocated as far as possible among the customers according to the incremental costs they impose on the water system. In the traditional approach, fairness was often defined rather narrowly and led to the allocation of (arbitrary) accounting costs to various consumers. Because the LRMC method deals with future costs over a long period, e.g., about 10 years, the resulting prices (in constant terms) tend to be quite stable over time. This smoothing out of costs over a long period is especially important because of capital indivisibilities or lumpiness of water system investments.

The use of economic opportunity costs (or shadow prices, especially for capital, labor, and fuel) instead of purely financial costs, and the consideration of externalities whenever possible, also underline the links between the LRMC method and efficient resource allocation (see Chapter 3 for details).

Practical Tariff-Setting

The first stage of the LRMC approach for water tariff-setting is the calculation of pure or strict LRMC that reflect the economic efficiency criterion. If price were set strictly equal to LRMC, consumers could indicate their willingness-to-pay for more consumption, thus signalling the justification of further investment to expand capacity.

Variations from LRMC

In the second stage of tariff-setting, ways are sought in which the strict LRMC may be adjusted to meet the other objectives, among which the most important is the financial requirement. There are several reasons why the actual prices set might diverge from LRMC:

1) To avoid a financial surplus or deficit:

If prices were set equal to strict LRMC under conditions where marginal costs are higher than average costs (during a period when the unit costs of supply are increasing), a financial surplus will be generated. In principle, financial surpluses of the utility may be taxed away by the state but, in practice, the pricing of water (which is considered a basic need), to raise central government revenues is likely to be politically unpopular and rarely applied. However, where they do occur, such surplus revenues can also be disposed of in a manner consistent with the other objectives. For example, connection charges could be subsidized without violating the LRMC price, or low-income consumers could be provided with a subsidized block of water to meet their basic requirement, thus satisfying sociopolitical objectives.

If, as in some cases, marginal costs are below average costs (e.g., due to economies of scale), then pricing at the strict LRMC will lead to a financial deficit, which will have to be made up, for example, by higher lump-sum connection charges, flat rate charges, or even government subsidies.

2) Where other pricing policies do not reflect marginal costs:

Another reason for deviating from the strict LRMC arises when prices elsewhere in the economy do not reflect marginal costs, especially in the case of substitutes and complements for piped water from the system. In such cases, departures from the strict marginal cost pricing rule for water services would be justified. For example, in some areas alternative sources of water (like private wells) may be available cheaply or exist already. In this case, second-best pricing of water below the first-best LRMC may be justified to prevent excessive use of the alternative forms of water, where significant externality costs exist (see the Case Study in Chapter 10).

3) Where short-run modifications in prices are necessary:

Since the computation of strict LRMC is based on the total water supply least-cost expansion program, LRMC may also need to be modified by short-term considerations if previously unforeseen events render the long-run system plan sub-optimal in the short-run. Typical examples include:

*   a sudden reduction in demand growth and a large excess of installed capacity, which may justify somewhat reduced water charges; or
*   a rapid increase in operating costs, which could warrant a short-term surcharge.
*   unforeseen water shortages, which may require higher water charges (based on the high SRMC or opportunity cost of water in the highest value alternative use), as a rationing mechanism.

A wider discussion of the mechanics of calculating adjusted LRMC tariffs for the special conditions under which they are desirable is contained in Section 8.4.

Limits on Tariff Structuring

As discussed earlier, the LRMC approach permits a high degree of tariff structuring. However, data constraints and the objective of simplifying metering and billing procedures usually impose a practical limit to differentiation of tariffs by (a) major customer categories (e.g., residential, industrial, commercial, special); (b) time-of-use (e.g., wet/dry season or peak/off-peak period); and (c) geographic location. Finally, various other constraints may also be incorporated into the LRMC-based tariff, such as the political requirement of having a uniform national tariff or subsidizing water supply. However, in each case, such deviations from LRMC will impose an efficiency cost on the economy.

A Summary of Benefits from LRMC

From a planning perspective, adoption of an LRMC based tariff has a number of clear advantages. In the first stage of calculating LRMC, the economic (first-best) efficiency objectives of tariff-setting are satisfied because the method of calculation is based on future economic resource costs (rather than sunk costs) and also incorporates economic considerations such as shadow prices and externalities. The structuring of marginal costs permits an efficient and fair allocation of the tariff burden on consumers. In the second stage of developing marginal cost-based tariffs, deviations from strict LRMC are considered in order to meet important financial and other social, economic (second-best), and political criteria. This second stage of adjusting strict LRMC is generally as important as the first-stage calculation, especially in the developing country context.

The LRMC approach provides an explicit framework for analyzing system costs and setting tariffs. If departures from the strict LRMC are required for non-economic reasons, then the economic efficiency cost of these deviations may be estimated, even on a rough basis, by comparing the impact of the modified tariff relative to (benchmark) strict LRMC. Furthermore, since the cost structure may be studied in considerable detail during the LRMC calculations, this analysis helps to pinpoint weaknesses and inefficiencies in the various parts of the water system, such as over-investment, unbalanced investment, or excessive losses at the production, transmission, and distribution levels in different geographic areas. This aspect is particularly useful in improving system-expansion planning.

Finally, it is obvious that given the tasks of water sector decisionmakers, any LRMC-based tariff is a compromise among many different objectives. Therefore, there is no "ideal" tariff. By using the LRMC approach, it is possible to revise and improve the tariff on a consistent and ongoing basis and, thereby, approach the optimum price over a period of several years, without subjecting long-standing consumers to "unfair" shocks in the form of large abrupt price changes.

Economics of Marginal Cost Pricing

The origins of marginal cost pricing theory date back as far as the path-breaking efforts of Dupuit (1844). Subsequently Hotelling (1938) and Ruggles (1959a, 1959b) have provided a comprehensive review of work in this area up to the 1940s. The development of the theory, especially for application in the public utility sectors, received a strong impetus from the work of Boiteux (1949), and others, from the 1950s onward. Recent work has led to more sophisticated investment models that permit determination of marginal costs, developments in peak-load pricing, and consideration of the effects of uncertainty and the costs of water shortages (see Chapter 4). This section consists of a review of the basic economic principles of marginal cost pricing and a summary of the current state of the art. Further details of the theory may be found in the references given earlier.

Basic Marginal Cost Theory

The rationale for setting price equal to marginal cost may be clarified with the simple supply-demand diagram shown in Figure 8.1. Let D_0 be the demand curve (which determines the liters of water demanded per year, at any given average price level), while S is the supply curve (represented by the marginal cost MC of supplying additional units of output).

At price p and demand Q, the total benefit of consumption is represented by the consumer's willingness-to-pay, i.e., the area under the demand curve OEFJ. The cost of supplying the output is the area under supply curve OAHJ. Therefore, the net benefit or total benefit minus supply cost, is given by the area AEFH. Clearly, the maximum net benefit AEG is achieved when price is set equal to marginal cost at the optimum market-clearing point G, i.e., (p_o, Q_o).

In mathematical terms, the net benefit is given by:

$$NB = \int_0^Q p(q)\,dq - \int_0^Q MC(q)\,dq \tag{8.1}$$

where p(Q) and MC(Q) are the equations of the demand and supply curves, respectively. Maximizing NB yields

$$\frac{d(NB)}{dQ} = p(Q) - MC(Q) = 0 \tag{8.2}$$

which is the point of intersection of the demand and marginal cost curves (p_o, Q_o).

Capital Indivisibilities and Peak Period Pricing

Following this static analysis, we now consider the dynamic effect due to the growth of demand from year 0 to year 1, which leads to an outward shift in the market demand curve from D_o to D_1 as shown in Figure 8.1. Assuming that the correct market-clearing price p_o was prevailing in year 0, excess demand equal to GK will occur in year 1. Ideally, the supply should be increased to Q_1 and the new optimum market-clearing price established at p_1. However, the available information concerning the demand curve D_1 may be incomplete, making it difficult to locate the point L.

Fortunately, the technical-economic relationships underlying the production function usually permit the marginal opportunity cost curve to be determined more accurately. Therefore, as a first step the supply may be increased to an

UNIT PRICE

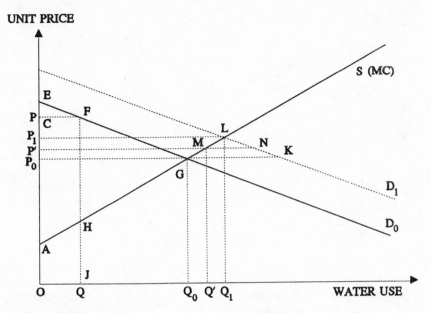

Figure 8.1 Dynamic Effects Due to Demand Curve Shifts

intermediate level Q', at the price p'. Observation of the excess demand MN indicates that both the supply and, if necessary, also the marginal cost price should be further increased. Conversely, if we overshoot L and end up in a situation of excess supply, then it may be necessary to wait until the growth of demand catches up with the over-supply. In this iterative manner, it is possible to move along the MOC curve towards the optimal market-clearing point. It should also be noted that, as we approach it, the optimum is also shifting with demand growth and therefore we may never hit this moving target. However, the basic guideline of pegging the price to the marginal opportunity cost of supply and expanding output until the market clears is still valid.

When the MC curve is based on marginal production costs, the effect of capital indivisibilities or lumpiness of investments causes difficulties. Thus, owing to economies of scale, investments for water systems (especially production facilities) tend to be large and long-lived. As shown in Figure 8.2, suppose that in year 0, the maximum supply capacity is QM_o, while the optimal price and output combination (P_o, Q_o) prevails, corresponding to the demand curve D_o and the short-run marginal cost curve SRMC (e.g., variable, operating and maintenance costs). As demand grows from D_o to D_1 over time and the limit of existing capacity is reached, the price must be increased to p_1

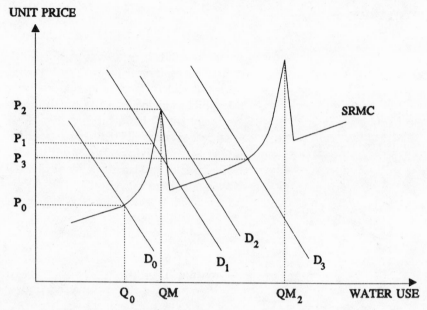

Figure 8.2 The Effect of Capital Indivisibilities on Price

to clear the market, i.e., "price-rationing" occurs. When the demand curve has shifted to D_2 and the price is P_2, plant is added on to increase the capacity to QM_2.

However, as soon as the capacity increment is completed and becomes a sunk cost, price should fall to the old trend line of SRMC. P_3 is the optimal price corresponding to demand D_3. Generally, the large price fluctuations during this process will be disruptive and unacceptable to consumers. This practical problem may be avoided by adopting a long-run marginal cost (LRMC) approach, and peak period pricing.

The basic peak period pricing model shown in Figure 8.3 has two demand curves; for example, D_{pk} could represent the monthly water demand during the peak season (or dry months) of the year when water use is greatest, while D_{op} would indicate the monthly off-peak demand during the remaining months, when demand is lower. The marginal cost curve is simplified assuming a single type of production source, with incremental operating and maintenance costs per unit of water supplied given by the constant a, and the incremental cost of capacity given by the constant b. The static diagram has been drawn to indicate that the pressure on capacity arises due to peak demand D_{pk}, while the off-peak demand D_{op} does not infringe on the capacity QM. The optimal pricing rule now has two parts corresponding to the two distinct rating periods (i.e., differentiated by the time of use):

UNIT PRICE

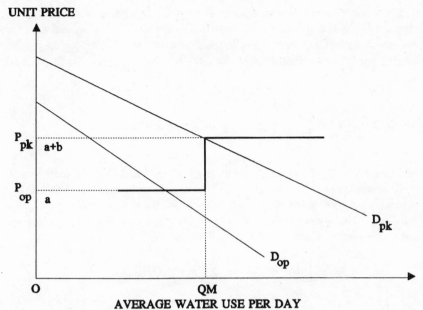

Figure 8.3 Peak Period Pricing Model

peak period price:

$$p_{pk} = a + b \qquad (8.3)$$

off-peak period price:

$$p_{op} = a \qquad (8.4)$$

The logic of this simple result is that peak period users, who are the cause of capacity additions, should bear full responsibility for the capacity costs as well as operating and maintenance costs, while off-peak consumers pay only the latter costs.

The economic rationale for peak period pricing may be demonstrated by extending the simple algebraic model presented earlier in equation (8.1). Consider two rates of consumption:

- a constant Q_1 m³/day during the off-peak season which is t_1 days long; and
- a steady Q_2 m³/day during the t_2 days of the peak period.

Let the investment cost be $K(Q_m)$ for a system that has maximum delivery capacity Q_m, while p_i is the price and MC_i is the short-run marginal cost (or operating cost) of supplying an additional unit of water during period i. The maximization of net benefits over the total period $t_1 + t_2$ may be formulated as:

$$Maximize \ \ NB = \sum_{i=1}^{2} t_i \left\{ \int_0^{Q_i} [p_i(q) - MC_i(q)]dq \right\} - K(Q_m) \tag{8.5}$$

with respect to Q_1, Q_2 and Q_m subject to $Q_i \leq Q_m$; and $Q_i \geq 0$; for i = 1,2.

If we assume that $[p_i(q) - MC_i(q)]$ is continuous and concave and that $K(Q_m)$ is continuous and convex, then the conditions for the Kuhn-Tucker theorem are satisfied. The above problem becomes therefore equivalent to finding the stationary points of the unconstrained Lagrangian:

$$L = NB - \sum_{i=1}^{2} u_i \cdot t_i \ (Q_i - Q_m) \tag{8.6}$$

where u_i are the Lagrange multipliers. Substituting for NB yields:

$$L = \sum_{i=1}^{2} t_i \left\{ \int_0^{Q_i} [p_i(q) - MC_i(q)]dq - u_i(Q_i - Q_m) \right\} - K(Q_m) \tag{8.7}$$

The first-order Kuhn-Tucker conditions for a stationary point are:

$$\frac{\partial L}{\partial Q} = t_i \ [p_i(Q_i) - MC_i(Q_i) - u_i] \ \leq \ 0 \tag{8.8a}$$

$$Q_i \ \frac{\partial L}{\partial Q_i} \ = \ 0 \tag{8.8b}$$

$$\frac{\partial L}{\partial Q_m} = (t_1 \cdot u_1 + t_2 \cdot u_2) - \frac{\partial K}{\partial Q_m} \ \leq \ 0 \tag{8.9a}$$

$$Q_m \ \frac{\partial L}{\partial Q_m} \ = \ 0 \tag{8.9b}$$

$$Q_i \ \leq \ Q_m \tag{8.10a}$$

$$u_i \ (Q_i - Q_m) \ = \ 0 \tag{8.10b}$$

and Q_1, Q_2, Q_m, u_1, u_2 all non-negative variables.

The rates of consumption Q_i are positive for all economically significant (or non-trivial) cases. From (8.10a) Q_m is then also positive. This observation and equations (8.9b) and (8.8b) imply that $(\partial L/\partial Q_m) = 0$; and $(\partial L/\partial Q_i) = 0$ for $i=1,2$; at the optimum. Therefore, rewriting (8.8a) as a strict equality and assuming $t_1 > 0$ and $t_2 > 0$, we get:

$$p_i(Q_i) = MC(Q_i) + u_i \quad for \quad i = 1,2 \tag{8.11}$$

Similarly, rewriting (8.9a) as a strict equality, yields :

$$t_1 \cdot u_1 + t_2 \cdot u_2 = \frac{\partial K}{\partial Q_m} \tag{8.12}$$

As far as the Lagrangian multipliers u_i are concerned, we can first consider the case that $u_1 = u_2 = 0$. According to (8.9a) this would mean that $\partial K/\partial Q_m = 0$ or the marginal cost of building extra capacity would be zero, which is not reasonable. A second case would be where both u_1 and u_2 were positive. From equation (8.10b) this would imply $Q_1 = Q_2 = Q_m$, i.e., the case where no distinct peak flow occurs. For the purposes of our study we can thus eliminate the two previous cases and remain with the situation where one u_i is strictly positive and the other one is zero. Conforming to our notation for the peak period, we retain $u_1 = 0$ and $u_2 > 0$. From (8.10b) we deduce for the off-peak period:

$$Q_1 < Q_m \tag{8.13}$$

and for the peak period:

$$Q_2 = Q_m \tag{8.14}$$

Clearly from (8.11), for the off-peak period: $p_1 = MC_1 =$ operating cost only. However for the peak period, (8.11) yields:

$$p_2 = MC_2 + u_2 \tag{8.15}$$

where u_2 has the usual interpretation of the shadow value of new capacity. This may be seen from (8.12), where $u_1 = 0$ and $u_2 = (\partial K/\partial Q_m)/t_2$, i.e., the marginal cost per unit of capacity per unit time.

We recall that at this optimum the marginal cost of adding to capacity $(\partial K/\partial Q_m)$ is exactly offset by the corresponding costs avoided by consumers due to improved quality of service and reduced shortages (see the water service quality optimizing model in Chapter 4).

Suppose the costs of shortages and service quality are ignored, and one were to set price equal to the short-run marginal cost (SRMC) of supply (i.e., operating costs only, ignoring capital costs). As mentioned earlier, this inevitably results in rapidly time-varying prices (Figure 8.1). Such fluctuations are undesirable because consumers can respond efficiently, only if the naive assumption is made that markets equilibrate quickly and costlessly. There is also a sociopolitical cost to frequent changes in the price of a service like water which is a basic need. In a recent paper, Swallow and Marin (1988) examined an LRMC based approach of the type described later in this chapter, consisting of a levelized weighted average of annual operating costs and (future) incremental investment expenditures. They conclude that this method provides price stability, while retaining about 99% of the efficiency benefits of the idealized SRMC pricing regime, over a range of practical water utility scenarios.

Extensions of Simple Models

The basic models presented so far must be extended to analyze the economics of real-world water supply systems. First, the usual procedure adopted in marginal cost pricing studies may require some iteration as shown in Figure 8.4., which is a simplified version of Figure 4.5. Typically, a deterministic long-range demand forecast is made assuming some given future evolution of prices. Then, using water system models and data, several plans are proposed to meet this demand at some fixed target service quality level (see Chapter 4). The cheapest or least-cost system expansion plan is chosen from these alternatives. Finally strict LRMC is computed on the basis of this least-cost plan and an adjusted LRMC tariff structure is prepared. If the new tariff that is to be imposed on consumers is significantly different from the original assumption regarding the evolution of prices, however, then this first-round tariff structure must be fed back into the model to revise the demand forecast and repeat the LRMC calculation.

Modifications Due to Uncertainties

In theory, this iterative procedure could be repeated until future demand, prices, and LRMC-based tariff estimates become mutually self-consistent. In practice, uncertainties in price elasticities of demand and other data may dictate a more pragmatic approach in which the LRMC results would be used after only one iteration to devise new water tariffs and to implement them. The demand behavior is then observed over some time period; the LRMC is re-estimated and tariffs are revised to move closer to the optimum, which may itself have shifted, as described previously. An extreme form of price feedback could result in a shift of the peak outside the original peak period,

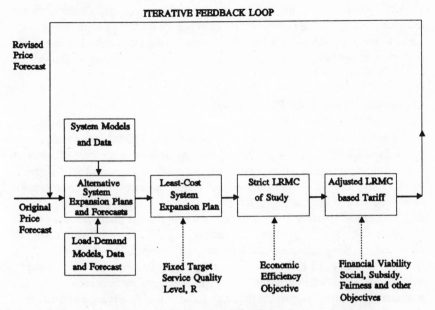

Figure 8.4 The Use of Price Feedback in Estimating LRMC Based Tariffs

especially if the latter was too narrowly defined (e.g., only one month of the year, in the seasonal model described earlier). That is, peak period pricing may shift the demand peak, from one pricing period (or season) to another. If sufficient data on the price elasticity of demand were available, theory indicates that each potential or secondary peak should be priced to keep its magnitude just below the available capacity level. Since the necessary information would rarely be available in practice, a combination of techniques including use of a sufficiently wide peak period or redefining the peak period to include both the actual and potential peaks, may be used to avoid the shifting peak problem.

Service Quality Issues

The inter-related issues of supply and demand uncertainty, safety margins, and service quality costs (discussed in Chapter 4) also raise complications. The least-cost system expansion plan to meet a water demand forecast is generally determined assuming some arbitrary service quality level. Therefore, marginal costs depend on the target quality of service, when in fact, economic theory suggests that water supply quality should also be treated as a variable to be optimized, and both price and service quality levels should be optimized simultaneously. The optimal price is the marginal cost price as described earlier, while the optimal service quality level is achieved when the marginal cost of capacity additions (to improve the quality of water supply) are equal to the expected value of economic cost savings to consumers due to the reduction in service quality costs (e.g., water supply shortages averted) by those capacity increments (see Chapter 4 for details).

Divergences Between SRMC and LRMC

Consider again the choice between SRMC and LRMC for pricing. We recall from Chapter 4 that, the SRMC may be defined as the cost of meeting additional water consumption, (including the costs of shortages) with capacity fixed. The LRMC is the cost of providing an increase in consumption (sustained indefinitely into the future) in a situation where optimal capacity adjustments are possible. When the system is optimally planned and operated (i.e., capacity and reliability are optimal), SRMC and LRMC coincide. However, if the system plan is temporarily suboptimal, significant deviations between SRMC and LRMC will have to be carefully resolved. For example, overestimation of future demand may result in significant excess capacity, and low marginal capacity costs in the near future, thus justifying a reduction in demand charges below the LRMC level. However, as peak demand grows and the system approaches optimality again, the capacity charges should rise smoothly towards LRMC. This transition could become undesirably abrupt if the initial reduction in demand charges was too large resulting in demand growth being overstimulated.

Joint Cost Allocation

When a water resource project gives rise to benefits that accrue to many purposes or outputs (including potable water supply), then the allocation of joint costs may become problematic (Eckstein 1958). For example, a large multipurpose reservoir could yield benefits in terms of potable water, irrigation, hydropower, navigation, flood control, fishing, and so on. Clearly, it is the total project cost which is most useful for the overall investment decision. Nevertheless, cost recovery and the efficient pricing of the various outputs are more directly affected by the exact apportioning of total project costs. Thus, if a multipurpose dam feeds an urban water supply system, the share of dam costs allocated to potable water will help determine the price of water to consumers.

There is no ideal method of allocating joint costs, so as to satisfy the requirements of economic efficiency, equity (or fairness), and practicality. One approach would be to simulate hypothetically, how incremental project costs might vary for a small change in a particular output (e.g., increasing the availability of potable water by raising the dam height). However, this procedure may also increase the outputs and benefits associated with other project purposes (e.g., flood control). It is the allocation of such truly joint costs that give rise to major problems.

A method that appears to be quite equitable, is the allocation of total project costs to different purposes in proportion to the corresponding benefits accruing to those purposes. However, this approach is difficult to apply, especially when (as is often the case), the benefit measurement procedure is not consistent or accurate across different outputs and purposes. This purely benefit-based allocation method has given rise to a variant called the separable costs and remaining benefits (SCRB) technique, which offers a reasonable compromise between efficiency, equity, and ease of application.

The SCRB technique is illustrated in Table 8.1, for the simple case of a project with two typical purposes (a dam that provides hydropower and drinking water). The procedure can be generalized easily to cases involving more outputs or purposes. The first step is to identify a set of single-purpose alternative schemes that will provide the same benefits as the multipurpose project. In our example, the two alternatives might be an equivalent thermal power plant and the pumping of the same volume of water from an underground aquifer, with cost adjustments for transport of the electricity and water to the desired point of delivery. The costs of the single-purpose alternatives (item 2) are compared to the corresponding benefits accruing to each purpose (item 3), and the smaller of these quantities (item 4) is selected. This procedure eliminates the danger of having to rely on unrealistic and expensive alternative projects.

The separable costs of the multipurpose project are estimated next (item 5). These costs are defined as those directly attributable to a specific purpose (e.g., transmission pipes that carry the potable water away from the dam), plus the portion of the joint costs (e.g., the dam) that is traceable to the inclusion of a specific purpose within the project. The remaining benefits (item 6) are defined as the difference between items 4 and 5. The residual joint costs (item 8) are the difference between the total project costs (item 1) and the separable costs (item 5). These residual joint costs are allocated to the different purposes (item 9) in direct proportion to the remaining benefits fraction (item 7). Finally, the sum of separable and allocated joint costs yields the total allocated costs (item 10).

The above process is unlikely to provide a very accurate apportionment of project costs, especially in the developing countries. However, such allocated costs are likely to amount to only a rather small fraction of the total costs of any given water supply system. Therefore, the impact of inaccuracies in the joint cost allocation exercise will not be too significant, on the economic and financial analysis of the water supply system.

274

TABLE 8.1 Separable Costs and Remaining Benefits (SCRB) Technique for Joint Cost Allocation: A Simple Two Purpose Example

Item	Project Purpose		
	A (Potable Water)	B (Hydropower)	Total
1. Total Multipurpose Project Costs			i
2. Alternative Single-Purpose Project Costs	a	b	
3. Benefits of Multipurpose Project	c	d	
4. Smaller of Item 2 or 3	c	b	
5. Separable Costs	e	f	(e+f)
6. Remaining Benefits (Item 4 - Item 5)	g=(c-e)	h=(b-f)	(g+h)
7. Remaining Benefits Fraction	[g/(g+h)]	[h/(g+h)]	1.0
8. Residual Joint Costs (Item 1 - Item 5)			k=[i-(e+f)]
9. Allocation of Residual Joint Costs	gk/(g+h)	hk/(g+h)	[i-(e+f)]
10. Total Allocated Costs (Item 5 + Item 9)	e+[gk/(g+h)]	f+[hk/(g+h)]	i

Environmental Impacts

Environmental considerations have to be included as much as possible in the determination of efficient water prices. As explained in Chapter 5, changes in the environment due to water and other sector activities, both negative and positive, can have considerable financial implications in terms of the ability to supply water to consumers at a given quality, quantity and cost. These factors must be included in the long-term calculation of costs to give a realistic estimate of the true costs of supplying water now and tomorrow. The concept of inter-generational equity is important in that logically, those responsible for externalities that have a future negative impact should bear a burden of the costs passed on to subsequent consumers. Pricing using LRMC provides a vehicle for this concept. For example, if the building of a new storage dam results in the flooding of land having ecological, recreational or agricultural value, then these costs should be reflected in LRMC. Similarly, if some of the water supply is derived from groundwater extraction, externality costs might be imposed on the economy in the form of damages caused to buildings or infrastructure due to land subsidence (see Chapter 4). Other long-term economic effects of groundwater extraction are the depletion costs and the deterioration of groundwater quality, which might impose further costs on future users of water, e.g., as the result of saline water intrusion (Munasinghe 1990). Costs are incurred in pumping from deeper depths and in the provision of relief or alternative supplies for communities reliant on low-cost appropriate pumping technologies that are rendered obsolete (for example, many of the hand-pumped hand-dug shallow wells in rural India).

While such environmental and depletion costs may be quite difficult to quantify, in certain cases they may already be included (at least partially) on the supply side, in terms of costs incurred to avoid environmental degradation or as a result of resource depletion. Costs associated with environmental protection are already being passed on to consumers in a number of developing countries (for instance, in Manila, the Philippines, where a 60% surcharge has been levied on the combined water and sewerage tariff to account for environmental protection). They are also included in the mitigation or preventive aspects of water supply project implementation and may already constitute up to 5% of development costs (as explained in the discussion of Environmental Assessment in Chapter 5). Using Manila as an example, Chapter 13 illustrates an approach to account for pollution costs in the case of groundwater extraction.

We might conclude from this brief discussion and those of Chapter 5 earlier that the total cost of using a water resource is generally the sum of three components:

1) the conventional resource cost of extraction, treatment, storage, bulk transmission, distribution and disposal;
2) the depletion cost due to higher expenditures imposed on future users of the same water source; and
3) the additional cost due to environmental degradation and damage, or cost of mitigating such adverse impacts.

Depending on the interpretation of definitions, there may be some overlap among these categories.

Shadow (Border) and Market Pricing

If the LRMC is calculated by using border shadow prices, it is necessary to make a further adjustment to convert this shadow priced LRMC into an equivalent optimal water price that will be perceived and interpreted by consumers like any other domestic market price. Thus, if only economic efficiency is considered, a typical expression for the optimal market price based on LRMC would be:

$$p_e* \quad = \quad (MCB_e / b) \qquad\qquad (8.16a)$$

where MCB_e is the LRMC calculated using border shadow prices (see Chapter 3).

As explained in Appendix A8.1, the value of b for a given consumer group depends on the expenditure pattern of these water users and, therefore, it is possible to have different prices P_e* for various categories of water consumers (e.g., residential, industrial), based on the same value of MCB_e.

It may sometimes be simpler to use an economy-wide average value of b, such as the standard conversion factor SCF, for all water consumers, especially when detailed information on different consumer categories is unavailable. Since usually SCF < 1 in such a case, the optimal market price is greater than the border priced LRMC, i.e.,

$$p_e* \quad > \quad MCB_e \qquad\qquad (8.16b)$$

Calculating Strict LRMC

Strict LRMC may be defined broadly as the incremental cost of optimal adjustments in the system expansion plan and system operations attributable to an incremental demand increase that is sustained into future. However, LRMC must be evaluated within a disaggregated framework. This structuring of LRMC is based chiefly on technical grounds and may include differentiation of marginal costs by time of use (season) or geographic area. The degree of structuring and sophistication of the LRMC calculation depends on data constraints and the usefulness of the results, given the practical problems of computing and applying a complex tariff (as previously outlined). Although in theory, the LRMC of serving each individual consumer at each moment in time may be estimated.

The calculation of strict LRMC is discussed below, with the structuring framework limited to one that is of operational value in a typical developing country. The methodology of computing LRMC is only summarized here because of space limitations, but points at which the computation may be pursued at a more sophisticated level are indicated in the text.

Cost Categories and Pricing Periods

Three broad categories of marginal costs may be identified for purposes of the LRMC calculations:

1) Marginal Capacity Costs:

- these are basically the investment costs of production, bulk transmission, and distribution facilities associated with supplying additional units. In the context of water supply pricing, the production and transmission cost analysis discussed below is done for typical bulk supply to the distribution system.

2) Marginal Operation and Maintenance Costs:

- marginal O & M costs are the costs of providing additional cubic meters of water.

3) Marginal Customer Costs:

- these are the incremental costs directly attributable to additional customers including costs of hook-up, metering, and billing.

Relevant other administrative and general (A & G) costs must also be allocated to these basic cost categories.

The first step in structuring is the selection of appropriate rating periods. By examining the patterns of demand imposed on the system, it is possible to determine periods during which demand presses on capacity, for example, in a given season of the year. Other aspects of structuring are introduced later in the discussion.

Estimating Average Incremental Costs (AIC)

Now we may proceed to estimate the Long-Run Marginal Cost (LRMC) of water supply. Usually the average incremental cost (AIC) of supply is a good approximation to LRMC. Briefly turn back to the schematic diagram of a typical water system shown in Figure 4.1. of Chapter 4. First, without differentiating between peak and off-peak supply periods, we may define the average incremental cost of water produced at the headworks by:

$$AIC_H \cdot \left[\sum_{t=L}^{T+L} \frac{Q_{1t}}{(1+r)^t} \right] = \left[\sum_{t=0}^{T} \frac{(I_{1t}+R_{1t})}{(1+r)^t} \right] \qquad (8.17a)$$

where:

I_{1t} = investment at the headworks in year t;
R_{1t} = incremental operating and maintenance (O&M) cost at the headworks in year t;
Q_{1t} = incremental water produced at the headworks in year t;
r = discount rate (e.g., opportunity cost of capital).

Thus the AIC is the unit cost which equates the present discounted value of water and the supply costs. Equation (8.17a) yields the result:

$$AIC_H = \frac{\displaystyle\sum_{t=0}^{T} \frac{(I_{1t}+R_{1t})}{(1+r)^t}}{\displaystyle\sum_{t=L}^{T+L} \frac{Q_{1t}}{(1+r)^t}} \qquad (8.17b)$$

In the above expression, the rationale for discounting I and R may be easier to understand than the case for discounting a physical quantity like Q. However, it is the monetary value of Q that is effectively discounted as can be seen from the original equation (8.17a).

Similarly, we may define the average incremental cost of water delivered through the: (a) trunk mains as AIC_T; (b) primary distribution as AIC_P; and (c) secondary distribution as AIC_S.

If we make allowances for losses (as defined in Figure 4.1), the AIC of water delivered at Level 2 is given by:

$$AIC_2 = \frac{AIC_H}{1-LF_1} \qquad (8.18a)$$

where $LF_1 = L_1/Q_1$ is the loss fraction at the headworks.

Similarly the AIC of water delivered at levels 3,4 and 5 are:

$$AIC_3 = \frac{AIC_2 + AIC_T}{1 - LF_2} \qquad (8.18b)$$

$$AIC_4 = \frac{AIC_3 + AIC_P}{1 - LF_3} \qquad (8.18c)$$

$$AIC_5 = \frac{AIC_4 + AIC_S}{1 - LF_4} \qquad (8.18d)$$

The above approach may be made somewhat more sophisticated by distinguishing between peak and off-peak supply. We recall that according to the peak demand pricing model developed earlier, the peak period price should include both investment and operating costs, while the off-peak price comprises only the operating costs.

Accordingly, we may define the peak period average incremental cost at the headworks by:

$$AICPK_H = \frac{\displaystyle\sum_{t=0}^{T} \frac{(I_{1t} + RPK_{1t})}{(1+r)^t}}{\displaystyle\sum_{t=L}^{T+L} \frac{QPK_{1t}}{(1+r)^t}} \qquad (8.19)$$

where:

RPK_{1t} = incremental O&M costs at the headworks in year t, to supply peak period water;

QPK_{1t} = incremental water produced at the headworks in year t, during the off-peak period.

Similarly, the off-peak AIC at the headworks may be defined by:

$$AICOP_H = \frac{\displaystyle\sum_{t=0}^{T} \frac{ROP_{1t}}{(1+r)^t}}{\displaystyle\sum_{t=L}^{T+L} \frac{QOP_{1t}}{(1+r)^t}} \qquad (8.20)$$

where:

ROP_{1t} = incremental O&M costs at the headworks in year t, to supply peak period water;

QOP_{lt} = incremental water produced at the headworks in year t, during the off-peak period.

All the equations (8.18a) through (8.18d) could be redefined in the same way to determine a set of peak and off-peak AIC at each level of the water supply system. The loss fraction (LF) is likely to be higher during the peak periods, (when pressure gradients and flow rates are greater) than during off-peak periods. If data is unavailable to discriminate between the two periods, then an average value of LF could be used for both peak and off-peak supply (as an approximation).

Next consider customer costs which are defined as those which can be readily allocated to users. There are two types: initial and recurrent:

- initial customer costs consist of nonrecurrent expenses attributable to items such as service connections, meters and labor for installation. These costs may be charged to the customer as a lump sum or distributed payments over several years; and
- recurrent customer costs that occur due to meter reading, billing, administrative and other expenses, could be imposed as a recurring flat charge, in addition to unit water charges.

Further disaggregation of costs to increase economic efficiency is possible by using "zonal pricing." In this approach, water prices increase as a function of the distance between a zone and a pumping station. The economic justification is that the cost of delivering water increases with distance due to increased energy for pumping and additional capital facilities required. When significant cost differences are not matched by differentiated rates, inefficiencies in development and use of water supply facilities are likely to occur (Schlenger 1986).

The World Bank Infrastructure Department reviewed projects initiated between 1966 and 1981 and found that the AIC of water (at 1988 US$) per cubic meter of water was $ 0.49 whereas the average tariff on water sold was $ 0.26. Since unaccounted for water averaged at 35% for all the projects, the effective price per cubic meter produced was $ 0.17 or only 1/3 of the incremental cost of production. A similar analysis for the period 1987-1990 yielded an AIC of US$ 0.55 (at 1988 US$) and an average price of $ 0.32 per cubic meter, not allowing for unaccounted for water (World Bank 1990).

Not only are AIC's generally greater than tariffs, but they are actively increasing due to the more difficult water supply conditions prevailing in many developing countries. According to Falkenmark et al. (1990), there is growing evidence that the AIC of urban water supplies are commonly 2 to 3 times greater than the cost of existing water supply schemes. Table 8.2 confirms this for a selected number of developing countries.

TABLE 8.2 AIC's of Existing and Future Water Supply Projects for Selected Developing Countries (1988 US$)

Country	Present Project	AIC $/m^3$	Future Project	AIC $/m^3$
Algeria-Algiers	Groundwater	0.23	Surface Water (raw)	0.50
Bangladesh-Dhaka	Groundwater	0.08	Surface water	0.30
China-Shenyang	Groundwater	0.04	Surface water	0.11
China-Yingkuo	Groundwater	0.07	Reservoir intakes	0.30
India-Hyderabad	Reservoir ph2	0.17	Reservoir ph3	0.62
India-Bangalore	Pumped (river)	0.10	Pumped (river)	0.22
Jordan-Amman	Groundwater	0.41	Surface - piped	1.33
Mexico-Mex. City	Groundwater	0.54	Pumped (river)	0.82
Peru-Lima	Surface	0.25	Inter-basin transfer	0.54

Source: Various World Bank reports.

Peak and Off-Peak Marginal Costs

Consider Table 8.3 which shows some typical examples of marginal costs of water supply. Although the developing country data do not differentiate between peak (dry) and off-peak (wet) seasons, the US and Australian data show how the per unit costs of water supplied during peak periods exceed those of off-peak periods, sometimes by a substantial margin.

Where appropriate and practical, the higher marginal costs of supply during peak demand periods should be reflected in tariff structures so that water users are confronted with them at such times. If they are not, consumption during peak periods would be larger and during slack periods somewhat lower. This point is illustrated in Figure 8.4, where as indicated earlier, the demand during the peak period D_{pk} is greater than off-peak demand D_{op}. If a uniform, non-differentiated tariff P_{av} was used that reflects some average of the off-peak and peak period marginal supply costs, the quantity consumed during the peak period would be equal to Q_1. However, if true peak periods costs P_{pk} were charged, consumption would be reduced to Q_m instead. As a result, overall capacity needs would be lower.

During the off-peak period, water consumption would tend to be correspondingly greater (i.e., increase from Q_2 to Q_4) because of the lower price P_{op} relative to the averaged-out price. Another reason for increased consumption during that period would be the partial, inter-temporal substitution from the higher-priced peak period to the off-peak period. Hence the consequence of a peak period tariff would be an overall reduction in needed total supply capacity together with a more efficient, i.e., more uniform,

TABLE 8.3   Typical Values for Marginal Costs of Water Supply
(current prices: 1986-87 for developing countries and 1979-80 for developed countries)

Country	Project	Marginal Cost (US$/ cu meter)
Brazil	Sao Paulo State Water Sector Project	0.35
Haiti	Port-Au-Prince Water Supply Project	0.30
Philippines	Metropolitan Manila Water Distribution Project	0.35
Saudi Arabia	Taif Madina	0.10 0.08
Nigeria	Lagos Water Supply Project	0.23
Yemen (Dem. Rep.)	Al Mukalla Water Supply Project	0.69
U.S.A.	New York State Water Supply	Winter : 1.21 Summer : 2.73
Australia	Perth Water Supply	Winter : 0.096 Summer : 0.176

Sources: Hanke 1981a, 1981b, Riziaza 1991, and World Bank data.

utilization of the remaining capacity. This would lead to overall reductions in marginal costs and resulting prices paid by water users.

Sewerage Charges and Pollution Externalities

Decisionmakers must not forget to consider the costs of dealing with wastewater generated by the provision of increasingly higher service levels of supply to a growing population. These are not static costs and vary considerably to the extent that they are borne by consumers themselves or by the wider community or public authority. They must be included in an appropriate water tariff or levied as a separate charge such as a sewer fee based on water consumption. Costs may be incurred in the form of building and running sanitation and treatment facilities, or in terms of the environmental costs generated by wastewater-related impacts such as drinking water supply pollution, reservoir eutrophication, loss of work though illness, or reduced property values, etc. Examples from Jakarta have shown that as service levels increase to consumers, costs to the municipality from handling wastewater decrease, as long as environmental impacts are essentially restricted to their community of origin. However, as environmental impacts of higher service levels extend beyond community boundaries (due to sewerage outflow), The Municipality of Jakarta and Government of Indonesia's costs increase. Linear increases in the amounts of wastewater generated by a higher service level have been seen to require exponential increases in collection and treatment costs (Gunnerson 1989).

The importance of considering the incremental costs of sanitation must not be underestimated. In fact, where sanitation is provided by a separate agency or is not integrated into the water supply plan, serious cost underestimates can be made. Effective sanitation is always more costly than the water supply from which it is generated. At a low service level (handpump and pit-latrines), the ratio is around 1.3:1 and is often absorbed by the users as a self-help input or through cost-recovery. As the service level rises from around 20 to 700 lcd, this ratio becomes around 15:1. The ratio for Jakarta is around 4.5:1 for communities with disposal of on-site waste to a surface drainage system (Gunnerson 1989)

The principles of charging for piped sewerage services are an extension of those described earlier for piped water supply, since the disposal of liquid wastes through a sewerage system is the logical complement to the provision of water via household connections. Mainstream opinion holds that if significant environmental externalities are likely to occur from provision of a water supply without a corresponding sanitation or sewerage collection, disposal and treatment system, then the cost of a such a system should be factored into the tariffs charged for water connection and consumption. The benefits in terms of health and welfare of providing a water system without a means of disposing of waste (as in the case in many developing countries as shown by the imbalance in rural and urban water coverage compared to sanitation) are questionable and often short-lived. The marginal cost of dealing with wastewater can be calculated by using the AIC method, based on investment cost required to conduct sewerage from the consumer through the collection system to the treatment plant (where relevant) and hence back into water courses. The basic AIC at each level of the sewerage system must be adjusted for losses. As pointed out in Chapter 4, leakages of outside effluents at various levels in the sewerage collection network actually increase the flow volume. Thus, in Figure 4.2 (Chapter 4), the AIC at level 8 is given by:

$$AIC_8 = AIC_7 + AICT_s \, (1+LF_7) \qquad (8.21)$$

where:

AIC_7 = average incremental cost at level 7;
$AICT_s$ = average incremental cost of trunk sewerage pipe.

The AIC of sewerage services estimated above can be added to the marginal costs of water supply to obtain a combined charge.

However, two particular issues arise which are worth considering. First, for the combined water and sewerage charge it is conceptually difficult to separate the benefit derived by consumers from each service, or to measure their willingness to pay for water and sewerage separately since they do not usually consider this to be two distinct decisions. This issue is important for investment analysis but is not so critical for pricing purposes. Consumers adjust their consumption of water to the point where, at the margin, they derive a benefit per unit of water used that equals the cost of both supply and disposal.

Second, externalities, which are probably much more important in the case of sewerage than water supply, relate to benefits enjoyed by those besides the customer who actually pays the bill. The aesthetic and health benefits enjoyed by the community at large, due to sewerage service, are usually obvious. However, this is a matter of degree because there are also indirect external health benefits enjoyed by the community due to water supply. While consumers should pay the marginal cost of all sewerage disposal wherever possible, there is therefore, an economic case for offering some form of subsidy to low-income consumers who cannot take into account the external benefits to the community at large in their willingness-to-pay decision (as well as in their ability-to-pay).

Consideration of sewerage charges also leads us logically to the general questions of charging for pollution. In principle, the contamination of surface or groundwater resources by wastewater or sewerage sludge will give rise to costs that should be included in the sewerage charges (see Chapter 4). This is often done on the established "polluter pays" principle.

Adjustments to Strict LRMC to Meet Other Objectives

As briefly explained earlier, once efficient water prices based on strict LRMC have been determined, the second stage of pricing to meet social, financial, political, and other constraints must be carried out. We note that efficient water prices deviate from the prices calculated on the basis of financial costs because shadow prices are used instead of the market prices. This is done to correct for distortions in the economy. Therefore, the constraints that force further departures from efficient prices (in the second stage of the pricing procedure) may also be considered as distortions that impose their own shadow values on the calculation.

Financial Viability

The financial constraints most often encountered relate to the revenue requirements of the sector, and are often embodied in criteria such as some target financial rate of return on assets, or an acceptable rate of contribution towards the future investment program. In principle, for state-owned water utilities, the most efficient solution would be to set price equal to marginal cost and rely on government subsidies (or taxes) to meet the utility's financial needs. Marginal cost pricing at the market clearing point also helps to restrain the tendency of a profit maximizing monopoly enterprise to equalize marginal revenue with marginal cost. In general, in most developing country projects financed by the World Bank, expected average tariffs are well below the continuing increase in the AIC of new service. This creates a need for heavy public sector subsidies, for example for Egypt these total in the range of US$ 5-10 billion per year (World Bank 1990).

In practice, some measure of financial autonomy and self-sufficiency is an important goal for the sector. Because of the premium that is placed on public funds, a marginal cost pricing policy which results in failure to achieve minimum financial targets for continued operation of the water sector, would rarely be acceptable. The converse and more typical case, where marginal cost pricing would result in financial surpluses well in excess of traditional revenue targets, often leads to consumer resistance. Therefore in either case, changes in revenues have to be achieved by adjusting the strict marginal cost based tariffs.

Financial Viability Criteria

A widely used criterion of financial viability is the utility's potential to earn an acceptable rate of return on assets, for example, the net operating income after taxes given as a fraction of net fixed assets in operation plus, in some cases, adequate working capital. In the case of private utilities, for example, in the US, the regulatory authorities have traditionally imposed a fair rate of return as an upper limit on earnings (and therefore, on average price per unit sold). Where utilities are government owned, as in most developing countries, the target rate of return is usually considered a minimum requirement to help resist sociopolitical pressures that tend to keep prices too low. If the asset base is defined in revalued terms, then this requirement is more consistent with the forward-looking approach of LRMC. Another future oriented financial criterion that is especially useful when the system expands rapidly, requires the utility to make a reasonable contribution to its future investment program from its own revenues. This self-financing ratio is often expressed by the amount of internally generated funds available after operating expenses and debt service, as a fraction of capital expenditures.

The application of the financial criteria often raises serious conceptual and practical problems. Thus, if a rate of return test is to be used, then the question of asset revaluation arises. The use of historical costs for working assets, typically original cost less depreciation, would tend to understate their value when capital costs are rising rapidly (for instance under conditions of high inflation). If assets are to be revalued, the cost of either:

- exactly reproducing the water system at today's prices; or
- replacing it with an equivalent system, also at today's prices;

might be used after netting out depreciation to allow for the loss of value corresponding to the economic and functional obsolescence of existing equipment. Significant difficulties of interpretation clearly will occur in the practical application of either application of either approach.

Adjustments of Tariffs to Achieve Financial Goals

Whichever criterion or combination of criteria is used, it is important that the initial tariffs based on strict LRMC be included in the utility's financial forecast. Then these first round tariffs may be adjusted through an iterative process until the chosen parameters of financial viability fall within the acceptable range. Although this process is usually quite ad hoc, some practical guidelines may be effectively used for reconciling strict LRMC and the revenue requirement. The relative adjustments to strict LRMC between major consumer categories like residential and industrial, as well as among the different rating periods (like peak and off-peak) within a given consumer category, will determine the share of the revenue burden to be borne by each user group in a given rating period.

The simplest practical method of adjustment, which also appears to be the most equitable, is to retain the relative structure of LRMC and vary the average rate level by equiproportional changes. In general, this procedure will not be economically efficient.

The Ramsay approach is based on the price elasticity of demand (i.e., the percentage change in demand for a one percent change in price). If the elasticity is low, the demand curve will be steep (see Figure 8.1), and a change in price will have only a small effect on water consumption. This is highly desirable when deviating from strict LRMC, because the change from the optimal water use level will be small. Such an analysis leads to the inverse elasticity rule where by the greatest (least) divergence from strict LRMC occurs for the consumer group and rating period where the price elasticity is lowest (highest). This is the most satisfactory adjustment procedure from the viewpoint of economic efficiency (Baumol and Bradford 1970). In the case of two goods, the following expression applies:

$$\frac{1 - LRMC_1/p_1}{1 - LRMC_2/p_2} = \frac{1/e_1 + 1/e_{12}}{1/e_{21}} \tag{8.22}$$

$LRMC_i$ and p_i are the strict LRMC and price, respectively, of good i; while:

$$e_i = (\frac{\partial Q_i}{\partial p_i}) / (\frac{Q_i}{p_i}) \tag{8.23}$$

$$e_{ij} = (\frac{\partial Q_i}{\partial p_j}) / (\frac{Q_i}{p_j}) \tag{8.24}$$

are the own and cross price elasticities, respectively, of demand Q with respect to price p (where o is the term for a partial differential). The two goods 1 and 2 may be interpreted as either the water consumption of two different consumer groups in the same rating period or the consumption of the same consumer group in two distinct rating periods. In practice, a larger number of consumer types and rating periods must be considered and application of the rule will be limited by lack of data on price elasticities (as explained in Chapter 6) and the need to use subjective estimates. This technique may appear to penalize some customers more than others, thus violating the fairness objective.

Adjustments involving lump-sum payments/rebates or changes in customer and connection charges are also consistent with economic efficiency provided consumers water usage is relatively unaffected by these procedures, i.e., consumption depends mainly on the variable, regular charges. However, the magnitude of the adjustments that can be made may not change revenues sufficiently. Another related approach for reducing revenues is to charge strict LRMC only for marginal consumption and reduce the price for an initial block of water use. These subsidies on customer charges or on the initial consumption block can also be tailored to satisfy the lifeline rate requirement for poor consumers (described in Section 8.4.2 below), but such measures tend to complicate the price structure.

In practice, an eclectic approach involving a combination of all the methods discussed above is most likely to be successful.

Failure to Recover Costs

The results of a recent study of water supply projects summarized in Table 8.4, indicate that revenues never reach the levels which were projected when the project was undertaken (Garn 1987). The reasons for this include inaccurate demand estimates, inappropriate technology or equipment design,

TABLE 8.4   Discrepancy Between Expected and Actual Cost Recovery for 54 Water
Supply Projects, Completed Before 1980

Year after loan effectiveness	Cost Recovery (average annual ratio of sales revenue to operation and maintenance costs)	
	Expected	Actual
1	1.74	1.63
2	1.82	1.44
3	1.98	1.37
4	2.10	1.68
5	2.07	1.56
6	2.09	1.61

Source: Garn 1987.

and a lack of community involvement in the planning process. For example, in the rural subsector of the Philippines, the Rural Water Works Development Corporation is the main institution for water and sanitation infrastructure provision. The monthly tariff rates for consumers are calculated to cover all operating costs, service debts and allow for a reasonable profit by charging level III water and sanitation system consumers (house and sewer connection) a higher tariff and allowing them to cross-subsidize smaller, poorer ones with level I systems (well and handpump, and latrine). However, the corporation has low overall collection efficiency, collecting only around 30% of its billings in 1986 (Montrone 1988a). Non-revenue water averaged around 50% in the last 17 years. Hence the financial viability of the corporation is undermined. Whilst consumers can afford to pay the tariffs which are 2 to 5% of their income, many consider the systems to be a government gift and are unwilling to pay (Montrone 1988b).

Another major reason that revenues fail to attain projected levels is that while the average customer could afford the monthly commodity charges, a high connection fee prevents initial hook-up. For this reason, in many water systems the funds necessary to provide the connection are now provided out of a special fund where customers can receive subsidized financing over a period of years, or included as an implicit part of the monthly service or commodity charge levied on all or a selected class of customers (World Bank 1985). For example, in Thailand, Village Public Health Development Revolving Funds are used to assist villagers in securing a water supply and sanitation system (usually water tanks and latrines). Repayment is made over 10 or 20 monthly installments with 1% interest per month (Tunyavanich 1988), although poor farmers may pay twice yearly after harvesting. To

TABLE 8.5   Terms and Conditions for Financing Connection Charges

Country	Year	Water	Sewer	Interest Rate	Years	Percent Financiable
Tunisia	1982	X		6.5	20	100
Guatemala	1986	X	X	10.00	5	100
Ecuador	1986	X		8.50	5	100
Indonesia	1985 (a)	X		0.00	5	50
India	1985 (b)	X		8.75	10	100

Source: World Bank data.
(a) Starting in 1989.
(b) Financing is available to qualified customers for all materials required to extend the water line from the property boundary to the tap inside the dwelling.

illustrate common examples of different financing methods, Table 8.5 shows the rates and terms for connection in five selected countries.

As inferred above, in many cases it is possible to set the connection fee so low that financing is not necessary, e.g., the current practice in Brazil. Ordinarily, it is desirable to require a small connection fee even if its financial benefit for the utility is negligible. This is because it gives the customer an opportunity to express his desire and willingness to pay for the service, and also signals him that the service will involve an ongoing financial obligation. Financial participation allows a consumer to exercise choice and to play a role in the planning, implementation and management of their individual supply system.

Katko (1990), discusses the following useful factors for successful cost-recovery:
- tariffs must be affordable to consumers;
- consumers must be willing to pay for water services;
- appropriate water charges and tariff structures must be developed; and
- the charges must be collected and channelled into the intended uses within the water sector.

Subsidized or Lifeline Rates

Sociopolitical or equity arguments are often advanced in favor of "lifeline" rates for water, especially where the costs of water consumption are high in comparison to the relevant income levels. While the ability of water utilities to act as discriminating monopolists permits such tariff structuring, the appropriateness of the "lifeline" rate policy and the size of the tariff blocks requires detailed analysis.

The Lifeline Rate Concept

It is generally recommended that a stepped tariff structure be adopted since it encourages consumers to save water and avoid misuse and wastage (WHO 1988). Care must be taken not to set the lower threshold (the lifeline level) too high such that the costs of supplying basic needs exceeds the ability of poor households to pay. In a study of tariff structures around the world, the WHO (1986) found that increasingly, progressive tariffs are being adopted. The number of countries doing so in the Americas was over 80%, in the Mediterranean and SE Asia over 60%, in Africa over 50% and in the Western Pacific around 40%.

In general, water resources planners have commonly assumed that a community should be provided with the highest level of service that can be obtained for less than 5% of the income of households in the community. For example, in the Philippines, urban centers of more than 20,000 inhabitants are served by Water Districts (WDs). Their tariff structures are generally calculated so that low-income families do not pay charges in excess of 5% of their income (Montrone 1988a). According to Katko (1990), an appropriate lifeline block for developing countries should be a minimum of 10-15 lcd.

The concept of a subsidized "social" block, or "lifeline" rate, for low-income consumers has another important economic rationale, based on the income redistribution argument. We clarify this point with the aid of Figure 8.5 which shows the respective demand curves AB and GH of low (I_1) and average (I_2) income domestic users, the social tariff P_s over the minimum consumption block 0 to Q_{min}, and marginal cost based price level p_e. If the actual tariff $p = p_e$ then the average household will be consuming at the "optimal" level Q2, but the poor household will not be able to afford the service. If increased benefits accruing to the poor have a high social weight or value, the consumer surplus portion ABF should be multiplied by the appropriate social weight (greater than unity). Then, although in nominal market prices the point A lies below p_e, the weighted distance OA could be greater than the marginal cost of supply. The adoption of the increasing block tariff shown in Figure 8.5, consisting of the lifeline rate ps, followed by the full tariff p_e, helps to capture this "weighted" consumer surplus of the poor user, but does not affect the optimal consumption pattern of the average consumer, if we ignore the income effect due to reduced expenditure of the average consumer for the first block of consumption, i.e., up to Q_{min}. In practice, the magnitude Q_{min} should be based on acceptable criteria for identifying "low-income" groups, and reasonable estimates of their minimum consumption levels (e.g., sufficient to supply basic requirements for drinking, washing and cooking).

In many developing countries where average water use is low, the base average water demand for a small community of 3000 people varies between

UNIT PRICE

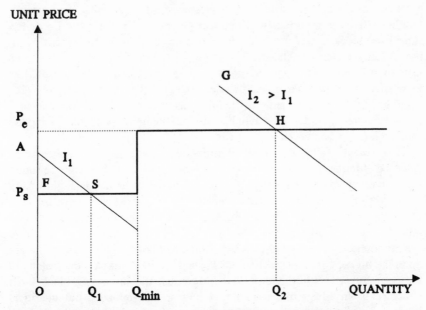

Figure 8.5 Welfare Economic Basis for Social Block and Lifeline Rates

2 and 4 cubic meters per capita per month, Qmin is usually under 1 cubic meter per capita per month. For the price p_s, one simple welfare model (see Appendix 8.1) yields:

$$p_s = [strict\ LRMC\ x\ (poor\ persons\ income/critical\ income)] \qquad (8.25)$$

where the critical income is like a nationally established poverty line. Sometimes, too low a service level is selected for the lifeline rate and households are not willing to pay for the service, for example, for an inconveniently located handpump. On the other hand, many will be willing to pay more than 5% of their income for a better service such as a house connection (Whittington et al. 1989).

Perversities of Lifeline Rates and Subsidized Blocks

The utility's revenue constraints and the ability to pay of the poor consumer would also be considered in determining ps and Q_{min}. This approach may be reinforced by an appropriate connections policy (e.g., subsidized house connections, etc.). From the viewpoint of economic theory, it would be more efficient to price all consumption at marginal cost, but provide lump sum subsidies to compensate poor consumers. However, this raises formidable practical problems of identifying and specifically targeting low-income families. This is notoriously difficult in practice. On the other hand, the subsidized block approach avoids the above problem by assuming that water use and income are correlated. Therefore, violation of this hypothesis could lead to regressive effects (i.e., poorer groups paying a higher price). In general, unless low-income beneficiaries are carefully targeted, the subsidies could end up benefitting better off families, as shown in Table 8.6. Perverse cross subsidies should also be avoided, such as the urban poor subsidizing the rural rich (see Chapter 9).

In a recent study of Ghana, Whittington (1990) explains how poorly designed lifeline rates and increasing block tariffs (IBT) can be quite regressive. Two reasons are pinpointed. First, households in high-density areas, who often share a single water connection, must pay more per unit under IBT structures than households that share a connection with only a few others. The second reason is that many low-income families do not have private connections and purchase water from neighbors, who in turn get caught up in the higher cost consumption blocks, and are likely to pass them along to the poor buyer. Whittington (1990) states that the increasing block tariff structure is an illustrative example of how a well-intended but uncritical transfer of policies from developed countries to the developing world can have unexpected and undesirable results. In the 1990 yearly review of the Water Supply and Sanitation Sector, the World Bank discussed the need to investigate the role of the tariff structure and the nature of punitive effects on low-income groups and the perversities of subsidization which can often benefit the wealthier consumers (World Bank 1990).

Cross Subsidization

The Nature of Subsidies

The issue of subsidization between different customer groups within a class arises because urban customers often subsidize rural customers by paying more in relation to the LRMC of their water supply than the latter. Large consumers are also made to cross subsidize smaller, usually lower-income consumers. In this manner, a uniform national tariff can be implemented to help accomplish certain specific policy goals, based on sociopolitical reasons such as maintaining a viable regional industrial or agricultural base, stemming rural to urban migration, or alleviating local political discontent. For example, in November 1985, Algeria instituted a uniform national water tariff despite the fact that the estimated average cost of water varied between 1987 US$ 0.23 and 0.58 (World Bank 1987). While the national tariff recovered the costs of the sector as a whole, it also resulted in local water companies having widely varying profits and losses. In Tunisia, the national water company,

TABLE 8.6 Beneficiaries of Subsidized Rural Water Services

Country	Income Level		
	Low	*Medium*	*High*
India			
Index of the density of water supply points per locality	0.8	1.9	2.5
Kenya			
Percentage of families with connections	34	54	66
Republic of Korea			
Percentage of families with connections	53	66	77
Colombia			
Percentage of families with connections	16	18	24

Source: Briscoe and de Ferranti 1988.

SONEDE, charges a uniform tariff that permits cross-subsidization among different water systems to avoid prohibitive charges in high-cost systems (World Bank 1982). Meanwhile, in the Hashemite Kingdom of Jordan, the government provides free water to nomadic populations at up to ten times the cost in the country's large cities (World Bank 1986). In Malawi, large consumers have been allowed to cross-subsidize lower lifeline rate consumers within a common national tariff that also allows the losses of unprofitable supply systems (i.e., costs higher than revenue raised by common national tariff) to be offset by profits generated by cheaper systems in areas where water source conditions are more favorable (Wyss 1988).

While the full economic benefits of such a course of action may be greater than the efficiency losses which arise from any divergence between actual price and strict LRMC, the rationale for such deviation from efficient prices must be thoroughly studied. For example, one advantage of cross-subsidization versus say, taxation, is that rate structures can be used to develop a direct scheme for transfers among customer groups. Tariffs which perform this cross subsidization within a customer class are highly useful in redistributing income, provided higher incomes and greater water consumption are positively correlated. Such a tariff is equivalent to a tax on consumption which can be collected in a discriminatory fashion, with little possibility of evasion.

However, subsidization across service sectors is generally difficult and not advisable. For example, if a state enterprise supplies both water and electric service, the tariffs for each should be independently determined. While it may seem unnecessary to perform this exercise as long as the combined revenues from both sources allows the enterprise to remain financially viable as a whole, over time it will become almost impossible to avoid sending incorrect price signals to individual customers. Also, if only one sector experiences a significant exogenous shock, i.e., when the electricity sector experiences a sharp increase in oil prices, then finding a justification for raising the price in both sectors may be a difficult task. For example, the state enterprise in Istanbul that provided water, electricity and transport services faced severe problems of this nature in the last decade.

Cross subsidization might also occurs over time when, due to tightened financial constraints, water utilities seek capital contributions from new water service customers. These are referred to as buy-in charges, latecomers' fees, connection charges, tap fees or system development charges (OECD 1987). Much controversy has risen in the United States around this issue, where proposals were tabled to make new customers pay more per unit of consumption than old customers (Hanke and Wenders 1982). Economically there is little reason to discriminate between old and new customers. The old customer's marginal unit of consumption is as much responsible for system extension as the new customer's first unit. Higher unit charges to new customers (beyond initial once-and-for-all hookup and other costs) effectively boils down to subsidizing the old consumers.

The Developing Country Context

Pressures to subsidize water supply are likely to be more significant in a developing country than a developed one, because of the high cost of water relative to incomes in the former. Also, the available administrative and fiscal machinery to redistribute incomes, or achieve regional and industrial development objectives by other means, is frequently ineffective in developing nations. For the same reason, it is particularly difficult to reform pricing policy where low incomes and a tradition of subsidized water supply combine to create extreme sociopolitical difficulties in raising prices to anywhere near marginal costs. The impact of local politics on water tariffs is often considerable. Many water authorities are only semi-autonomous and their pricing policies are subject to approval from directors, councils or governments. Their political influences often result in postponement, reduction or cancellation of proposed tariff increases (Summerfield 1988). In practice, price changes have to be gradual, bearing in mind the costs which may be imposed on those who have already incurred expenditures on equipment and made other decisions, while expecting little or no change in traditional water pricing policies. The efficiency costs of gradualism can be seen as an implicit shadow value placed upon the social benefits that result from this policy.

Previously, many development projects were aimed at providing free water supplies to poor urban and rural communities as a basis for further socioeconomic development. Notwithstanding the problems created for the sustainability of systems due to the lack of a sense of ownership or responsibility amongst recipients, in most developing countries where full coverage is far from attained, the supply of free water to any given consumer implies that the service will not be extended to others who have an equal right to it (WHO 1988). The mainstream opinion is now that users should pay for their water, both for connection to supply systems and for continued use. Whilst poorer consumers should not necessarily pay full costs, they should pay a proportion at least, depending on the potential for cross-subsidization. However, since poor households are growing at a much faster rate than large consumers, this potential for cross-subsidy based on differential tariffs is receding.

The macroeconomic type argument that water price increases may be inflationary is rarely valid because even in developing countries, the costs of water use are usually a small proportion of most household's income and of industrial production costs. In contrast, the over-stimulation of demand and lack of funds to expand supply, resulting from low water prices are potentially much more serious long-run problems that should not be ignored.

Perhaps the biggest drawback facing cross subsidization in developing countries is that each year, its scope is being reduced as a result of the imbalance between the fast-growing low-income population and the stagnating or declining large consumers group.

Metering Decision and Price Complexity

The Relationship Between Tariffs, Metering and Billing

Owing to both the practical difficulties and the economics of metering and billing, the tariff structure may have to be simplified. Another crucial factor is that the tariff structure must be comprehensible to the average customer. Otherwise, individuals will not be able to adjust their consumption according to the price signals. Therefore, the number of customer categories, consumption blocks, and fixed charges will have to be limited. On the other hand, more detailed price structures could indicate price signals to consumers, more efficiently.

Seasonal tariffs could be instituted and metered by standard volumetric metering equipment without significant additional costs. Seasonal tariffs can be justified on equity as well as efficiency grounds, because consumers would be confronted by the true seasonal supply costs of their consumption. Seasonal price differentials may not always lead to major substitutions from peak to off-peak periods uses, especially when postponing water consumption for several months could be rather impractical. The main effects on consumption might come from a genuine reduction in demand in response to the higher seasonal price (i.e., a movement along a given demand curve).

Metering of residential demand over short periods (days or weeks) is a more difficult problem because the costs of an average sized household water meter would increase several fold. Thus, the use of time-of-use metering devices would not be economically justified for residential users in low-income countries, if the net benefits realized through savings in water used were less than the increased costs of the more complex metering. The costs of time-of-use metering are much less of a problem for larger users, such as large commercial establishments or industrial plants, because the added costs of metering are likely to be small relative to the amount of water consumed. Most peak period pricing schemes, therefore, have concentrated on such users, although several developed countries have attempted to apply such tariffs in the residential sector as well.

The degree of sophistication of metering, for example, by time of use, should be determined by the net benefit of metering, the practical problems of installation and maintenance, ease of billing, and so on. The arguments for metering are twofold, equity and efficiency (OECD 1987). The equity argument for metering is that it permits volumetric charging, which means payment according to the quantity of water used. The economic rationale for making the metering decision depends on the net benefit of metering based on a cost-benefit analysis that compares the lower supply costs of reduced consumption with the cost of metering and billing plus the decrease in net consumption benefits (see Appendix 8.1 for details).

Although the residential sector is often a major contributor to the extra peak period costs, the use of peak period metering is unlikely to be justified for the household sector. This means that peak period pricing schemes can only be partially applied. On equity as well as efficiency grounds the full utility system marginal cost differential between off-peak and peak periods should not be charged against those users that can be metered. To achieve economically efficient consumption patterns among them, they should be confronted with no more than their proportional share of the total added costs of peak period supplies. For example, if metered users account for, say, 40% of total peak period consumption, their peak period tariffs should be raised to cover 40%, but no more, of the added costs of peak period supply. The other 60% should added into the averaged-out LRMC-based uniform tariffs of the remaining groups. It should be noted that the three prices charged to the various user groups -- off-peak and peak period prices to users with appropriate metering, average prices to all others -- should be based on the respective long-run marginal costs, i.e., total incremental costs including the costs of new investments, as described earlier.

Two part tariffs, consisting of a fixed capacity charge and volumetric water charges are widely used in order to reflect the higher costs of peak-load supplies. The fixed portion of such tariffs are usually based on the installed capacity of equipment (size of processing equipment) or the maximum capacity of the supply connection (size of supply pipe). Another alternative is to install metering devices that register the maximum demand (or flow rates) in a given meter reading interval. While such tariffs are relatively easy to implement and administer, they do not really solve the peak-load problem. This is so because the capacity charge is invariant with respect to time. In other words, the charge is the same regardless of the period of time in which the full installed capacity is utilized. No incentive exists to users to reduce consumption during peak periods. Hence, while overall installed user capacity might be lower in response to prevailing capacity charges, consumption patterns of installed capacity would not be affected. Time-of-use metering, therefore, is a more preferable demand management and pricing tool.

The discussion in this section has proceeded as if there existed only one basic type of user and marginal cost and two periods of on-peak or off-peak. This is an obvious simplification. Many different user classes exist, and the marginal costs of supply to them will differ as well. Peak demand periods may well be broken down into more discriminating time periods to better reflect variations in the marginal costs of supply.

The Nature of Metering

To reiterate briefly, the degree of sophistication of metering depends on the practical problems of installation and maintenance, and the net benefit of metering, based on a cost benefit analysis that compares the lower supply costs of reduced consumption with the cost of metering plus the decrease in net consumption benefits (Lund 1988, Munasinghe 1990b). Recently, advanced solid-state technology (including use of microprocessors) is being examined to implement sophisticated metering, automatic meter reading, demand management techniques and pricing structures (Gestler 1985, Schweppe et al. 1987). In contrast, some developing countries may lack technically skilled labor for installation and maintenance of sophisticated meters, or even reliable meter readers. Therefore, choice of appropriate metering is usually very country specific, and is likely to involve many practical considerations.

Despite these country-specific requirements, at least for urban water systems in developing countries it is always preferable to meter at both ends of the distribution system. This is because historically the amount of unaccounted for water in these systems greatly exceeds that found in comparable systems in industrial countries. Thus, metering provides a reliable method to compare the amount of water produced to the amount actually delivered to customers and, thereby, losses can be estimated and steps taken to reduce them when they exceed a predetermined level. It is also postulated that metering water use discourages waste, even at standposts where no money is charged, and in this way acts as a powerful psychological agent to promote efficient use of resources (Sims 1978).

As a useful summary, the WHO (1988) has itemized the pros and cons of metering water supplies to consumers as a cost-recovery mechanism in the developing country context:

1) Pros of metering water supply:

- increase in revenue;
- equity;
- reduction of misuse and wastage;
- conservation of water resources;
- more accurate economic costing and pricing providing signals to increase and decrease consumption;
- use of a single parameter (volume);
- differential tariff structures according to volume consumed;
- possibility to calculate meaningful lifeline rates, to predict average revenue and growth in demand;
- improvement of the commercial accounting organization, management and control of a public utility; and
- better technical control of water supply systems (subject to adequate master metering -- i.e., identification of system losses).

2) Cons of metering water supply:

- cost (acquisition in foreign currency, installation, preventive maintenance, inspection, repairs);
- consumers' reactions to defective meters (vandalism, non-payment);
- irregular income (as opposed to fixed rates);
- high levels of under-registration and other technical problems (adaptation to local conditions);
- logistic and other difficulties related to inspection and reading (on which billing and collection depend);
- high level of accuracy required prior to computerization;
- billing system purely volumetric and impersonal perhaps not adapted to equity objectives; and
- poor reliability of supply may be an obstacle to consumers' willingness to pay for metered consumption.

Common Tariff Forms

Probably the most common form of tariff is the unit charge based on the customer's consumption over a given period of time, typically one month. Unit charges may also be varied according to the volume of water consumed, yielding two basic types of block tariff structures. Incorporation of the increasing block structure in applying the LRMC-based methodology has already been discussed, particularly in the section on social or subsidized prices.

Decreasing Block Tariffs

Rationale

The decreasing block tariff, in which the initial slab of consumption has the highest price followed by successively cheaper blocks has been widely used especially for households and small consumers with simple metering. Such rate structures were widely used by the 1950s, for example, they were recommended by the Water Rates Committee of the American Water Works Association (AWWA 1957). The rationale for this policy included arguments that:

- the utility could recover some of the fixed customer costs through the high priced initial block even though water consumption was low;
- the first block corresponded to the high cost of supplying the customers during peak period for water demand, whereas additional consumption was mainly caused by off-peak appliance use that could be supplied at relatively low cost;
- the utility should encourage increased consumption to realize economies of scale in production;
- price discrimination could be used to extract the maximum revenue from smaller users who had low price elasticities of demand while also encouraging consumption of larger users who were more sensitive to high prices; and
- if temporary excess capacity existed, for example, when new plants are developed, higher consumption should be encouraged to collect the maximum potential revenues.

Broader Considerations

All of these arguments ignore the fact that if any portion of the decreasing block tariff is significantly below LRMC, it signals the consumer that water is much cheaper than it really is, thus encouraging wasteful consumption. A more appropriate pricing policy recognizes at least the following:

- if customer costs must be recovered then single or recurring fixed charges should be used;
- unless there is clear evidence that customers with greater consumption (in a given user category) impose lower costs on the system, any additional water consumed by all consumers will be equally costly to supply. Therefore, there would be little basis for price discrimination according to consumption level;
- even if economies of scale exist at the aggregate level of the utility, they do not apply in the case of the variable costs to individual customers. In fact, few utilities currently exhibit any economies of scale, and real unit costs of supply in the long run are rising;
- it must not be generally assumed that the consumption of larger users would be more sensitive to price;
- using up any short-run excess capacity is costly in the long run, because if demand growth is unduly stimulated, investments in capacity expansion must be advanced; and
- the decreasing block rate tends to be regressive and unfair, because it penalizes poorer consumers who generally use less, but must pay higher prices per unit purchased (see also, earlier discussion of lifeline tariffs and increasing block tariffs).

Fixed Charges

Fixed charges are most often related to consumer costs as described earlier. A lump-sum payment may be levied to cover the initial cost of providing the service connection or, as discussed above, the repayment period may be spread over several years to provide relief to customers. Recurrent fixed costs are charged to meet the costs of meter reading, billing, and other repetitive expenses. In some cases, the charge based on the capacity of a consumer's connection is also called a fixed charge, but this is usually a proxy for the capacity cost which should be included in the variable charge.

Surcharges and Adjustment Clauses

Surcharges or adjustment clauses are also becoming increasingly common. This permits the utility to quickly pass on to the consumer any unforeseen increases in operating costs. Ideally, any changes in relative input prices would require re-estimation of strict LRMC followed by changes in the tariff structure, but the legislative procedure to achieve the latter may take a long time. A convenient short-run adjustment clause can, meanwhile, provide much needed financial relief when cost inflation is significant, as is the case in many developing countries today.

References

Abu Rizaizi, O.S. 1991. "Residential Water Usage: A Case Study of the Major Cities of the Western Region of Saudi Arabia." *Water Resources Research*. 37, pp. 667-671.

AWWA. 1957. *Water Rates Manual*. New York: American Water Works Association.

Baumol, W.J., and D. Bradford. 1970. "Optimal Departures From Marginal Cost Pricing." *American Economic Review*. 67, pp. 350-365.

Boiteux, M. 1949. "La tarification des demandes en pointe." *Revue Generale de l'Electricite*. 58.

Bowers, J. 1990. *Economics of the Environment -- The Conservationists' Response to the Pearce Report*. British Association of Nature Conservationists.

Dupuit, P. 1932. "De l'Utilite' et de sa Mesure." *Annales Des Ponts et Chausees*. Vol. 8, 1844, reprinted in *La Reforma Soziale*. Turin, Italy.

Eckstein, O. 1958. *Water Resource Development*. Cambridge, MA: Harvard University Press.

Falkenmark, M., M. Garn, and R. Cesti. 1990. *Water Resource: A Call for New Ways of Thinking*. INUWS Paper. Washington DC: The World Bank.

Garn, H.A. 1987. *"Patterns in the Data Reported on Completed Water Supply Projects*. Washington DC: The World Bank.

Gestler, D.J. 1985. "Centralized Meter Reading: An Overview of Developments to the Present" in Proceedings *AWWA Seminar on Customer Metering Practices*. Annual Conference, Washington DC. Denver: American Water Works Association.

Gunnerson, C.G. 1989. *Responding to Diseconomies of Scale in Water Supply and Sanitation*. Unpublished Extension of Paper Presented at the Conference on Water and the City. Chicago: APWA.

Hanke, S.H. and J.T. Wenders. 1982. "Costing and Pricing for Old and New Customers." *Public Utilities Fortnightly*.

_____. 1981a. "On the Marginal Cost of Water Supply." *Water/Engineering & Management*. pp. 60-63.

_____. 1981b. "Distribution System Leak Detection and Control" in *Water Engineering and Management, Reference Handbook 81*. pp. R-107-108.

Hotelling, H. 1938. "The General Welfare in Relation to Problems of Taxation and of Railway and Utility Rates." *Econometrica*. 6, pp. 242-269.

Katko, T.S. 1990. "Cost Recovery in Water Supply In Developing Countries." *Water Resources Development*. 6, pp. 86-94.

Lund, J.R. 1988. "Metering Utility Services: Evaluation and Maintenance." *Water Resources Research*. 24, pp. 802-81.

Montrone, G.E. 1988a. "CWS Organization in the Philippines." Annex V/VII in *WHO Draft Guidelines on Cost Recovery in Community Water Supply and Sanitation. Preliminary Draft Report of the Third Informal Consultation on Institutional Development*. Geneva: World Health Organization.

_____. 1988b. "Cost Recovery in the Philippines." Annex V/IX in *WHO Draft Guidelines on Cost Recovery in Community Water Supply and Sanitation*.

Preliminary Draft Report of the Third Informal Consultation on Institutional Development. Geneva: World Health Organization.

Munasinghe, M. 1990. *Managing Water Resources to Avoid Environmental Degradation*. ENV Paper No. 41. Washington DC: The World Bank.

_____. 1990. "The Pricing of Water Services in Developing Countries." *Natural Resources Forum*. 15.

OECD. 1987. *Pricing of Water Services*. Paris: Organization for Economic Co-operation and Development.

Ruggles, N. 1959a. "The Welfare Basis of the Marginal Cost Pricing Principle." *Rev. of Economic Studies*. 17, pp. 29-46.

_____. 1959b. "Recent Developments in the Theory of Marginal Cost Pricing." *Rev. of Economic Studies*. 17, pp. 107-126.

Schlenger. D.L. 1986. *The Application of Zonal Pricing To a Metropolitan Water Utility*. Doctoral Dissertation. Chapel Hill: University of North Carolina.

Schweppe, F., M. Caramanis, R. Tabors, and R. Bohn. 1987. *Spot Pricing of Electricity*. New York: Kluwer Publishing Co.

Sims, J.H. 1978. "The Sociopsychology of Responses to Resource Issues" in D. Holtz and S. Sebastian (eds.). *Municipal Water Systems*. Bloomington: Indiana University Press.

Summerfield, M.T. 1988. "Water Demand Management in Cities of Kenya, Pakistan and Syria." Annex V/III in *WHO Draft Guidelines on Cost Recovery in Community Water Supply and Sanitation. Preliminary Draft Report of the Third Informal Consultation on Institutional Development*. Geneva: World Health Organization.

Swallow, S.K., and C.M. Marin. 1988. "Long-Run Price Inflexibility and Efficiency Loss for Municipal Water Supply." *Journal of Environmental Economics and Management*. 15, pp. 233-47.

Tunyanavich, N. 1988. "Use of Revolving Funds in Thailand." Annex IX/II in *WHO Draft Guidelines on Cost Recovery in Community Water Supply and Sanitation. Preliminary Draft Report of the Third Informal Consultation on Institutional Development*. Geneva: World Health Organization.

Whittington, D., M. Mujwahuzi, G. McMahon, and C. Kyeongae. 1990. *A Note on the Use of the Increasing Block Water Tariff Structures in Developing Countries*. Infrastructure and Urban Development Department Working Papers. Washington DC: The World Bank.

_____. 1989. *Willingness to Pay for Water in Newala District, Tanzania: Strategies for Cost Recovery. WASH Field Report No. 246*. Arlington: Water and Sanitation for Health Project.

WHO. 1988. *Draft Guidelines on Cost Recovery in Community Water Supply and Sanitation. Preliminary Draft Report of the Third Informal Consultation on Institutional Development*. Geneva: World Health Organization.

_____. 1986. *The International Drinking Water Supply and Sanitation Decade, Review of National Progress (as of December 1983)*. Geneva: World Health Organization.

World Bank. 1990. *Water Supply and Sanitation -- FY90 Sector Review*. Infrastructure Department. Washington DC: The World Bank.

_____. 1987. *Algeria: Second National Water Supply & Sewerage Project*. Staff Appraisal Report No. 6582a. Washington DC: The World Bank.

_____. 1986. *Hashemite Kingdom of Jordan: Jordan Water Supply and Sewerage Project*. Staff Appraisal Report No. 6056-JO. Washington DC: The World Bank.

Wyss, D.K. 1988. "CWS Accounting and Commercial Practices in Malawi." Annex IX/III in *WHO Draft Guidelines on Cost Recovery in Community Water Supply and Sanitation. Preliminary Draft Report of the Third Informal Consultation on Institutional Development.* Geneva: World Health Organization.

Appendix 8.1

Model for Optimal Water Pricing
Using Shadow Prices

In this appendix, a general expression for the socially optimal price for water is developed, based on shadow prices, to compensate for distortions in the economy. From the general equation, results for optimal water pricing are derived for cases which reflect:

- a perfectly competitive economy (classical result);
- efficient prices, including economic second-best considerations; and
- subsidized social prices or lifeline rates for poor consumers.

The supply and demand for water is shown in Figure A8.1.1, where S is the supply curve represented by the marginal cost of supply (evaluated at domestic market prices), and D is the corresponding demand curve for a specific consumer. Starting with the initial combination of price and consumption (p,Q), consider the impact of a small price reduction (dp), and the resultant increase in demand (dQ), on the net social benefits of water consumption.

Before evaluating the net social benefit of this price change, let us define the shadow-pricing framework. First, suppose we calculate the long-run marginal cost of supply MC without shadow-pricing, i.e., in market prices. Then a_p is defined as the water conversion factor (ECF) that transforms MC into the corresponding real economic resource cost, i.e., with correct shadow-pricing, the LRMC is $MCB_e = (a_p \cdot MC)$. Second, we assign a specific social weight W_c to each marginal unit of consumption (valued in market prices) of a given individual i in the economy. For example, if this user of water is poor, the corresponding social weight may be much larger than for a rich customer, to reflect society's emphasis on the increased consumption of low-income groups. Third, if the given individual's consumption of goods and services other than water (valued in market prices) increased by one unit, then the shadow-priced marginal cost of economic resources used (or the shadow cost to the economy) is b_c.

As a result of the price reduction, the consumer is using dQ units more of water, which has a market value of $(p \cdot dQ)$ (i.e., area IFGH). However, the consumer's income has increased by the amount $[pQ - (p-dP) \cdot (Q+dQ)]$, and assuming none of it is saved, this individual's consumption of other goods and services will increase by the amount $(Q \cdot dp - p \cdot dQ)$, also valued in market prices (i.e., area BEFG minus area IFGH). Therefore, the consumer's total

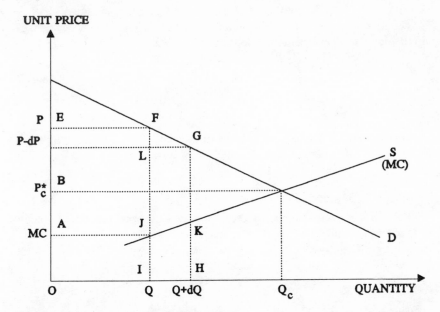

Figure A8.1.1 Supply and Demand for Water

consumption, water plus other goods, will increase by the net amount $(Q \cdot dp)$ in market prices. This is the traditional increase in consumer surplus benefits. The shadow value of this increased consumption is $[W_c \cdot (Q \cdot dp)]$, where W_c is the social weight appropriate to this consumer's income/consumption level.

Next consider the resource costs of these changes in consumption. The shadow cost of increasing the supply of water A is $(a_p \cdot MC \cdot dQ)$, (i.e., a_p times area IJKH), and the resources used up to provide $[b_c \cdot (A \cdot dp - p \cdot dQ)]$ (i.e., the other additional goods consumed), where a_p is the conversion factor for water, and b_c is the conversion factor for other goods consumed by this consumer. Finally, the income change of the producer of water (if any) must also be considered but this effect may be ignored if we assume quite plausibly that the producer is the government.

The total increase in net social benefits due to the water price decrease is given by:

$$NB = W_c(p \cdot dQ) - a_p(MC \cdot dQ) + (W_c - b_c)(Q \cdot dp - p \cdot dQ) \qquad (A8.1.1)$$

Therefore:

$$\frac{dNB}{dp} = Q[(W_c - b_c) + n \cdot b_c] - n \cdot a_p \cdot (\frac{MC}{p}) \qquad (A8.1.2)$$

where $n = (p \cdot dQ)/Q \cdot dp)$ is the elasticity of demand (magnitude).

The necessary first order condition for maximizing net social benefits, is $d(NB)/dp = 0$. This yields the optimal price level:

$$p^* = \frac{a_p \cdot MC}{b_c + (W_c - b_c)/n} \qquad (A8.1.3)$$

This expression may be reduced to a more familiar form, by making some simplifying assumptions outlined in the following cases:

Case 1

There is a perfectly competitive economy, where market prices and shadow prices are the same and income-transfer effects are ignored, i.e., no social weighting. Therefore, $a_p - W_c = b_c = 1$, and equation (A8.1.3) reduces to

$$p_c^* = MC \qquad (A8.1.4)$$

This is the classical marginal cost pricing result where net social benefits are maximized when price i set equal to marginal cost at the market-clearing point (p^*_c, Q_c) in Figure A8.1.1.

Case 2

Income-transfer effects are ignored because the marginal social benefit of consumption is equal to the marginal social cost to the economy of providing this consumption. Therefore, $W_c = b_c$, and equation (A8.1.3) becomes:

$$p_e^* = (a_p \cdot MC)/b_c = MCB_e/b_c \qquad (A8.1.5)$$

This is the optimal efficient price that emphasizes the efficient allocation of resources and neglects income-distributional considerations.

As mentioned earlier, the long-run marginal cost of water (MCB_e) may usually be evaluated in a straightforward manner (i.e., in the case of a non-tradable like water, by applying the appropriate shadow prices to the least-cost mix of technically-determined inputs used in production). However, the conversion factor b_c depends crucially on the type of consumer involved.

For residential consumers of water, bc represents the consumption conversion factor (CCF), which reflects the resources cost or shadow value of one (market-priced) unit of the household's marginal consumption basket. If the CCF < 1, then:

$$p_e^* > MCB_e \qquad (A8.1.6)$$

If it is not possible to determine the consumption patterns of specific consumer groups, then bc could be defined very broadly as the average conversion factor for all water users, e.g., the SCF, as discussed in the text.

Case 3

This is the most general case. Equation (A8.1.3) is the optimal water price when shadow prices are used that incorporate income-distributional concerns.

Consider the case of a group of very poor consumers for whom we may assume: $W_c >> b_c (n - 1)$. Therefore, equation (A8.1.3) may be written:

$$p_s^* = n \cdot MCB_e / W_c \qquad (A8.1.7)$$

An even greater simplification is possible if it is assumed that n = 1, thus:

$$p_s^* = MCB_e / W_c \qquad (A8.1.8)$$

For illustration, suppose that the income/consumption level of these poor consumers (c) is 1/3 the critical income/consumption level ($\underline{c}$) which is like a poverty line. Then a simple expression for the social weight is:

$$W_c = \underline{c}/c = 3 \qquad (A8.1.9)$$

Therefore, the "lifeline" rate or subsidized tariff appropriate to this group of low-income consumers is:

$$p_s^* = MCB_e / 3 \qquad (A8.1.10)$$

Appendix 8.2

Peak Period Pricing and the
Metering Decision

Figure A8.2.1 depicts the analysis underlying the metering decision to implement a two-period, time-of-use tariff for water supply. D_{pk} and D_{op} are the demand curves for an average day during the peak and off-peak seasons of the year, each season lasting D days and (365 - D) days, respectively. If a simple uniform price P_{av} is levied throughout the use, the seasonal consumption will be $Q_1 \cdot D$ and $Q_2 \cdot (365 - D)$ cubic meters respectively during the peak and off-peak periods. Instead, if a two-period tariff (P_{pk}, P_{op}) is charged during the peak and off-peak seasons, the corresponding levels of consumption will be $Q_3 \cdot D$ and $Q_4 \cdot (365 - D)$. Suppose that the LRMC of supplying a cubic meter of water during the peak and off-peak periods are MC_{pk} and MC_{op}, respectively, where the former includes both capacity and operating costs and the latter includes only the operating cost.

The net annual consumption benefit of the uniform tariff is given by:

$$
\begin{aligned}
NB_I &= B_I - C_I \\
&= [\{OGIJ\} \cdot D + \{OFRM\} \cdot (365-D)] \\
&\quad - [Q_1 \cdot D \cdot MC_{pk} + Q_2 \cdot (365-D) \cdot MC_{op}]
\end{aligned}
\tag{A8.2.1}
$$

Where the symbol {...} denotes the relevant area indicated.

Similarly, the net annual consumption benefit of the two-period tariff is given by:

$$
\begin{aligned}
NB_{II} &= B_{II} - C_{II} \\
&= [\{OGHL\} \cdot D + \{OFNK\} \cdot (365-D)] \\
&\quad - [Q_3 \cdot D \cdot MC_{pk} + Q_4 \cdot (365-D) \cdot MC_{op}]
\end{aligned}
\tag{A8.2.2}
$$

Therefore, the increment or change in net annual benefits is:

$$
\begin{aligned}
\Delta NB &= NB_{II} - NB_I \\
&= [\{MRNK\} \cdot (365-D) - \{LHIJ\} \cdot D] \\
&\quad + [(Q_2-Q_4) \cdot (365-D) \cdot MC_{op}] + [(Q_1-Q_3) \cdot D \cdot MC_{pk}]
\end{aligned}
\tag{A8.2.3}
$$

A further simplification is possible if it is assumed that the two-period tariff reflects strict LRMC; that is $P_{pk} = MC_{pk}$ and $P_{op} = MC_{op}$. Then, $(Q_4 - Q_2) \cdot MC_{op} = \{MSNK\}$, and $(Q_1 - Q_3) \cdot MC_{pk} = \{LHTJ\}$. Therefore, the following result is obtained:

PRICE PER UNIT

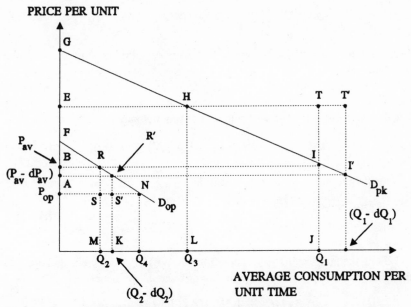

Figure A8.2.1 Economics of the Complexity of Price Structuring

$$\Delta NB = [\{HTI\} \cdot D] + [\{SRN\} \cdot (365 - D)] \qquad (A8.2.4)$$

We now introduce the time dimension into the analysis. Let the stream of incremental net annual consumption benefits computed as described above during each year of the lifetime (T years) of the metering installed, be denoted by $\Delta NB_1, \ldots, \Delta NB_t, \ldots, \Delta NB_T$.

Similarly let the difference between the two streams of metering and billing costs (installation, maintenance, administration, etc.) associated with the two-period and uniform tariffs be $\Delta C_1, \ldots, \Delta C_t, \ldots, \Delta C_T$ over the lifetime T of the metering. If the condition:

$$\sum_{t=1}^{T} \frac{(\Delta NB_t - \Delta C_t)}{(1+r)^t} > 0 \qquad (A8.2.5)$$

is satisfied, implementation of the two-period price structure would be economically justified.

Even if the decision to install more complex metering is negative, further analysis is helpful. Thus, it is clear from equation (A8.2.4) that applying the uniform price P_{av} instead of the strict LRMC prices $P_{pk} = MC_{pk}$ and $P_{op} = MC_{op}$, will result in an annual loss of net efficiency benefits:

$$\Delta NB_1 = [\{HTI\} \cdot D] + [\{SRN\} \cdot (365-D)] \qquad (A8.2.6)$$

The level of P_{av} may be adjusted, however, to minimize this loss of net benefits.

Suppose that a reduction in price from P_{av} to $(P_{av} - dP_{av})$ results in increased water consumption given by $(Q_1 + dQ_1)$ and $(Q_2 + dQ_2)$ in periods 1 and 2 respectively. The new annual net benefits may be written:

$$\Delta NB_2 = [\{HT'I\} \cdot D] + [\{S'R'N\} \cdot (365-D)] \qquad (A8.2.7)$$

The change in net efficiency benefit is:

$$
\begin{aligned}
d(\Delta NB) &= \Delta NB_2 - \Delta NB_1 \\
&= [(MC_{pk}-p_{av}) \cdot dQ_1 \cdot D] - [(p_{av}-MC_{op}) \cdot dQ_2 \cdot (365-D)]
\end{aligned}
\qquad (A8.2.8)
$$

Using the familiar first-order condition $d(\Delta NB)/dP_{av} = 0$ yields the optimal uniform price that will minimize the loss of annual net benefits:

$$p_{av}^* = \frac{[D \cdot (dQ_1/dP_{av}) \cdot MC_{pk} + [(365-D) \cdot (dQ_2/dP_{av}) \cdot MC_{op}]}{[D \cdot (dQ_1/dP_{av})] + [(365-D) \cdot (dQ_2/dP_{av})]} \qquad (A8.2.9)$$

This result may be generalized. Thus, suppose the tariff analyst wishes to consolidate n pricing periods during the years, where D_i is the duration, Q_i is the average daily consumption, and MC_i is the LRMC during the ith period. The optimal uniform price would be:

$$p_{av}^* = \frac{\sum_{i=1}^{n} [H_i \cdot (dQ_i/dP_{av}) \cdot MC_i]}{\sum_{i=1}^{n} [H_i \cdot (dQ_i/dP_{av})]} \qquad (A8.2.10)$$

Note that derivatives of the form $D_i.(dQ_i/dP_{av})$ refer to a change in consumption during a given pricing period i due to a uniform change in price across all the pricing periods that need to be consolidated under the single price regime. Generally, in most countries, information on demand would be inadequate to determine the magnitude of such derivatives accurately. In this case, a practical approximation might be:

$$p_{av}^{*} = \frac{\sum_{i=1}^{n} [H_i \cdot Q_i \cdot MC_i]}{\sum_{i=1}^{n} [H_i \cdot Q_i]} \qquad (A8.2.11)$$

Here the uniform price is set equal to the weighted average LRMC using the consumption levels in the different pricing periods as the weights.

9

Rural and Low-Cost Water Supply

The rigorous analysis of supply and demand, as well as pricing policy, on a systematic basis has so far been presented mostly in the context of centralized piped and pumped water supply systems for larger population centers. However, in the 1980s, due to the initiatives of the International Drinking Water Supply and Sanitation Decade, considerable attention has been focused on the problems of rural and low-cost water supply and sanitation development applicable to the growing and increasingly marginalized rural communities (see also Chapter 1). Prior to the 1980s, the rate of water supply development was not keeping pace with population growth in many developing countries (Saunders and Warford 1980). Those systems that were constructed frequently suffered breakdowns with resulting water supply shortages and interruptions. Sanitation had been even more neglected in comparison, with few viable solutions offered to the problems of safe, and environmentally sound sewerage disposal in dispersed rural communities. The Water Decade sought to focus the efforts of the donor community and national governments on the widespread introduction of low-cost, appropriate technologies. Significant lessons have been learned which can be applied to development efforts in the 1990s and beyond. These include the need to switch attention from external aid driven development to internal cost-recovery based development, in particular permitting maximum advantage to be made of the capabilities of the private sector, non-governmental organizations and beneficiaries themselves. The main policy and technology issues specific to low-cost rural system development are discussed in this chapter.

Rural Water Supply and Development

For many decades, rural water supply has been promoted by enthusiasts as a major driving force for the development of the rural areas of the third world. The expectations, particularly in the 1960s and 1970s, included:

- rapid economic growth and improvements in the quality of rural life, especially of the poor;
- improved health and hygiene;
- increasing use of water for productive activities in agriculture, industry, and commerce; and
- modernization and other attitudinal changes.

Such hopes were not surprising, given that water resource development has played a significant role in improving living conditions in rural areas of the developed nations. This was particularly true for agricultural development in terms of domestic food production and production of valuable revenue-generating export crops.

On the other hand, skeptics were quick to point out numerous potential problems that might interfere with such optimistic scenarios. In fact, many of their concerns have been realized. Some of the difficulties that continue to plague rural water supply efforts in many developing countries, include:

- scarcity of capital, especially of foreign exchange;
- high costs and poor quality of supply;
- disappointing demand growth;
- low benefits and productivity gains; and
- perverse distributional effects, with benefits favoring the rich rather than the poor.

A number of studies and assessments of rural water supply programs have been carried out during the past decade, by the developing countries as well as donors of foreign aid. Sufficient time has now elapsed to build up a body of experience and information, based on the evolution of rural water supply efforts in the developing countries, especially those that had launched early initiatives in this area. Therefore, it is now possible to establish a more convincing, realistic, and balanced picture of both the promises and pitfalls facing rural water supply development in the 1990s and beyond.

Some Features of Rural Water Supply

In 1988, the world's population numbered over 5.0 billion, of which roughly 4 billion lived in the developing countries (World Bank 1990). Given that over 65 percent of the latter live in rural areas, usually under difficult conditions, the magnitude of the rural water supply and development problem is very great.

The status of water supply in the developing world has been summarized in Chapter 1, and includes a detailed breakdown of rural water supply availability by major geographic region (see especially Table 1.2). This table shows that wide variations exist in the degree of rural water and sanitation services provided among different regions of the world. There are similar differences among the individual countries within a given region. Table 9.1 shows the access to safe water supply in rural areas of selected developing countries in 1980 prior to the International Decade. The projected estimates of achievements by the year 2000 are also listed. It is clear that variations, both regional and global are striking. For example, Bangladesh and Pakistan are relatively similar in size and sociocultural background but have markedly different levels of access to safe water. According to the figures presented in Chapter 1, Latin America and the Mediterranean appear to be best served, and East Africa the worst. There does appear to be a general link between high levels of access to water in rural areas and the period of time for which serious rural water supply efforts have been pursued with strong government support in a given country. This point was previously raised in discussions on institutional frameworks in Chapter 2.

For a more specific picture of variations within a single region, the WASH Project has recently prepared country profiles for 20 African nations (WASH 1989). Their data on water supply and sanitation coverage is summarized in Table 9.2, which shows the degree of improvement (and hence investment) required to boost coverage levels in the water sector. Although this data is for both rural and urban areas, they are still revealing because Africa is still predominantly rural. The coverage levels in rural areas would be much lower than the overall national coverage. With coverage for water supply and sanitation averaging 38 % and 21 % respectively for this broad cross-section of countries (whose GNP per capita varies from US$ 150 to US$ 910), the task is clearly considerable. Some countries have much farther to go than others, for example Ivory Coast has only 37 % lacking access to safe water, whereas Uganda has 86 % lacking access. The degree to which sanitation has lagged behind water development can clearly be seen, with only 4 of the 20 countries having a greater coverage for sanitation than for water.

At a very general level, there are several salient points that have emerged through the analysis of past experience. First, rural water supply is a tool for national socioeconomic development, and should be treated like any other policy instrument. In particular, it should be subject to the same rational analysis, and closely coordinated with the other policy tools available to the government of a developing country, to meet national objectives and goals.

Second, in a related vein, the integrated rural development approach (which can be considered as a smaller-scale application of the IWRP concept) has proved itself in many instances. For example, health improvements depend on education, consumer awareness, water supply, sanitation, economic development, etc. (see Lindskog and Lundqvist 1989). Water supply alone is unlikely to automatically entail development, and may in fact be costly and ineffective if developed in isolation. In many earlier development projects,

TABLE 9.1   Rural Population and Water Supply for Selected Countries

Region Country	Rural Population		1980 Rural Access to Safe Water %
	1980 *(millions)*	*2000* *(estimate)*	
East Africa			
Ethiopia	27.4	41.9	2
Kenya	14.4	28.4	4
Malawi	5.4	9.2	29
West Africa			
Burkina Faso	5.7	9.2	23
Nigeria	64.1	107.9	25
Latin America			
Brazil	39.4	31.1	57
Mexico	23.3	24.7	51
East Asia & the Pacific			
Indonesia	117.4	129.9	18
Philippines	30.3	38.1	33
South Asia			
Bangladesh	79.0	119.2	55
India	527.5	632.4	20
Pakistan	62.7	88.6	17
Mediterranean			
Egypt	22.8	29.5	50
Tunisia	3.0	3.1	25

Source: After A. A. Churchill 1987.

water supply had been considered the entry point or catalyst on which subsequent wider and broader regional socioeconomic development would hinge. However, it is now felt that a set of infrastructural services would be much more likely to result in greater benefits and welfare improvements through synergistic effects. Such a comprehensive package would include not only water supply, but also some or all of the following:

- agricultural extension services and inputs;
- rural and agricultural credit;
- irrigation;
- incentives for small business, agro-industries, and cottage industries;
- roads and transport;
- schools and educational facilities;

TABLE 9.2   Population, Water Supply and Sanitation Data for 20 African Countries

Country	Population 1988 millions	Lacking Water millions	Lacking Sanitation millions	Lacking Water %	Lacking Sanitation %
Benin	4.5	2.1	2.9	46.7	64.4
Burkina Faso	8.5	2.9	7.5	34.1	88.2
Burundi	5.2	3.9	2.2	75.0	42.3
Cameroon	10.5	5.5	6.0	52.4	57.1
Guinea	6.9	5.2	6.0	75.4	87.0
Ivory Coast	11.9	4.4	9.3	37.0	78.2
Kenya	23.3	16.5	16.7	70.8	71.7
Liberia	2.5	1.2	2.0	48.0	80.0
Malawi	7.7	4.6	4.7	59.7	61.0
Mali	8.7	6.5	6.9	74.7	79.3
Niger	7.2	3.9	6.6	54.2	91.7
Nigeria	112.0	68.1	100.7	60.8	89.9
Rwanda	7.1	3.6	3.1	50.7	43.7
Senegal	7.3	3.5	4.1	47.9	56.2
Sudan	24.0	15.4	20.4	64.2	85.0
Swaziland	0.7	0.6	0.5	89.6	74.6
Tanzania	24.3	16.0	8.9	65.8	36.6
Togo	3.3	1.3	2.9	39.4	87.9
Uganda	16.4	14.1	14.7	86.0	89.6
Zaire	33.3	21.9	30.4	65.8	91.3
	Total 325.3	*Total* 201.2	*Total* 256.5	*Average* 61.9	*Average* 78.9

Source: WASH 1989.

- hospitals and health care facilities;
- rural markets;
- communications facilities;
- rural electrification; and
- other services.

Sanitation should be added to this list if it is not implicitly integrated into the water supply development program.

Third, rural water issues cannot be separated from the overall context in which they are embedded. Although some decoupling is possible, rural water supply must be analyzed (to the extent possible) within an integrated framework that includes the broader water resources sector, and the overall macro-economy. At the same time, rural water supply and rural development are inextricably intertwined, and rural development itself is only one aspect of overall national development. Planners in developing countries must decide the relative priorities of projects and how a given level of coverage can be achieved with the available government investment, or increasingly, with private and community resources.

Fourth and finally, recognition of the dynamic nature of rural water supply is an important key to successful implementation. The institutional framework, demand forecasting, design and planning of networks, operation and maintenance practices, methods of financing, assessment of socioeconomic benefits and costs, and other aspects must be tailored to the often rapid evolution and growth of rural demand and the system that serves them. Focusing on the start-up phase of a new rural water supply scheme and initial investment is only the first step. Continued attention must be paid to financing and maintaining the level of services to water consumers in the scheme area over a long period of time, as load growth continues. Operation and maintenance programs for rural and low-cost water supply and sanitation schemes have been poorly developed up to now and require greater attention in the future (Bastemeijer and Visscher 1990).

In this connection, the issue of timing is also important. For example, rural water supply benefits may be best realized in areas which have already reached a certain level of development. Therefore, it may be prudent sometimes to begin only with minimum water supply facilities (e.g., a few wells), to achieve immediate health related and other social benefits in a particularly depressed area, while delaying the introduction of a more sophisticated system until other complementary elements of infrastructure are in place, or local incomes have increased further. By contrast, excessive delays in supplying water to relatively advanced rural areas may force villagers to rely on less effective and unsafe alternatives such as polluted sources. This may be a much more costly supply option from the long-term national economic viewpoint, and thus should be preempted by accelerating the provision of water to such areas. The perspective taken in relation to these issues will vary considerably from country to country based on political as well as economic considerations.

Status of Rural Water Supply in Developing Countries

For the purposes of economic planning, it is rather difficult to define the term rural water supply very precisely, because it is interpreted and used with wide variations, in different countries. Frequently, rural water supply schemes are defined in terms of local administrative units, mainly for convenience of implementation. For example, the Indonesian government uses the kabupaten (or provinces) as the basic geographic unit, broken down further into three types of rural agglomerations: swasembada, swakarya, and swadaya desa (villages). Similarly, there are thanas in Bangladesh, villages in Colombia, douars and communes in Morocco, and barrios and towns in the Philippines. Such rural communities range from groups of 10 or more houses (Tunisia) and dispersed groups of farms (Brazil), to small towns exceeding 40,000 inhabitants (Thailand and the Philippines).

Broadly defined, rural water supply schemes would generally cover regions where agricultural activity (including agro-industries) was dominant, the ratio of labor to capital used in production was high, and incomes were low on average, relative to urban areas. Water use intensities would also be relatively low, because the number of connections per km of line, and the water use per connection tend to be small relative to urban areas. At the same time, costs per connection and per liter supplied would be significantly higher, operation and maintenance more problematic, and the quality of supply lower. Often small or medium sized towns (population up to 50,000) in a rural area may be included in rural water schemes, or suburban areas of larger cities. In fact, from the socioeconomic and demographic viewpoint, the rural-urban gradation may often be continuous, and the terminology "regional water supply" is sometimes used to indicate programs covering a mix of rural farms, villages and small towns. From the planning and engineering design perspective, the load and customer density are among the chief parameters which would help to distinguish between urban and rural water supply systems.

Water can be introduced into a rural area in several ways:

- private isolated sources such as wells or boreholes powered by a variety of means including muscle power, or diesel or electric motors, serving a single consumer (for example a business enterprise, farm or small village);
- private isolated sources serving several consumers who are connected by a local pipeline system, for example a small community;
- public supplies from a centrally supplied system; and
- mixed systems dependent on the nature and distribution of available/potable water sources (i.e., regional and local groundwater, artesian springs and surface water).

Typically, these are not distinct ways to introduce water into a rural area. Rather, they might sometimes occur sequentially when more than one supply option exists, or systems can be upgraded along with socioeconomic developments. This procedure involving several phases of water supply can be thought of as an initial building up of demand for rural water, by means of more individual private supplies, up to a point where it becomes economically feasible (in most cases) to connect to a public central network.

We conclude this section by reviewing some of the broad impacts of rural water supply. While many recent studies of past rural water supply efforts in the developing countries are available, the disciplines and viewpoints of the authors, and the rigor with which the data has been collected and analyzed, vary widely. Sometimes, different analysts have provided conflicting interpretations of the same set of facts. Nevertheless, the following broad consensus appears to have emerged concerning the impact of water supply on the rural areas of the Third World. More specific benefits and their measurement are discussed at greater length in Chapter 3.

Related Developments in Other Sectors

Rural water supply promotes agricultural development best when certain complementary inputs such as electricity, agricultural and financial services, and others mentioned earlier, are also available. However, subsidized water supply prices may conceal the reality that the economic costs of a public water system may often exceed the costs of alternative sources.

Rural water supply may help to stimulate agro-industrial and commercial activity, although the direction of causality is not completely clear. In other words, rural areas that are ready for sustained growth are likely to be selected early to benefit from water supply, and will also exhibit rapid demand growth.

Real Impacts

Domestic consumers perceive a significant improvement in their living conditions, mainly due to the improved quality and quantity of water available, for which they are willing-to-pay far more than their incomes might suggest. Health and other social benefits could accrue to individuals, especially where other factors such as literacy, basic education in public health, and income levels, are favorable (Saunders and Warford 1976). Water supply improvements do have considerable potential to help improve health. However, several attempts to measure the impact of water supply and sanitation on improved health have been inconclusive. The main reason is that, in order for the potential to be fully realized, sanitation, hygiene and hygienic behavior are as important for health as clean water (Falkenmark 1982, Briscoe and de Ferranti 1988, Cairncross 1989).

As far as the willingness-to-pay is concerned for sewerage services, Churchill (1987) found that rural water consumers are much less willing to contribute a significant share of the costs of improving sewerage services, on a sustained basis, than are urban consumers.

Reading skills, literacy levels, and education are positively correlated with households connected to water systems, but the direction of causality is not clear. Thus, more ambitious and motivated families may be the ones who would acquire a water connection first.

Limitations

Demand growth and beneficial impacts are often hampered by not recognizing the dynamic nature of rural water supply. Poor planning, inadequate maintenance and follow-up, overloading of systems, and poor supply quality, are some of the undesirable consequences. There is a tendency for the benefits of rural water supply to accrue mainly to the more prosperous villages and better off and influential persons (wealthy landowners, politicians, and local officials), unless the program is well designed and the poorer beneficiaries carefully targeted. In such circumstances, rural water supply generally may not be a good method for achieving income redistributional or social-equity oriented objectives. Furthermore, care must be exercised to ensure that perverse effects do not occur, such as water revenues obtained from the urban poor being utilized to subsidize the rural rich. This problem was previously discussed in Chapter 7.

There is little or no evidence for many of the other major benefits that are proposed, like increased employment opportunities, reduced rural to urban migration, and so on. Increased access to water may however, result in modest increases of income through gardening, small animal husbandry, and other productive activities. Women who may have had to previously walk large distances to collect water, are likely to have more time for productive work, once piped water is made available.

More systematic ex-post analysis of rural water supply schemes in the developing countries is important, in order to resolve some of these ambiguities, and tailor future programs to be more effective in the widely varying conditions found in different parts of the world.

Rural Water Sources and Their Management

Selection of Water Sources

The sources of rural water supply differ somewhat from those of the urban water supply. Urban centers usually have access to perennial rivers, to large surface water reservoirs or major underground aquifers. They exploit these sources using relatively standardized, centralized technologies based on piped distribution and private and public tap facilities, often metered and subject to user tariffs (as previously explained). In the rural setting, the general strategy is to make use of whichever resource is available with whatever technology is appropriate for local socioeconomic and technical conditions. However, there is an order of preference which is usually:

- artesian groundwater piped by gravity (spring protection and gravity feed systems) requiring no treatment prior to consumption;

- pumped groundwater requiring no treatment prior to consumption (using village level operation and maintenance handpumps - see Arlosoroff et al. 1987);
- rainwater harvested from rooftops or other impermeable surfaces and stored hygienically in tanks; and
- surface water sources requiring treatment prior to consumption.

The systems are prioritized on the basis of the minimum treatment philosophy which recognizes the problems of establishing and sustaining effective water treatment facilities under developing country rural conditions (Myhrstad and Haldorsen 1984, WHO 1989). An example is the experience with slow-sand filtration in Latin America which has not effectively solved the operation and maintenance difficulties that lead to poor water quality control (WASH 1990). Sources selected under the minimum treatment strategy generally are those that are well protected by natural buffers (uninhabited catchment area, protective soil and rock layers, etc.) or which can be protected by management interventions. However, both of these are becoming increasingly difficult to find or protect under conditions of rising populations and environmental pressures (Lee and Bastemeijer 1991).

The four sources listed are also prioritized on the basis of least-cost per capita investments to achieve a given level of supply and coverage. They contrast with the urban setting in which frequently large surface water sources requiring treatment are selected because of their size, proximity and reliability. Because of the absence of suitable sources in the first two categories, many rural villagers have to rely on the last two options involving small rainwater catchments, or minor rivers with intermittent and erratic flows.

A problem arises for rural communities when they are positioned downstream of large urban centers and share the same source such as a large river or a regional aquifer. City dwellers, because of their legislative, technical or economic power, often deprive downstream users of water during periods of shortage or due to their long-term water abstraction habits (as explained in Chapter 5). Local authorities tend to favor meeting the water demand of the cities rather than those of rural areas. A clear example is the 1985 depletion of the River Niger at Niamey, the capital of the Niger Republic. The 600,000 inhabitants of the city rely heavily on the Niger for their water supply. As a direct result of the catastrophic failure of the 1984-85 rainy season, in which the lowest rainfall on record was registered (since measurements began in the early 1900s), the riverflow from October 1984 till May 1985 was the smallest ever observed. A computer model projected that the river would run dry for the first time in recorded history (Buydens 1985). The authorities responded quickly to the hydrological warnings and had a temporary earth-fill dam constructed across the river, thus creating an upstream reservoir with an estimated capacity of 2 million cubic meters. This volume was sufficient to bridge the critical period before the arrival of the first rainfall of the new rainy season. The direct victims of the special measure were the downstream village dwellers, who severely suffered from the negative externality imposed upon them by the dam, since virtually no water was released and their water supply almost entirely depended on the river.

Villagers are not worse off than the city populations, in all cases, especially in comparison to the poorer urban population groups. In many countries, it is the wealthier villages which receive priority in the allocation of water supply, because they are the most influential in making their demands. It may be the case that the populations of such villages are actually in less need of support than the inhabitants of urban slums.

Rural Water Supply Institutions

We conclude with some observations on rural water supply institutions, that supplement the more general discussion in Section 2.5. Some key issues that need to be considered by countries which are reviewing existing institutional frameworks for water supply, or setting up new ones, include the following:

- the case for a strong central agency versus a more decentralized approach must be examined in the light of the acceptability of localized bodies and their ability to coordinate activities and cooperate with other agencies;
- if a central rural water supply organization is set up, it should be strong enough to support a long-term, nationwide program, or if it is a part of an existing utility or institution, it should have the commitment to rural water supply and the local organizational infrastructure necessary to implement and follow up the program; and
- the drive to expand water supply facilities to reach new customers could have important effects on existing water sector organizations, especially urban utilities. In particular, competition for scarce financial and skilled manpower resources must be avoided, where this could lead to the further deterioration of already poor quality water service to existing consumers, coupled with unsatisfactory execution of new water supply programs.

Water Vending and Kiosk Systems in Rural and Urban Areas

Millions of poor people in both the urban and rural areas of developing countries obtain water from commercial vendors who deliver it to their homes. People moving into slums and settlements on the fringes of rapidly expanding urban areas often must rely on vendors until the piped system is expanded, if ever. Water vending systems can become quite elaborate. In Onitsha, Nigeria, a city of 700,000 inhabitants, the vast majority obtains its water through a vending system. During the dry season households obtain approximately 2.96 million gallons per day (mgd) from this vending system, for which they pay about US$ 28,000. At the same time, in 1987, the public water utility was supplying about 1.5 mgd for which it only managed to collect about US$ 1,100 in revenues (Whittington et al. 1989a).

Some water vending systems are very well organized. All systems have one or more of three types of vendors (Whittington et al. 1989b):

- wholesale vendors, who obtain water from some source and sell it to distributing vendors;
- distributing vendors, who obtain water from a source or a wholesale vendor and sell it to consumers, door-to-door. They may include households with storage facilities who sell water to their neighbors; and
- direct vendors who sell water to consumers coming to the source to purchase water.

The latter type is the so called kiosk system, where the water is dispersed from a piped distribution system or isolated source (like a well). In some cases, where the vending system is expensive and unreliable, a planned development of the kiosk system might provide a good alternative, in the absence of affordable metered private connections (Whittington et al. 1990).

Customers of vended water often pay high prices for the services. Households sometimes pay over 10% of their monthly income for such water service, as compared to 1-5% for most piped water systems (Zaroff and Okun 1984). In hard to access villages, the prices charged for a bucket of water may be as high as an entire day's wages in agriculture, according to Whittington et al. (1989c). Some researchers argue that the principal reason for this phenomenon is a combination of the high cost of delivery and monopolistic pricing policies on the part of the vendors (Whittington et al. 1990). The vendors often make only a fair return on their labor and capital investments, without exorbitant profits. This suggests that government regulation of vending policies may not be necessary or advisable. In villages, people may have sufficient income to afford vended water at least part of the time and thus save significant time required for fetching water from a distant source. In a study of a village in Kenya (Whittington et al. 1989b), it was found that the majority of the inhabitants chose to pay for their water and obtain it from the kiosk system, either directly by walking to a kiosk or indirectly by purchasing it from a vendor, rather than hauling it free from a more distant open well or handpump. The choice is based on both water quality and convenience of supply (time-saved) considerations.

The same study also revealed that households using vendors value their time at a higher rate than the current market wage for unskilled labor. In this respect, a survey of vending practices in an area can be a useful indicator of the choice of technology and the ability and willingness to pay for water services amongst different groups in a community. Households who place a high value on their time are unlikely to make use of a new handpump, but might be willing to pay for the installation of yard taps. Individuals that previously were collecting water from kiosks, open wells or handpumps, and did not make use of existing water vending services, reveal that the price charged by the vendor is an upper bound on their benefits for any specific type of water service (Whittington et al. 1989b). Willingness-to-pay is highly correlated with the level of consumer income. Different studies on water demand reveal that poorer consumers are willing to pay a higher proportion of their income for better water supply services than are their richer neighbors (see e.g., Briscoe and de Ferranti 1988). Other factors that determine the willingness to pay are family characteristics, the convenience, reliability and perceived quality of existing versus proposed water supplies (see also Chapter 7 for a model that relates water demand to the quality of supply). In many project assessments, water taken from traditional sources is considered free, whereas it actually costs a significant amount in terms of time and labor as testified by willingness-to-pay studies. When people buy water even though they have access to traditional supplies, they clearly value the increased quality and the time saved in collection, equal to or more highly than the price paid for kiosk supplies.

Techno-Economic Considerations

Area Selection

While the qualitative links between rural water supply and other characteristics of rural areas have been examined in several recent studies (see Chapter 1), no systematic analyses of the quantitative relationships between such variables and the returns to rural water supply projects appear to have been done. It would be useful to carry out a study of past rural water supply programs, and use standard statistical techniques (such as regression analysis, or discriminant analysis) to determine the relative weights or importance of specific rural indicators, in ensuring the success of rural water supply efforts. The results of such an ex-post analysis would be helpful in future area selection and targeting of rural water supply investments. However, these relatively simple approaches would only serve as preliminary screening devices, aimed at eliminating the obviously uneconomic rural water projects and indicating rough priorities for those that remain. The surviving rural water supply schemes would still have to be subjected to detailed project evaluation and cost-benefit analysis, as described in Chapter 3.

At this stage, it is useful to examine how individual projects are usually defined within an overall national or regional rural water supply program. A typical rural water scheme will invariably include as its core, the source and primary and secondary distribution networks (see Chapter 4 for details). However, the scope of the project may be expanded to incorporate other upstream investments such as bulk water supply facilities and source protection measures designed to prevent environmental deterioration, as well as downstream components ranging from house-plumbing and water using devices and equipment to complementary infrastructure associated with the integrated rural development approach. From the geographic viewpoint also, rural water supply programs span the spectrum from individual connections, through household groups, single villages and village clusters, up to large areas or regions.

The foregoing suggests that the definition of a rural water supply project is therefore likely to be quite case specific, and determined on the basis of convenience in identifying the costs and benefits associated with a given package of investments, in a particular location. However, there is a danger that the aggregate analysis of large areas containing many consumers might mask significant variations at a more detailed level. Therefore, it is advisable (provided the necessary data is available), that a two stage approach be used, in which macro-level evaluation of a large rural water supply project is supplemented by the micro-level analysis of smaller components and sub-components (especially low load density and thinly populated areas), to help refine the scope of the scheme.

Approaches to Rural Water Supply

Some specific strategic approaches to rural water supply include:

- *Integrated rural development* -- water is treated as only one component of a wider package of infrastructure;
- *Area coverage* -- comprehensive networking seeks to quickly provide water supply to as many customers as possible within the designated project area. More modified approaches may first adopt a backbone distribution system, with increasing numbers of consumers being added on over a phased time period;
- *Network extension* -- water supply is based on proximity to existing networks and their relative ease of extension. Each separate branch addition is judged on its own merits;
- *Isolated sources* -- water supply in extremely remote areas, is based on relative cheapness and abundance of local water sources; and

- *Intensification* -- concentrating on increasing both connection rates and water usage rates per connection in already supplied areas.

Most of these approaches, whilst efficient from a financial or technical sense, do not focus on the situations in which the greatest social benefits are to be gained. The last three, for example, focus on conditions where significant infrastructure or resource potential already exists. This must be borne in mind by decisionmakers who wish to maximize social benefits. Cairncross (1989) indicates that many rural water supply schemes involving individual house connections benefits consumers who already have a water source within 100 to 200 meters of their home.

Whatever the strategic approach preferred, specific decisions concerning the pace and timing of rural water schemes, selection of areas to be supplied, investment and cost recovery policy, and pricing and connections policy, require more detailed analysis. For example, projected national rural water supply targets over the planning period will depend on the current extent of coverage, the resources and implementation capability available, and the sociopolitical pressures for water in rural areas. Similarly, quantitative criteria for ranking areas for water supply may be developed and used in conjunction with other more judgmental factors, e.g., by sector policymakers carrying out indicative planning and resource allocation exercises. Thus, where data is available, a formula of the following type could be used for ranking:

$$\textit{Rural Water Merit Value} \; = \; \sum_i W_i \cdot C_i \qquad\qquad (9.1)$$

where:

W_i = the weight assigned to characteristic C;
C_i = the i th characteristic of the rural area under consideration.

In practice, a wide variety of indicators or characteristics and weights may be used, depending on the local conditions and data availability. In some cases, it might be the relative socioeconomic disadvantage that qualifies a rural area for public sector development capital.

The diversity of water sources that may be used in the rural setting, and an indication of their range of application are discussed in the next section.

Low-Cost Service and Appropriate Technology

The Suitability of Appropriate Technologies

The economic framework developed in earlier chapters should be applied systematically to select technological options. However, before doing such a full-fledged analysis, some rough screening is desirable. In one such approach, the appropriateness of a technology may be judged against four criteria:

1) its technical suitability in terms of design, construction, operation and maintenance;
2) its economic suitability in terms of capital cost, running costs and replacement costs;
3) its social suitability in terms of its acceptance and sustained use by the community at a service level they find sufficient; and
4) its environmental suitability in terms of sustainability, susceptibility to negative external impacts and its own actual impact on environmental conditions.

According to a review of nearly ten years of experience by the USAID WASH project (WASH 1990), in order for a technology to be suitable for use in a particular location it must pass several tests:

- it must be conceptually and physically within the capabilities of the persons responsible for the operation and repair of the system;
- spare parts and equipment must be available in order to maintain and repair the chosen technology, preferably of local manufacture; and
- the cost of operating the technology must be within the financial means of the responsible institution (or community group) for operation, maintenance and replacement.

They indicate appropriateness to be a site-specific context varying between developing countries, regions and even villages.

Appropriate technologies are not necessarily modern inventions (such as the Tara handpump). Some have been used for many years. Techniques of water delivery, in particular, were developed over millennia. Unfortunately, the first water supply programs in official aid programs tended to put too much emphasis on technologically "elegant," but relatively untried options. These early attempts paid insufficient attention to improving existing local techniques, such as gravity systems, e.g., fed by a series of springs or river water. Excessive attention was placed on technical considerations without considering environmental and socioeconomic factors. However, expensive failures, such as the first experiences with the use of handpumps (elaborated further below), eventually convinced most external donors of the importance of properly investigating the local geophysical and sociological environment in order to assess whether a certain technology would prove to be really appropriate. It is accepted now that additional prerequisites for successful implementation of new technologies are the training of local technicians to operate and maintain equipment, and an effective dialogue with the targeted consumers. Some researchers have pointed out that the ultimate beneficiaries of such projects, if properly informed about the various options, may be best qualified to make judgements about the appropriateness of the technology to suit their needs (Feachem et al. 1983). However, they rarely participate in selecting the technology, while external donors and experts (often far removed from the site) make these critical decisions.

Quite often technical, institutional or financial obstacles, stifle the successful implementation of appropriate technologies. In particular, the adherence to excessively high standards has been cited as a major culprit for inappropriate and excessively costly water supply and water treatment projects (Gakenheimer and Brando 1987, Kalbermatten and Middleton 1991). Though it is a classical case in rural dwellings, urban areas seem to be even more affected.

The conventional scapegoats are the engineering consultant and contractor from the developing countries. By focusing on sophisticated technical standards, proven useful in the developed countries, they may overlook secondary project objectives, such as employment creation in low-income areas. Consultants, have little incentive to minimize project costs and thus to readjust their frame of problem solving in terms of appropriate technologies. Nevertheless, a growing part of the international engineering community is trying to advocate the use of appropriate standards.

At the same time it has been observed that in the developing countries themselves, certain factors favor the use of high standards. First, there is the national technical engineering elite who studied the developed country standards (often abroad), and prefer to opt for prestigious modernist complexity in design and construction. Use and dissemination of appropriate standards is often left to "second-rank" engineers of lesser professional status, and who attended trade-oriented schools. The behavior of international and domestic engineers is reinforced by that of government agencies, elected officials and suppliers of materials. Government agencies prefer failure-proof, maintenance free construction because of their central position in bearing responsibility for failures and the traditionally low budgets for operation and maintenance.

Elected officials who ultimately legislate the industry standards, may prefer to leave technical matters with the engineers, and secondly they may favor the use of high technology as an indication of their devotion to progressive development (Gakenheimer and Brando 1987). The international agencies could play a major potential role in providing balanced advice on appropriate technologies.

Overview of Appropriate Technologies for Water Supply

A number of useful overviews of appropriate technologies for rural water supply (and sanitation) have been published over the last decade. A catalyst of many efforts to apply and refine appropriate technologies at the project level was the early World Bank work of Kalbermatten et al. (1981). A more recent publication is that of Morgan (1990) which focuses on the practical aspects of handpump and well construction as well as low-cost sanitation. ITDG have focused on a whole range of appropriate technology issues in the water sector through their journals "Appropriate Technology" and "Waterlines."

Water Extraction

The archetype of appropriate technology used in supplying water to low-income users in both rural and urban fringe areas, is the handpump. Handpumps are most commonly used for shallow or small-diameter wells which supply up to about 200 people (see Table 9.3). Originally, handpumps were expected to provide one of the simplest and least costly techniques for water supply. However, by the early 1980s, failure rates of 70 percent were reported in projects initiated several years earlier (Churchill 1987). The major reported cause of poor performance was the lack of appropriate maintenance. Other problems were related to the wrong selection of pump types for a given environment, the poor quality of manufacturing and their misuse in the field (Arlosoroff 1985). This raised the question of how "appropriate" technology handpumps really were. Nevertheless, international agencies such as the World Bank, WHO, UNDP, and UNICEF perceive improvements in handpumps as one of the best approaches to providing a low-cost but adequate water supply. Acknowledging the lessons of the past, due attention has been given (by means of laboratory tests and field trials) to develop light pumps, manufactured by regular machine-tools and extruding machines (Arlosoroff et al. 1987). The pumps should be standardized, simple to operate, easy to dismantle, and have locally made components, while trained village operators should be able to maintain and repair the pumps, adequately (Arlosoroff 1985).

Since the handpump is only one, albeit a major, component in the water supply system, it will only work efficiently if the technical problems relating to the other components can be properly handled as well. In this respect, critical attention needs to be given to the design of boreholes. For example, very poor gravel packing and well screen design have been the rule rather than the exception in many past projects.

One successful example of introducing a technology appropriate for use by villagers is the case of the Tara handpump in Bangladesh. The pump's main features are its simplicity, low cost, and ease of maintenance. It has been specifically designed to make maximum use of local materials and skills available in Bangladesh. In 1987, it was adopted as the standard handpump for installation in areas of the country where the depth from the surface to the water table exceeded the normal suction limit for handpumps (about 7.5m), but was less than 12m. The design of the pump made full use of the favorable hydrogeology of Bangladesh (i.e., the combination of plentiful shallow water and a subsoil of sand and silt, that allows easy drilling). The favorable user acceptance level is indicated by consistently high utilization, an insignificant level of complaints, and negligible vandalism. The capital costs for the full system (pump and tubewell) are in the region of US$ 3-4 per user, while maintenance costs are in the range of US$ 0.05-0.10 per user per year (Kjellerup et al. 1989). The use of Tara pumps has contributed significantly to the relatively high water supply coverage level achieved in Bangladesh (see Table 9.1).

Water Storage

Low-cost measures to accumulate and store surface and groundwater during the wet season, for consumption in dryer periods are important. If no mitigatory steps are taken, the demand for water in dry periods tends to deplete aquifers and surface reservoirs, long before the first rainfalls of the next wet season. Villagers are then forced to resort to more expensive and sophisticated deep-well pumping, if they are fortunate enough to have such alternatives at their disposal in the first place. Or else they must return to poor quality traditional sources at increasingly distant locations. In many areas of Asia and Africa, rainwater is collected from rooftops and surface catchments for storage and later use. Rainwater harvesting is a method of evening out variations in water availability both in space, by making a more local supply of water available for all or part of the year, and in time, by storing water during rainy periods for use during dry (Lee and Visscher 1990). In some cases, it is a means of supplying higher quality water when alternative sources are contaminated. Surface water is often polluted with human and other wastes, while groundwater may contain high concentrations of fluoride, nitrates or iron making it unpalatable.

One common household system is to catch runoff from household rooftops and store the water in ferrocement containers ranging from 2 m³ to 30 m³ depending on the length of dry season and water needs of users (see Hasse 1989). Lee and Visscher (1990) document a number of examples of rooftop systems from five African countries. They range from 1 m³ to 100 m³. In Asia, upwards of 3 million households get their primary water supply from several 2 m^3 cement jars storing rooftop runoff and built for less than US$ 50 each (Tuyanavich and Hewison 1990). Other surfaces suitable for harvesting include large bare rock outcrops and areas of cleared ground which have an impermeable surface (Lee and Visscher 1991). Whilst the quality of collected water is not always acceptable by WHO guideline standards, many rural communities value it as a resource due to its convenience, proximity and its relative quality compared to available alternatives.

Examples of surface runoff systems are the several thousand small stone dams built on the Cape Verde islands to capture the rainfall that otherwise would be lost as water surface runoff (Agrhymet 1987). Although the annual rainfall on the Cape Verde islands is of the order of magnitude of 400 mm, most of it occurs in two or three downpours. The dams are ingeniously built as a series of cascades, and are constructed such that evaporation is attenuated.

In some regions, groundwater reservoirs may have some distinct advantages over surface reservoirs, like lower construction and maintenance costs, fewer losses by evaporation or seepage, less risk of pollution, reduced inundation of potentially arable land, and lower health hazards related to the presence of disease-vectors such as mosquitos or snails. One low-cost technique of groundwater storage, which has been known for centuries is the groundwater dam. This is a form of controlled, local groundwater recharge and capture. Nilsson (1985, 1988) gives some examples of very simple and inexpensive subsurface dams in Asian and African developing countries. The basic purpose of a groundwater dam is to store water below ground level (typically at locations along a seasonal river bed). Water is retained behind a clay or masonry dam built down into and across the sand-filled river bed in a reservoir contained by the virtually impermeable layers below (either rock or clay). The stored groundwater can then be accessed easily by shallow wells and simple handpumps, or by a gravity pipe (in the case of sub-surface dams that are extended to a greater height above the river bed to catch more water and sand, often called Sand Dams). These are a good examples of how various low-cost technologies can complement one another. Lee and Visscher (1991) detail the practical design and construction aspects of sub-surface dam construction as does the Government of India (1990). The usefulness of groundwater dams depends on the presence of favorable hydrogeological conditions. Therefore, preliminary hydrogeological studies should precede any subsurface dam construction.

Water Treatment

Conventional water treatment plants carry out several basic operations, including rapid mixing, flocculation, sedimentation, filtration and disinfection (see Chapter 4). They are often too costly and technology-intensive for application to developing country rural settings. Low-cost alternatives have been implemented most successfully in the filtration component. A well established appropriate technology is the slow-sand filtration (Visscher et al. 1987). This type of filtration is an efficient method for the removal of organic matter and pathogenic organisms, as well as inorganic suspended matter present in surface water. More technical details are presented by Visvanathan (1985). A typical slow sand filtration plant can serve 1500 to 3000 people. The design is relatively simple and local materials can be readily used to constitute the necessary coarse filter media, e.g., coarse gravel, crushed stones or even crushed coconut shells, as well as locally available sand. Operation and maintenance can be carried out by trained local technicians who act as system caretakers (Visscher et al. 1987). Most slow-sand filter operations include a pre-treatment facility for removal of turbidities that might otherwise deteriorate the filter, and sometimes require continuous chlorination of filtered water to provide a multi-barrier system against possible disease transmission.

Other common forms of water treatment used in rural areas include simple pot chlorination of wells and rainwater storage containers, and of course boiling of water by individual households (IRC 1988).

The most common form of large wastewater treatment system is the waste stabilization pond which comprises a series of shallow lakes through which sewerage water flows (Cairncross and Feacham 1983). Treatment occurs through natural physical, chemical and biological processes and no machinery or energy is required. However, the majority of wastewater in many developing countries is still discharged directly into water bodies, creating considerable environmental externalities for downstream communities in terms of health and water treatment costs (see Chapter 5). Wastewater treatment technologies are discussed extensively in Fresenius et al. (1989) and stabilization by Pearson et al. (1987).

Wastewater treatment clearly goes hand-in-hand with a sanitation system for the collection and delivery of wastewater to the treatment location. Where domestic wastewater produced in a community is in excess of roughly 45 m³ per hectare per day, off-site, rather than on-site sanitation systems are required, in which waste is transported out of the area by a conventional sewerage system to a location where it can be more safely handled. This may involve one or more of the techniques described above depending on the socioeconomic conditions. One important alternative and low-cost sanitation technology in rural areas is the latrine. A variety of types exist for a range of socioeconomic, cultural and hydrological conditions. The ventilated improved pit-latrine is generally the preferred technology by water sector authorities. Latrines have been widely discussed in the development literature and project reports. A useful recent publication is that of Morgan (1990). ITDG's Waterlines magazine has closely documented the development of appropriate sanitation technologies over the last 10 years. A main environmental concern associated with this technology is that on-site sanitation should not be a mechanism for surface or groundwater contamination due to poor siting and construction. This frequently is the case, however, and results predominately in nitrate and faecal contamination of groundwater (Lewis et al. 1980). Other appropriate sanitation technologies for rural application include the pour-flush toilet and the septic tank system (Kalbermatten et al. 1981, Cairncross and Feacham 1983).

Water Distribution

Water distribution systems convey water from the source to the point of use, sometimes via intermediate treatment or storage facilities. For most rural situations in developing countries, the distribution system is kept as simple as possible. Wherever feasible, gravity pipe networks are preferred, with intermediate storage and break-pressure stations only where necessary to augment peak supply capabilities and to ensure the structural integrity of the pipeline system, respectively. With these preferred systems, water is conveyed wholly under the force of gravity without any additional electric or diesel-powered pumping stations. Consequently, most water sources are fairly local, perhaps only tens of kilometers away. However, some transmission main pipelines may run for longer distances of several hundred kilometers if the source is of regional importance (for example, pipeline supplies from Kilimanjaro snowmelt into Tanzania or Kenya). Consequently, the most common source of supply are the highland artesian springs protected by a spring cap (Archambault et al. 1987) or dammed mountain rivers. Here, the catchment and source are relatively protected and isolated from human interference, and the required pressure head is available. Examples of countries with significant numbers of gravity flow systems include Zambia, Malawi and Sri Lanka.

In some cases where gravity systems are not feasible, groundwater is used. Water is pumped from drilled boreholes or tubewells and distributed to nearby villages by pipeline. An example of a country committed to this system of supply and distribution is Botswana, who have received technical assistance from the Swedish International Development Agency SIDA (UNICEF 1989). In other countries, no reticulation system is added to abstraction wells and instead, consumers access water directly by means of well-head pumps, mostly manually operated handpumps.

Pipeline distribution systems have one of three types of consumer connections attached:

1) the individual household connection -- this is usually metered and consumers are subject to a tariff;

2) the communal public standpost connection -- this is usually unmetered and often water is supplied free of charge due to the difficulties of revenue collection (Cairncross 1989, Grover 1983); and

3) the water vendor kiosk connection -- from which water is sold to customers through an intermediary attendant (see previous discussion).

According to Grover (1983), where individual, house connections exist, they are costly and account for about 50-70% of the capital cost of the water supply systems. More recently, many projects have imposed connection charges on individuals receiving house connections, as explained in Chapter 7. However, the full cost is not always passed on to consumers. In many developing countries, the water authority assists villagers in installing and financing domestic connections.

The major advantage of distribution systems with house connections is the convenience for the user and the reduced risk of contamination. Over the last decade, significant data has been collected to suggest that the further the potable water source is from the home, the more likely it is that contamination will occur between the supply point (i.e., the communal standpost perhaps 200 meters away from the home) and the mouth of the consumer. Opportunity for contamination occurs during collection, transport in domestic containers, and storage in the house prior to consumption. Home connections also make the collection of revenues from the user more effective. They contribute to greater water consumption and improved levels of hygiene through the convenience of having a reliable on-site source of water. However, house connections make it necessary to provide adequate drainage, and wherever possible, an effective form of on-site or centralized sanitation system is required for the disposal of wastewater and sewerage.

Because of the expense involved, in many rural communities (and some low-income urban areas), water distribution systems tend to be more limited. Instead of individual house connections water authorities often prefer standpipe or standpost arrangements. Ideal technical requirements for public standposts are that they are no more than 50 to 150 meters away from any household. However, in many semi-arid regions with difficult hydrological and landscape conditions, the target distance within which all households should have a year-round reliable, improved source of water is between 500 and 2000 meters (e.g., Tanzania and Kenya).

Generally, communal standposts are designed to serve up to 100-200 households. Each standpost is equipped with one or more taps, depending upon the number of households to be served, and a concrete apron designed to collect spillage and conduct it to a drain or soakaway pit. In their current use, however, some serious drawbacks have been observed. Standpipes are often subject to vandalism, which could be overcome by better community participation. In addition, water losses can be considerable in the case of leaky or open taps which, if coupled to inadequate drainage, can cause health hazards. Furthermore, as previously explained, the users of standpipes may obtain only small amounts of water which can be contaminated by dirty containers, during transport to the house and through improper storage. Finally, it is very difficult to collect revenues from the users of standpipes (Grover 1983).

As far as the economic issues related to connections are concerned, a recent study in Brazil (Briscoe et al. 1990) revealed that the potential price charged for using water from a public tap would have little effect on the revenues of the utility. The same study indicates that, given the negative income elasticity of demand for use of public taps, it is the poor who are the principal beneficiaries of free public taps. Therefore, there appears to be scope to improve the equity of rural water supply systems by charging high tariffs for the house connections used mainly by the better off, and providing free public taps which are used mainly by the poor (thus establishing a cross subsidizing mechanism). These issues were previously discussed in Chapter 7.

Applicability of Technologies

The handpump, rainwater catchment system, subsurface dam, slow-sand filter and standpipe are representative of the low-cost techniques currently in vogue worldwide in the water supply sector for rural areas and for some fringe or low-income urban settings. Table 9.3. presents an overview of their range of applicability, as well as some addition examples of appropriate technologies.

Rural Water Pricing Policy

Subsidies and Benefit Distribution

Because sociopolitical and other considerations play a relatively significant role in the determination of rural water policy, the general framework for tariff setting described in Chapter 7 has to be adapted to the rural context. The special issues that arise in the pricing of rural water supply are discussed below.

Governments invariably seek to build up rural water demand as rapidly as possible, starting from a very low level, in order to achieve early gains in health and social benefits, as well as to accelerate the recovery of the relatively high costs of rural water schemes. Therefore, the initial connection fee or price should not be allowed to become a significant barrier to entry, given the context of the relatively low in comes of rural households and the high LRMC of supply. Often, a policy of promotional pricing well below LRMC, and subsidized connection charges, is adopted for an initial period, to encourage

TABLE 9.3 (a)　Examples of Appropriate Technologies in Water Supply

Type of Technology	Technical Specifications	Application Advantages	Limitations	References
W A T E R S U P P L Y				
Gravity System	Fed by springs or rivers, water conveyed by pipes or earthen channels	• Natural water supply • No energy required • Easy to maintain	• Vulnerable to erratic flows	Archambault et al, 1987
Handpumps Suction pump	For shallow wells (lift less than 7.5 m)	• Easy to operate and maintain	• Serves only 150 to 200 people	Arlosoroff, 1984, 87 Churchill, 1987
Lift pump	For deep wells (lift up to 180 m)	• Access to deeper groundwater	• Operation and maintenance is somewhat complicated	Okun et al, 1987
Turbine and centrifugal pumps	Driven by motors Versatile use for both shallow and deep wells, by multi-staging of turbines	• High efficiency • Easily adaptable to local hydrogeology by combining the number, size and speed of impellers	• Requires skilled operation and maintenance • Dependent on energy	Okun et al, 1987

TABLE 9.3 (b) Examples of Appropriate Technologies in Water Storage

Type of Technology	Technical Specifications	Application Advantages	Limitations	References
WATER STORAGE				
Rain-water catchment	Rainfed reservoir	• Natural water supply • Easy to maintain	• Dependent on amount of rainfall • Losses due to seepage and evaporation • Possible health hazards	Lee & Visscher 1990, 1991 Hasse, 1989
Subsurface dam	Constructed below ground level to arrest flow in natural aquifer	• Inexpensive and local material can be used in construction	• Requires longer term preliminary studies	Nilsson, 1985, 88 G. of India, 1990
Water harvesting	Soil surface is made nearly impervious to reduce the infiltration of water in the soil	• Natural water supply • Easy to maintain	• Depends on availability of waterproofing agents (asphalt, oil)	Ishaq, 1985 Reij et al, 1988

TABLE 9.3 (c) Examples of Appropriate Technologies in Water Treatment and Distribution Systems

Type of Technology	Technical Specifications	Application Advantages	Limitations	References
WATER TREATMENT				
Slow sand filters	Water moves through a multi-media bed that filters out debris, organic material and some pathogens	• Efficient removal • Construction can make use of local materials • Easy to operate and maintain	• Serves only a limited number of people • Only apt to treat water with a low turbidity	Visvanatha et al, 1985 Visscher et al, 1985
Sea water supplies filter system	Box device that transforms the river or seabed into a natural filter	• Can treat highly turbid rivers • Can serve a large urban population	• Installation, operation and repair are somewhat complicated	Visvanatha et al, 1985
WATER DISTRIBUTION SYSTEMS				
Standpipes	Public access pipe with typically one or more taps, concrete pad and soakage pit	• Low investment cost	• Serves only 100-200 households • Subject to vandalism, waterlosses, drainage problems	Grover, 1983 Okun et al, 1987

the rapid growth of demand and popularize the use of water supply in rural areas. This is sometimes coupled with financial incentives and subsidies to consumers, to help in the installation of plumbing, storage tanks and other water-related equipment, especially where this could lead to new or more productive uses of water. The lifeline block, described earlier in Chapter 6 may be set more generously (relative to LRMC) for rural users, than for urban ones.

In some countries, the LRMC of supply may vary quite widely, especially where there are many independent systems. However, uniform national water pricing policies are frequently implemented, based on egalitarian and sociopolitical arguments. If this results in effective cross-subsidization of rural water users in high LRMC areas, by urban consumers in low LRMC areas, then additional issues may arise. First, the deviations from LRMC have efficiency costs, and give wrong price signals to users. Second, perverse effects may occur unless the subsidies are carefully targeted, with poor urban households subsidizing the water supply consumption of better-off rural users. Third, the reasons for the cross-subsidy must be well justified, quantitatively if possible. For example, if the governments objective is to improve the quality of rural life and stem rural to urban migration, a serious effort should be made to estimate the corresponding efficiency benefits. Fourth, as mentioned earlier, it may be better to focus on promoting productive use of water in rural areas, as discussed before. Since these consumers are likely to be more able and willing to pay higher prices, the resulting revenues could be used to subsidize tariffs to poorer households. Fifth and finally, as discussed earlier, even relatively poor consumers often signal how highly they value at least a minimum quantity of water for personal use, through the high prices that they are willing to pay to water vendors.

In some cases, it may be justifiable to subsidize publicly supplied water, in order to wean uninformed or less educated domestic consumers away from traditional but unsafe sources, thereby realizing significant health and other social benefits. The foregoing suggests that there are good reasons in favor of subsidizing water supply consumption in rural areas. At the same time, some subsidization schemes can often lead to ill-conceived policies that defeat the original objectives, if the justification is not based on systematic and rational analysis along the lines indicated earlier. In particular, even where promotional prices are used, it should be recognized that this is a transitional phase, and prices should be raised to more normal levels as the market matures and local incomes rise. This will permit more effective and earlier cost recovery, and the ability to expand rural water systems into newer and more disadvantaged areas.

Community Financing

Until recently, central governments have tended to act as monopolistic providers of water and sanitation services, with little input from the private sector (Churchill 1987). External funders have supported this situation based on the assumption that only a large supplier has the capacity to realize the economies of scale inherent in water systems. Increasingly, however, decisionmakers are realizing that whilst this may be the case for some urban contexts in the developing world, it is not necessarily true for rural systems which do not exhibit the same economies -- due to their largely piece-meal, small-scale nature. The role of local communities in deciding on, developing, and financing their own water supply systems is becoming larger.

Increasingly, the attention of developing countries and their international donors is focusing on cost-recovery as a basic component of rural water supply projects. Since 1985, the WHO has organized a working group on cost recovery in community water supply comprised of members from the donor community and senior officials from the water and related sectors of 21 developing countries. The aim of the group has been to formulate guiding principles and frameworks for agency-managed systems, and for community and household-based water supply and sanitation (WHO 1988a and 1988b).

The guiding managerial and financial principles formulated for agencies and applicable to most rural supply situations include:

- water sector agencies should be granted financial autonomy and operate on a commercial basis;
- agencies should practice cost-control by selecting an appropriate scale of investment and technology applicable to the supply context, and by minimizing non-revenue water, maximizing revenue collection, and implementing preventive maintenance to ensure continued supplies;
- supplies should be tailored to consumers needs, while willingness-to-pay guidelines should be used to determine appropriate tariff policies;
- liquidity should be maintained by fixing the tariff level at the point where all cash needs are covered, and avoiding projects that might undermine sector financial viability;
- the principles of long-run marginal cost recovery should be adopted, especially for large consumers (i.e., those who can effectively decrease their consumption in response to price signals); and
- charges should be levied on users to recover the costs of sewerage/drainage systems, and on those who privately abstract water from common sources.

As far as the mechanisms of cost recovery are concerned, the basic concept is that in most developing countries where full coverage of water supply and

TABLE 9.4 Financing Options for Piped Systems

Option	Circumstance	Purpose	Implementor	Procedure
voluntary funds	in communities with a tradition of fund-raising, seasonal income, and a good knowledge of payments according to household capacity and benefits	financial contributions to construction; occasional larger contributions to maintenance and repair of simple systems with public water points	traditional leadership, voluntary organizations, e.g. women's groups, tap organizations	targets are set and funds collected periodically through meetings, house-to-house collections, bazars, etc.; funds are collected in advance when required
general community	in communities with own source of income and a water supply with public facilities	annual maintenance and repair, financial contributions to construction; depreciation and expansion where possible	local government, community water committee or subcommittee	reservation of funds based on the estimated costs and net annual income of the community; cost-reduction or income generation where necessary
cooperative funds	water supply initiated and financed through production cooperative or village revolving fund; no direct payments for water used	annual maintenance and repairs; repayment of construction loan; depreciation and expansion where possible	cooperative's executive committee, community water commitee or subcommittee	reservation of funds based estimated costs and income from cooperative ventures and/or member fees; cost-reduction or income generation where necessary
flat rates	families have private taps, or share taps with well-defined social group, have fairly reliable incomes, and benefit more or less equally	repayment of community loan for construction; annual maintenance and repairs; depreciation and expansion where possible	water committee or subcommittee, board of water users cooperative, local government, tap users' committee	project agency advises on rate for approval by users; rates are collected and administered by the local water organization
graded rates	in communities with appreciable differences in water use and benefits and sufficient community spirit to divide user households into different payment categories	repayment of community loan for construction; annual maintenance and repairs; depreciation and expansion where possible	community water organization with support from promoters or other social experts assisting the project agency	private tap owners are classified in high and low categories, using local indicators of water use and wealth; users sharing taps may pay lower or equivalent individual rate

TABLE 9.4 (continued)

Option	Circumstance	Purpose	Implementor	Procedure
mixed systems	in communities with large differences in payment capacity and water use, with high and low-income households living in separate sections	repayment of community loan for construction; annual maintenance and repairs; depreciation and expansion where possible	water agency with community water committee or subcommittee	surplusses or private taps are used to finance the costs of free public taps in poorer sections
water metering	in large communities with limited water resources and an efficient administration	repayment of community loan for construction; annual maintenance and repairs; depreciation and expansion where possible	water agency and/or community water organization	meter reading, billing and rate collection by separate workers, or payment through banks, at central government offices or local branches
vending instead of a piped distribution network	in communities where a socially valuable vending system can be improved, where other solutions are technically, economically or politically impossible	contribution toward financing of the recurrent costs of the agency, and financing of vendor service costs, including upkeep of hygiene and simple repair	water agency paid operators, women's groups or water sellers' cooperative	water is sold from metered taps at controlled prices; when buying prices are subsidized, selling prices may equal private rates, the difference forming the vendors' income
vending as part of a piped distribution network	in communities where group connections or cross subsidies between private and public taps have not worked	contribution towards financing of the recurrent costs of public taps and the service of the vendors, including upkeep of hygiene and simple repairs	water agency paid operators or scio-economically appropriate concessionnaires, e.g. women heads of households	.
coin-operated taps	not recommended because of their great sensitivity to breakdown and interference			
direct or indirect water taxes	in communities where the transfer of sufficient funds to the water organization is assured and taxation can be related to water use and costs	annual maintenance and repair; repayment of construction loan; depreciation and expansion where possible	local government service organization for a specific area, e.g. a low-cost housing scheme	taxes are used exclusively for financing one or several basic services; categories of payment are based on level of service or housing conditions

Source: van Wijk-Sijbesma 1987.

sanitation is far from attained, the provision of free water to any given consumer implies that the service will not be extended to others who have an equal right to it (WHO 1989a). Therefore, consumers should be expected to provide part, if not all of the costs of supplying their water, based on their willingness to pay and the need to produce an equitable and appropriate distribution of economic and social benefits. The mechanisms through which costs can be recovered from rural and low-income urban communities are neatly summarized by van Wijk (1987) and endorsed by the WHO working group. They are reproduced here in Table 9.4 and provide a useful overview for water supply decisionmakers considering possible financing options for piped supplies.

Two important questions concerning cost-recovery from rural communities are (Churchill 1987):

1) do rural households have enough income (or resources) overall to be able to contribute toward covering the costs of water supply and sanitation services?; and
2) is a large enough fraction of their income (or resources) available in a form that can be accepted in payment (for example, cash, or labor and materials for constructing and maintaining service improvements?

Decisionmakers must assess whether significant portions of capital investment can be offset by selection of technologies that allow a high proportion of self-help or cash-in-kind contributions to achieving target coverage levels.

On a sobering note, the implementation of cost-recovery programs is hampered by poor data concerning the influence of costs of water on water use. Whilst willingness-to-pay studies are gradually being performed, they are still few and far between. More seriously, there is little published data on the elasticity of demand for water among low-income groups in developing countries, although this information is central to the issue of cost recovery (Cairncross 1989).

References

Agrhymet. 1987. *The 1986 Annual Hydrological Review for CILLS Countries*. World Meteorological Organization. Niamey, Republique du Niger: Centre Agrhymet Publications.

Archambault, J., C. Cédou, and N. Camphuis. 1987. *Le captage des sources*. Dossier No 10, Le Point Sur. Paris, France: Association Française des Volontaires du Progrès/GRET.

Arlosoroff, S., G. Tschannerl, D. Grey, W. Journey, A. Karp, O. Langenegger, and R. Roche. 1987. *Community Water Supply: The Hand Pump Option*. Washington DC: The World Bank.

_____, 1985. "Management and Techniques for Low-Cost, Low-Discharge Rural Water Supply" in *Water Resources for Rural Areas and Their Communities*. Vth World Congress on Water Resources. Brussels: IWRA. pp. 75-83.

Bastemeijer, T., and J.T. Visscher. 1990. *Maintenance Systems for Rural Water Supplies. Occasional Paper 8*. The Hague: IRC.

Briscoe, J., P. Furtado de Castro, C. Griffing, J. North, and O. Olson. 1990. *Towards Equitable and Sustainable Rural Water Supplies: A Contingent Valuation Study in Brazil*. Draft Paper. Washington DC: The World Bank.

_____, and D. de Ferranti. 1988. *Water for Rural Communities: Helping People Help Themselves*. Washington DC: The World Bank.

Buydens, W. 1985. *A Depletion Model for the River Niger at Niamey. Technical Note*. Niamey, Republique du Niger: Centre Agrhymet Publications.

Cairncross, S. 1989. "Water Supply and Sanitation: An Agenda for Research." *J. Trop. Med. and Hyg*. 92, pp. 301-314.

_____, and R.G. Feacham. 1983. *Environmental Health Engineering in the Tropics*. New York: John Wiley.

Churchill, A.A. 1987. *Rural Water Supply and Sanitation : Time for a Change. World Bank Discussion Paper No 18*. Washington DC: The World Bank.

Falkenmark, M. (ed.). 1982. *Rural Water Supply and Health: The Need For a New Strategy*. Summary of Papers and Discussions From the United Nations Interregional Seminar on Rural Water Supply, Uppsala, Sweden, 6-17 October 1980. Uppsala, Sweden: Scandinavian Institute of African Studies.

Feachem, R.F., D.J. Bradley, H. Garelick, and D.D. Mara. 1983. *Sanitation and Disease: Health Aspects of Excreta and Wastewater Management*. New York: John Wiley.

Fresenius, W., W. Schneider, B. Bohnke, and K. Popponghaus. 1989. *Wastewater Technology -- Origin, Collection, Treatment and Analysis of Wastewater*. Springer-Verlag/GTZ.

Gakenheimer, R., and C.H.J. Brando. 1987. *Infrastructure Standards in: Shelter, Settlement and Development*. L. Rodwin (ed.). United Nations, International Year of Shelter for the Homeless. Boston, MA: Allen and Unwin. pp. 131-50.

Government of India. 1990. *Rainwater Harvesting*. Department of Rural Development Report. New Delhi, India: Ministry of Agriculture.

Grover, B. 1983. *Water Supply and Sanitation Project Preparation Handbook, Vol 1: Guidelines. World Bank Technical Paper No 12*. Washington DC: The World Bank.

Hasse, R. 1989. *Rainwater Reservoirs Above Ground Structures for Roof Catchment*. GATE Publication. Wiesbaden: Friedr. Vieweg & Sohn.

IRC. 1988. *Community Self-Improvement in Water Supply and Sanitation. Training Series 5*. The Hague: IRC.

Ishaq, A.M. 1985. "Water Harvesting for Rural Areas in Saudi Arabia" in *Water Resources for Rural Areas and Their Communities*. Vth World Congress on Water Resources. Brussels: IWRA. pp. 1297-1306.

Kalbermatten, J.M., D.S. Julius, C.G. Gunnerson et al. 1981. *Appropriate Technology for Water and Sanitation*. 12 Volumes. Washington DC: The World Bank.

_____, and R.N. Middleton. 1991. *Future Directions in Water Supply and Waste Disposal*. Kalbermatten Associates, Inc.

Kjellerup, B., W.K. Journey, and K.M. Minnatullah. 1989. *The Tara Handpump: The Birth of a Star. Water and Sanitation Discussion Paper Series, DP No 1.* Washington DC: UNDP/The World Bank.

Lee, M.D., and T.F. Bastemeijer. 1991. *Drinking Water Source Protection: An Overview of Problems, Causes, Experiences and Needs. Occasional Paper 15.* The Hague, The Netherlands: IRC International Water and Sanitation Centre.

_____, and J.T. Visscher. 1990. *Water Harvesting in Five African Countries. Occasional Paper Series 14.* The Hague: IRC/UNICEF.

_____, and J.T. Visscher. 1991. *Water Harvesting - A Guide for Decisionmakers and Planners.* Forthcoming Technical Paper Series. The Hague: IRC.

Lewis, W.J., S.D. Foster, and B.S. Drasar. 1980. *The Risk of Pollution by On-Site Sanitation in Developing Countries -- A Literature Review. Report No. 01/82.* Duebendorf, Switzerland: IRCWD.

Lindskog, P., and J. Lundqvist. 1989. *Why Poor Children Stay Sick.* Research Report No 85. Uppsala, Sweden: Scandinavian Institute of African Studies.

Morgan, P. 1990. *Rural Water Supplies and Sanitation.* London: Macmillan.

Myhrstad, J.A., and O. Haldorsen. 1984. "Drinking Water in Developing Countries - The Minimum Treatment Philosophy: A Case Study." *Aqua.* 2, pp. 86-90.

Nilsson, A. 1988. *Groundwater Dams for Small-Scale Water Supply.* London: IT Publications.

_____. 1985. "Siting of Ground-water Dams for Rural Water Supply in Developing Countries: Hydrogeological and Planning Aspects" in *Water Resources for Rural Areas and Their Communities.* Vth World Congress on Water Resources. Brussels: IWRA. pp. 1287-1296.

Okun, D.A., and W.E. Ernst. 1987. *Community Piped Water Supply Systems in Developing Countries. World Bank Technical Paper No 60.* Washington DC: The World Bank.

Pearson, H.W., D.D. Mara, and C.R. Bartone. 1987. "Guidelines for The Minimum Evaluation of the Performance of Full-Scale Waste Stabilization Systems." *Water Research.* 21, pp. 1067-1075.

Reij, C., P. Mulder, and L. Begemann. 1988. *Water Harvesting for Plant Production. World Bank Technical Paper No 91.* Washington DC: The World Bank.

Saunders, R., and J.J. Warford. 1980. *Village Water Supply.* Baltimore, MD: John Hopkins University Press.

Tuyanavich, N., and K. Hewison. 1990. "Rural Water Supply, Sanitation and Health Education in Thailand: Can Success Follow Success?" *Waterlines.* 8, pp. 6-9.

UNICEF. 1989. *Children, Women and Development in Botswana: A Situation Analysis.* Consultant's Report for The Joint GOB/Unicef Programme Planning and Co-ordinating Committee. Gaborone, Botswana: UNICEF/Government of Botswana.

van Wijk, C. 1987. *What Price Water? -- User Participation in Paying for Community-Based Water Supply.* The Hague: IRC Water and Sanitation Centre.

Visscher, J.T., R. Paramasivam, A. Raman, and H.A. Heijnen. 1987. *Slow-Sand Filtration for Community Water Supply. Technical Paper 24.* The Hague: IRC.

Visvanathan, C., and S. Vigneswaran. 1985. "Water Filtration Technologies for Developing Countries" in *Water Resources for Rural Areas and Their Communities.* Vth World Congress on Water Resources. Brussels: IWRA. pp. 1265-1274.

WASH. 1990. *Lessons Learned From the WASH Project: Ten Years of Water and Sanitation Experience in Developing Countries.* Washington DC: Water and Sanitation for Health Project.

_____. 1989. *Water and Sanitation Sector Profiles of Twenty African Countries.* *WASH Field Report 291.* Washington DC: Water and Sanitation for Health Project.

Whittington, D., D.T. Lauria, and X. Mu. 1989a. *Paying for Urban Services: A Study of Water Vending and Willingness to Pay for Water in Onitsha, Nigeria. Report INU 40.* Washington DC: The World Bank.

_____, D.T. Lauria, D.A. Okun, and X. Mu. 1989b. "Water Vending Activities in Developing Countries: A Case Study of Ukunda, Kenya." *Water Resources Development.* 5, pp. 158-168.

_____, M. Mujwahuzi, G. McMahon, and K. Choe. 1989c. *Willingness to Pay for Water in Newala District, Tanzania: Strategies for Cost Recovery. WASH Field Report No. 246.*

_____, A. Okorafor, A. Okore, and A. McPhail. 1990. *Cost Recovery Strategy for Rural Water Delivery in Nigeria. PRE Working Papers.* Washington DC: The World Bank.

WHO. 1989. *UNEP/WHO Project on Control of Drinking Water Quality in Rural Areas.* Report of a Review Meeting at the WHO Collaborating Centre for the Protection of Drinking Water Quality and Human Health, Robens Institute, Guilford, 31-10-4/11. Geneva: World Health Organization.

_____. 1988a. *Managerial and Financial Principles for Water Supply and Sanitation Agencies.* WHO/CWS/89.5. Report of The Fourth Consultation on Institutional Development Working Group on Cost Recovery. I. Geneva: World Health Organization.

_____. 1988b. *Principles and Models to Achieve Sustainable Community Water Supply and to Extend Household Sanitation.* WHO/CWS/89.6. Report of The Fourth Consultation on Institutional Development Working Group on Cost Recovery. II. Geneva: World Health Organization.

World Bank. 1990. *World Development Report 1990.* Oxford University Press.

Zaroff, B., and D.A. Okun. 1984. "Water Vending in Developing Countries." *Aqua.* 5, pp. 289-295.

10

Africa: Economic Analysis of
a Typical Water Supply Project

In this chapter, a simplified economic analysis is presented to justify a classical water supply project in an African township (Munasinghe 1977). As explained in Chapter 3, such a cost-benefit analysis usually consists of several inter-related steps: demand forecast; least-cost investment program; internal economic rate of return; incremental cost of supply; and price level. The emphasis in this chapter is on how demand, cost and revenue data should be used effectively for decisionmaking, rather than on how this information was generated. More detailed practical examples of demand forecasting, cost estimation and pricing are provided in subsequent case study chapters. Environmental considerations are also not included in this first case study, to simplify the presentation.

Demand Forecast

The demand forecast for the township area encompassed by the project is shown in Table 10.1. In the first two columns, total population and total demand are provided to give an indication of overall system size. The incremental demand refers to water which must be supplied via new investments, inclusive of the sources required to replace existing ones which are expected to go out of service in the future. Thus, the increase in total demand from year 1 to year 2 is only 413 m^3 per day (i.e., 4548-4135), but the total incremental demand met (from new investments) is 700 m^3 per day, because of existing sources that have to be replaced. By year 11, the total demand and the total incremental demand met are identical (8763 m^3 per day), since all existing sources would have gone out of service. Incremental demand is the important quantity for this calculation, and is broken down by major consumer category. Domestic consumers are the most important followed by government and finally, industrial users.

348

TABLE 10.1 Demand Forecast

Year	Total Population (10³)	Total Demand (m³/day)	Incremental Demand m³/day				Water Unaccounted For (%)	Total Incremental Supply (m³/day)
			Household	Government	Industrial	Total		
0 (present)	121.5	3717	0	0	0	0	20	0
1	125.7	4135	0	0	0	0	20	0
2	130.1	4548	420	210	70	700	20	875
3	134.6	4983	900	450	150	1500	20	1875
4	139.4	5416	1356	678	226	2260	20	2825
5	144.2	5904	1860	930	310	3100	20	3875
6	149.0	6350	2328	1164	388	3880	19	4790
7	153.9	6796	2760	1380	460	4600	19	5679
8	158.9	7250	3030	1515	505	5050	19	6235
9	164.2	7647	3476	1737	579	5793	19	7152
10	169.7	8134	4035	2017	672	6724	18	8200
11	175.3	8763	5258	2629	876	8763	18	10687
12	180.9	9328	5597	2798	933	9328	18	11376
13	187.0	9892	5935	2968	989	9892	18	12063
14	193.1	10600	6360	3180	1060	10600	18	12927
15	199.6	11300	6780	3390	1130	11300	18	13780
16	207.0	12000	7200	3600	1200	12000	18	14634
17	Forecast uncertain beyond this period		6667	3333	1111	11111	18	13550
18			6173	3086	1029	10288	18	12546
19			5716	2858	952	9526	18	11617
20			5292	2646	882	8820	18	10756

The percentage of water unaccounted for is the fraction of water produced which is not consumed. It decreases steadily due to improvements to the system, better billing etc. Total incremental supply is equal to the sum of total demand and unaccounted for water. We note that incremental demand (and supply) begin in year 2, only after the corresponding investments which had started in year 0 (Table 10.2) have become operational. The 20 year time horizon chosen is sufficient to ensure that due to the cumulative effects of discounting, events occurring beyond this period have negligible impact on the results of the analysis. In fact, by year 16 all existing facilities are operating at full capacity. Thereafter, no new sources are considered, and the incremental demand met by the existing sources declines steadily due to wear and tear.

Least-Cost Investment Program

For illustrative purpose, we assume that the two best feasible alternative system expansion programs or sequences for meeting the demand, are as follows:

- a borehole followed by a reservoir and more boreholes; or
- a reservoir followed by a series of boreholes.

There are ample supplies of both groundwater and surface water available, so that cost complications due to depletion effects (e.g., lowering of the water table and increased pumping costs) do not arise.

In the case of this African township (as in most practical cases) there are more than two alternatives. However, we focus on a comparison of these two different expansion options below, with the understanding that the same principles may be used to compare more than two alternatives.

The cost breakdowns associated with each alternative are given in Tables 10.2 and 10.3. Although certain system costs which are common to both alternatives (e.g., distribution, operation and maintenance and connection costs) may be netted out without affecting the results of the least-cost analysis, these costs have been included in the tables because they will be required for the rate of return and marginal cost computations which follow.

The system of efficiency shadow pricing described in Chapter 3 is followed in Table 10.2. All costs are given in local currency units (L), in real 1990 prices. The reference official exchange rate is US$ 1 = L1.

The two columns marked "Direct Imports" are net of duties and taxes, and converted directly into border prices (using the official exchange rate). Investments supplied through the local construction sector are converted from domestic to border prices using the construction conversion factor of 0.85.

TABLE 10.2 Supply Costs for Alternative 1

| | Investment Costs (10³ L) (1) | | | Operation And Maintenance Costs (10³ L) (1) | | | | | | | | Total Cost (10³ L) |
| | Direct | Local Construction (3) | | Direct | Local Investment Goods (4) | | Electricity (5) | | Local Labor (6) | | |
Year	Imports (2)	Dom.P.	Border P.	Imports (2)	Dom.P.	Border P.	Dom.P.	Border P.	Dom.P.	Border P.	Border Prices
0	150	50	42.6	0	0	0.0	0	0.0	0	0.0	192.6
1	45	15	12.8	0	0	0.0	0	0.0	0	0.0	57.8
2				3	6	5.4	6	4.8	15	12.8	26.0
3				7	14	12.6	14	11.2	35	29.8	60.6
4	400	267	227.0	10	20	18.0	20	16.0	50	42.5	713.5
5	300	200	170.0	18	32	28.8	32	25.6	80	68.0	610.4
6				25	44	39.6	44	35.2	110	93.5	199.3
7				33	56	50.4	56	44.8	140	119.0	247.2
8				38	60	54.0	60	48.0	150	127.5	267.5
9				60	88	79.2	88	70.4	220	187.0	396.6
10	75	25	21.3	70	96	86.4	96	76.8	240	204.0	533.5
11				85	106	95.4	106	84.8	265	225.3	490.5
12	30	20	17.0	102	114	102.6	114	91.2	285	242.3	585.1
13	150	50	42.5	110	125	112.5	125	100.0	315	267.8	782.8
14				115	136	122.4	136	108.8	340	289.0	635.2
15				119	145	130.5	145	116.0	360	306.0	671.5
16				110	134	120.6	134	107.2	335	284.8	622.6
17				102	124	111.6	124	99.2	316	268.6	581.4
18				94	113	101.7	113	90.4	280	238.0	524.1
19				87	105	94.5	105	84.0	260	221.0	486.5
20				80	97	87.3	97	77.6	240	204.0	448.9

(1) All Costs are in real 1990 Local currency units (L). The official exchange rate is US$ 1 = L1.
(2) Net of duties and taxes; therefore already in border prices.
(3) Construction conversion factor = 0.85, for general inputs from the local construction sector (includes labor).
(4) Investment conversion factor = 0.9, for aggregate of locally purchased (small) investment items.
(5) Electricity conversion factor = 0.8, for electricity input, ideally, the border price should reflect the long-run marginal cost of supply of electricity.
(6) Labor conversion factor or shadow wage rate (SWR) = 0.85, this is a weighted average of: unskilled SWR = 0.55 and skilled SWR = 0.95.

TABLE 10.3 Supply Costs for Alternative 2

| | Investment Costs (10³ L) | | | Operation And Maintenance Costs (10³ L) | | | | | | | Total Cost (10³ L) |
| | Direct | Local Construction | | Direct | Local Investment Goods | | Electricity | | Local Labor | | |
Year	Imports	Dom.P.	Border P.	Imports	Dom.P.	Border P.	Dom.P.	Border P.	Dom.P.	Border P.	Border Prices
0	300	200	170.0	0	0		0		0		470.0
1	200	133	113.1	0	0		0		0		313.1
2				6	3	2.7	2	1.6	10	8.5	18.8
3				14	7	6.3	4	3.2	25	21.5	45.0
4				20	10	9.0	6	4.8	35	29.8	63.6
5				32	20	18.0	14	11.2	60	51.0	112.2
6				44	32	28.8	28	22.4	90	76.5	171.7
7				56	48	43.2	42	33.6	110	93.5	226.3
8	30	20	17.0	60	56	50.4	50	40.0	150	127.5	324.9
9	75	25	21.3	88	85	76.5	81	64.8	195	165.8	491.4
10				92	96	86.4	95	76.0	250	212.5	466.9
11	120	40	34.0	97	106	95.4	106	84.8	275	233.8	665.0
12				103	114	102.6	114	91.2	300	255.0	551.8
13	150	50	42.5								782.8
14											635.2
15					Operating and maintenance costs are the same as in Table 10.2						671.5
16					from the 13th year onwards.						622.6
17	30	20	17.0								628.4
18											524.1
19											486.5
20											448.9

(1) See Table 10.2 for explanatory footnotes.

TABLE 10.4   Comparison of Water System Expansion Alternatives

	Present Value of Total Costs $(10^3 L)$		
Discount Rate (%)	Alternative 1	Alternative 2	Difference
0	9134	8721	413
5	5267	4971	296
10	3321	3134	187
20	1649	1639	10
30	1018	1129	-111

Internal Economic Rate of Return (IERR) = 20.5%.
Opportunity Cost of Capital = 10% to 12%.

Similarly, an investment conversion factor of 0.9 applies to locally purchased investment goods used in operation and maintenance.

Domestic priced electricity inputs used mainly for pumping have been converted to border prices using the electricity conversion factor of 0.8. In this way, the border price of electricity is adjusted to reflect the long-run marginal cost (LRMC) of supply (see Chapter 7 for details). Finally, a shadow wage rate (SWR) or labor conversion factor of 0.85 is used to border price local labor inputs. This aggregate SWR is a weighted average of 75% skilled labor (with SSWR=0.95) and 25% unskilled labor (USWR=0.55). Finally, all the columns involving direct imports and border priced costs are added together in the last column, to yield the total costs of alternative 1 in border prices. Exactly the same procedure is followed in Table 10.3, where the costs of the second alternative are analyzed.

The present values (PV) of the cost streams for both alternatives are given in Table 10.4, for several different discount rates. It is clear that alternative 2 is better than alternative 1 for discount rates ranging from 0 to 20%. The opportunity cost of capital for this specific example falls in the range 10% to 12%. Therefore, the second investment program involving construction of the surface water reservoir first, is chosen as the least-cost alternative.

Internal Economic Rate of Return (IERR)

Based on the above analysis, construction of the reservoir and associated facilities becomes the desired scheme. The costs associated with the water supply project under consideration are shown in Table 10.5, (e.g., capital costs for reservoir construction in years 0 and 1, and for renovation in years 8 and 17). The border pricing procedure used here is the same as in Tables 10.2 and 10.3.

TABLE 10.5 Project Costs

	Investment Costs (10³ L)			Operation And Maintenance Costs (10³ L)							Total Cost (10³ L)
	Direct	Local Construction		Direct	Local Investment Goods		Electricity		Local Labor		
Year	Imports	Dom.P.	Border P.	Imports	Dom.P.	Border P.	Dom.P.	Border P.	Dom.P.	Border P.	Border Prices
0	300	200	170.0	0	0		0		0		470.0
1	200	133	113.1	0	0		0		0		313.1
2				6	3	2.7	2	1.6	10	8.5	18.8
3				14	7	6.3	4	3.2	25	21.3	45.0
4				20	10	9.0	6	4.8	35	29.8	63.6
5				32	20	18.0	14	11.2	60	51.0	112.2
6				44	32	28.8	28	22.4	90	76.5	171.7
7				56	48	43.2	42	33.6	110	93.5	226.3
8	30	20	17.0	60	56	50.4	50	40.0	150	127.5	324.9
9				88	85	76.5	81	64.8	195	165.8	395.1
10				88	85	76.5	81	64.8	195	165.8	395.1
11				88	85	76.5	81	64.8	195	165.8	395.1
12				88	85	76.5	81	64.8	195	165.8	395.1
13				88	85	76.5	81	64.8	195	165.8	395.1
14				88	85	76.5	81	64.8	195	165.8	395.1
15				88	85	76.5	81	64.8	195	165.8	395.1
16				88	85	76.5	81	64.8	195	165.8	395.1
17	30	20	17.0	80	78	70.2	74	59.2	180	153.0	409.4
18				73	71	63.9	67	53.6	166	141.1	331.6
19				67	64	57.6	61	48.8	153	130.1	303.5
20				61	58	52.2	56	44.8	141	119.9	277.9

(1) See Table 10.2 for explanatory footnotes.

TABLE 10.6   Project Benefits (Partial)

| | Incremental Consumption due to Project (m³/day) | | Incremental Consumption Benefits due to Project | | | | Total (10³ L/year) |
| | | | Household (L/day) | | Government & Industrial (L/day) | | |
Year	Household	Government & Industrial	Domestic Prices (1)	Border Prices (2)	Domestic Prices (3)	Border Prices (4)	Border Prices
0	0	0	0.0	0.0	0.0	0.0	0.0
1	0	0	0.0	0.0	0.0	0.0	0.0
2	420	280	134.4	107.5	78.4	66.6	63.6
3	900	600	288.0	230.4	168.0	142.8	136.2
4	1356	904	433.9	347.1	253.1	215.1	205.2
5	1860	1240	595.2	476.2	347.2	295.1	281.5
6	2328	1552	745.0	596.0	434.6	369.4	352.4
7	2760	1840	883.2	706.6	515.2	437.9	417.7
8	3030	2020	969.6	775.7	565.6	480.8	458.6
9	3476	2316	1,112.3	889.8	645.6	548.8	525.1
10	3476	2316	1,112.3	889.8	645.6	548.8	525.1
11	3476	2316	1,112.3	889.8	645.6	548.8	525.1
12	3476	2316	1,112.3	889.8	645.6	548.8	525.1
13	3476	2316	1,112.3	889.8	645.6	548.8	525.1
14	3476	2316	1,112.3	889.8	645.6	548.8	525.1
15	3476	2316	1,112.3	889.8	645.6	548.8	525.1
16	3476	2316	1,112.3	889.8	645.6	548.8	525.1
17	3218	2144	1,029.8	823.8	600.3	510.2	486.9
18	2980	1986	953.6	762.9	556.1	472.6	451.0
19	2759	1839	882.9	706.2	515.0	437.7	417.5
20	2555	1702	817.6	654.1	476.6	405.0	386.6

(1) Average household tariff = L 0.32 per m³ is the proxy for benefits (in domestic prices).
(2) Consumption conversion factor = 0.8.
(3) Average government and industrial tariff = L 0.28 per m³ is the proxy for benefits (in domestic prices).
(4) Standard conversion factor = 0.85; used due to uncertainty regarding alternative consumption patterns of government and industry.

In this example, the project itself is a distinct part of the larger least-cost investment program shown in Table 10.3. However, such a separation of the program into many distinct components may not always be possible. In such cases, the project would be defined to include the entire investment program (i.e., project and program are identical).

Table 10.6 contains the incremental benefit stream, corresponding to the costs in Table 10.5. These benefits are only partial because incremental revenues are used as a proxy for benefits whereas consumer surplus and external benefits have been ignored (see Chapter 3 for details). Incremental consumption benefits associated with the project begin in year 2 (i.e., after 2 years of initial investment), and increase steadily up to the year 9 when the new facilities are fully utilized. After year 17, the incremental output supplied from the project starts to decline as the plant ages. The incremental water used by households (in m^3) is multiplied by the average household tariff of L0.32 per m^3 to obtain the corresponding benefit (in domestic prices). This domestic priced benefit must be converted to border prices by applying the consumption conversion factor of 0.8 (see Chapter 3).

Similarly, the government and industrial water use benefits (in domestic prices) are calculated after multiplying the physical water consumption by the average government and industrial user tariff of L0.28 per m^3. These benefits are converted to border prices using the standard conversion factor of 0.85 (since we do not have a specific conversion factor for government and industry).

The household, government and industrial benefits are added together to yield the total border priced project benefits in the last column of Table 10.6. We note that these benefits are a minimum measure of consumer willingness-to-pay.

The IERR for the project is 13.6%, which equates the present values of the cost and benefit streams computed in the last columns of Tables 10.5 and 10.6 (see Chapter 3 for details). The opportunity cost of capital (OCC) lies in the range 10 to 12%, as indicated earlier. Based on the following analysis, it is possible to draw some interesting general conclusions from a comparison of the IERR and the OCC.

First, we note that the incremental cost of supply (ICS) based on this project alone could be used as a rough approximation to average LRMC. ICS may be defined by the expression:

$$ICS = \frac{PVC(OCC)}{PVD(OCC)} \tag{10.1}$$

where PVC(OCC) = present value of project costs discounted at OCC, and PVD(OCC) = present value of incremental demand discounted at OCC.

By definition, the present value of costs and of incremental benefits are equal when IERR is the discount rate. In other words:

$$PVC(IERR) = PVB(IERR) \qquad (10.2)$$

but:

$$PVB(IERR) = p \cdot PVD(IERR) \qquad (10.3)$$

where p is the constant average price per unit of water sold (assumed to be consistent with the forecast demand).

Equations (10.2) and (10.3) yield:

$$p = \frac{PVC(IERR)}{PVD(IERR)} \qquad (10.4)$$

It is straightforward to show that IERR > OCC implies that p > ICS and vice versa. Therefore, for this project the average tariff level is somewhat higher than the incremental cost of supply (since IERR = 13.6% > OCC = 10 to 12%).

Incremental Cost of Supply and
Average Price Level

Of much greater relevance for efficient allocation of resources in the sector is the long-run marginal cost (LRMC) of water based on the entire system expansion plan (Table 10.3). Since the investments are lumpy, Average Incremental Cost (AIC) may be used to estimate LRMC, as explained in more detail in Chapter 6.

To summarize, the AIC is calculated by computing:

- the sum of the present discounted values of incremental costs each year, for years 0 to T;
- the sum of the present discounted values of incremental supply each year, for years 0 to T; and
- the ratio A/B.

The values of AIC for this case range from L0.210 to 0.222 per m³ of water in border prices for discount rates of 10 to 12%. As described in Chapter 3, dividing this AIC value by the standard conversion factor (SCF = 0.85) for governmental and industrial consumers, yields the benchmark marginal cost range of $AIC_{G,I}$ = L0.248 to 0.261 per m^3, in domestic prices, which may be compared with the existing average tariff level. Similarly, using the consumption conversion factor (CCF = 0.8) for household consumers, we find: AIC_H = L0.263 to 0.278 per m^3.

The prevailing average tariff levels are L0.28 and 0.32 per m^3 of water respectively for government/industrial and household consumers, both of which are slightly higher than the corresponding benchmark values of AIC_H and $AIC_{G,I}$, calculated above. This confirms the tentative conclusion regarding the level of average tariffs made in the previous paragraph, based on the project IERR calculation alone.

If financial, sociopolitical and other constraints permit it, we could be justified in urging a small decrease in overall tariff levels, based solely on economic efficiency considerations. However, detailed recommendations on both the level and structure of tariffs ought to be made only after a thorough tariff study as described in Chapter 7.

References

Munasinghe, M. 1977. *Economic Analysis of Water Supply Projects: A Case Study of an African Township*. Public Utilities Department Report. Washington DC: The World Bank.

11

Brazil: National Water Supply Policy and Evaluation of the São Paulo Water Utility

Introduction

This chapter describes the main issues in the Brazilian water and sewerage sector, as well as details of the overall strategy to address these problems. It also presents a case study involving SABESP, the water utility in the State of São Paulo. Brazil provides a useful example to illustrate the problems and achievements of the water and sanitation sector in developing countries.

The demand for basic sanitation services in urban areas of Brazil has been growing faster than supply. The ability of the sector to meet the needs for these services over the next several decades is uncertain in view of financial constraints in the country. Since its establishment in 1968, the National Water and Sanitation Program (PLANASA) has achieved impressive goals, adding over 55 million new water connections and over 24 million new sewerage connections to the Brazilian water and sanitation system. However, demand has outpaced supply because of rapid urbanization and an accelerated household formation which will generate nine million new urban households by the turn of the century.

Meeting national sector goals of 90% coverage in water supply and 65% in sewerage will require a restoration of future rates of investment to former levels. In addition, the new constitution and the fiscal and administrative reforms promulgated in 1988 resulted in greater financial resources and responsibilities for states and municipalities, but diminished the federal government's own expenditures in the sector. Although the effects of the

This chapter was prepared with the assistance of E. Rodriguez, C. Velez, M. Sheehan, G. Yepes and T. Campbell.

reform are not yet clearly known, with this receding federal role, state and municipal entities must become more active and efficient in both resource mobilization and allocation.

In the past, emphasis has been placed on the strengthening of sector financial viability and the institutional capacities of the State Water Companies (SWCs), throughout Brazil. The study in the second part of this chapter summarizes the efforts to pursue this strategy, in the case of SABESP, the São Paulo state-owned water and sewerage company. Specific activities described include the financing of a portion of its five-year investment program, increasing the efficiency of public sector investment planning and decisionmaking, and generally strengthening the financial and institutional relationship between SABESP and the State of São Paulo. A comprehensive case study of water and sewerage pricing for SABESP is provided subsequently in Chapter 12. SABESP has made progress over the past decade in closing the service deficits in the sector. The evidence presented below shows that it is in a good position to meet the new challenges of extending service to secondary cities and towns, especially among the urban poor, where most of Brazil's new water connections are needed during the next decade.

Population

Although the overall rate of population growth in Brazil has slowed to under three percent per year, urbanization rates will continue to exert pressure on basic infrastructure. The total population of the country (close to 150 million in 1989), is expected to reach nearly 180 million by the turn of the century. Over 74% (110 million) of this total is presently living in cities, and nearly 80% will be urban by the year 2000 (see Table 11.1).

The distribution of population has had a pronounced effect on the demand for infrastructure for the following reasons:

- rural populations are nearly steady, and even declining in some regions;
- the rates of growth and population totals are unevenly distributed in the country. The heaviest urban populations are found in the South and Southeast regions;
- although the Northeast has the largest percentage of poor, the largest absolute numbers of urban poor are found in the South and Southeast;
- the relatively "bottom heavy" age distribution of the population pyramid implies that household formation rates are 20% higher than urban growth rates as a whole. This signifies an even higher demand for infrastructure connections than would be suggested merely by urban population growth alone; and
- the urbanization process is increasing the number of secondary and tertiary cities and towns. This fact has complicated the administrative

TABLE 11.1   Urban and Rural Populations Historic (1970 to 1980) and Projected (1985 to 2000)

Years	Millions of Inhabitants			% of Total Population		
	Total	Urban	Rural	Total	Urban	Rural
1970	95.9	53.6	42.3	100.0	56.0	44.0
1980	121.3	82.0	39.3	100.0	67.6	32.4
1985	135.6	97.6	38.0	100.0	72.0	28.0
1990	150.4	112.7	37.7	100.0	74.9	25.1
1995	165.1	128.0	37.1	100.0	77.5	22.5
2000	179.5	143.1	36.4	100.0	79.7	20.3

Source: Luiz Armando de Madeiros Frias, 1988.

Note: The adjusted 1970 and 1980 population figures and the projections
               for total resident population are from: IBGE/Centro Latinao
               Americano de Demografia--CELAGDE, Brasil: Estimaciones de
               Poblacion 1950-2025, Fasciculo F/BRA 1, Julio 1984.

burden of meeting the need for water and sanitation, given the present emphasis on decentralization.

Service Coverage and Performance

Brazil has one of the most impressive records in expansion of water services in any Latin American country. Over the past two decades, more than 55 million people have been connected to water and another 24 million to sanitation services. By 1989, as a result of this effort, 87% of the urban households were connected to water and 39% to sanitation services, as opposed to coverage levels in 1968 of 50% and 30%, respectively. The rate of service growth in water has outpaced population and even urbanization rates overall. Sanitation services have lagged behind water because water is the first priority and because sanitation including treatment is more expensive and harder to finance from internal resources (see Table A11.1). Sewerage and wastewater disposal is a major problem in most low-income and slum/shanty-towns giving rise to significant adverse environmental impacts on the health conditions of residents and downstream communities.

The regional distribution of water and sanitation services in the PLANASA system in 1988, is given in Table 11.2. Service levels have dropped perceptibly in the recent past. Projections based on 1985 survey data show that merely to maintain present levels of water and sanitation service nearly

TABLE 11.2   Regional Distribution of Urban Service Levels, 1988

| | Population Receiving Service | | | |
| | Water | | Sewerage | |
Region	Number (millions)	% Served (1)	Number (millions) (2)	% Served (3)
North	2.5	72.5	0.1	5.2
Northeast	16.8	80.6	2.9	17.7
Southeast	35.2	90.0	19.6	48.8
South	11.4	88.9	2.2	19.4
Centerwest	6.4	85.9	2.5	38.9
Total Brazil	72.3	82.6	27.3	37.8

(1)   Service fraction is given as the percentage of total urban population.
(2)   Refers only to water-borne sewerage, not to other forms of waste-water disposal.
(3)   Service fraction is given as the percentage of urban population with water.

Source: Caixa Economica Federal.

650 thousand new households must be connected each year to water, and more than 1.85 million to sanitation systems, between 1985 and 1990.   The performance of the principal SWCs in Brazil, with respect to water supplied, losses, average unit price and operating costs, return on assets, and consumers per employee, are given in Table A11.2.   In general, there is a marked difference in performance (e.g., compare losses of return on assets) between SWC in the poorer north and richer south, with the latter showing marked superiority.

National Water and Sewerage Policies

Sector Policies

Much of the reason for the priority given to investments in the water sector is founded on the need for basic infrastructure and protection of public health. The progress made in water connections over the past several decades is reflected in improvements in health indicators. Child mortality and morbidity, two indicators sensitive to sanitation services, have improved by about 17%

nationwide since 1970. However, as suggested earlier, these improvements are found mostly in large cities and regions where not only are water services more widespread, but three other key indicators: health services; education; and income are also better. Marked differences in health levels by region and income level remain to be addressed. For instance, child mortality among the poorest neighborhoods in all Brazilian cities is 60 to 70% higher than the average for urban Brazil. Continued improvements in the living conditions of the poor will require increased investments in water and increased emphasis on sanitation.

Brazil has adopted PLANASA goals of reaching 90% of the overall urban population with water and 65% with sanitation by the turn of the century. New emphasis is being given to waste disposal. However, the large financial requirements implied by these goals, combined with a number of policy constraints, make it unlikely that the goals can be met. To achieve even more modest targets, a range of policy and financial issues need to be addressed, including overall policy formulation, long range planning, sector coordination, and tariffs. The new program seeks to address the most important among these policy issues, especially those relating to public sector efficiency and institutional arrangements.

PLANASA and the National Tariff Law (NTL)

Most of the past progress in this sector has been the result of the national PLANASA program. Established in 1968, PLANASA greatly improved planning and programming, establishing a national tariff law, standardizing accounting practices and procedures, setting up criteria for program screening and appraisal, and building information systems. The PLANASA system is anchored by a central financial and technical intermediary, the Caixa Economica Federal (CEF), which plans, coordinates, and lends directly to states and water companies for capital investments. CEF funds are also channeled indirectly through the State Water and Sewerage Funds (FAEs), which are revolving funds set up to maintain sources of financing for sector investments at the state level. Inflation and the economic crisis in Brazil since 1983 have eroded the financial viability of the system. Recently, the water companies have managed to avoid major capital depreciation and serious reductions in service levels through capital transfers directly from state governments, and as of 1987-1988, by raising real tariff levels.

With the exception of investment made in municipalities that have not joined PLANASA, this program has been the sole source of financing for water and sanitation in urban areas. Since 1968, PLANASA has invested more than US$ 11 billion in the sector (68.4% in water and 31.6% in sanitation), benefitting nearly 80 million people in more than 4,000 communities. Almost two-thirds of these investments came from the central government (the CEF and its predecessor in the sector, the National Housing Bank (BNH)), nearly a quarter from the states (a portion of which had been lent to the states by CEF), and the rest from grants and outside financing. PLANASA investment represents more than 80% of Brazil's total investment in water and sewerage.

One of PLANASA's most important achievements, has been the promulgation of the National Tariff Law (NTL). This law has proved to be effective mainly from the financial point of view (i.e., by helping to define appropriate average tariff levels). However, it contains some deficiencies with regard to the treatment of price structure. Notably, the NTL does not use marginal cost concepts and fails to provide a systematic basis for determining:

- the degree of cross-subsidization for the financing of services to the poor;
- the relationship between water and sewerage charges; and
- the appropriate structure of charges to be applied to different types of water consumers.

To remedy this situation, the Brazilian authorities launched a program (in 1988), to examine the level and structure of water supply and sewerage tariffs. Six SWCs in Brazil that are responsible for almost half the total water sales: SABESP, SANEPAR, COPASA, COSANPA, CAGECE and SANESUL (see Table A11.2 in Appendix 11), are carrying out detailed studies of their marginal cost structures with a view to ultimately revising their tariff structure (see Chapter 12 for specific details).

SABESP Case Study

A principal focus of past efforts in the Brazilian water sector had been to nurture sector financial viability and the institutional capabilities of SWCs to plan and execute investments and operate their systems. Starting in 1989, the federal government began to transfer considerably greater resources and responsibilities to states and municipalities while curtailing its own direct expenditures and activities in the sector. In line with these policies, the specific program described in the following case study works within the broader framework of PLANASA, to support measures and investments in the state of São Paulo, that will encourage economic growth and social development. More specifically, it seeks to strengthen the capacity of SABESP to carry out more efficient planning of investments, improved internal revenue mobilization, and increased efficiency of operations, while covering urgently needed extension of services (see Table 11.3 for overall targets).

TABLE 11.3   SABESP's Overall Targets (1989-1993)

Indicator	1988	1993	Increment
State Urban Population (millions)	28.4	33.7	5.3
SABESP			
Total Urban Population (millions)	18.9	21.5	2.6
Water Supply			
Serviced Population (millions)	17.0	19.4	2.4
(percentage)	90	90	--
Persons/Family	4.3	4.2	--
Connections (millions)	3.19	3.67	0.48
Families (millions)	3.96	4.68	0.72
Metered connections (%)	91	93	--
Production (Mm³/year)	1937	2122	185
Consumption, billed (Mm³/year)	1167	1333	166
Block sales (Mm³/year)	287	329	42
Unaccounted for water (%)	25	22	-3
Sewerage			
Serviced Population (millions)	11.5	14.4	2.9
(percentage)	61	67	6
Persons/Family	4.3	4.3	--
Connections (millions)	1.89	2.32	0.43
Families (millions)	2.68	3.29	0.61

In the following sections, we examine the demand projections, least-cost investment plan, and SABESP's status (including its financing plan). The chapter concludes with a rigorous cost-benefit analysis (CBA) of one specific part of the investment program.

Water Demand Forecast

Water supply and sewerage service demand projections have been made by administrative region (see Figure 11.1) which includes: the São Paulo Metropolitan Region (RMSP) Integrated System; the RMSP Isolated System; the Baixada Santista; the Interior Large and Medium Cities (CMG); and the Interior Small Communities (CPP). As shown in Tables 11.4 and 11.5, the accurate design of water systems by specific small areas requires detailed and disaggregate projections to be made, assuming that:

• annual population growth rates, daily water consumption per person, household sizes, and persons per connection, will remain constant;

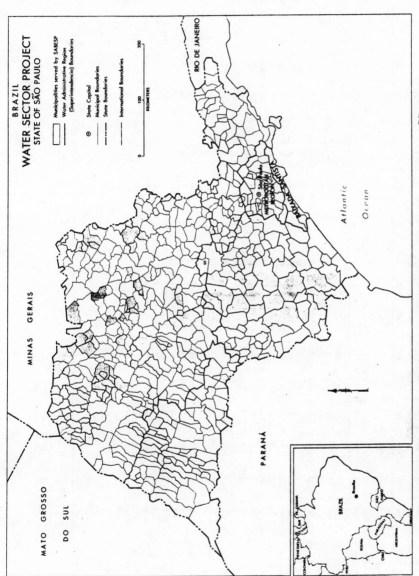

Figure 11.1 Water Sector Projects by Administrative Region for the State of São Paolo

TABLE 11.4 SABESP's Projected Water Demand (millions m³)

Description	1988	1989	1990	1991	1992	1993	1994	1995	1996	1997	1998	1999	2000*	2001	2002	2003	2004	2005-18
RMSP: Integrated System																		
Urban Population (thousands)	12,385.0	12,653.0	12,930.0	13,163.0	13,405.0	13,650.0	13,898.0	14,148.0	14,361.0	14,576.0	14,795.0	15,016.0	15,241.0	15,241.0	15,241.0	15,241.0	15,241.0	15,241.0
Coverage Level (%)	90.0	90.3	90.6	90.9	91.2	91.5	91.5	91.5	91.5	91.5	91.5	91.5	91.5	91.5	91.5	91.5	91.5	91.5
Urban Pop Served (thousands)	11,147.0	11,426.0	11,715.0	11,955.0	12,225.0	12,490.0	12,717.0	12,945.0	13,140.0	13,337.0	13,537.0	13,740.0	13,946.0	13,946.0	13,946.0	13,946.0	13,946.0	13,946.0
Annual Cons/Cap (m³/p-yr)	76.7	76.7	76.7	76.7	76.7	76.7	76.7	76.7	76.7	76.7	76.7	76.7	76.7	76.7	76.7	76.7	76.7	76.7
Persons Per Household (units)	4.2	4.2	4.2	4.2	4.2	4.2	4.2	4.2	4.2	4.2	4.2	4.2	4.2	4.2	4.2	4.2	4.2	4.2
HH Per Connection (units)	1.3	1.3	1.3	1.3	1.3	1.3	1.3	1.3	1.3	1.3	1.3	1.3	1.3	1.3	1.3	1.3	1.3	1.3
End of Yr Connect (thousands)	2,041.0	2,093.0	2,146.0	2,191.0	2,239.0	2,288.0	2,329.0	2,371.0	2,407.0	2,443.0	2,479.0	2,516.0	2,554.0	2,554.0	2,554.0	2,554.0	2,554.0	2,554.0
End Yr Inc. Conn. (thousands)	NA	51.6	104.5	150.4	198.1	246.5	288.1	330.0	365.7	401.7	438.4	475.4	513.1	513.1	513.1	513.1	513.1	513.1
Water Cons.: Final Users	845.0	866.0	887.0	908.0	928.0	948.0	967.0	984.0	1,000.0	1,015.0	1,031.0	1,046.0	1,062.0	1,070.0	1,070.0	1,070.0	1,070.0	1,070.0
Water Cons.: Bulk Sale Cons.	244.0	251.0	258.0	266.0	274.0	282.0	291.0	300.0	312.0	324.0	337.0	330.0	363.0	363.0	363.0	363.0	363.0	363.0
Water Cons.: Special Contracts	43.0	43.0	44.0	46.0	47.0	49.0	50.0	52.0	53.0	55.0	56.0	58.0	58.0	58.0	58.0	58.0	58.0	58.0
Water Consumption	1,132.0	1,160.0	1,189.0	1,219.0	1,248.0	1,277.0	1,306.0	1,334.0	1,364.0	1,393.0	1,423.0	1,452.0	1,482.0	1,490.0	1,490.0	1,490.0	1,490.0	1,490.0
Incremental Water Consum.	NA	27.8	57.1	86.8	115.7	145.4	174.2	201.8	231.7	260.9	290.6	320.3	350.5	358.4	358.4	358.4	358.4	358.4
Average Losses Level (%)	23.0	22.5	22.0	21.5	21.0	20.5	20.0	20.0	20.0	20.0	20.0	20.0	20.0	20.0	20.0	20.0	20.0	20.0
Water Production	1,470.0	1,496.0	1,524.0	1,553.0	1,579.0	1,607.0	1,633.0	1,667.0	1,705.0	1,741.0	1,778.0	1,815.0	1,853.0	1,863.0	1,863.0	1,863.0	1,863.0	1,863.0
Incremental Water Production	NA	26.5	54.4	82.6	109.4	136.8	162.7	197.3	234.6	271.2	308.2	345.4	383.1	393.0	393.0	393.0	393.0	393.0
RMSP: Isolated System																		
Urban Population (thousands)	121.0	124.0	127.0	131.0	135.0	140.0	144.0	149.0	149.0	149.0	149.0	149.0	149.0	149.0	149.0	149.0	149.0	149.0
Coverage Level (%)	60.0	60.0	62.0	64.0	67.0	70.0	73.0	76.0	76.0	76.0	76.0	76.0	76.0	76.0	76.0	76.0	76.0	76.0
Urban Pop Served (thousands)	72.6	74.4	78.7	83.8	90.5	98.0	105.1	113.2	113.2	113.2	113.2	113.2	113.2	113.2	113.2	113.2	113.2	113.2
Annual Cons/Cap (m³/p-yr)	58.4	58.4	58.4	58.4	58.4	58.4	58.4	58.4	58.4	58.4	58.4	58.4	58.4	58.4	58.4	58.4	58.4	58.4
Persons Per Household (units)	4.2	4.2	4.2	4.2	4.2	4.2	4.2	4.2	4.2	4.2	4.2	4.2	4.2	4.2	4.2	4.2	4.2	4.2
HH Per Connection (units)	1.0	1.0	1.0	1.0	1.0	1.0	1.0	1.0	1.0	1.0	1.0	1.0	1.0	1.0	1.0	1.0	1.0	1.0
End of Yr Connect (thousands)	16.8	17.2	18.2	19.4	20.9	22.7	24.3	26.2	26.2	26.2	26.2	26.2	26.2	26.2	26.2	26.2	26.2	26.2
End Yr Inc. Conn. (thousands)	NA	0.4	1.4	2.6	4.1	5.9	7.5	9.4	9.4	9.4	9.4	9.4	9.4	9.4	9.4	9.4	9.4	9.4
Water Consumption	4.2	4.3	4.5	4.7	5.1	5.5	5.9	6.4	6.6	6.6	6.6	6.6	6.6	6.6	6.6	6.6	6.6	6.6
Incremental Water Consum.	NA	0.1	0.3	0.5	0.9	1.3	1.7	2.2	2.4	2.4	2.4	2.4	2.4	2.4	2.4	2.4	2.4	2.4
Average Losses Level (%)	32.0	31.5	31.0	30.5	30.0	29.5	29.0	28.5	28.0	28.0	28.0	28.0	28.0	28.0	28.0	28.0	28.0	28.0
Water Production	6.2	6.3	6.5	6.8	7.3	7.8	8.4	8.9	9.2	9.2	9.2	9.2	9.2	9.2	9.2	9.2	9.2	9.2
Incremental Water Production	NA	0.1	0.3	0.3	0.6	1.1	1.6	2.2	2.7	3.0	3.0	3.0	3.0	3.0	3.0	3.0	3.0	3.0

TABLE 11.4 (continued)

Description	1988	1989	1990	1991	1992	1993	1994	1995	1996	1997	1998	1999	2000*	2001	2002	2003	2004	2005-18
Rainais Services																		
Urban Population (thousands)	2,236.0	2,305.0	2,378.0	2,434.0	2,493.0	2,556.0	2,620.0	2,685.0	2,753.0	2,821.0	2,892.0	2,964.0	3,038.0	3,114.0	3,192.0	3,272.0	3,353.0	3,437.0
Coverage Level (%)	96.0	96.0	96.0	96.0	96.0	96.0	96.0	96.0	96.0	96.0	96.0	96.0	96.0	96.0	96.0	96.0	96.0	96.0
Urban Pop Served (thousands)	2,144.0	2,213.0	2,283.0	2,337.0	2,393.0	2,454.0	2,515.0	2,578.0	2,643.0	2,708.0	2,776.0	2,845.0	2,916.0	2,989.0	3,064.0	3,141.0	3,219.0	3,300.0
Annual Cons/Cap (m³/p-yr)	50.0	50.0	50.0	50.0	50.0	50.0	50.0	50.0	50.0	50.0	50.0	50.0	50.0	50.0	50.0	50.0	50.0	50.0
Persons Per Household (units)	5.0	5.0	5.0	5.0	5.0	5.0	5.0	5.0	5.0	5.0	5.0	5.0	5.0	5.0	5.0	5.0	5.0	5.0
HH Per Connection (units)	1.9	1.9	1.9	1.9	1.9	1.9	1.9	1.9	1.9	1.9	1.9	1.9	1.9	1.9	1.9	1.9	1.9	1.9
End of Yr Connect (thousands)	243.0	250.0	258.0	264.0	271.0	278.0	285.0	292.0	299.0	307.0	314.0	322.0	330.0	338.0	347.0	355.0	364.0	373.0
End Yr Inc. Conn. (thousands)	NA	7.5	15.4	21.5	27.9	34.7	41.7	48.7	56.1	63.5	71.2	79.1	87.1	95.4	103.8	112.5	121.4	130.5
Water Consumption	105.0	108.9	112.4	115.5	118.2	121.2	124.2	127.3	130.5	133.8	137.1	140.5	144.0	147.6	151.3	155.1	159.0	163.0
Incremental Water Consum.	NA	3.9	7.4	10.5	13.2	16.2	19.2	22.3	25.5	28.8	32.1	35.5	39.0	42.6	46.3	50.1	54.0	58.0
Average Losses Level (%)	37.0	37.0	36.0	35.0	34.0	33.0	32.0	31.0	30.0	29.0	28.0	27.0	26.0	26.0	26.0	26.0	26.0	26.0
Water Production	166.7	172.9	175.6	177.7	179.2	180.9	182.7	184.5	186.4	188.4	190.4	192.5	194.7	199.5	204.5	209.6	214.9	220.2
Incremental Water Production	NA	6.2	8.9	11.0	12.5	14.2	16.0	17.8	19.7	21.7	23.7	25.8	28.0	32.8	37.8	42.9	48.2	53.5
Interior: Large and Medium Cities (CMG)																		
Urban Population (thousands)	3,518.0	3,671.0	3,827.0	3,979.0	4,139.0	4,302.0	4,474.1	4,653.0	4,839.2	5,032.7	5,234.0	5,443.4	5,661.1	5,661.1	5,661.1	5,661.1	5,661.1	5,661.1
Coverage Level (%)	87.0	87.0	87.0	87.0	87.0	87.0	87.0	87.0	87.0	87.0	87.0	87.0	87.0	87.0	87.0	87.0	87.0	87.0
Urban Pop Served (thousands)	3,060.7	3,193.8	3,329.5	3,461.7	3,600.9	3,742.7	3,892.4	4,048.1	4,210.1	4,378.5	4,553.6	4,735.8	4,925.2	4,925.2	4,925.2	4,925.2	4,925.2	4,925.2
Annual Cons/Cap (m³/p-yr)	59.0	59.0	59.0	59.0	59.0	59.0	59.0	59.0	59.0	59.0	59.0	59.0	59.0	59.0	59.0	59.0	59.0	59.0
Persons Per Household (units)	4.3	4.3	4.3	4.3	4.3	4.3	4.3	4.3	4.3	4.3	4.3	4.3	4.3	4.3	4.3	4.3	4.3	4.3
HH Per Connection (units)	1.0	1.0	1.0	1.0	1.0	1.0	1.0	1.0	1.0	1.0	1.0	1.0	1.0	1.0	1.0	1.0	1.0	1.0
End of Yr Connect (thousands)	724.6	756.1	788.3	819.6	852.3	886.1	921.5	958.4	996.7	1,036.6	1,078.1	1,121.2	1,166.0	1,166.0	1,166.0	1,166.0	1,166.0	1,166.0
End Yr Inc. Conn. (thousands)	NA	31.5	63.7	95.0	127.9	161.5	196.9	233.8	272.1	312.0	353.5	396.6	441.4	441.4	441.4	441.4	441.4	441.4
Water Consumption	176.8	184.5	192.4	200.3	208.3	216.6	225.2	234.2	243.6	253.4	263.5	274.0	285.0	290.6	290.6	290.6	290.6	290.6
Incremental Water Consum.	NA	7.7	15.6	23.5	31.5	39.8	48.4	57.4	66.8	76.6	86.7	97.2	108.2	113.8	113.8	113.8	113.8	113.8
Average Losses Level (%)	27.5	27.5	26.5	26.0	25.5	25.0	25.0	25.0	25.0	25.0	25.0	25.0	25.0	25.0	25.0	25.0	25.0	25.0
Water Production	243.9	254.5	261.8	270.7	279.7	288.9	300.3	312.3	324.8	337.8	351.3	365.4	380.0	387.4	387.4	387.4	387.4	387.4
Incremental Water Production	NA	10.6	17.9	26.8	35.8	45.0	56.4	68.4	80.9	93.9	107.4	121.5	136.1	143.5	143.5	143.5	143.5	143.5

TABLE 11.4 (continued)

Description	1988	1989	1990	1991	1992	1993	1994	1995	1996	1997	1998	1999	2000*	2001	2002	2003	2004	2005-18
Interior: Small Communities (CIPP)																		
Urban Population (thousands)	664.0	693.0	724.0	748.0	778.0	814.0	846.6	880.4	915.6	952.3	990.4	990.4	990.4	990.4	990.4	990.4	990.4	990.4
Coverage Level (%)	79.7	80.0	80.0	80.0	80.0	80.0	80.0	80.0	80.0	80.0	80.0	80.0	80.0	80.0	80.0	80.0	80.0	80.0
Urban Pop Served (thousands)	529.2	554.4	579.2	598.4	622.4	651.2	677.2	704.3	732.5	761.8	792.3	792.3	792.3	792.3	792.3	792.3	792.3	792.3
Annual Cons/Cap (m³/p-yr)	55.9	55.9	55.9	55.9	55.9	55.9	55.9	55.9	55.9	55.9	55.9	55.9	55.9	55.9	55.9	55.9	55.9	55.9
Persons Per Household (units)	3.5	3.5	3.5	3.5	3.5	3.5	3.5	3.5	3.5	3.5	3.5	3.5	3.5	3.5	3.5	3.5	3.5	3.5
HH Per Connection (units)	1.0	1.0	1.0	1.0	1.0	1.0	1.0	1.0	1.0	1.0	1.0	1.0	1.0	1.0	1.0	1.0	1.0	1.0
End of Yr Connect (thousands)	160.9	168.5	176.0	181.9	189.2	197.9	205.9	214.1	222.6	231.6	240.8	240.8	240.8	240.8	240.8	240.8	240.8	240.8
End Yr Inc. Conn. (thousands)	NA	7.6	15.1	21.0	28.3	37.0	45.0	53.2	61.7	70.7	79.9	79.9	79.9	79.9	79.9	79.9	79.9	79.9
Water Consumption	29.6	30.3	31.7	32.9	34.1	35.6	37.1	38.6	40.2	41.8	43.4	44.3	44.3	44.3	44.3	44.3	44.3	44.3
Incremental Water Consum.	NA	0.7	2.1	3.3	4.5	6.0	7.5	9.0	10.6	12.2	13.8	14.7	14.7	14.7	14.7	14.7	14.7	14.7
Average Losses Level (%)	31.0	30.0	29.0	28.0	27.0	26.0	26.0	26.0	26.0	26.0	26.0	26.0	26.0	26.0	26.0	26.0	26.0	26.0
Water Production	42.9	43.3	44.6	45.7	46.7	48.1	50.2	52.2	54.3	56.4	58.7	59.9	59.9	59.9	59.9	59.9	59.9	59.9
Incremental Water Production	NA	0.4	1.7	2.8	3.8	5.2	7.3	9.3	11.4	13.5	15.8	17.0	17.0	17.0	17.0	17.0	17.0	17.0
SABESP																		
Urban Population (thousands)	18,924.0	19,446.0	19,986.0	20,455.0	20,950.0	21,462.0	21,983.0	22,515.0	23,018.0	23,531.0	24,060.0	24,563.0	25,080.0	25,155.0	25,233.0	25,313.0	25,395.0	25,479.0
Coverage Level (%)	89.6	89.8	90.0	90.2	90.4	90.6	90.6	90.6	90.5	90.5	90.5	90.5	90.5	90.5	90.5	90.5	90.6	90.6
Urban Pop Served (thousands)	16,953.0	17,461.0	17,985.0	18,446.0	18,932.0	19,435.0	19,907.0	20,389.0	20,839.0	21,299.0	21,773.0	22,226.0	22,693.0	22,766.0	22,840.0	22,917.0	22,996.0	23,076.0
Annual Cons/Cap (m³/p-yr)	85.4	85.4	85.4	85.4	85.4	85.4	85.4	85.4	85.4	85.4	85.4	85.4	85.4	85.4	85.4	85.4	85.4	85.4
Persons Per Household (units)	4.3	4.3	4.3	4.3	4.3	4.3	4.3	4.3	4.3	4.3	4.3	4.3	4.3	4.3	4.3	4.3	4.3	4.3
HH Per Connection (units)	1.2	1.2	1.2	1.2	1.2	1.2	1.2	1.2	1.2	1.2	1.2	1.2	1.2	1.2	1.2	1.2	1.2	1.2
End of Yr Connect (thousands)	3,186.0	3,285.0	3,386.0	3,477.0	3,573.0	3,672.0	3,765.0	3,861.0	3,951.0	4,044.0	4,139.0	4,227.0	4,317.0	4,326.0	4,334.0	4,343.0	4,352.0	4,361.0
End Yr Inc. Conn. (thousands)	NA	99.0	200.0	291.0	387.0	486.0	579.0	675.0	765.0	858.0	953.0	1,041.0	1,131.0	1,140.0	1,148.0	1,157.0	1,166.0	1,175.0
Water Cons.: Final Users	1,161.0	1,194.0	1,228.0	1,262.0	1,294.0	1,327.0	1,359.0	1,391.0	1,421.0	1,451.0	1,481.0	1,512.0	1,542.0	1,559.0	1,562.0	1,566.0	1,570.0	1,574.0
Water Cons.: Bulk Sale Cons.	244.0	251.0	258.0	266.0	274.0	282.0	291.0	300.0	312.0	324.0	337.0	350.0	363.0	363.0	363.0	363.0	363.0	363.0
Water Cons.: Special Contracts	43.0	43.0	43.0	44.0	46.0	47.0	49.0	50.0	52.0	53.0	55.0	56.0	58.0	58.0	58.0	58.0	58.0	58.0
Water Consumption	1,447.0	1,488.0	1,530.0	1,572.0	1,614.0	1,656.0	1,699.0	1,740.0	1,785.0	1,828.0	1,873.0	1,918.0	1,962.0	1,980.0	1,983.0	1,987.0	1,991.0	1,995.0
Incremental Water Consum.	NA	41.0	83.0	125.0	167.0	209.0	252.0	293.0	338.0	381.0	426.0	471.0	515.0	533.0	536.0	540.0	544.0	548.0
Average Losses Level (%)	25.0	24.6	24.0	23.4	22.9	22.3	21.9	21.8	21.7	21.6	21.6	21.5	21.4	21.4	21.4	21.4	21.4	21.5
Water Production	1,930.0	1,973.0	2,013.0	2,054.0	2,092.0	2,132.0	2,174.0	2,225.0	2,279.0	2,333.0	2,388.0	2,442.0	2,497.0	2,519.0	2,524.0	2,529.0	2,534.0	2,540.0
Incremental Water Production	NA	43.0	83.0	124.0	162.0	202.0	244.0	295.0	349.0	403.0	458.0	512.0	567.0	589.0	594.0	599.0	604.0	610.0

* Urban population, population served and related figures remained constant after this year due to system saturation.

TABLE 11.5   SABESP's Projected Demand for Sewage Collection and Effluent Treatment (millions m³)

Description	1988	1989	1990	1991	1992	1993	1994	1995	1996	1997	1998	1999	2000-18
RMSP: Integrated System													
Urban Population (thousands)	12,385.0	12,653.0	12,930.0	13,163.0	13,405.0	13,650.0	13,650.0	13,650.0	13,650.0	13,650.0	13,650.0	13,650.0	13,650.0
Coverage Level (%)	59.0	64.1	66.8	68.2	68.4	68.7	68.7	68.7	68.7	68.7	68.7	68.7	68.7
Urban Pop. with Sewage Collected (thousands)	7,305.0	8,104.0	8,642.0	8,982.0	9,174.0	9,381.0	9,381.0	9,381.0	9,381.0	9,381.0	9,381.0	9,381.0	9,381.0
Persons Per Household (units)	4.2	4.2	4.2	4.2	4.2	4.2	4.2	4.2	4.2	4.2	4.2	4.2	4.2
Households Per Connection (units)	1.5	1.5	1.5	1.5	1.5	1.5	1.5	1.5	1.5	1.5	1.5	1.5	1.5
End of Year Connections (thousands)	1,144.0	1,270.0	1,354.0	1,407.0	1,437.0	1,469.0	1,469.0	1,469.0	1,469.0	1,469.0	1,469.0	1,469.0	1,469.0
End of Year Incremental Connec. (thousands)	NA	125.0	210.0	263.0	293.0	325.0	325.0	325.0	325.0	325.0	325.0	325.0	325.0
Sewage Collected / Water Consumption	0.9	0.9	0.9	0.9	0.9	0.9	0.9	0.9	0.9	0.9	0.9	0.9	0.9
Sewage Collected	504.2	559.5	596.6	620.0	633.3	647.5	647.6	647.6	647.6	647.6	647.6	647.6	647.6
Incremental Sewage Collected	NA	55.3	92.4	115.8	129.1	143.3	143.4	143.4	143.4	143.4	143.4	143.4	143.4
Effluent Treated	249.1	263.1	277.9	293.5	310.0	327.4	345.8	365.3	385.8	407.5	430.4	454.5	480.1
Incremental Effluent Treated	NA	14.0	28.8	44.4	60.9	78.3	96.7	116.2	136.7	158.4	181.3	205.4	231.0
RMSP: Isolated System													
Urban Population (thousands)	121.0	124.0	127.0	131.0	135.0	140.0	140.0	140.0	140.0	140.0	140.0	140.0	140.0
Coverage Level (%)	21.1	30.7	47.5	63.5	66.9	75.3	75.4	75.4	75.4	75.4	75.4	75.4	75.4
Urban Pop. with Sewage Collected (thousands)	25.5	38.0	60.3	83.1	90.3	105.5	105.5	105.5	105.5	105.5	105.5	105.5	105.5
Persons Per Household (units)	4.2	4.2	4.2	4.2	4.2	4.2	4.2	4.2	4.2	4.2	4.2	4.2	4.2
Households Per Connection (units)	1.0	1.0	1.0	1.0	1.0	1.0	1.0	1.0	1.0	1.0	1.0	1.0	1.0
End of Year Connections (thousands)	5.9	8.8	14.0	19.2	20.9	24.4	24.4	24.4	24.4	24.4	24.4	24.4	24.4
End of Year Incremental Connec. (thousands)	NA	2.9	8.1	13.3	15.0	18.5	18.5	18.5	18.5	18.5	18.5	18.5	18.5
Sewage Collected / Water Consumption	0.9	0.9	0.9	0.9	0.9	0.9	0.9	0.9	0.9	0.9	0.9	0.9	0.9
Sewage Collected	1.3	2.0	3.2	4.4	4.7	5.5	5.5	5.5	5.5	5.5	5.5	5.5	5.5
Incremental Sewage Collected	NA	0.7	1.9	3.1	3.4	4.2	4.2	4.2	4.2	4.2	4.2	4.2	4.2
Effluent Treated	4.4	5.2	6.2	7.3	8.6	10.2	12.0	14.2	16.2	19.9	23.5	27.8	32.8
Incremental Effluent Treated	NA	0.8	1.8	2.9	4.2	5.8	7.6	9.8	12.4	15.5	19.1	23.3	28.4

TABLE 11.5 (continued)

Description	1988	1989	1990	1991	1992	1993	1994	1995	1996	1997	1998	1999	2000-18
Baixada Santista													
Urban Population (thousands)	2,236.0	2,305.0	2,378.0	2,434.0	2,493.0	2,556.0	2,556.0	2,556.0	2,556.0	2,556.0	2,556.0	2,556.0	2,556.0
Coverage Level (%)	53.4	55.2	57.9	61.7	65.2	65.7	65.6	65.6	65.6	65.6	65.6	65.6	65.6
Urban Pop. with Sewage Collected (thousands)	1,195.0	1,273.0	1,376.0	1,501.0	1,625.0	1,678.0	1,678.0	1,678.0	1,678.0	1,678.0	1,678.0	1,678.0	1,678.0
Persons Per Household (units)	5.0	5.0	5.0	5.0	5.0	5.0	5.0	5.0	5.0	5.0	5.0	5.0	5.0
Households Per Connection (units)	3.9	3.9	3.9	3.9	3.9	3.9	3.9	3.9	3.9	3.9	3.9	3.9	3.9
End of Year Connections (thousands)	61.6	65.6	70.9	77.4	83.8	86.5	86.5	86.5	86.5	86.5	86.5	86.5	86.5
End of Year Incremental Connec. (thousands)	NA	4.0	9.3	15.7	22.2	24.9	24.9	24.9	24.9	24.9	24.9	24.9	24.9
Sewage Collected / Water Consumption	0.7	0.7	0.7	0.7	0.7	0.7	0.7	0.7	0.7	0.7	0.7	0.7	0.7
Sewage Collected	41.8	44.6	48.2	52.5	56.9	58.7	58.7	58.7	58.7	58.7	58.7	58.7	58.7
Incremental Sewage Collected	NA	2.8	6.4	10.7	15.1	16.9	16.9	16.9	16.9	16.9	16.9	16.9	16.9
Effluent Treated	47.3	50.1	53.1	56.2	59.6	63.1	66.8	70.8	75.0	79.4	84.1	89.1	94.4
Incremental Effluent Treated	NA	2.8	5.8	8.9	12.3	15.8	19.5	23.5	27.7	32.1	35.8	41.8	47.1
Interior: Large and Medium Cities (CMG)													
Urban Population (thousands)	3,518.0	3,671.0	3,827.0	3,979.0	4,139.0	4,302.0	4,302.0	4,302.0	4,302.0	4,302.0	4,302.0	4,302.0	4,302.0
Coverage Level (%)	73.8	72.1	71.7	69.9	68.1	66.5	66.5	66.5	66.5	66.5	66.5	66.5	66.5
Urban Pop. with Sewage Collected (thousands)	2,597.0	2,662.0	2,745.0	2,780.0	2,820.0	2,859.0	2,859.0	2,859.0	2,859.0	2,859.0	2,859.0	2,859.0	2,859.0
Persons Per Household (units)	4.3	4.3	4.3	4.3	4.3	4.3	4.3	4.3	4.3	4.3	4.3	4.3	4.3
Households Per Connection (units)	1.0	1.0	1.0	1.0	1.0	1.0	1.0	1.0	1.0	1.0	1.0	1.0	1.0
End of Year Connections (thousands)	580.8	595.2	613.7	621.6	630.5	639.4	639.4	639.4	639.4	639.4	639.4	639.4	639.4
End of Year Incremental Connec. (thousands)	NA	14.0	33.0	41.0	50.0	59.0	59.0	59.0	59.0	59.0	59.0	59.0	59.0
Sewage Collected / Water Consumption	0.9	0.9	0.9	0.9	0.9	0.9	0.9	0.9	0.9	0.9	0.9	0.9	0.9
Sewage Collected	137.9	141.3	145.7	147.6	149.7	151.8	151.8	151.8	151.8	151.8	151.8	151.8	151.8
Incremental Sewage Collected	NA	3.4	7.8	9.7	11.8	13.9	13.9	13.9	13.9	13.9	13.9	13.9	13.9
Effluent Treated	6.9	8.5	10.6	13.1	16.2	20.0	24.8	30.7	38.0	47.0	58.2	72.0	89.1
Incremental Effluent Treated	NA	1.6	3.7	6.2	9.3	13.1	17.9	23.8	31.1	40.1	51.3	65.1	82.1

TABLE 11.5 (continued)

Description	1988	1989	1990	1991	1992	1993	1994	1995	1996	1997	1998	1999	2000-18
Interior: Small Communities (CPR)													
Urban Population (thousands)	664.0	693.0	724.0	748.0	778.0	814.0	814.0	814.0	814.0	814.0	814.0	814.0	814.0
Coverage Level (%)	53.7	52.1	50.9	49.9	48.6	46.8	46.8	46.8	46.8	46.8	46.8	46.8	46.8
Urban Pop. with Sewage Collected (thousands)	356.7	360.8	368.8	373.0	378.3	381.1	381.1	381.1	381.1	381.1	381.1	381.1	381.1
Persons Per Household (units)	3.5	3.5	3.5	3.5	3.5	3.5	3.5	3.5	3.5	3.5	3.5	3.5	3.5
Households Per Connection (units)	1.0	1.0	1.0	1.0	1.0	1.0	1.0	1.0	1.0	1.0	1.0	1.0	1.0
End of Year Connections (thousands)	98.0	99.1	101.3	102.5	103.9	104.7	104.7	104.7	104.7	104.7	104.7	104.7	104.7
End of Year Incremental Connec. (thousands)	NA	1.1	3.3	4.5	5.9	6.7	6.7	6.7	6.7	6.7	6.7	6.7	6.7
Sewage Collected / Water Consumption	0.9	0.9	0.9	0.9	0.9	0.9	0.9	0.9	0.9	0.9	0.9	0.9	0.9
Sewage Collected	17.9	18.2	18.6	18.8	19.0	19.2	19.2	19.2	19.2	19.2	19.2	19.2	19.2
Incremental Sewage Collected	NA	0.3	0.7	0.9	1.1	1.3	1.3	1.3	1.3	1.3	1.3	1.3	1.3
Effluent Treated	5.4	6.0	6.8	7.6	8.5	9.6	10.7	12.1	13.5	15.2	17.1	19.1	21.5
Incremental Effluent Treated	NA	0.7	1.4	2.2	3.2	4.2	5.4	6.7	8.2	9.8	11.7	13.8	16.1
SABESP													
Urban Population (thousands)	18,924.0	19,446.0	19,986.0	20,455.0	20,950.0	21,462.0	21,462.0	21,462.0	21,462.0	21,462.0	21,462.0	21,462.0	21,462.0
Coverage Level (%)	60.7	64.0	66.0	67.1	67.2	67.1	67.1	67.1	67.1	67.1	67.1	67.1	67.1
Urban Pop. with Sewage Collected (thousands)	11,479.0	12,438.0	13,192.0	13,719.0	14,087.0	14,405.0	14,405.0	14,405.0	14,405.0	14,405.0	14,405.0	14,405.0	14,405.0
Persons Per Household (units)	4.3	4.3	4.3	4.3	4.3	4.3	4.3	4.3	4.3	4.3	4.3	4.3	4.3
Households Per Connection (units)	1.4	1.4	1.4	1.4	1.4	1.4	1.4	1.4	1.4	1.4	1.4	1.4	1.4
End of Year Connections (thousands)	1,891.0	2,038.0	2,154.0	2,228.0	2,276.0	2,324.0	2,324.0	2,324.0	2,324.0	2,324.0	2,324.0	2,324.0	2,324.0
End of Year Incremental Connec. (thousands)	NA	148.0	264.0	338.0	386.0	434.0	434.0	434.0	434.0	434.0	434.0	434.0	434.0
Sewage Collected / Water Consumption	0.9	0.9	0.9	0.9	0.9	0.9	0.9	0.9	0.9	0.9	0.9	0.9	0.9
Sewage Collected	703.0	766.0	812.0	843.0	864.0	883.0	883.0	883.0	883.0	883.0	883.0	883.0	883.0
Incremental Sewage Collected	NA	57.0	103.0	134.0	155.0	174.0	174.0	174.0	174.0	174.0	174.0	174.0	174.0
Effluent Treated	313.0	333.0	354.0	378.0	403.0	430.0	460.0	493.0	529.0	569.0	613.0	663.0	718.0
Incremental Effluent Treated	NA	20.0	41.0	65.0	90.0	117.0	147.0	180.0	216.0	256.0	300.0	349.0	405.0

- sewerage connections will increase at a higher rate than water connections; and
- unaccounted-for-water will diminish at reasonable rates over the period.

The corresponding overall investments for 1989-93 have been designed to meet these water supply and sewerage demands in the 416 municipalities served by SABESP in the state of São Paulo: 29 in the RMSP, 10 in the Baixada Santista and 377 in the Interior. These activities will enable SABESP to extend water supply and sewerage services significantly, covering additional populations of about 2.4 million in water and 2.9 million in sewerage by 1993 (the increment of population served with water will rise to 6.1 million by 2004). Between 1989 and 1993, the water supply coverage level will remain approximately constant at its present level of 90%, and the sewerage coverage will increase to 67% from its present level of 61%. It is estimated that over 40% of the beneficiaries with water and 37% of the beneficiaries with sewerage are in the poverty group.

SABESP's Overall Investments and Financing Plan

The overall investments of SABESP are expected to be US$ 1,717 million, during the period 1989-93. The management's main objectives are to:

- help optimize the allocation of scarce sector resources through better investment planning, and marginal cost analysis and pricing;
- increase SABESP's operational efficiency and financial health;
- improve environmental and health conditions in São Paulo's urban areas through water service and wastewater disposal;
- help develop new strategies to improve SABESP's ability to implement projects with high social importance but not necessarily high financial returns; and
- support government efforts in decentralization by commitment of resources from the State of São Paulo and SABESP.

Activities during the period 1989-1993 will increase the company's capacity to mobilize investment resources internally. SABESP is expected to contribute, as a minimum, counterpart funds amounting to 11% of the planned investments or 32% of the total program costs (13% and 37% respectively, including interest during construction) during the period 1989-1993. The studies of the marginal cost of water and sewerage services constitute an important tool for planning, subproject selection, and cost analysis; and also will enable SABESP to design a more efficient pricing policy (see Chapter 12). SABESP's planning and programming will be further supported by the detailed monitoring of its performance by the State of São Paulo.

Description of the Specific Program

The more specific investment program (1989-93) that we analyze in this study amounts to US$ 600 million, and represents about 35% of the total of US$ 1,717 that will be invested by SABESP in the State of São Paulo during the same period. The specific 10-point program includes:

1) construction of the first stage of the South West Water Supply Scheme to increase raw water supply for the RMSP by 3 m³/s, which includes:
   - three dams that form two impounding reservoirs with about 214 million m³ (Alto and Medio Capivari and Embura);
   - an outflow control structure and channel at Embura; and
   - a pumping station to transfer 5 m³/s of water from Medio to Alto Capivari reservoirs;
2) improvements to the water production installations of Cabucu, Guarau and Alto Coitia in the RMSP;
3) construction of about 2,000 km of water transmission and distribution pipelines, an aggregate capacity of about 100,000 m³ of storage tanks and 200,000 water connections in RMSP;
4) construction, extension and/or improvement of water systems in about 50 medium-sized cities and about 200 small towns;
5) construction of 2 km of interceptors, a pumping station and a 1.8 m³/s sewerage treatment plant in the city of São Jose dos Campos;
6) construction and/or extension of sewerage systems and sewerage treatment facilities in about 19 medium-sized cities and 50 small towns;
7) institutional development, including technical assistance, materials and works for an unaccounted-for water reduction program; other improvements in operational and commercial systems of SABESP, such as in the user's cadastre and metering;
8) an assessment of and a program for financing appropriate investments in municipal wastewater pollution in the State of São Paulo;
9) staff training; and
10) consultant services for engineering, designs and supervision of construction.

Costs and Financing of the Specific Program

The cost of the specific program is estimated to be US$ 600 million equivalent, excluding interest during construction (For details see Appendix Table A11.3). The foreign exchange requirement is estimated to be US$ 150 million. Costs are based on December 1988 prices, and include an average of 7% for physical contingencies and price contingencies of 5.3% per year for 1989 and 1990 and 4.1% for 1991 and thereafter. Costs include direct taxes (about US$ 40 million). Cost estimates for major subprojects are based on bills of quantities and unit prices prepared by consultants and SABESP. Estimates for other subprojects are based on unit costs of similar works recently bid. The costs of the institutional development activities are estimated in accordance with prevailing costs of materials and services.

The financial success of the program depends largely on the self-financing capacity of SABESP. This is a departure from practices in the past where investments were done with near total debt financing. Under the program, SABESP must provide a minimum counterpart cash contribution amounting to 32% of the program (37% including interest during construction). A World Bank loan to SABESP amounting to US$ 280 million equivalent is financing the foreign component plus local costs, amounting to 22% of the estimated program cost. SABESP's investments are US$ 1,117 million, for other projects outside the specific program (for details see Appendix Table A11.4.

Program preparation and implementation is well under way. Designs for extensions of water distribution or sewerage systems in many cases follow existing master plans and only minor revisions are needed. Designs for medium-sized and small communities, in most cases, require a lead time of only two to three months. Works in RMSP include the construction of three dams, which would require satisfactory environmental impact reports (RIMAs) and relocation studies (see the ensuing section on project evaluation).

Institutional Framework and Financial Status

SABESP was created in 1973 (State of São Paulo 1973), by the fusion of the then-separate water and sewerage companies, Companhia Metropolitana de Aguas de São Paulo (COMASP) and Companhia Metropolitana de Saneamento de São Paulo (SANESP). SABESP is a limited corporation, 93% owned by the State of São Paulo, through the Department of Water and Electricity (DAEE).

SABESP is governed by a management council (Diretoria) comprised of the Executive President and Department Directors. The Governor of the state appoints the President for a four-year term. The Diretoria is ultimately responsible to an Administrative Council, comprising nine members, with responsibility for such functions as ex-ante approval of investment programs and issuing of new shares. There is also a Financial Council, consisting of five members, responsible inter-alia for approving ex-post all budgets and financial policy. The structure is common to most Brazilian state-owned companies (for details, see Appendix Figure A11.1).

In 1989, SABESP staff numbered about 21,000. Distribution of personnel among various functions is shown in Figure A.11.1. One indicative measure of employee efficiency of a water utility is the number of consumers per employee. For SABESP, this ratio was 206 in 1987, which is higher than the

TABLE 11.6   Monitoring Indicators

	(Actual) 1988	1989	1990	1991	1992	1993	1994	1995
Operational								
Water & Sewerage Connections/Employee	207	215	220	227	232	235	238	242
Population Served-Water (%)	90	90	90	90	90	90	90	90
Population Served-Sewerage (%)	61	64	66	67	67	67	67	67
Unaccounted for Water (%)	25	25	24	24	23	22	22	22
Sewerage Treated (%) (1)	20	21	22	23	24	25	26	27
Sewerage Collected (%) (2)	45	46	47	48	49	50	51	52
Financial								
Operating Ratio	0.67	0.61	0.59	0.57	0.56	0.56	0.54	0.54
Rate of Return (%) (3)	8	12	8	9	10	11	11	12
Debt/(Debt+Equity) (4)	0.64	0.63	0.61	0.59	0.56	0.53	0.50	0.50
Accounts Rec. Comparator	109	95	92	84	78	70	65	60
Net Internal Cash as % of Total Investment	11	13	15	17	18	20	25	30

Notes:
(1)   volume treated/volume water consumed
(2)   volume collected/volume water consumed
(3)   revalued assets, 1990 and thereafter
(4)   long-term debt

sector average of 181 for the same period (see Appendix Table A11.2). During the next few years, this ratio would continue to improve (Table 11.6). A program for institutional development, including training, technical assistance, and managerial skills upgrading, forms a prominent part of the Managerial Development Program (PDE) to be undertaken within the proposed program.

Water services have been constitutionally delegated to the municipalities; therefore SABESP, like all SWCs in Brazil, operates under concessions granted by the municipal governments.   Under the PLANASA system, standard concession contracts have been developed with a duration of 30 years and the possibility of renewal.   SABESP's area of responsibility covers 416 (or 73%) of the municipalities in the state, covering about 66% of the state's urban population.   Six municipalities receive water in bulk (paying directly and charging their consumers).

TABLE 11.7   Exchange and Inflation Rates for Brazil

Year	End Year Exchange Rate (1)		Average Exchange Rate (1)		Domestic Inflation Rate (%)	U.S. Inflation Rate (%)
1983	984.00	Cr$/US$	577.00	Cr$/US$	-	-
1984	3,184.00	"	1,848.00	"	224	4.0
1985	10,490.00	"	6,200.00	"	235	4.0
1986(2)	14.90	Cz$/US$	13.66	Cz$/US$	65	5.0
1987	72.25	"	39.23	"	416	9.8
1988	765.30	"	262.01	"	1037	4.6
1989(3)	11.36	NCz$/US$	2.83	NCz$/US$	1782	4.6
1990	177.06	"	68.55	"	1476	6.1

(1)   Brazilian currency units are: Cruzerio (Cr$), Cruzado (Cz$) and Novo Cruzado (NCz$).
(2)   February, 1986 (Cruzado Plan): Cz$ 1 = Cr$ 1000.
(3)   January, 1989 (Summer Plan): NCz$ 1 = Cz$ 1000.

SABESP employs a computerized, double-entry, cost-center accounting system developed under PLANASA and used by many SWCs in Brazil. Major accounting procedures are consistent with internationally-accepted standards.   Inflation and exchange rate adjustments need special attention because these corrections are very large, as shown in Table 11.7.   Monthly closings are completed within 30 days, and the results circulated as a management report.   Year-end closings are finalized within three months of year's end.   Private external auditors annually review SABESP's financial statements.

Customer meters are read monthly by company staff (on a rotating basis by region), and bills processed internally.   SABESP has serious problems due to the long billing period (from meter reading to due date) and a poor accounts receivable records, due both to non-payment of municipal bulk consumers and the company's inability to cumulatively adjust consumer bills for inflation. These circumstances have contributed to liquidity problems (see below).   The new program proposes measures to improve the accounts receivable situation, and performance standards regarding billing and collection (see Table 11.6).

SABESP's Past and Present Financial Situation

The financial situation of all Brazilian SWCs has been seriously affected by the country's unstable economic environment since 1983 which have included:

- high inflation rates (nearly 1,000% in 1988, and over 2000% in 1989);
- periodic differentials between inflation indexes; and

- price freezes associated with the macroeconomic adjustment plans of 1986, 1987 and 1989.

Although Brazilian corporate law provides for inflation accounting (Government of Brazil 1978), the magnitude of the macroeconomic shocks, and the variance in movement of the adjustment indexes, have made it difficult to make line-by-line comparative interpretations of historical financial statements or precise conclusions regarding SWC profitability (see for example, rate of return information for 1987, in Appendix Table A.11.2).

SABESP's financial performance during the period 1984-1987 was weak due largely to low federal government-set retail tariffs, which lagged behind inflation. More detailed financial information for SABESP (income statement, balance sheet and flow of funds) is provided in Appendix Tables A11.5, A11.6 and A11.7. Other factors included escalating operating costs, particularly chemicals and electric power. These factors were exacerbated by the debt service burden related to investments made under PLANASA and large investments in sewerage treatment in RMSP (SANEGRAN) undertaken without a certain financing plan. This led SABESP to rely on contributions from the state government in the form of direct equity injections to cover working capital, and debt service assistance to partially cover SANEGRAN investments. During this time, SABESP barely covered its operational costs, depreciation charges and financial expenses, and did not generate sufficient revenue to meet the National Tariff Law (NTL), despite a financial recuperation plan designed to achieve this goal.

However, this performance must be viewed in the context of the sector as a whole. SABESP's 1984-1987 average operating ratio (i.e., operating costs before debt service, depreciation and other financing charges) was 75%. This value was far healthier than the sector average of nearly 100% for the same period. Also, SABESP's rate of return on remunerable investments in 1987 of 3.7% was significantly better than the sector average of -1.4%. Other ratios (see Table 11.3) similarly demonstrate the comparatively strong financial performance and position of SABESP in the sector (see Appendix Table A11.2 for details).

During 1988, financial health throughout the sector improved with the de-facto transfer of authority for tariff-setting, from the federal to the state governments, due to the constitutional reform. While the real average tariff had gradually increased under federal control during the early 1980s, the macroeconomic crisis of the mid-1980s resulted in substantial erosion, with the average tariff reaching a low in 1986 of just 65% of the real 1982 level. During 1987-1988, water and sewerage tariffs increased about 105% in real terms, to a combined average of US$ 0.37/m3 as of December, 1988. This has led to substantially improved operating results in 1988, as demonstrated by the rate of return on remunerable investment of over 8%, and compliance with the targets established in the financial recuperation plan as well as with the NTL.

The inability to make inflationary corrections on consumer bills, however, has led during the past year to liquidity problems. SABESP presently requires only a one-time penalty charge on overdue accounts. With accelerated inflation during 1988, accounts receivable from operations, as measured by the average collection period, climbed to 110 days. In addition, SABESP has had three bulk municipal consumers with long-term (over one year) outstanding bills.

To remedy this situation, SABESP intends to:

- reduce its average (year-end) number of days accounts receivable to not more than 70 by the end of 1993, following the gradual improvements shown in the Monitoring Indicators (Table 11.6);
- by end-1990, adjust overdue accounts for inflation, or take other measures which would reduce the financial losses resulting from overdue bills; and
- ensure that bulk supply consumers' individual days accounts receivable at year-end do not exceed the yearly averages stipulated in (a) above.

Company net fixed assets at end-1988 were about US$ 2,600 million. These consist mainly of water and sewerage systems. Because of the book-value distortions caused by inflation adjustments during the past decade, it is likely that SABESP's assets are undervalued. This has serious implications for SABESP's tariff-setting policy (which is based on a return on assets), and the annual inflation adjustments which have been responsible for large losses in the past years.

Therefore the company is carrying out a study on the fiscal implications of its physical inventory and asset value. The study is based on current replacement costs and useful asset life and the results would be incorporated into the company's financial statements by fiscal year 1990. In addition, SABESP would update this revaluation no later than every four years. Because of off-setting equity entries, this step would improve the capital structure of the company, which had a debt/equity ratio of 63/37 as of end-1988, in addition to providing a more accurate base for tariff-setting and for yearly inflation adjustments.

SABESP's Future Financial Performance

Financial forecasts for the period 1989-1995 (Table 11.12) are based on conservative assumptions, including a continuation of constrained investment resources under PLANASA; maintenance of existing water coverage levels and a small increase in sewerage coverage; and constant tariffs in real terms (for details see Appendix Tables A11.5, A11.6 and A11.7). The investment program provides least-cost solutions, with the non-program components financed by the CEF and by the State's FAE at levels equivalent to annual payments. Any increases in the combined average tariff level for water and sewerage services brought about by improvements in:

- the structure of SABESP's tariff schedule (resulting from the ongoing marginal cost studies, mentioned earlier); and/or
- its consumer cadastre (estimated in 1989 to yield a 6% real increase in the average tariff);

would yield increased internal cash, and enable SABESP to further improve its self-financing ratio. Real tariff increases have not been considered, however, because there exists a risk of tariff erosion in real terms (as during the period 1984-1987) due to Brazil's macroeconomic situation. Further, SABESP's historic financial performance demonstrates that it is capable of coping with difficult macroeconomic circumstances and maintaining a position of relative financial strength in the sector.

To further strengthen its financial situation, the company will seek to:

- comply with the requirements of the National Tariff Law (i.e., to cover all operating costs, depreciation charges and debt service costs, within the limit of a maximum 12% remuneration on assets); and
- generate sufficient internal cash to cover annually no less than 32% of the total projected costs excluding interest during construction, and in 1993 and thereafter would generate sufficient internal cash to cover annually not less than 20% of it's total investment program.

In addition, SABESP's debt/equity ratio will not exceed 70/30 in 1989, 65/35 in 1990 and 60/40 in 1991 and thereafter, while its debt service coverage ratio will not fall below 1.5 during the program period. Maintenance of the current tariff level in real terms over the program period would enable SABESP to continue to meet the requirements of the NTL, meet its minimum counterpart cash contribution, and comply with the other target financial ratios.

As the major shareholder, the State has an obligation to ensure the financial solvency of the SWC. This has meant both injections of working capital and payment of debt service, as well as contribution of counterpart funds for specific investments and contributions to the FAEs (See Appendix Table A11.8 for details of capital transfers from the State to the sanitation sector).

Under favorable economic conditions, this increased direct contribution would be expected to continue during the program period, and would be a major source of funding for the non-program investments. However, with the financial tightening at the federal level in the late 1980s, the adequacy of state funds (a large percentage of which are borrowed at a federal level) has become an issue. For this reason the financing plan for the proposed program relies on a conservative amount of state equity funds of just 21% of total program costs, and the financing plan for the global investment program of the company would be reviewed annually. The monitoring indicators summarized in Table 11.6 would form the main basis for evaluating SABESP's performance, in the coming years.

Project Evaluation

Selection Criteria

The specific investment program and costs have been described earlier. In addition, SABESP will use the following criteria for selection of subprojects:

*   least-cost alternative; and
*   long-run average incremental cost (see Chapter 12).

The justification of each individual subproject will be made using marginal costs calculated on the basis of the investment program of the subproject and its complementary works. Water projects will be approved only if the SWCs average water tariff, present or in the near future, exceeds 75% of the marginal cost of providing the service to the smallest type of consumers connected to the system. Sewerage subprojects will be approved only if the SWCs average sewerage tariff, present or in the near future, exceeds 60% of the marginal cost of providing the service (i.e., sewerage collection, transportation and treatment, if available) to the smallest type of consumers connected to the system.

The use of marginal costs simplifies program selection, provides useful information regarding cost and tariff structures, and is easy for policymakers to understand and apply. In addition, marginal cost data generate useful statistics for the companies on investment costs, operating and commercial expenses, and on cost differentials between regions and cities.

Projects not satisfying the above conditions but which are designed for minimum cost may be accepted on a case-by-case basis. The analysis would consider, inter-alia:

*   poverty levels and health conditions;
*   the lack of alternative water sources;
*   the problems of recovering costs through tariffs; and
*   an evaluation of benefits in other sectors of the economy.

Such projects are likely to be in towns where urban poverty prevails, and large investments are needed to compensate for imbalances created by the lack of previous investments.

Economic Cost-Benefit Analysis

In Table 11.8, incremental revenues from the sales of future water and sewerage services (made available as a result of the investments), have been used as a proxy for the benefits of the specific program. As explained in detail in Chapter 3, incremental revenues are a minimum measure of benefits, since:

- they underestimate "willingness-to-pay," by excluding consumer surplus (which cannot be measured in light of available information); and
- there are important non-quantifiable benefits which in any case are not likely to be captured by "willingness-to-pay," notably better public health and a better quality of life which result from improved water supply and sanitation.

Program costs also summarized in Table 11.8, are based on the investment program described earlier.

An internal rate of return (IRR) has been calculated for water and sewerage as a joint service, since in many cases consumers pay a combined bill for both. Although separate charges are provided in the tariff structures for water and sewerage (see next chapter on tariffs), it is not possible to identify the "willingness-to-pay" for each service separately. All costs and revenues are expressed in constant market prices (US$ of December 1988), including all complementary investments necessary to achieve the full benefits of the program. Investments not related to incremental benefits (such as plant replacement or major maintenance) have been excluded from the analysis.

The calculated IRR is 12% for water and sewerage combined, using January 1989 average tariffs (US$ 0.34/m^3 for water and US$ 0.36/m^3 for sewerage) as a proxy for economic benefits. The return is moderately sensitive to increases in costs or decreases in revenues: an increase of 10% in costs combined with a 10% decrease in revenues, for example, reduces the return to 9% (see Table 11.9).

Environmental Impact

There are a number of environmental aspects of the SABESP program. First, three dams need to be constructed. The environmental consequences of the dams have been investigated on a preliminary basis already. Further detailed impact studies are being carried out, since SABESP is required by

TABLE 11.8 SABESP's Estimated Revenues, Costs and Benefits (US$ millions as of December 1988)

Description	1988	1989	1990	1991	1992	1993	1994	1995	1996	1997	1998	1999	2000	2001	2002	2003	2004	2005	2006-18
Water																			
Estimated Sales (millions m³)	1,535.6	1,579.1	1,623.6	1,668.2	1,712.8	1,757.3	1,803.0	1,846.5	1,894.2	1,939.9	1,987.6	2,035.4	2,082.1	2,101.2	2,104.4	2,108.6	2,112.8	2,117.1	2,117.1
Average Tariff (US$/m³)	0.3351	0.3351	0.3351	0.3351	0.3351	0.3351	0.3351	0.3351	0.3351	0.3351	0.3351	0.3351	0.3351	0.3351	0.3351	0.3351	0.3351	0.3351	0.3351
Total Direct Revenue	514.6	529.1	544.1	559.0	574.0	588.9	604.2	618.8	634.8	650.1	666.1	682.1	697.7	704.1	705.2	706.6	708.0	709.4	709.4
Total Indirect Revenue	11.6	11.6	12.3	13.6	15.6	18.4	20.5	22.8	25.4	28.3	31.5	35.1	39.0	43.2	47.7	52.7	58.3	64.4	64.4
Total Revenue	526.2	540.7	556.4	572.6	589.6	607.3	624.7	641.6	660.2	678.4	697.6	717.1	736.7	747.3	752.9	759.3	766.3	773.8	773.8
Incremental Revenue	0.0	14.5	30.2	46.4	63.4	81.1	98.5	115.4	134.0	152.2	171.4	190.9	210.5	221.1	226.7	233.1	240.1	247.6	247.6
Sewerage																			
Estimated Sales (millions m³)	746.4	813.3	862.1	895.0	917.3	937.5	937.5	937.5	937.5	937.5	937.5	937.5	937.5	937.5	937.5	937.5	937.5	937.5	937.5
Average Tariff (US$/m³)	0.3375	0.3375	0.3375	0.3375	0.3375	0.3375	0.3375	0.3375	0.3375	0.3375	0.3375	0.3375	0.3375	0.3375	0.3375	0.3375	0.3375	0.3375	0.3375
Total Direct Revenue	266.8	290.7	308.2	320.0	327.9	335.1	335.1	335.1	335.1	335.1	335.1	335.1	335.1	335.1	335.1	335.1	335.1	335.1	335.1
Total Indirect Revenue	6.0	6.4	7.0	7.8	8.9	10.5	11.4	12.4	13.4	14.6	15.9	17.2	18.7	20.6	22.7	25.0	27.6	30.4	30.4
Total Revenue	272.8	297.1	315.2	327.7	336.9	345.6	346.5	347.5	348.6	349.7	351.0	352.4	353.9	355.7	357.8	360.2	362.7	365.6	365.6
Incremental Revenue	0.0	24.3	42.4	54.9	64.1	72.8	73.7	74.7	75.8	76.9	78.2	79.6	81.1	82.9	85.0	87.4	89.9	92.8	92.8
Water & Sewerage																			
Total Direct Revenue	781.4	819.9	852.3	879.0	901.9	924.0	939.3	953.9	969.9	985.2	1,001.2	1,017.2	1,032.9	1,039.3	1,040.3	1,041.7	1,043.2	1,044.6	1,044.6
Total Indirect Revenue	17.6	17.9	19.3	21.4	24.6	28.9	31.9	35.2	38.9	42.9	47.4	52.3	57.8	63.8	70.4	77.7	85.8	94.8	94.8
Total Revenue	799.0	837.8	871.6	900.3	926.4	952.9	971.2	989.1	1,008.8	1,028.1	1,048.6	1,069.5	1,090.6	1,103.0	1,110.7	1,119.5	1,129.0	1,139.4	1,139.4
Incremental Revenue	0.0	38.8	72.6	101.3	127.4	153.9	172.2	190.1	209.8	229.1	249.6	270.5	291.6	304.0	311.7	320.5	330.0	340.4	340.4
Water Investment Cost	27.7	133.0	148.1	155.3	151.2	145.6	41.1	42.1	39.7	40.8	41.9	38.8	39.8	5.2	5.2	5.3	5.3	5.4	0.0
Water AOM Fixed Incr. Cost	0.0	2.7	4.7	7.3	9.3	11.3	13.6	16.0	18.4	20.7	23.2	25.5	27.9	28.1	28.2	28.3	28.4	28.6	28.6
Water AOM Oper. Incr. Cost	0.0	1.3	2.5	3.7	4.8	6.0	7.3	8.8	10.4	12.0	13.6	15.3	16.9	17.6	17.7	17.9	18.0	18.2	18.2
Water Incremental Cost	27.7	136.9	155.2	166.3	165.3	162.9	61.9	66.8	68.5	73.6	78.7	79.5	84.6	50.8	51.1	51.4	51.8	52.1	46.7
Sewerage Investment Cost	67.7	156.8	176.5	147.1	125.7	121.9	0.0	0.0	0.0	0.0	0.0	0.0	0.0	6.0	6.0	6.0	6.0	6.0	0.0
Sewerage AOM Fixed Inc Cst	0.0	0.5	1.0	1.5	1.9	2.3	2.8	3.3	4.0	4.5	5.0	5.4	5.9	6.0	6.0	6.0	6.0	6.1	6.1
Sewerage AOM Op. Inc. Cost	0.0	0.0	0.0	0.0	0.0	0.0	0.0	0.0	0.0	0.0	0.0	0.0	0.0	0.0	0.0	0.0	0.0	0.0	0.0
Sewerage Incremental Cost	67.7	157.3	177.4	148.6	127.6	124.2	2.8	3.3	4.0	4.5	5.0	5.4	5.9	6.0	6.0	6.0	6.0	6.1	6.1
Water & Sewerage Incr. Cost	95.4	294.3	332.6	314.8	292.9	287.1	64.7	70.1	72.4	78.0	83.7	85.0	90.6	56.8	57.1	57.5	57.8	58.2	52.8
Water Incremental Revenue	0.0	14.5	30.2	46.4	63.4	81.1	98.5	115.4	134.0	152.2	171.4	190.9	210.5	221.1	226.7	233.1	240.1	247.6	247.6
Sewerage Incremental Revenue	0.0	24.3	42.4	54.9	64.1	72.8	73.7	74.7	75.8	76.9	78.2	79.6	81.1	82.9	85.0	87.4	89.9	92.8	92.8
Water & Sewerage Incr. Rev.	0.0	38.8	72.6	101.3	127.4	153.9	172.2	190.1	209.8	229.1	249.6	270.5	291.6	304.0	311.7	320.5	330.0	340.4	340.4
Water Incremental Net Benefit	(27.7)	(122.4)	(125.0)	(119.9)	(101.9)	(81.8)	36.5	48.6	65.5	78.6	92.6	111.4	125.9	170.3	175.6	181.7	188.3	195.5	200.9
Sewerage Incr. Net Benefit	(67.7)	(133.0)	(135.5)	(93.6)	(63.5)	(51.4)	70.9	71.5	71.8	72.5	73.3	74.1	75.2	76.9	79.0	81.4	83.9	86.7	86.7
Water&Sewerage Inc Net Ben	(95.4)	(255.5)	(260.1)	(213.5)	(165.5)	(133.2)	107.5	120.0	137.3	151.1	165.9	185.5	201.0	247.3	254.6	263.0	272.2	282.2	287.6

TABLE 11.9   Sensitivity of the IRR to Changes in Costs and Revenues

Revenue Change (%)	Cost Change (%)					
	0			+ 10		
	Water	Sewerage	W & S	Water	Sewerage	W & S
0	14.0	9.9	12.3	12.4	8.6	10.8
-10	12.3	8.5	10.7	10.7	7.3	9.3

Federal Law (Government of Brazil 1986) to prepare a rigorous and comprehensive environmental impact report (RIMA) according to state guidelines.

A second environmental aspect taken up in this program concerns pollution control of municipal wastewater discharged into various bodies of water in the state. SABESP's record is better than most other Brazilian SWCs in providing wastewater treatment, and they are already in the advanced diagnostic phases of a study of the state's nine water basins. Under the new program, SABESP will carry out a further study including the detailed assessment of the degree of treatment required for sewerage effluents in the state, their benefits and costs and the sources of revenues to meet the recommended investments and their operational costs.

Finally, the program finances sewerage in much greater proportions in middle-sized towns than in the past, in spite of the fact that the recent deterioration in water supply, make water delivery systems the first priority. SABESP's wastewater treatment includes facilities at São Jose dos Campos, a medium-sized city on the Paraiba, and one of the most polluted in Brazil, as well as investments in many small communities in order to avoid water pollution problems in the future.

Urban Poverty Impact

The urban poor constitute a significant fraction of the beneficiaries of this program. Urban poor are defined in Brazil as families earning a monetary income of three regional minimum salaries or less. Taking into account the duration of the program, about 2.4 million poor (about 40% of all beneficiaries) will be connected to water supply, and 1.1 million poor (about 37% of total beneficiaries) will receive sewerage services.

Risks

There are no serious technical risks associated with this program, but other risks are:

- the unknown effects of inter-governmental financial reforms on the state's revenues, and their impact on counterpart funds;
- the impact of inflation on program costs, tariff levels and the financial viability of the company; and
- political interference in the setting of tariffs and priorities for investments.

Fiscal reforms are expected to benefit São Paulo State proportionally more than other states, diminishing the risk to counterpart funds. In 1988, tariffs were raised to adequate levels in real terms and the state and SABESP should continue the successful strategy of frequent small tariff increases to maintain the real value of tariffs. In addition, close supervision of progress, the annual review of the investment program and financial situation, and prompt completion and implementation of tariff studies would further mitigate these risks.

Conclusion

The foregoing analysis helps us to confirm that the specific investment program reviewed is acceptable from the economic, financial and technical points of view, subject to the results of more detailed environmental impact assessments of several aspects of the project identified earlier.

References

Luis Armando de Medeiros Frias. 1988. *Projeções da Popilaçâo Residente e do Número de Domicilios Particulares Ocupados: 1985-2020. Textos para Discussáo.* DPE-88 005. São Paulo.

Government of Brazil. 1978. *National Law No. 6404.* Brasilia: Government of Brazil.

Government of Brazil. 1986. *Resolution 001.* Brasilia: Government of Brazil.

State of São Paulo. 1973. *State Law No. 119.* São Paulo: State of São Paulo.

Appendix 11

Relevant SABESP and São Paulo State Data

TABLE A11.1   Basic Sanitation, Simulated "Deficits" for Brazil: 1985-90
(thousands of Units)

Characteristic	Adjusted deficits: 1985 (4)			Simulation: Rate of Growth (5) Absolute & Relative Deficits: 1990		
	Total	Urban	Rural	Total	Urban	Rural
TOTAL HOUSEHOLDS	30,900	23,100	7,800	35,900	27,900	8,000
Not Connected to General Water Network						
Absolute		2,978	n.a.		3,627	n.a.
% of Units		13.0			13.0	
Without Piped Water (1)						
Absolute	9,725	4,046	5,679	10,711	4,887	5,825
% of Units	31.5	17.5	72.8	29.8	17.5	72.8
Without General Sewer System or Septic Tank (2)						
Absolute	16,007	8,917	7,090	18,041	10,769	7,272
% of Units	51.8	38.6	90.9	50.3	38.6	90.9
Without Any Sanitary Facility (3)						
Absolute	6,652	2,541	4,111	7,285	3,069	4,216
% of Units	21.5	11.0	52.7	20.3	11.0	52.7

Source: IBGE, PNAD-85, adjusted for 1985 recount.

(1)   Without piped water from the general network,well or spring.
(2)   Without general sewer system or septic tank or with shared facility.
(3)   Without any facility or with shared facility.
(4)   Adjusted using total from Table 10.1. Due to rounding, the urban and rural deficits do not always sum to exactly the total.
(5)   Assumes that the number of households served grows at the same rate as the number of rural and urban households.

TABLE A11.2   Financial Status of State Water Companies (SWCs)

State	Company	Volume Billed ('000 m³)	Losses (%)	Average Tariff (US$/m³)	Operation Costs (US$/m³)	Return on Assets (%)	Consumers per Employee
Alagoas	CASAL	43,989	16.1	0.397	0.415	-3.5	150
Amazonas	COSAMA	56,632	54.8	0.443	0.398	-1.6	122
Bahia	EMBASA	284,956	25.0	0.369	0.368	-2.2	152
Ceara	CAGECE	108,831	26.7	0.266	0.274	-8.3	217
Espiritu Santo	CESAN	130,579	30.7	0.308	0.257	2.9	193
Maranhao	CAEMA	49,560	42.0	0.276	0.502	-13.7	92
Mato Grosso	SANEMAT	57,407	42.7	0.498	0.502	-7.0	136
Para	COSANPA	126,650	37.6	0.178	0.220	-13.3	172
Paraiba	CAGEPA	91,566	22.4	0.264	0.262	-4.9	155
Pernambuco	COMPESA	241,193	22.5	0.280	0.264	1.2	197
Piaui	AGESPISA	49,553	32.4	0.337	0.320	-1.8	158
R G do Norte	CAERN	59,577	39.1	0.297	0.313	-5.4	152
Sergipe	DESO	54,824	24.4	0.378	0.246	3.6	161
AVERAGE NORTH		104,255	32.0	0.330	0.334	-4.1	158
Federal District	CAESB	151,585	35.1	0.336	0.290	3.1	186
Goias	SANEAGO	200,518	–	0.264	0.263	-1.3	107
M G do Sul	SANESUL	70,489	29.0	0.337	0.289	-1.0	228
Minas Gerais	COPASA	533,869	–	0.232	0.202	5.5	239
Parana	SANEPAR	309,548	27.0	0.370	0.282	3.7	291
R G do Sul	CORSAN	268,398	13.5	0.428	0.310	5.8	242
Rio de Janeiro	CEDAE	1,466,642	17.7	0.202	0.173	1.0	237
Santa Catarina	CASAN	149,146	18.2	0.300	0.245	3.2	190
Sao Paulo	SABESP	1,587,529	24.9	0.384	0.260	3.8	206
AVERAGE SOUTH		526,414	23.6	0.317	0.257	2.7	214
AVERAGE SECTOR		276,956	29.1	0.325	0.303	-1.4	181

Notes: Data gathered during mid-November, 1988; Source:CAIXA ECONOMICA FEDRAL, Rio de Janiero.   Not included are Acre (SANACRE), Amapa (CAESA), Rondonia (CAERO) and Roraima.

TABLE A11.3   Specific Program Costs (US$ million equivalent)

	1989	1990	1991	1992	1993	TOTAL	% of Base
A. São Paulo Metropolitan							
Region	7.6	32.4	52.1	58.9	46.4	197.4	39.7
1. Water supply:	7.6	32.4	52.1	58.9	46.4	197.4	39.7
Production	1.4	6.7	13.1	15.4	15.3	51.9	10.4
Sudoeste	0.0	3.8	6.7	8.7	10.5	29.8	6.0
Rio Grande	1.0	1.8	1.7	1.9	1.9	8.3	1.7
Cabucu	0.0	0.0	0.7	1.8	2.9	5.2	1.0
Cantareira	0.4	0.7	2.7	1.6	0.0	5.6	1.1
Alto Cotia	0.0	0.3	1.3	1.3	0.0	3.6	0.6
Transmission	3.1	14.1	18.6	22.6	11.1	68.9	13.9
Storage	1.8	3.1	3.2	2.2	1.2	11.5	2.3
Distribution	1.3	3.5	17.2	19.4	18.8	65.1	13.1
B. Interior	33.7	39.7	45.6	46.5	46.5	211.9	42.6
1. Water supply:	23.8	24.3	28.0	29.4	30.1	135.6	27.3
Vegetative growth	14.4	14.1	14.8	16.6	13.3	73.0	14.7
Medium-Sized Cities	6.2	7.0	11.4	11.0	14.9	50.3	10.1
Housing Program	1.1	1.2	0.0	0.0	0.0	2.3	0.5
Small Cities	2.2	2.1	2.0	1.9	1.9	10.1	2.0
2. Sewerage:	9.8	15.4	17.7	17.0	16.4	76.3	15.3
Vegetative growth	4.0	5.6	5.4	5.2	5.0	25.0	5.0
Medium-Sized Cities	1.1	4.7	4.6	4.4	4.2	19.0	3.8
Housing Program	1.8	1.6	0.0	0.0	0.0	3.4	0.7
Small Cities	2.9	2.8	2.7	2.6	2.5	13.4	2.7
São Jose dos Campos	0.0	0.7	5.1	4.9	4.7	15.4	3.1
C. Supervision of Construction	7.3	7.0	6.7	6.4	6.2	33.6	6.8
D. Institutional Development	10.3	11.8	11.1	10.7	10.0	54.0	10.9
Total Program Base Cost	58.8	90.8	115.6	122.6	109.1	496.9	100.0
Physical Contingencies	4.1	6.4	8.1	8.6	7.6	34.8	7.0
Price Contingencies	1.6	7.3	14.5	21.0	23.9	68.3	13.7
Total Program Cost	64.5	104.5	138.2	152.2	140.6	600.0	120.7
Interest During Construction	1.1	4.0	8.4	13.7	18.8	46.0	9.3
Total Financing Requirements	65.6	108.6	146.6	165.8	159.4	646.0	130.0

TABLE A11.4   Other Investment Costs (US$ million equivalent)

	1989	1990	1991	1992	1993	TOTAL	% of Base
A. São Paulo Metropolitan Region	164.7	165.5	136.4	106.8	122.9	696.3	73.8
1. Water Supply:	48.9	43.0	36.7	23.5	29.8	182.0	19.3
Production	22.0	18.7	14.2	11.4	13.1	79.4	8.4
Transmission	9.7	1.3	1.5	0.6	0.0	13.1	1.4
Reservation	2.7	3.3	2.7	1.0	0.9	10.6	1.1
Distribution	10.0	9.0	2.0	0.6	2.5	24.2	2.6
Rehabilitation & Improvement	2.2	7.0	10.5	4.4	6.2	30.2	3.2
Others (own resources)	2.5	3.8	5.7	5.5	7.1	24.5	2.6
2. Sewerage:	115.8	122.5	99.7	83.3	93.1	514.4	54.6
Interception & Treatment	7.6	3.4	13.1	43.3	49.0	116.4	12.3
Collectors	105.5	116.3	83.2	35.4	37.2	377.7	40.1
IDB Program	83.9	102.4	58.4	0.0	0.0	244.7	26.0
Others	21.6	13.9	24.8	35.4	37.2	133.0	14.1
Rehabilitation & Improvement	1.2	1.4	2.0	2.6	4.8	12.0	1.3
Others (own resources)	1.5	1.4	1.3	1.9	2.2	8.3	0.9
B. Interior	30.3	35.6	24.2	23.9	15.9	130.0	13.8
1. Water Supply	14.2	15.1	7.8	7.5	7.3	51.8	5.5
2. Sewerage	13.9	18.4	13.1	12.6	0.6	58.6	6.2
Operation & Maintenance							
3. Programs	2.2	2.1	3.3	3.9	8.1	19.6	2.1
C. Supervision of Construction	16.4	15.6	15.1	14.5	14.0	75.6	8.0
D. Institutional Development	10.4	7.1	6.8	6.6	10.0	41.0	4.3
Total Other Investments Base Cost	221.9	223.8	182.5	151.8	162.9	942.9	100.0
Physical Contingencies	15.5	15.7	12.8	10.6	11.4	66.0	7.0
Price Contingencies	5.9	18.1	22.8	26.0	35.7	108.6	11.5
Total Other Investment Cost	243.3	257.6	218.1	188.4	210.0	1,117.5	118.5
Interest During Construction	2.3	3.5	3.9	4.8	5.5	20.0	2.1
Total Other Financing Requirements	245.6	257.6	218.1	188.4	210.0	1,117.5	118.5
Total Combined Program Base Costs	280.8	314.7	298.1	274.3	272.0	1,439.8	100.0
Physical Contingencies	19.7	22.0	20.9	19.2	19.0	100.8	7.0
Price Contingencies	7.4	25.5	37.3	47.0	59.7	176.9	12.3
Total Combined Program Cost	307.8	362.2	356.2	340.6	350.7	1,717.5	119.3
Interest during construction	3.4	7.5	12.3	18.5	24.3	6.0	4.6
Total Combined Program Financing Requirements	311.2	369.7	368.5	359.0	375.0	1,783.5	123.9

Note: Due to high inflation in Brazil during appraisal period (Nov.1988), investment costs are shown in US $(Dec.1988).   Physical contingencies average about 7 % of base costs. Price contingencies are calculated according to IBRD OMS (Oct.1988).   Direct taxes of US$ 40 million on the IBRD project and US$ 77 million on the other investment are included in the base costs.

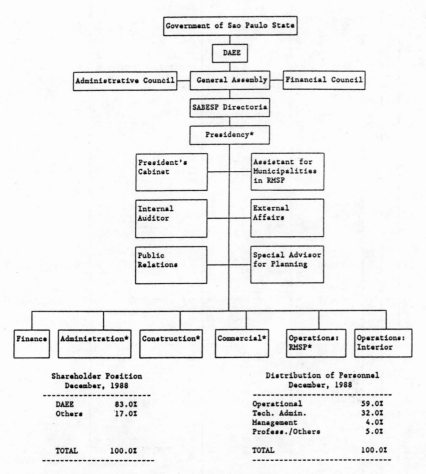

Figure A11.1 SABESP's Organization Chart

TABLE A11.5 SABESP Income Statement (Current US$ millions)

	historic				est.		projected					
	1984	1985	1986	1987	1988	1989	1990	1991	1992	1993	1994	1995
Water billed (Mm³)	1,164	1,161	1,143	1,411	1,460	1,500	1,541	1,585	1,627	1,669	1,708	1,739
Sewage billed (Mm³)	407	430	457	726	746	813	862	895	917	938	956	975
Avg. Tariff (US$ / m³)	0.14	0.15	0.13	0.18	0.30	0.33	0.34	0.36	0.37	0.39	0.40	0.42
Operating Revenues	277.9	285.5	312.8	402.8	665.7	771.3	844.1	908.2	973.2	1,043.2	1,110.6	1,183.7
Water	176.8	180.1	195.9	252.3	416.4	488.1	528.1	565.2	604.1	645.2	687.1	728.3
Final	164.4	167.5	182.2	234.7	384.4	453.9	491.1	525.7	561.8	600.1	639.0	677.4
Block	12.4	12.6	13.7	17.7	32.0	34.2	37.0	39.6	42.3	45.2	48.1	51.0
Sewerage	94.2	97.7	107.8	140.9	230.2	264.6	295.4	319.2	340.6	362.4	384.8	408.6
Other	7.0	7.7	9.2	9.6	19.0	18.5	20.5	23.7	28.5	35.6	38.7	46.8
Operating Expenses	149.7	161.1	169.0	267.4	382.4	399.8	424.0	441.6	460.0	481.9	499.5	517.8
Personnel	105.4	111.0	112.8	167.6	253.0	259.7	273.4	284.6	296.3	308.5	321.1	334.3
Materials	9.5	11.2	14.1	18.7	22.1	25.9	27.8	29.5	31.3	33.2	35.2	37.4
Chemicals	4.2	4.9	6.4	8.2	9.2	11.6	12.6	13.6	14.7	15.8	17.0	18.4
Other Materials	5.3	6.3	7.8	10.5	12.9	14.3	15.2	15.9	16.6	17.4	18.2	19.6
Third Parties	32.8	36.5	38.3	69.0	98.6	105.5	114.0	118.7	123.5	131.3	134.2	137.1
Electricity	17.7	19.4	21.3	28.6	45.4	48.6	52.5	54.7	56.9	62.0	62.0	92.6
Other Third Parties	15.2	17.1	17.1	40.4	53.1	56.9	61.5	64.0	66.6	69.3	72.2	75.1
General	1.9	2.4	3.6	11.7	8.1	8.0	8.0	8.0	8.0	8.0	8.0	8.0
Fiscal	0.1	0.1	0.2	0.7	0.6	0.7	0.7	0.8	0.8	0.9	0.9	1.0

TABLE A11.5 (continued)

	historic					est.	projected					
	1984	1985	1986	1987	1988	1989	1990	1991	1992	1993	1994	1995
Depreciation & Provisions	46.1	50.6	51.6	60.1	62.0	74.5	85.4	95.5	105.6	117.4	123.6	129.3
Depreciation	44.2	48.6	50.4	56.3	54.2	66.4	76.8	87.2	97.2	109.4	115.7	121.5
Provision for Bad Debt	1.8	2.0	1.2	3.9	7.8	8.0	8.5	8.4	8.3	8.0	7.9	7.9
Operating Income	82.2	73.7	92.3	75.3	221.5	297.0	334.7	371.0	407.6	443.9	487.5	536.6
Net Non-Operating Expenses	(0.9)	(18.8)	(1.8)	(68.0)	(2.7)	(16.1)	(16.0)	(14.0)	(12.0)	(9.0)	(9.6)	(9.0)
Net Financial Expenses	(125.8)	(62.9)	(74.8)	(67.7)	(104.0)	(100.9)	(111.8)	(119.8)	(135.7)	(151.2)	(157.7)	(162.2)
Net Inflation Adjustment	122.1	(3.7)	(38.3)	(49.7)	(205.6)	0.0	0.0	0.0	0.0	0.0	0.0	0.0
Pre-Tax Income	77.6	(11.7)	(22.6)	(110.1)	(90.8)	180.1	206.9	237.2	260.0	283.7	320.7	365.4
Net Income Tax Charge	2.9	0.0	0.0	2.4	1.3	54.0	62.1	71.2	78.0	85.1	96.2	109.6
Net Revenue (Loss)	74.7	(11.7)	(23.4)	(112.5)	(92.2)	126.0	144.9	166.1	182.0	198.6	224.5	255.8
Ratios:												
Operating Ratio (OpCost+Depc+DServ)/Revs (NTL compliance)	0.7	0.74	0.7	0.81	0.67	0.61	0.6	0.59	0.58	0.57	0.56	0.55
	1.36	1.17	1.05	1.11	0.9	0.87	0.83	0.84	0.85	0.85	0.85	0.83
RoR Avg Net Assets (Un-revalued basis)	0.06	0.05	0.05	0.04	0.08	0.12	0.14	0.15	0.15	0.15	0.15	0.15

Note:
The unusually high inflation adjustment of 1988 masks the significant improvement in performance, generated by a 67 percent real increase in average tariffs. This improvement can be seen in the financial ratios, and in operating income. Inflation adjustments have not been forecast; however, until the asset revaluation in 1990, these effects could have a negative impact on SABESP's projected booked net revenues.

TABLE A11.6 SABESP Balance Sheet (Current US$ millions)

	historic					est.	projected					
	1984	1985	1986	1987	1988	1989	1990	1991	1992	1993	1994	1995
Assets	2,238.2	2,431.6	3,109.1	3,183.9	3,012.4	3,319.1	3,689.3	4,044.5	4,374.4	4,666.0	4,975.8	5,296.1
Current Assets	97.6	110.3	102.8	165.6	260.8	297.1	335.4	357.8	364.2	341.6	378.9	436.3
Cash	9.3	17.9	17.9	11.9	18.0	40.7	43.4	45.8	48.3	50.9	53.7	56.6
Accounts Receivable	54.4	58.2	42.4	95.1	198.1	200.7	212.7	209.0	208.0	200.1	197.8	194.6
Uninvoiced Receivable	18.0	20.3	35.1	35.0	38.7	42.4	46.4	49.9	53.5	57.4	61.1	65.1
Inventory	6.5	3.2	4.7	4.0	3.2	6.2	7.7	6.8	6.3	6.5	10.5	10.5
Deferred Payments & Other	9.4	10.8	2.7	19.6	2.7	7.0	7.0	7.0	7.0	7.0	7.0	7.0
Short-term Investment	0.0	0.0	0.0	0.0	0.0	0.0	18.1	39.2	41.2	19.8	48.9	102.5
Total Fixed Assets	2,140.6	2,321.3	3,006.3	3,018.2	2,751.6	3,022.0	3,353.9	3,686.7	4,010.2	4,324.4	4,596.9	4,859.8
Net Fixed Assets	1,486.2	1,543.1	1,932.8	1,939.3	1,657.5	1,952.6	2,234.9	2,563.0	2,886.2	3,200.0	3,488.4	3,751.2
Gross Fixed Assets	1,711.8	1,816.6	2,316.1	2,349.5	2,050.5	2,396.9	2,739.1	3,135.7	3,537.3	3,939.5	4,326.4	4,697.4
Less: Accumulated Dep.	(225.6)	(273.5)	(383.3)	(410.2)	(393.0)	(444.3)	(504.2)	(572.7)	(651.1)	(739.5)	(838.0)	(946.1)
Work in Progress	645.1	762.7	1,055.8	1,061.9	1,087.8	1,034.2	1,083.7	1,088.5	1,088.8	1,089.2	1,073.3	1,073.3

TABLE A11.6 (continued)

	historic					est.	projected					
	1984	1985	1986	1987	1988	1989	1990	1991	1992	1993	1994	1995
Liabilities & Equity	2,238.2	2,431.6	3,109.1	3,183.9	3,012.4	3,319.2	3,689.3	4,044.5	4,374.4	4,666.0	4,976.2	5,298.8
Current Liabilities	162.0	192.9	192.6	182.9	249.3	237.0	268.2	286.7	310.9	333.5	353.8	355.2
Accounts Payable	71.2	37.7	53.2	54.8	78.2	80.0	84.8	88.3	92.0	96.4	99.9	103.6
Current Port. of L-T Debt	69.2	135.4	109.8	90.2	97.6	81.1	107.1	123.3	140.7	160.0	174.0	174.0
Suppliers & 3rd Party	21.6	19.9	29.6	37.9	73.6	76.0	76.3	75.1	78.2	77.1	79.9	77.7
Total Long-Term Debt	1,151.7	1,247.1	1,700.6	1,837.0	1,664.6	1,940.2	2,081.1	2,201.8	2,283.6	2,330.0	2,295.3	2,260.7
Less: Current Portfolio	69.2	135.5	109.8	90.2	97.6	81.1	107.1	123.3	140.7	160.0	174.0	174.0
Total L-T Debt	1,584.9	1,382.6	1,810.5	1,927.2	1,762.2	2,021.3	2,188.2	2,325.1	2,424.2	2,522.0	2,487.3	1,452.7
Other L-T Liabilities	65.5	64.0	54.7	77.8	154.2	30.9	25.0	25.0	25.0	25.0	25.0	25.0
Equity	859.0	927.6	1,161.2	1,086.1	944.2	1,111.1	1,314.9	1,531.0	1,755.0	1,977.6	2,302.1	2,657.8
Capital	217.3	302.1	708.3	287.3	125.5	245.5	357.5	467.5	577.5	677.5	777.5	877.5
Reserves	475.7	623.4	468.4	881.6	922.7	924.2	924.2	924.2	924.2	924.2	924.2	924.2
Earnings Reserve	8.3	8.7	0.0	0.0	0.0	0.0	0.0	0.0	0.0	0.0	0.0	0.0
Retained Earnings/Losses	157.7	(6.5)	(15.4)	(82.8)	(104.0)	(58.7)	33.2	139.3	253.2	375.8	600.3	856.1
Ratios:												
Current Ratio	0.6	0.6	0.5	0.9	1.0	1.3	1.3	1.2	1.2	1.0	1.1	1.2
Debt:Equity Ratio	0.57	0.57	0.59	0.63	0.64	0.64	0.61	0.59	0.57	0.54	0.50	0.46
A/R Comparator	71	74	49	86	109	95	92	84	78	70	65	60

TABLE A11.7 SABESP Flow of Funds (Current US$ millions)

| | historic | | | | | est. | | projected | | | | | Total |
	1984	1985	1986	1987	1988	1989	1990	1991	1992	1993	1994	1995	1989-93
Total Sources	264.2	275.5	309.6	310.1	311.5	574.6	665.3	698.5	731.1	774.8	698.0	739.5	3,417.3
Internal Sources	122.6	103.5	140.1	61.2	51.0	293.4	333.5	373.0	414.9	459.2	498.0	539.5	1,873.9
Net Income (Loss) After Tax	74.7	(11.7)	(23.4)	(112.5)	(92.2)	126.0	144.9	166.1	182.0	198.6	224.5	255.8	817.5
Plus:													
Depreciation	44.2	48.6	50.4	56.3	54.2	66.4	76.8	87.2	97.2	109.4	115.7	121.5	437.1
Monetary Variation	1,491.4	1,563.7	782.2	2,347.6	4,196.3	0.0	0.0	0.0	0.0	0.0	0.0	0.0	0.0
Monetary Correction	(1,613.5)	(1,560.0)	(743.9)	(2,297.9)	(4,211.4)	0.0	0.0	0.0	0.0	0.0	0.0	0.0	0.0
Financial Charges	125.8	62.9	74.8	67.7	104.0	100.9	111.8	119.8	135.7	151.2	157.7	162.2	619.3
Other	0.0	0.0	0.0	0.0	0.0	0.0	0.0	0.0	0.0	0.0	0.0	0.0	0.0
External Sources	141.6	172.0	169.5	248.9	260.4	254.2	331.9	325.5	316.2	315.7	200.0	200.0	1,543.4
Debt::	76.5	95.4	101.6	159.9	168.1	134.2	219.9	215.5	206.2	215.7	100.0	100.0	991.4
CEF	0.0	0.0	0.0	0.0	0.0	28.0	62.5	70.0	60.0	79.5	50.0	50.0	300.0
FAE	0.0	0.0	0.0	0.0	0.0	28.0	62.5	70.0	60.0	79.5	50.0	50.0	300.0
IDB	0.0	0.0	0.0	0.0	0.0	41.2	55.6	14.6	0.0	0.0	0.0	0.0	111.4
IBRD	0.0	0.0	0.0	0.0	0.0	37.0	39.3	60.9	86.2	56.7	0.0	0.0	280.0
Equity:	64.2	75.6	65.4	87.3	92.4	120.0	112.0	110.0	110.0	100.0	100.0	100.0	552.0
Shareholder's Inc.	51.9	49.7	42.7	42.6	49.8	94.0	85.0	84.0	86.0	77.0	100.0	100.0	426.0
Capital Increases	12.3	26.0	22.8	44.7	42.6	0.0	0.0	0.0	0.0	0.0	0.0	0.0	0.0
IBRD Counterpart	0.0	0.0	0.0	0.0	0.0	26.0	27.0	26.0	24.0	23.0	0.0	0.0	126.0
Other Asset Increase	1.0	1.0	2.5	1.6	0.0	0.0	0.0	0.0	0.0	0.0	0.0	0.0	105.9

TABLE A11.7 (continued)

| | historic | | | | | est. | projected | | | | | | Total |
	1984	1985	1986	1987	1988	1989	1990	1991	1992	1993	1994	1995	1989-93
Total Applications:	202.9	192.9	260.5	321.2	311.5	570.3	670.4	700.9	733.6	777.4	700.4	742.9	3,452.6
Capital Expenditures	145.6	196.7	233.8	263.3	292.7	292.8	391.8	401.3	401.8	402.7	376.0	376.0	1,890.4
Proposed Project	0.0	0.0	0.0	0.0	0.0	64.5	104.5	138.2	152.2	140.6	0.0	0.0	600.0
Other Investments	130.6	179.2	212.6	240.4	261.2	208.3	257.6	228.1	208.4	215.0	350.0	350.0	1,117.4
Interest During Const.	2.5	0.5	0.1	2.9	2.5	3.4	7.5	12.3	18.5	24.3	5.0	5.0	66.6
Cap'd Admin. Costs	12.5	17.0	21.0	20.0	29.0	16.6	22.2	22.7	22.7	22.8	21.0	21.0	107.6
(Inc)/Dec in Working Cap	(125.9)	(128.0)	(83.4)	(64.3)	(133.3)	(48.7)	(7.1)	(4.0)	17.7	45.3	(17.0)	(56.0)	3.3
Other Liability Inc.	0.4	0.8	1.5	1.3	0.0	127.7	92.8	76.7	55.1	37.6	21.4	83.9	389.9
Debt Service	182.8	123.4	108.7	120.9	152.2	198.5	192.9	226.9	258.9	291.8	320.0	339.0	1,169.9
Interest	125.8	62.9	74.8	67.7	104.0	100.9	111.8	119.8	135.7	151.2	160.0	165.0	619.3
Amortization	57.0	60.5	33.9	53.2	48.2	97.6	81.1	107.1	123.3	140.7	160.0	174.0	549.7
(Inc)/Dec in Cash						(22.7)	(5.1)	(2.4)	(2.5)	(2.6)	(2.8)	(2.9)	59.9
Cash Beginning Year						18.0	40.7	45.8	48.2	50.7	53.3	56.1	
Cash End Year					18.0	40.7	45.8	48.2	50.7	53.3	56.1	59.0	
Ratio:													
Debt Service Coverage	0.7	0.8	1.3	0.5	0.3	1.5	1.7	1.6	1.6	1.6	1.6	1.6	1.6

TABLE A11.8   Transfers From the State to the Sanitation Sector
(Current US$ millions)

	Historic				Estimated	
	1984	1985	1986	1987	1988	1989
Total Revenues	4,363.5	5,720.3	8,957.0	8,693.1	7,842.4	8,000.0
Total Transfers to Sanitation	85.6	95.0	94.8	116.2	159.2	147.6
To SABESP	60.3	76.1	66.4	85.6	125.6	137.6
To FAE	25.3	18.8	28.4	30.6	33.6	10.0
% of Total Revenues to Sanitation	2.0	1.7	1.1	1.3	2.0	1.8
% Share to SABESP	70.4	80.2	70.1	73.6	78.9	93.2
% Share to FAE	29.6	19.8	29.9	26.4	21.1	6.8

12

Brazil: Water Pricing Policy and Marginal Costs

In this chapter, we first review the existing national water and sewerage tariff policies in Brazil. Next, we examine the specific situation in São Paulo State by estimating SABESP's long-run marginal costs (LRMC) of supply and comparing this LRMC to the existing tariff structure.

Current Water and Sewerage Tariff Policies in Brazil

Brazilian water supply and sewerage tariff structures are based on the National Tariff Law or NTL (see Chapter 11), and more specific implementation criteria defined by the Caixa Economica Federal (CEF).

General Pricing Criteria

Existing tariff setting criteria are based on two general objectives: (i) financial equilibrium; and (ii) social equity. These two aspects are explained below in greater detail. Financial equilibrium requires utilities to generate revenues sufficient to meet service costs, SC (De Azevedo et al. 1984). SC is defined as the sum of:

- exploitation expenses -- operating, maintenance, commercial, administrative and fiscal expenses (DEX);
- annual allowances for depreciation, doubtful accounts (excluding a reserve for it) and amortization of expenses (DPA); and

---

This chapter was prepared with the assistance of C. Velez.

$$Rev \geq DEX + DPA + RI$$

$$RI > DS$$

$$DPA \leq \underline{Rev - DEX - DS} \rightarrow \text{will at least allow Investment} = \text{depreciation}$$

- remuneration for investment (RI) -- the acknowledged investment in operating and immobilized fixed assets times an authorized remuneration rate.

The remuneration for investment should be at least equal to the debt service (interest payments and capital amortization due in a given period of time). The actual annual remuneration rate should be equal to or smaller than 12%.

The current Brazilian socioeconomic policy on water supply and sewerage tariffs requires utilities to take into account users' ability to pay (De Azevedo et al. 1984; Accorsi 1987). Rate structures are established using minimum consumption levels and increasing block tariffs. Assumptions underlying this philosophy are that:

- households may not be classified as commercial or industrial customers; and
- family income is positively correlated with water consumption.

Additionally, this approach explicitly denies subsidies to commercial and industrial customers, and suggests a neutral tariff (a tariff equal to the utility's service cost) for public users. In view of their complexity and importance, the social equity guidelines are discussed in greater detail below.

Social Equity Guidelines

Each relevant guideline is first defined and then the issues arising from its application are discussed.

Minimum Residential Bill

The first guideline establishes that there should be a minimum water residential bill not exceeding 0.35 OTN (Obrigacoes do Tesouro Nacional), and a minimum water and sewerage residential bill not exceeding 0.50 OTN (1 OTN - US\$ 6.91). In 1983, the actual average minimum bill for both residential water supply and sewerage reached 70% of the above maximum authorized by the law. By 1986, this figure was reduced to less than 60%, while the actual average minimum residential bill for water supply alone was about 50% of the corresponding maximum limit.

Residential Minimum Consumption Level (MCL)

A second guideline establishes that:

- the minimum residential consumption level corresponding to the minimum bill should be at least equal to 10m³ per household per month; and
- this volume should be based on the quantity of water a family requires for maintaining the minimum indispensable health and sanitary conditions.

In 1989, 18 SWCs had their minimum household consumption level (MCL) at 10m³/month, one had it at 12 m³/month, and two at 20 m³/month. The concentration at 10 m³/month is a relatively recent trend.

Usually, the main reason for including MCLs (at a fixed price) in a rate schedule is that it allows utilities a full or partial recovery of customer-related fixed costs. Pursuit of this objective with low-income households contributes to significant departures from the objective of improving poor families' welfare, especially when implemented too aggressively. In many cases, residential, commercial, industrial, and public customers who can afford to pay the utilities' service cost are being subsidized.

Residential Consumption Blocks

A third guideline establishes that residential consumption should be differentiated, through an increasing block tariff structure. The consumption ranges for blocks vary significantly not only from one utility to another, but also between areas being served by the same utility (for example, the institute CAERN has three different schedules). Thus, typically, the second block ranges from 11 m³/month to 15m³/month in 9 SCWs, from 11 m³/month to 20 m³/month in 6 SWCs, from 16m³/month to 30m³/month in 3 SCWs, and exhibits 8 different ranges in the remaining 12 SCWs.

Relationship of Residential Water Use to Family Income and Other Variables

Practical implementation of current Brazilian public policy on water supply and sewerage tariffs is based on the assumption that family income and water consumption are positively correlated. Minimum bills, minimum consumption levels, and consumption blocks, are all rate schedule elements because of this critical assumption. However, if the assumption is not accurate, the entire pricing structure based on social considerations may become regressive with some well-off households being subsidized. Since residential rates are generally smaller than marginal costs, a large majority of households are subsidized. This gives water utilities considerable scope for increasing revenues just by eliminating unnecessary subsidies now being granted to high-income families.

This assumption has been examined in a recent study which concluded that water consumption is not an appropriate variable for the purpose of ensuring progressive tariffs, because of its weak correlation with family income (Accorsi 1987). The correlation coefficient found for these two variables was only 0.21.

Table 12.1 shows average household water consumption by income level for a typical Brazilian water utility company, SANEPAR (in the State of Parana). The small differences between averages (especially among the first four categories), as well as the large standard deviation for all income levels, are worth noting. The household water consumption distribution for each income level category is shown in Table 12.2 and illustrated in Figure 12.1. The small range falling between 7 m³/month and 15 m³/month includes almost half of SANEPAR's residential consumers.

A practical consequence of using water consumption as a proxy for household income in water supply pricing may be that resulting tariff structures are not as progressive as had been planned originally. In some cases, these tariff structures may even be regressive. Hence, there is a growing concern in Brazil about the fairness of existing water supply and sewerage tariffs. However, it would be wrong to argue that the solution is to make the tariff structure more progressive, sharply increasing the rates belonging to higher consumption blocks. This proposal may make the tariff structure appear progressive for the average poor family. However, upon closer examination, it will surely aggravate the situation for many middle income and some poor households.

In the above mentioned study, residential water consumption (RWC) could not be satisfactorily explained by other variables. Geographical location and the city size did not explain the differences between water consumption of households located in different cities. Finally, explanatory variables such as: number of water exits (points), number of people living in each house, number of rooms, the area of each house, and the type of construction, also failed to explain the variations in RWC among SANEPAR consumers.

Non-Residential Tariffs

A fourth guideline establishes that tariffs should be differentiated by final usage, and that average commercial and industrial rates should be greater than the utility's average price.

A fifth guideline establishes that commercial, industrial, and public minimum consumption levels should be set, such that the minimum consumption rate is smaller than the remaining rates in that category. Additionally, commercial and industrial minimum rates should be greater than the utility's average tariff, and the public usage minimum price should be greater than the residential minimum rate.

TABLE 12.1   SANEPAR's Household Water Consumption and Income

Household Income (Y) (Minimum Salaries (MS) per Month) (1)	Households		Household Water Consumption (m³/month)		
	#	%	Mean	Standard Deviation	Deviation Coefficient
Y < 1 MS	338	6.2	10.4	12.3	118
1 MS < Y < 2 MS	806	14.9	11.0	7.7	70
2 MS < Y < 5 MS	1969	36.4	12.3	7.5	61
5 MS < Y < 10 MS	1228	22.7	15.7	11.0	70
10 MS < Y < 20 MS	674	12.5	22.5	18.5	82
20 MS < Y	419	7.3	32.3	24.6	76
Total	5434	100.0	15.5	13.8	89

(1) One Minimum Salary (MS) = US$ 60.42 (end 1988).
Source: Accorsi 1987.

TABLE 12.2   SANEPAR's Household Water Consumption Distribution

Water Consumption (W) m³/month	Household Income Level (Y) (%)					
	Y < 1MS (1)	1MS < Y Y < 2MS	2MS < Y Y < 5MS	5MS < Y Y < 10MS	10MS < Y Y < 20MS	20MS < Y
W < 3	15	12	7	5	3	2
3 < W < 6	18	15	12	9	4	2
6 < W < 10	31	31	29	20	13	0
10 < W < 15	21	24	28	27	20	16
15 < W < 25	12	14	19	26	33	29
25 < W < 50	3	4	5	11	19	30
50 < W	0	0	0	2	8	21
Total	100	100	100	100	100	100

(1) One Minimum Salary (MS) = US$ 60.42 (end 1988).
Source: Accorsi 1987.

Differentiating between commercial, industrial, or public customers based on their water consumption level has negative effects on the resource allocation process. Minimum consumption levels for non-residential customers seek to accommodate some households owning a small family business, who are classified as commercial or industrial customers. However, such complexities could be avoided with a better tariff structure that automatically took care of this classification process. Households having small family business within or

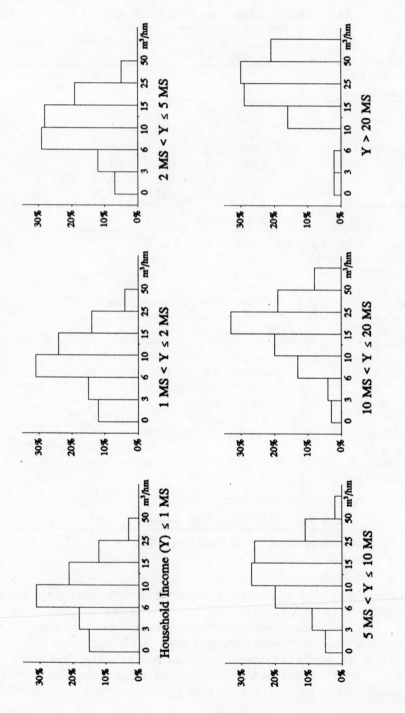

Figure 12.1 SANEPAR's Household Water Consumption Distribution

attached to their homes should find themselves better off when classified as residential customers. Likewise, households having a larger than normal family business should find themselves better off when classified as non-domestic customers.

Non-Metered Consumption

Twelve (12) SWCs charge non-metered residential customers only with their authorized minimum bills. The remaining companies bill them using their rate schedules, and water consumption estimates based on the following criteria:

- dwellings' area in m^2 (5);
- dwelling construction type (3);
- number of rooms (2);
- number of water exits (1); and
- a combination of more than one of the above (1).

Most non-residential water consumption is metered, and unmetered customers are generally low volume water users. SWCs use one of the following criteria to estimate unmetered water consumption:

- establishment area in m^2;
- economic activity;
- arbitrary minimum consumption level;
- number of water exits; and
- a combination of more than one of the above criteria.

Special Contracts

Special contracts exist between non-residential customers and eight of the SWCs. These contracts usually guarantee a minimum amount of water to be supplied to the customer concerned. In this case, the customer negotiates his rates outside the usual rate schedule. The volume of water sold under this kind of agreement represents a significant share for some companies, despite the small number of customers involved.

Sewerage Rates

Sewerage and water supply tariff structures are symmetric, with sewerage rates applied as a surcharge varying from 35% and 100% of water rates. Currently, there are 15 SWCs applying a 100% surcharge, 9 applying 80%,

2 applying 60%, 2 applying 50%, and one each applying 90%, 75%, and 35%, respectively.

Sewerage rates are not based on supply costs, but on financial needs. Explicit charges for treatment do not exist. Systems without treatment have rates significantly larger than costs, while systems with treatment have costs much greater than rates. Generally, the sewerage component generally provides a large cross-subsidy to the water supply components, given that in most utilities only a small portion (if at all) of the collected sewerage is treated.

Complementary Guidelines

A long-term objective of each utility is to serve the whole population within its franchise area. Therefore, as a means of facilitating access to their services, most utilities do not charge connection fees from customers. In cases where such charges are levied, they cover materials, labor, and the meter cost, if applicable.

A typical SWC usually has several water supply and sewerage systems with different supply costs which are aggregated and consolidated for financial and pricing purposes. Therefore, SWC rate schedules and levels are applied uniformly to all their customers, independent of the individual system which is serving them. This pricing feature introduces a cross-system subsidization element among customers belonging to different water systems within a given utility. Furthermore, differences in the interest rate PLANASA applies to the different SWCs introduces another cross-subsidization element among utilities.

Efficient Allocation of Resources

Water supply and sewerage pricing criteria are complemented by investment planning criteria that seek to achieve an efficient allocation of resources. Utilities are required to expand their systems choosing the least-cost alternative, and water projects are accepted only if the utility's water average tariff (WAT) is larger than 0.75 of the project's marginal cost (MC), for those cases involving populations larger than 50,000 people. The WAT should be larger than 0.75 of the project's marginal cost (MC), for those cases involving population larger than 5,000 people but smaller than 50,000 people. Sewerage projects are accepted only if the utility's sewerage average tariff is at least equal to 0.60 MC. However, a project that does not satisfy these conditions may still be accepted if it is possible to demonstrate that there are "special social benefits" resulting from its execution.

SABESP'S Marginal Costs and
Tariff Structure

The following is a preliminary comparison of SABESP's existing tariff structure and estimated LRMC of its water and sewerage systems. While this analysis is not a substitute for a full-scale marginal cost based tariff study, it is possible to identify most of the main issues, as summarized below. These issues need to be investigated further through a more detailed tariff study.

Marginal Cost Pricing Analysis

Long-run marginal costs (LRMC) for the project's own investments as well as complementary works have been estimated using the average incremental cost or AIC approach (see Chapter 8). SABESP's water and sewerage LRMC have been estimated for each of the five regions into which its market is divided: RMSP's Integrated System, RMSP's Isolated Systems, Baixada Santista, Interior's Large and Medium Cities (CMG) and Interior's Small Communities (CPP).

Demand Forecasts and Capacity Expansion

As explained in Chapter 7, demand projections were estimated using: expected population growth rates; fixed targets for service coverage; constant parameters for annual per-capita consumption, number of people per household and number of households per residential connection; and declining percentages of average losses. Therefore, demand forecasts implicitly assume a price elasticity equal to zero. Disaggregated projections for each market of SABESP and for the whole company are shown in Table 11.4 and 11.5. The nominal capacities of SABESP's water and sewerage treatment stations and their expected use level in each year are shown in Tables 12.3 and 12.4.

Incremental Costs

Water investments are divided into production (which includes water intake, treatment and unaccounted-for water control), transmission, reservoirs, primary distribution, secondary distribution and connections. Sewerage investments are divided into connections, collectors, main collectors, interceptors and treatment. All investments are expressed in prices of December 1988 and include engineering and physical contingencies. Complementary investments to be made by the SWCs after project execution are mainly house connections and secondary water distribution pipes and sewerage collectors. SABESP's investment programs for water and sewerage are shown in detail in Tables 12.5 and 12.6. Table 12.7 presents an

TABLE 12.3 SABESP's Water Treatment Capacity

| System | Nominal Treatment Capacity | | | | | | | | | | | | | | | | | |
| | Actual | | | | | Projected | | | | | | | | | | | | |
	1988	1989	1990	1991	1992	1993	1994	1995	1996	1997	1998	1999	2000	2001	2002	2003	2004	2005
RMSP: Integrated System																		
Cantareira / Eta Guarau	22.00	26.00	26.00	26.00	26.00	26.00	26.00	26.00	26.00	26.00	26.00	26.00	26.00	26.00	26.00	26.00	26.00	26.00
Guarapiranga / Eta Abv	10.50	10.50	10.50	10.50	10.50	10.50	10.50	10.50	10.50	10.50	10.50	10.50	10.50	10.50	10.50	10.50	10.50	10.50
Rio Claro / Eta Casa Grande	3.70	3.70	3.70	3.70	3.70	3.70	3.70	3.70	3.70	3.70	3.70	3.70	3.70	3.70	3.70	3.70	3.70	3.70
Rio Grande / Eta Rio Grande	3.50	3.50	3.50	3.50	3.50	3.50	3.50	3.50	3.50	3.50	3.50	3.50	3.50	3.50	3.50	3.50	3.50	3.50
Alto Cotia / Eta Alto Cotia	0.80	0.80	0.80	0.80	0.80	0.80	0.80	0.80	0.80	0.80	0.80	0.80	0.80	0.80	0.80	0.80	0.80	0.80
Baixo Cotia / Eta Baixo Cotia	0.50	0.50	0.50	0.50	0.50	0.50	0.50	0.50	0.50	0.50	0.50	0.50	0.50	0.50	0.50	0.50	0.50	0.50
Riberao Estiva	0.02	0.02	0.02	0.02	0.02	0.02	0.02	0.02	0.02	0.02	0.02	0.02	0.02	0.02	0.02	0.02	0.02	0.02
Alto Tiete	-	-	-	-	5.00	5.00	5.00	5.00	5.00	5.00	5.00	5.00	5.00	5.00	5.00	5.00	5.00	5.00
Sucoeste	-	-	-	-	-	2.70	2.70	2.70	2.70	2.70	2.70	2.70	2.70	2.70	2.70	2.70	2.70	2.70
Cabucu / Engordador	-	-	-	-	-	0.50	0.50	0.50	0.50	0.50	0.50	0.50	0.50	0.50	0.50	0.50	0.50	0.50
Nominal Capacity (m^3/s)	41.02	45.02	45.02	45.02	50.02	53.22	53.22	53.22	53.22	53.22	53.22	53.22	53.22	53.22	53.22	53.22	53.22	53.22
Nominal Capacity (millions m^3)	1,293.6	1,419.8	1,419.8	1,419.8	1,577.4	1,678.3	1,678.3	1,678.3	1,678.3	1,678.3	1,678.3	1,678.3	1,678.3	1,678.3	1,678.3	1,678.3	1,678.3	1,678.3
Expected Production (millions m^3)	1,470.0	1,496.0	1,524.0	1,553.0	1,579.0	170.0	1,633.0	1,667.0	1,705.0	1,741.0	1,778.0	1,815.0	1,853.0	1,863.0	1,863.0	1,863.0	1,863.0	1,863.0
Expected Overloading (times)	1.1364	1.0537	1.0734	1.0939	1.0010	0.9575	0.9730	0.9932	1.0159	1.0373	1.0594	1.0814	1.1042	1.1100	1.1100	1.1100	1.1100	1.1100
RMSP: Isolated System																		
Nominal Capacity (m^3/s)	0.18	0.19	0.22	0.24	0.25	0.26	0.26	0.26	0.26	0.26	0.26	0.26	0.26	0.26	0.26	0.26	0.26	0.26
Nominal Capacity (millions m^3)	5.74	6.05	7.00	7.63	7.95	8.26	8.26	8.26	8.26	8.26	8.26	8.26	8.26	8.26	8.26	8.26	8.26	8.26
Expected Production (millions m^3)	6.20	6.30	6.50	6.80	7.30	7.80	8.40	8.90	9.20	9.20	9.20	9.20	9.20	9.20	9.20	9.20	9.20	9.20
Expected Overloading (times)	1.0802	1.0405	0.9284	0.8910	0.9186	0.9440	1.0166	1.0772	1.1135	1.1135	1.1135	1.1135	1.1135	1.1135	1.1135	1.1135	1.1135	1.1135

TABLE 12.3   (continued)

| System | Nominal Treatment Capacity | | | | | | | | | | | | | | | | | |
| | Actual | | | | | Projected | | | | | | | | | | | | |
	1988	1989	1990	1991	1992	1993	1994	1995	1996	1997	1998	1999	2000	2001	2002	2003	2004	2005
Private Services																		
Nominal Capacity (m^3/s)	5.40	5.40	6.00	6.15	6.15	6.75	6.75	6.75	6.75	6.75	6.75	6.75	6.75	6.75	6.75	6.75	6.75	6.75
Nominal Capacity (millions m^3)	170.29	170.29	189.22	193.95	193.95	212.71	212.71	212.71	212.71	212.71	212.71	212.71	212.71	212.71	212.71	212.71	212.71	212.71
Expected Production (millions m^3)	166.70	172.90	175.00	177.70	179.20	180.90	162.70	184.50	186.40	186.40	190.40	192.50	194.70	199.50	204.50	209.60	214.60	220.20
Expected Overloading (times)	0.9789	1.0153	0.9280	0.9162	0.9240	7.0000	0.8589	0.8674	0.8763	0.8857	0.8951	0.9050	0.9153	0.9379	0.9614	0.9854	1.0103	1.0352
Interior: Large and Medium Cities (CMG)																		
Nominal Capacity (m^3/s)	6.80	7.40	8.49	9.79	10.99	11.61	11.61	11.61	11.61	11.61	11.61	11.61	11.61	11.61	11.61	11.61	11.61	11.61
Nominal Capacity (millions m^3)	214.44	235.26	267.74	308.74	346.58	366.13	366.13	366.13	366.13	366.13	366.13	366.13	366.13	366.13	366.13	366.13	366.13	366.13
Expected Production (millions m^3)	243.90	254.50	261.80	270.70	279.70	288.90	300.30	312.30	324.80	337.80	351.30	365.40	380.00	387.40	387.40	387.40	387.40	387.40
Expected Overloading (times)	1.1374	1.0818	0.9778	0.8768	0.8070	0.7891	0.8202	0.8530	0.8871	0.9226	0.9595	0.9980	1.0379	1.0581	1.0581	1.0581	1.0581	1.0581
Interior: Small Communities (CPP)																		
Nominal Capacity (m^3/s)	1.40	1.53	1.61	1.71	1.74	1.82	1.82	1.82	1.82	1.82	1.82	1.82	1.82	1.82	1.82	1.82	1.82	1.82
Nominal Capacity (millions m^3)	44.15	48.34	50.87	53.99	55.00	57.24	57.24	57.24	57.24	57.24	57.24	57.24	57.24	57.24	57.24	57.24	57.24	57.24
Expected Production (millions m^3)	42.90	43.30	44.60	45.70	46.70	48.10	50.20	52.20	54.30	56.40	58.70	59.90	59.90	59.90	59.90	59.90	59.90	59.90
Expected Overloading (times)	0.9717	0.8957	0.8768	0.8465	0.8491	0.8404	0.8770	0.9120	0.9487	0.9854	1.0255	1.0465	1.0465	1.0465	1.0465	1.0465	1.0465	1.0465

TABLE 12.4 SABESP's Sewage Treatment Capacity

System	Nominal Treatment Capacity												
	Actual					Projected							
	1988	1989	1990	1991	1992	1993	1994	1995	1996	1997	1998	1999	2000
RMSP: Integrated System													
Nominal Capacity in m³/s	9.20	9.49	9.60	9.76	10.70	15.22	15.22	15.22	15.22	15.22	15.22	15.22	15.22
Nominal Capacity in millions of m³	290.1	299.3	302.7	307.8	337.4	480.0	480.0	480.0	480.0	480.0	480.0	480.0	480.0
Expected Effluent Treated in millions of m³	249.1	263.1	277.9	293.5	310.0	327.4	345.8	365.3	385.8	407.5	430.4	454.5	480.1
Expected Overloading (times)	0.8586	0.8791	0.9179	0.9536	0.9187	0.6821	0.7204	0.7611	0.8038	0.8490	0.8967	0.9469	1.0003
RMSP: Isolated Systems													
Nominal Capacity in m³/s	0.14	0.32	0.50	0.68	0.86	1.04	1.04	1.04	1.04	1.04	1.04	1.04	1.04
Nominal Capacity in millions of m³	4.4	10.1	15.8	21.4	27.1	32.8	32.8	32.8	32.8	32.8	32.8	32.8	32.8
Expected Effluent Treated in millions of m³	4.4	5.2	6.2	7.3	8.6	10.2	12.0	14.2	16.8	19.9	23.5	27.8	32.8
Expected Overloading (times)	0.9966	0.5153	0.3932	0.3404	0.3171	0.3110	0.3659	0.4330	0.5122	0.6068	0.7165	0.8476	1.0000
Baixada Santista													
Nominal Capacity in m³/s	3.10	3.10	3.36	3.36	4.89	6.19	6.19	6.19	6.19	6.19	6.19	6.19	6.19
Nominal Capacity in millions of m³	97.8	97.8	106.0	106.0	154.2	195.2	195.2	195.2	195.2	195.2	195.2	195.2	195.2
Expected Effluent Treated in millions of m³	47.3	50.1	53.1	56.2	59.6	63.1	66.8	70.8	75.0	79.4	84.1	89.1	94.4
Expected Overloading (times)	0.4838	0.5125	0.5011	0.5304	0.3865	0.3232	0.3422	0.3627	0.3842	0.4067	0.4308	0.4564	0.4836
Interior: Large & Medium Cities (CMG)													
Nominal Capacity in m³/s	0.22	0.34	0.47	0.47	2.27	2.84	2.84	2.84	2.84	2.84	2.84	2.84	2.84
Nominal Capacity in millions of m³	6.9	10.7	14.8	14.8	71.6	89.6	89.6	89.6	89.6	89.6	89.6	89.6	89.6
Expected Effluent Treated in millions of m³	6.9	8.5	10.6	13.1	16.2	20.0	24.8	30.7	38.0	47.0	58.2	72.0	89.1
Expected Overloading (times)	0.9945	0.7927	0.7152	0.8838	0.2263	0.2233	0.2769	0.3428	0.4243	0.5248	0.6498	0.8039	0.9948
Interior: Small Communities (CPP)													
Nominal Capacity in m³/s	0.20	0.20	0.20	0.20	0.21	0.80	0.80	0.80	0.80	0.80	0.80	0.80	0.80
Nominal Capacity in millions of m³	6.3	6.3	6.3	6.3	6.6	25.2	25.2	25.2	25.2	25.2	25.2	25.2	25.2
Expected Effluent Treated in millions of m³	5.4	6.0	6.8	7.6	8.5	9.6	10.7	12.1	13.5	15.2	17.1	19.1	21.5
Expected Overloading (times)	0.8562	0.9513	1.0781	1.2050	1.2835	0.3805	0.4241	0.4796	0.5351	0.6025	0.6778	0.7571	0.8520

TABLE 12.5 SABESP's Water Investment Program (US$ millions as of December 1988)

Description	1988	1989	1990	1991	1992	1993	1994	1995	1996	1997	1998	1999	2000	2001	2002	2003	2004	2005
RMSP: Integrated System																		
Alto Tietê	9.47	15.66	12.28	12.59	10.07	10.77	0.00	0.00	0.00	0.00	0.00	0.00	0.00	0.00	0.00	0.00	0.00	0.00
Cantareira (GUARAU)	10.65	8.26	6.84	3.46	2.21	4.36	0.00	0.00	0.00	0.00	0.00	0.00	0.00	0.00	0.00	0.00	0.00	0.00
Cantareira (CABUCU)	0.00	0.00	0.00	0.79	1.89	3.37	0.00	0.00	0.00	0.00	0.00	0.00	0.00	0.00	0.00	0.00	0.00	0.00
Guarapiranga (ABV)	7.61	1.72	2.46	3.41	3.02	0.00	0.00	0.00	0.00	0.00	0.00	0.00	0.00	0.00	0.00	0.00	0.00	0.00
Rio Grande	0.00	1.21	2.13	2.01	2.27	2.18	0.00	0.00	0.00	0.00	0.00	0.00	0.00	0.00	0.00	0.00	0.00	0.00
Alto Cotia	0.00	0.00	0.41	1.57	1.51	0.00	0.00	0.00	0.00	0.00	0.00	0.00	0.00	0.00	0.00	0.00	0.00	0.00
Sudoeste	0.00	0.00	4.50	7.97	10.20	12.34	0.00	0.00	0.00	0.00	0.00	0.00	0.00	0.00	0.00	0.00	0.00	0.00
Production Reinforcement & Expansion	27.73	26.85	28.61	31.69	31.18	33.01	0.00	0.00	0.00	0.00	0.00	0.00	0.00	0.00	0.00	0.00	0.00	0.00
Unaccounted Water Control Program	0.00	13.74	15.34	16.06	10.54	9.76	0.00	0.00	0.00	0.00	0.00	0.00	0.00	0.00	0.00	0.00	0.00	0.00
Total Investment in Incremental Production	27.73	40.95	43.96	47.76	41.72	42.77	0.00	0.00	0.00	0.00	0.00	0.00	0.00	0.00	0.00	0.00	0.00	0.00
Transmission Pipes	0.00	15.08	18.08	23.05	25.74	12.28	0.00	0.00	0.00	0.00	0.00	0.00	0.00	0.00	0.00	0.00	0.00	0.00
Reservoirs	0.00	4.09	5.35	4.92	2.19	1.09	0.00	0.00	0.00	0.00	0.00	0.00	0.00	0.00	0.00	0.00	0.00	0.00
Primary Distribution Pipes	0.00	1.96	4.11	5.00	5.25	5.68	3.48	3.51	2.99	3.02	3.08	3.11	3.16	0.00	0.00	0.00	0.00	0.00
Secondary Distribution Pipes	0.00	4.58	9.59	11.65	12.24	13.25	8.13	8.20	6.98	7.05	7.18	7.25	7.38	0.00	0.00	0.00	0.00	0.00
Connections	0.00	6.61	6.50	5.41	5.40	5.27	4.52	4.56	3.88	3.92	4.00	4.04	4.11	0.00	0.00	0.00	0.00	0.00
Total Investment in Incremental Water Supply	27.73	72.92	87.59	97.78	92.54	80.34	16.14	16.27	13.86	13.99	14.26	14.39	14.64	0.00	0.00	0.00	0.00	0.00
Reposition & Major Maintenance	0.00	3.43	9.95	13.67	5.93	7.84	0.00	0.00	0.00	0.00	0.00	0.00	0.00	0.00	0.00	0.00	0.00	0.00
Total Investment in Water Supply	27.73	76.35	97.54	111.45	98.47	88.18	16.14	16.27	13.86	13.99	14.26	14.39	14.64	0.00	0.00	0.00	0.00	0.00
RMSP: Isolated Systems																		
Production	0.00	0.39	0.82	0.39	0.26	0.25	0.00	0.00	0.00	0.00	0.00	0.00	0.00	0.00	0.00	0.00	0.00	0.00
Unaccounted Water Control Program	0.00	0.05	0.05	0.05	0.05	0.04	0.00	0.00	0.00	0.00	0.00	0.00	0.00	0.00	0.00	0.00	0.00	0.00
Transmission Pipes	0.00	0.00	0.00	0.63	0.76	0.73	0.00	0.00	0.00	0.00	0.00	0.00	0.00	0.00	0.00	0.00	0.00	0.00
Reservoirs	0.00	0.34	0.57	0.39	0.38	0.36	0.00	0.00	0.00	0.00	0.00	0.00	0.00	0.00	0.00	0.00	0.00	0.00
Primary Distribution Pipes	0.00	0.01	0.02	0.02	0.02	0.02	0.14	0.16	0.00	0.00	0.00	0.00	0.00	0.00	0.00	0.00	0.00	0.00
Secondary Distribution Pipes	0.00	0.15	0.31	0.38	0.39	0.43	0.32	0.37	0.00	0.00	0.00	0.00	0.00	0.00	0.00	0.00	0.00	0.00
Connections	0.00	0.05	0.12	0.14	0.17	0.19	0.18	0.20	0.00	0.00	0.00	0.00	0.00	0.00	0.00	0.00	0.00	0.00
Total Investment in Incremental Water Supply	0.00	0.99	1.89	2.01	2.03	2.03	0.64	0.73	0.00	0.00	0.00	0.00	0.00	0.00	0.00	0.00	0.00	0.00
Reposition & Major Maintenance	0.00	0.09	0.12	0.16	0.15	0.18	0.00	0.00	0.00	0.00	0.00	0.00	0.00	0.00	0.00	0.00	0.00	0.00
Total Investment in Water Supply	0.00	1.08	2.01	2.16	2.18	2.21	0.64	0.73	0.00	0.00	0.00	0.00	0.00	0.00	0.00	0.00	0.00	0.00

TABLE 12.5 (continued)

Description	1988	1989	1990	1991	1992	1993	1994	1995	1996	1997	1998	1999	2000	2001	2002	2003	2004	2005
Baixada Santista																		
Production	0.00	1.98	2.69	1.82	0.85	1.20	0.00	0.00	0.00	0.00	0.00	0.00	0.00	0.00	0.00	0.00	0.00	0.00
Unaccounted Water Control Program	0.00	4.53	0.85	0.82	0.79	5.02	0.00	0.00	0.00	0.00	0.00	0.00	0.00	0.00	0.00	0.00	0.00	0.00
Transmission Pipes	0.00	6.02	6.02	3.01	3.95	5.39	0.00	0.00	0.00	0.00	0.00	0.00	0.00	0.00	0.00	0.00	0.00	0.00
Reservoirs	0.00	0.05	0.05	0.13	1.07	1.46	0.00	0.00	0.00	0.00	0.00	0.00	0.00	0.00	0.00	0.00	0.00	0.00
Primary Distribution Pipes	0.00	0.28	0.34	0.31	0.57	0.67	0.67	0.67	0.67	0.67	0.67	0.67	0.67	0.67	0.67	0.67	0.67	0.67
Secondary Distribution Pipes	0.00	1.09	1.36	1.26	2.31	2.67	2.67	2.67	2.67	2.67	2.67	2.67	2.67	2.67	2.67	2.67	2.67	2.67
Connections	0.00	1.02	2.10	1.55	1.56	1.60	1.63	1.67	1.71	1.76	1.80	1.84	1.89	1.86	1.89	1.95	2.00	2.04
Total Investment in Incremental Water Supply	0.00	14.98	13.41	8.89	11.11	18.02	4.97	5.01	5.05	5.10	5.14	5.18	5.23	5.20	5.23	5.29	5.34	5.38
Reposition & Major Maintenance	0.00	0.00	0.00	0.00	0.00	0.00	0.00	0.00	0.00	0.00	0.00	0.00	0.00	0.00	0.00	0.00	0.00	0.00
Total Investment in Water Supply	0.00	14.98	13.41	8.89	11.11	18.02	4.97	5.01	5.05	5.10	5.14	5.18	5.23	5.20	5.23	5.29	5.34	5.38
Interior: Large and Medium Cities (CMG)																		
Production	0.00	6.30	6.88	7.36	6.01	7.48	0.00	0.00	0.00	0.00	0.00	0.00	0.00	0.00	0.00	0.00	0.00	0.00
Unaccounted Water Control Program	0.00	6.64	5.64	5.42	5.21	7.35	0.00	0.00	0.00	0.00	0.00	0.00	0.00	0.00	0.00	0.00	0.00	0.00
Transmission Pipes	0.00	2.44	2.86	3.72	3.08	6.47	0.00	0.00	0.00	0.00	0.00	0.00	0.00	0.00	0.00	0.00	0.00	0.00
Reservoirs	0.00	3.07	6.33	5.36	3.75	1.66	0.00	0.00	0.00	0.00	0.00	0.00	0.00	0.00	0.00	0.00	0.00	0.00
Primary Distribution Pipes	0.00	2.00	1.24	1.35	1.54	1.31	1.50	1.56	1.62	1.69	1.75	1.82	1.89	0.00	0.00	0.00	0.00	0.00
Secondary Distribution Pipes	0.00	11.34	7.04	7.68	8.72	7.39	8.47	8.83	9.17	9.55	9.93	10.32	10.72	0.00	0.00	0.00	0.00	0.00
Connections	0.00	6.14	5.91	5.54	5.60	5.48	5.78	6.03	6.26	6.52	6.78	7.04	7.32	0.00	0.00	0.00	0.00	0.00
Total Investment in Incremental Water Supply	0.00	37.93	35.91	36.46	33.91	37.13	15.75	16.42	17.04	17.75	18.47	19.18	19.93	0.00	0.00	0.00	0.00	0.00
Reposition & Major Maintenance	0.00	0.00	0.00	0.00	0.00	0.00	0.00	0.00	0.00	0.00	0.00	0.00	0.00	0.00	0.00	0.00	0.00	0.00
Total Investment in Water Supply	0.00	37.93	35.91	36.46	33.91	37.13	15.75	16.42	17.04	17.75	18.47	19.18	19.93	0.00	0.00	0.00	0.00	0.00

TABLE 12.5 (continued)

Description	1988	1989	1990	1991	1992	1993	1994	1995	1996	1997	1998	1999	2000	2001	2002	2003	2004	2005
Interior: Small Communities (CPP)																		
Production	0.00	1.90	1.59	2.16	1.90	1.80	0.00	0.00	0.00	0.00	0.00	0.00	0.00	0.00	0.00	0.00	0.00	0.00
Unaccounted Water Control Program	0.00	1.17	4.00	3.85	3.70	1.29	0.00	0.00	0.00	0.00	0.00	0.00	0.00	0.00	0.00	0.00	0.00	0.00
Transmission Pipes	0.00	0.45	0.58	0.65	0.46	0.28	0.00	0.00	0.00	0.00	0.00	0.00	0.00	0.00	0.00	0.00	0.00	0.00
Reservoirs	0.00	0.51	0.35	0.40	0.37	0.38	0.00	0.00	0.00	0.00	0.00	0.00	0.00	0.00	0.00	0.00	0.00	0.00
Primary Distribution Pipes	0.00	0.02	0.02	0.02	0.05	0.04	0.03	0.03	0.03	0.03	0.03	0.00	0.00	0.00	0.00	0.00	0.00	0.00
Secondary Distribution Pipes	0.00	1.32	1.97	2.50	4.45	3.46	2.80	2.86	2.97	3.14	3.21	0.00	0.00	0.00	0.00	0.00	0.00	0.00
Connections	0.00	0.82	0.76	0.57	0.68	0.78	0.72	0.74	0.76	0.81	0.83	0.00	0.00	0.00	0.00	0.00	0.00	0.00
Total Investment in Incremental Water Supply	0.00	6.18	9.28	10.15	11.61	8.04	3.55	3.63	3.76	3.98	4.07	0.00	0.00	0.00	0.00	0.00	0.00	0.00
Reposition & Major Maintenance	0.00	0.19	0.23	0.17	0.16	0.33	0.00	0.00	0.00	0.00	0.00	0.00	0.00	0.00	0.00	0.00	0.00	0.00
Total Investment in Water Supply	0.00	6.37	9.50	10.32	11.77	8.36	3.55	3.63	3.76	3.98	4.07	0.00	0.00	0.00	0.00	0.00	0.00	0.00
SABESP																		
Production	27.73	37.42	40.59	43.45	40.21	43.74	0.00	0.00	0.00	0.00	0.00	0.00	0.00	0.00	0.00	0.00	0.00	0.00
Unaccounted Water Control Program	0.00	26.13	25.89	26.20	20.27	23.46	0.00	0.00	0.00	0.00	0.00	0.00	0.00	0.00	0.00	0.00	0.00	0.00
Transmission Pipes	0.00	23.99	27.54	31.05	33.99	25.16	0.00	0.00	0.00	0.00	0.00	0.00	0.00	0.00	0.00	0.00	0.00	0.00
Reservoirs	0.00	8.07	12.66	11.20	7.76	4.95	0.00	0.00	0.00	0.00	0.00	0.00	0.00	0.00	0.00	0.00	0.00	0.00
Primary Distribution Pipes	0.00	4.27	5.73	6.71	7.43	7.71	5.81	5.93	5.31	5.41	5.53	5.60	5.72	0.67	0.67	0.67	0.67	0.67
Secondary Distribution Pipes	0.00	18.48	20.27	23.47	28.11	27.20	22.40	22.93	21.79	22.41	23.00	20.23	20.77	2.67	2.67	2.67	2.67	2.67
Connections	0.00	14.64	15.40	13.21	13.42	13.33	12.84	13.20	12.62	13.00	13.41	12.92	13.31	1.86	1.89	1.95	2.00	2.04
Total Investment in Incremental Water Supply	27.73	133.00	148.07	155.28	151.20	145.55	41.05	42.06	39.71	40.82	41.93	38.75	39.81	5.20	5.23	5.29	5.30	5.38
Reposition & Major Maintenance	0.00	3.71	10.30	14.00	6.24	8.35	0.00	0.00	0.00	0.00	0.00	0.00	0.00	0.00	0.00	0.00	0.00	0.00
Total Investment in Water Supply	27.73	136.70	158.37	169.28	157.44	153.90	41.05	42.06	39.71	40.82	41.93	38.75	39.81	5.20	5.23	5.29	5.30	5.38

TABLE 12.6   SABESP's Sewerage Investment Program (US$ millions as of December 1988)

Description	1988	1989	1990	1991	1992	1993
RMSP: Integrated System						
Connections	2.38	7.55	6.83	5.34	2.06	1.99
Collectors	24.90	78.79	67.59	45.58	25.56	23.67
Main Collectors	9.01	28.50	47.95	30.01	8.12	7.49
Interceptors	15.51	2.09	0.00	1.68	24.61	20.46
Final Disposal & Treatment	15.90	4.95	2.71	11.77	23.28	33.80
Sewerage Related Investment	**67.70**	**121.87**	**125.08**	**94.38**	**83.63**	**87.41**
RMSP: Isolated Systems						
Connections	0.00	0.54	0.91	0.88	0.27	0.54
Collectors	0.00	5.73	9.83	7.15	3.43	6.43
Main Collectors	0.00	0.00	0.00	6.12	0.95	2.20
Interceptors	0.00	0.00	0.00	0.00	0.00	0.00
Final Disposal & Treatment	0.00	1.67	1.19	1.53	1.47	1.41
Sewerage Related Investment	**0.00**	**7.94**	**11.93**	**15.67**	**6.13**	**10.59**
Baixada Santista						
Connections	0.00	3.89	3.16	1.17	1.16	0.44
Collectors	0.00	2.98	4.92	4.73	3.88	1.04
Main Collectors	0.00	1.28	2.11	2.03	1.66	0.45
Interceptors	0.00	0.61	1.00	0.36	0.31	0.38
Final Disposal & Treatment	0.00	1.35	5.56	10.41	10.64	1.90
Sewerage Related Investment	**0.00**	**10.11**	**16.76**	**18.69**	**17.65**	**4.22**
Interior: Large & Medium Cities (CMG)						
Connections	0.00	2.90	3.75	2.68	2.89	2.91
Collectors	0.00	5.61	4.39	3.33	3.75	3.84
Main Collectors	0.00	2.18	1.71	1.30	1.46	1.49
Interceptors	0.00	2.50	4.48	3.18	1.97	2.40
Final Disposal & Treatment	0.00	1.91	5.61	4.77	5.29	6.22
Sewerage Related Investment	**0.00**	**15.10**	**19.93**	**15.25**	**15.36**	**16.88**
Interior: Small Communities (CPP)						
Connections	0.00	0.21	0.39	0.20	0.24	0.13
Collectors	0.00	1.24	1.48	1.36	0.79	0.60
Main Collectors	0.00	0.31	0.37	0.34	0.20	0.15
Interceptors	0.00	0.00	0.12	0.23	0.33	0.18
Final Disposal & Treatment	0.00	0.00	0.41	0.93	1.38	1.76
Sewerage Related Investment	**0.00**	**1.76**	**2.77**	**3.06**	**2.94**	**2.82**
SABESP						
Connections	2.38	15.08	15.04	10.26	6.61	6.02
Collectors	24.90	94.35	88.22	62.15	37.41	35.59
Main Collectors	9.01	32.27	52.13	39.78	12.40	11.79
Interceptors	15.51	5.20	5.62	5.45	27.21	23.43
Final Disposal & Treatment	15.90	9.88	15.47	29.42	42.06	45.10
Sewerage Related Investment	**67.70**	**156.78**	**176.48**	**147.06**	**125.70**	**121.92**

TABLE 12.7 SABESP's Fixed Administrative, Operation and Maintenance (ADM) Incremental Costs (US$ millions as of December 1988)

Description	1989	1990	1991	1992	1993	1994	1995	1996	1997	1998	1999	2000	2001	2002	2003	2004	2005-18
RMSP: Integrated System																	
Water Production	0.67	1.18	1.85	2.35	2.86	3.45	4.04	4.64	5.24	4.85	6.47	7.09	7.09	7.09	7.09	7.09	7.09
Water Transmission	0.35	0.61	0.96	1.22	1.48	1.79	2.09	2.41	2.72	3.04	3.36	3.68	3.68	3.68	3.68	3.68	3.68
Water Primary Distribution	0.15	0.26	0.41	0.52	0.04	0.77	0.90	1.04	1.17	1.31	1.44	1.58	1.58	1.58	1.58	1.58	1.58
Water Secondary Distribution	0.50	0.87	1.37	1.74	2.11	2.55	2.99	3.43	3.88	4.33	4.79	5.25	5.25	5.25	5.25	5.25	5.25
Water Connections	0.40	0.70	1.09	1.39	1.69	2.04	2.39	2.75	3.11	3.47	3.83	4.20	4.20	4.20	4.20	4.20	4.20
Total Water Fixed AOM Costs	2.07	3.61	5.68	7.23	8.78	10.59	12.42	14.26	16.12	18.00	19.89	21.80	21.80	21.80	21.80	21.80	21.80
Sewage Connections	0.06	0.10	0.16	0.21	0.25	0.31	0.36	0.41	0.47	0.52	0.58	0.63	0.63	0.63	0.63	0.63	0.63
Sewage Collection	0.16	0.29	0.45	0.57	0.69	0.84	0.98	1.13	1.28	1.43	1.58	1.73	1.73	1.73	1.73	1.73	1.73
Sewage Main Collection	0.08	0.13	0.21	0.26	0.32	0.39	0.45	0.52	0.58	0.65	0.72	0.79	0.79	0.79	0.79	0.79	0.79
Sewage Interception	0.04	0.06	0.12	0.15	0.18	0.22	0.26	0.30	0.34	0.38	0.42	0.46	0.46	0.46	0.46	0.46	0.46
Sewage Treatment	0.08	0.14	0.22	0.28	0.35	0.42	0.49	0.56	0.63	0.71	0.78	0.86	0.86	0.86	0.86	0.86	0.86
Total Sewerage Fixed AOM Costs	0.42	0.74	1.16	1.48	1.80	2.17	2.54	2.92	3.30	3.69	4.07	4.47	4.47	4.47	4.47	4.47	4.47
Total Water and Sewerage	2.49	4.36	6.84	8.71	10.58	12.76	14.96	17.18	19.42	21.69	23.97	26.27	26.27	26.27	26.27	26.27	26.27
RMSP: Isolated System																	
Water Production	0.00	0.00	0.01	0.01	0.01	0.00	0.01	0.01	0.01	0.01	0.01	0.01	0.01	0.01	0.01	0.01	0.01
Water Transmission	0.00	0.00	0.00	0.00	0.00	0.00	0.01	0.01	0.01	0.01	0.01	0.01	0.01	0.01	0.01	0.01	0.01
Water Primary Distribution	0.00	0.00	0.00	0.00	0.00	0.00	0.00	0.00	0.00	0.00	0.00	0.00	0.00	0.00	0.00	0.00	0.00
Water Secondary Distribution	0.00	0.00	0.00	0.00	0.01	0.01	0.01	0.01	0.01	0.01	0.01	0.01	0.01	0.01	0.01	0.01	0.01
Water Connections	0.01	0.01	0.02	0.02	0.01	0.01	0.01	0.01	0.01	0.01	0.01	0.01	0.01	0.01	0.01	0.01	0.01
Total Water Fixed AOM Costs	0.01	0.01	0.02	0.02	0.02	0.03	0.03	0.04	0.04	0.04	0.04	0.04	0.04	0.04	0.04	0.04	0.04
Sewage Connections	0.00	0.00	0.00	0.00	0.00	0.00	0.00	0.00	0.00	0.00	0.00	0.00	0.00	0.00	0.00	0.00	0.00
Sewage Collection	0.00	0.00	0.00	0.00	0.00	0.00	0.00	0.00	0.00	0.00	0.00	0.00	0.00	0.00	0.00	0.00	0.00
Sewage Main Collection	0.00	0.00	0.00	0.00	0.00	0.00	0.00	0.00	0.00	0.00	0.00	0.00	0.00	0.00	0.00	0.00	0.00
Sewage Interception	0.00	0.00	0.00	0.00	0.00	0.00	0.00	0.00	0.00	0.00	0.00	0.00	0.00	0.00	0.00	0.00	0.00
Sewage Treatment	0.00	0.00	0.00	0.00	0.00	0.00	0.00	0.00	0.00	0.00	0.00	0.00	0.00	0.00	0.00	0.00	0.00
Total Sewerage Fixed AOM Costs	0.00	0.00	0.00	0.00	0.01	0.01	0.01	0.01	0.01	0.01	0.01	0.01	0.01	0.01	0.01	0.01	0.01
Total Water and Sewerage	0.01	0.01	0.02	0.02	0.03	0.04	0.04	0.05	0.05	0.05	0.05	0.05	0.05	0.05	0.05	0.05	0.05

TABLE 12.7 (continued)

Description	1989	1990	1991	1992	1993	1994	1995	1996	1997	1998	1999	2000	2001	2002	2003	2004	2005-18
Bairrada Services																	
Water Production	0.04	0.07	0.11	0.14	0.18	0.21	0.25	0.29	0.32	0.36	0.40	0.44	0.47	0.51	0.55	0.59	0.63
Water Transmission	0.02	0.04	0.06	0.08	0.09	0.11	0.13	0.15	0.17	0.19	0.21	0.23	0.25	0.27	0.29	0.31	0.33
Water Primary Distribution	0.01	0.02	0.03	0.03	0.04	0.05	0.06	0.07	0.08	0.09	0.09	0.10	0.11	0.12	0.13	0.14	0.15
Water Secondary Distribution	0.03	0.05	0.08	0.11	0.13	0.16	0.18	0.21	0.24	0.26	0.29	0.32	0.35	0.38	0.41	0.44	0.47
Water Connections	0.02	0.04	0.07	0.09	0.10	0.13	0.15	0.17	0.19	0.22	0.24	0.26	0.29	0.31	0.33	0.36	0.38
Total Water Fixed AOM Costs	0.13	0.22	0.35	0.45	0.54	0.65	0.77	0.88	1.00	1.11	1.23	1.35	1.47	1.59	1.71	1.83	1.95
Sewage Connections	0.00	0.01	0.01	0.01	0.01	0.02	0.02	0.03	0.03	0.03	0.04	0.04	0.04	0.05	0.05	0.05	0.06
Sewage Collection	0.01	0.02	0.03	0.03	0.04	0.05	0.06	0.07	0.08	0.09	0.10	0.11	0.12	0.13	0.14	0.15	0.16
Sewage Main Collection	0.00	0.01	0.01	0.02	0.02	0.02	0.03	0.03	0.04	0.04	0.05	0.05	0.05	0.06	0.06	0.07	0.07
Sewage Interception	0.00	0.00	0.01	0.01	0.01	0.01	0.02	0.02	0.02	0.02	0.03	0.03	0.03	0.03	0.04	0.04	0.04
Sewage Treatment	0.03	0.04	0.07	0.09	0.11	0.13	0.15	0.25	0.25	0.25	0.26	0.26	0.26	0.26	0.26	0.27	0.27
Total Sewerage Fixed AOM Costs	0.03	0.04	0.07	0.09	0.11	0.13	0.15	0.40	0.42	0.44	0.46	0.48	0.51	0.53	0.55	0.57	0.59
Total Water and Sewerage	0.15	0.27	0.42	0.54	0.65	0.78	0.92	1.28	1.42	1.55	1.69	1.83	1.97	2.11	2.26	2.40	2.55
Interior: Large and Medium Cities (CMG)																	
Water Production	0.13	0.23	0.36	0.46	0.56	0.68	0.80	0.91	1.03	1.15	1.27	1.39	1.39	1.39	1.39	1.39	1.39
Water Transmission	0.07	0.12	0.19	0.24	0.29	0.35	0.41	0.48	0.54	0.60	0.67	0.73	0.73	0.73	0.73	0.73	0.73
Water Primary Distribution	0.03	0.05	0.08	0.10	0.13	0.15	0.18	0.21	0.23	0.26	0.29	0.32	0.32	0.32	0.32	0.32	0.32
Water Secondary Distribution	0.10	0.17	0.27	0.34	0.42	0.50	0.59	0.58	0.77	0.85	0.95	1.04	1.04	1.04	1.04	1.04	1.04
Water Connections	0.06	0.14	0.22	0.28	0.33	0.40	0.47	0.54	0.61	0.69	0.76	0.83	0.83	0.83	0.83	0.83	0.83
Total Water Fixed AOM Costs	0.41	0.71	1.12	1.43	1.73	2.09	2.45	2.82	3.18	3.56	3.93	4.31	4.31	4.31	4.31	4.31	4.31
Sewage Connections	0.01	0.02	0.03	0.04	0.05	0.06	0.07	0.08	0.09	0.10	0.11	0.12	0.12	0.12	0.12	0.12	0.12
Sewage Collection	0.03	0.06	0.09	0.11	0.14	0.17	0.19	0.22	0.25	0.28	0.31	0.34	0.34	0.34	0.34	0.34	0.34
Sewage Main Collection	0.01	0.03	0.04	0.05	0.06	0.06	0.09	0.10	0.11	0.13	0.14	0.15	0.15	0.15	0.15	0.15	0.15
Sewage Interception	0.01	0.02	0.02	0.03	0.04	0.04	0.05	0.06	0.07	0.08	0.09	0.10	0.10	0.10	0.10	0.10	0.10
Sewage Treatment	0.02	0.03	0.04	0.06	0.07	0.08	0.10	0.11	0.12	0.14	0.15	0.17	0.17	0.17	0.17	0.17	0.17
Total Sewerage Fixed AOM Costs	0.08	0.15	0.23	0.29	0.35	0.43	0.50	0.57	0.64	0.72	0.80	0.87	0.88	0.88	0.88	0.88	0.88
Total Water and Sewerage	0.49	0.86	1.35	1.72	2.09	2.52	2.95	3.39	3.83	4.27	4.37	5.18	5.19	5.19	5.19	5.19	5.19

TABLE 12.7 (continued)

Description	1989	1990	1991	1992	1993	1994	1995	1996	1997	1998	1999	2000	2001	2002	2003	2004	2005-18
Interior: Small Communities (CPP)																	
Water Production	0.02	0.03	0.04	0.06	0.07	2.08	0.10	0.11	0.13	0.14	0.14	0.14	0.14	0.14	0.14	0.14	0.14
Water Transmission	0.01	0.01	0.02	0.03	0.04	0.04	0.05	0.06	0.07	0.08	0.08	0.08	0.08	0.08	0.08	0.08	0.08
Water Primary Distribution	0.00	0.01	0.01	0.01	0.01	0.02	0.02	0.03	0.03	0.03	0.03	0.03	0.03	0.03	0.03	0.03	0.03
Water Secondary Distribution	0.01	0.02	0.03	0.04	0.05	0.06	0.07	0.08	0.09	0.10	0.10	0.10	0.10	0.10	0.10	0.10	0.10
Water Connections	0.01	0.02	0.03	0.03	0.04	0.05	0.06	0.07	0.08	0.09	0.09	0.09	0.09	0.09	0.09	0.09	0.09
Total Water Fixed AOM Costs	0.05	0.09	0.14	0.17	0.21	0.26	0.30	0.35	0.39	0.44	0.44	0.44	0.44	0.44	0.44	0.44	0.44
Sewage Connections	0.00	0.00	0.00	0.01	0.01	0.01	0.01	0.01	0.01	0.01	0.01	0.01	0.01	0.01	0.01	0.01	0.01
Sewage Collection	0.00	0.01	0.01	0.01	0.02	0.02	0.02	0.03	0.03	0.04	0.04	0.04	0.04	0.04	0.04	0.04	0.04
Sewage Main Collection	0.00	0.00	0.01	0.01	0.01	0.01	0.01	0.01	0.02	0.02	0.02	0.02	0.02	0.02	0.02	0.02	0.02
Sewage Interception	0.00	0.00	0.00	0.00	0.00	0.00	0.01	0.01	0.01	0.01	0.01	0.01	0.01	0.01	0.01	0.01	0.01
Sewage Treatment	0.00	0.00	0.01	0.01	0.01	0.01	0.01	0.01	0.02	0.02	0.02	0.02	0.02	0.02	0.02	0.02	0.02
Total Sewerage Fixed AOM Costs	0.01	0.02	0.03	0.04	0.04	0.05	0.06	0.08	0.09	0.09	0.10	0.10	0.10	0.10	0.10	0.10	0.10
Total Water and Sewerage	0.06	0.11	0.17	0.21	0.26	0.31	0.36	0.43	0.48	0.53	0.54	0.54	0.54	0.54	0.54	0.54	0.54
SABESP	3.20	5.60	8.80	11.20	13.60	16.40	19.24	22.33	25.20	28.10	30.97	33.87	34.02	34.16	34.31	34.45	34.60

SABESP's total AOM fixed costs were distributed between regions based on their 1988 estimated water production. AOM fixed costs were distributed between activities based on SABESP's estimated breakdown for the RMSP.

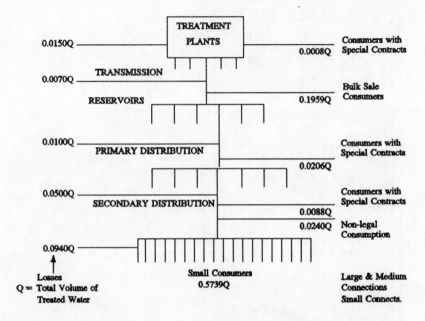

Figure 12.2 Simplified Diagram of the RMSP Water Supply Integrated System for the Year 1994

estimation of its fixed administrative, operating and maintenance (AOM) incremental costs.

AIC has been calculated at an annual opportunity cost of capital (OCC) of 10% for each level in the chain from production to final delivery (water) or disposal (sewerage). Figure 12.2 is a more specific version of the basic framework described in Chapter 4 (Figure 4.1). It shows a simplified diagram of the RMSP water supply integrated system for year 1994. SABESP's AIC of water supply and sewerage are shown in Table 12.8 and 12.9, calculated using the methodology of Chapter 7.

LRMC for treated water delivered at treatment plants, transmission pipes, primary and secondary distribution pipes, and meters have been estimated by adding and adjusting the corresponding AIC for losses. LRMC for sewerage collected and transported to the reception point has been estimated by adding the AICs at each level of collection and treatment, and then adjusting for reverse leakage (i.e., seepage of outside effluents into the sewerage system). SABESP's complete LRMC structure for these services is shown in Tables 12.10 and 12.11.

TABLE 12.8 SABESP's Average Incremental Costs (AIC) for Water Supply Service (US$ as of December 1988)

Treated Water Level	Investment US$ (10⁶)	Fixed AOM US$ (10⁶)	Inv. + Fixed AOM US$ (10⁶)	Water Product m³ (10⁶)	AIC (Before Losses) US$ / m³	Average Loss %	Loss Adjustment Factor
RMSP: Integrated System							
Treatment Plants	191.88	40.06	231.94	2065.74	0.1123	1.50	1.0152
Transmission Pipes	71.18	20.80	91.98	2064.06	0.0446	0.70	1.0070
Primary Distribution Pipes	39.78	8.93	48.71	1638.54	0.0297	1.00	1.0101
Secondary Distribution Pipes	60.13	29.67	89.80	1574.37	0.0570	5.00	1.0526
Connections	35.04	23.73	58.77	1253.92	0.0469	9.40	1.1038
RMSP: Isolated Systems							
Treatment Plants	1.84	0.08	1.92	18.29	0.1050	2.18	1.0222
Transmission Pipes	1.44	0.06	1.50	18.10	0.0829	1.02	1.0103
Primary Distribution Pipes	1.80	0.01	1.81	17.82	0.1016	1.45	1.0147
Secondary Distribution Pipes	1.58	0.07	1.65	16.40	0.1006	7.25	1.0782
Connections	0.70	0.07	0.77	13.54	0.0569	13.63	1.1578
Baixada Santista							
Treatment Plants	15.82	2.87	18.69	226.53	0.0825	2.40	1.0246
Transmission Pipes	18.75	1.50	20.25	223.67	0.0905	1.12	1.0113
Primary Distribution Pipes	6.22	0.67	6.89	219.82	0.0313	1.60	1.0163
Secondary Distribution Pipes	17.61	2.12	19.73	200.28	0.0985	8.00	1.0870
Connections	13.50	1.72	15.22	160.59	0.0948	15.04	1.1770
Interior: Large & Medium Cities (CMG)							
Treatment Plants	48.59	7.87	56.46	730.01	0.0773	1.88	1.0191
Transmission Pipes	13.49	4.12	17.61	723.32	0.0243	0.88	1.0088
Primary Distribution Pipes	26.41	1.79	28.20	713.79	0.0395	1.25	1.0127
Secondary Distribution Pipes	60.95	5.87	66.82	665.36	0.1004	6.25	1.0667
Connections	41.31	4.69	46.00	568.71	0.0809	11.75	1.1331
Interior: Small Communities (CPP)							
Treatment Plants	17.67	0.87	18.54	89.62	0.2069	1.95	1.0199
Transmission Pipes	1.86	0.48	2.34	88.77	0.0264	0.91	1.0092
Primary Distribution Pipes	1.71	0.19	1.90	87.54	0.0217	1.30	1.0132
Secondary Distribution Pipes	16.90	0.63	17.53	81.36	0.2155	6.50	1.0695
Connections	4.55	0.54	5.09	68.96	0.0738	12.22	1.1392

TABLE 12.9 SABESP's Average Incremental Costs (AIC) for Sewerage Service (US$ as of December 1988)

Sewage Level	Investment US$ (10⁶)	Fixed AOM US$ (10⁶)	NPV at r = 10% Inv. + Fixed AOM US$ (10⁶)	Sewage m³ (10⁶)	Effluent m³ (10⁶)	AIC (Before Adjustment for Water Metering) US$ / m³	Effluent Adjustment Factor
RMSP: Integrated System							
Connections	21.54	3.56	25.10	1,198.82		0.0209	
Collectors	218.79	9.77	228.56	1,198.82		0.1907	
Main Collectors	107.29	4.47	111.76	1,198.82		0.0932	
Interceptors	48.18	2.59	50.77		1,224.38	0.0415	2.2222
After Treatment	63.37	4.85	68.22		1,224.38	0.0557	2.2222
RMSP: Isolated Systems							
Connections	2.42	0.01	2.43	33.40		0.0728	
Collectors	25.04	0.01	25.05	33.40		0.7500	
Main Collectors	6.61	0.01	6.62	33.40		0.1982	
Interceptors	0.00	0.00	0.00		131.25	0.0000	2.2222
After Treatment	5.54	0.01	5.55		131.25	0.0423	2.2222
Baixada Santista							
Connections	8.09	0.26	8.35	132.07		0.0632	
Collectors	13.63	0.72	14.35	132.07		0.1087	
Main Collectors	5.84	0.32	6.16	132.07		0.0466	
Interceptors	2.12	0.18	2.30		512.22	0.0045	2.2222
After Treatment	22.09	1.27	23.36		512.22	0.0456	2.2222
Interior: Large & Medium Cities (CMG)							
Connections	11.53	0.69	12.22	112.04		0.1091	
Collectors	16.18	1.92	18.10	112.04		0.1615	
Main Collectors	6.29	0.86	7.15	112.04		0.0638	
Interceptors	11.21	0.55	11.76		361.04	0.0326	2.2222
After Treatment	17.42	0.95	18.37		361.04	0.0509	2.2222
Interior: Small Communities (CPP)							
Connections	0.90	0.07	0.97	10.17		0.0954	
Collectors	4.29	0.23	4.52	10.17		0.4444	
Main Collectors	1.07	0.12	1.19	10.17		0.1170	
Interceptors	0.61	0.06	0.67		79.17	0.0085	2.2222
After Treatment	3.07	0.12	3.19		79.17	0.0403	2.2222

TABLE 12.10 SABESP's Marginal Cost Structure for Water Supply (US$ as of December 1988)

Treated Water Level	Capacity Cost US$ / m³	Operating Cost US$ / m³	Consumption Cost US$ / m³	Non-Recurrent Customer Cost US$ / Connection	US$ / Consumer
RMSP: Integrated System					
Treatment Plants	0.1140	0.0303	0.1442	Variable	Variable
Transmission Pipes	0.1597	0.0305	0.1901	Variable	Variable
Primary Distribution Pipes	0.1913	0.0308	0.2221	Variable	Variable
Secondary Distribution Pipes	0.2614	0.0324	0.2938	Variable	Variable
Connections	0.3094	0.0358	0.3452	113.49	87.30
RMSP: Isolated Systems					
Treatment Plants	0.1073	0.0305	0.1378	Variable	Variable
Transmission Pipes	0.1921	0.0308	0.2229	Variable	Variable
Primary Distribution Pipes	0.2980	0.0312	0.3293	Variable	Variable
Secondary Distribution Pipes	0.4298	0.0337	0.4635	Variable	Variable
Connections	0.5036	0.0390	0.5426	112.77	109.49
Baixada Santista					
Treatment Plants	0.0845	0.0305	0.1151	Variable	Variable
Transmission Pipes	0.1771	0.0309	0.2079	Variable	Variable
Primary Distribution Pipes	0.2118	0.0314	0.2432	Variable	Variable
Secondary Distribution Pipes	0.3373	0.0341	0.3714	Variable	Variable
Connections	0.4096	0.0401	0.4497	229.04	120.55
Interior: Large & Medium Cities (CMG)					
Treatment Plants	0.0788	0.0304	0.1092	Variable	Variable
Transmission Pipes	0.1041	0.0306	0.1347	Variable	Variable
Primary Distribution Pipes	0.1454	0.0310	0.1764	Variable	Variable
Secondary Distribution Pipes	0.2622	0.0331	0.2953	Variable	Variable
Connections	0.3065	0.0375	0.3440	168.55	161.29
Interior: Small Communities (CPP)					
Treatment Plants	0.2110	0.0304	0.2414	Variable	Variable
Transmission Pipes	0.2395	0.0307	0.2702	Variable	Variable
Primary Distribution Pipes	0.2647	0.0311	0.2958	Variable	Variable
Secondary Distribution Pipes	0.5135	0.0332	0.5468	Variable	Variable
Connections	0.5939	0.0379	0.6318	93.49	93.49

Analysis of SABESP's Existing Tariffs

The tariff structure in SABESP's systems is presented in Table 12.12. Overall, the existing average water rates and the combined average rates for water and sewerage are in line with the long-run marginal costs in the RMSP and in the Baixada Santista, as may be seen in Table 12.13. While there are

TABLE 12.11 SABESP's Marginal Cost Structure for Sewerage Service (US$ as of December 1988)

Sewage Level	Sewerage Cost US$ / m³	Non-Recurrent Customer Cost	
		US$ / Connection	US$ / Consumer
RMSP: Integrated System			
Connections	0.0030	80.46	53.64
Collectors	0.1936	NA	NA
Main Collectors	0.2868	NA	NA
Interceptors	0.3790	NA	NA
After Treatment	0.5028	NA	NA
RMSP: Isolated Systems			
Connections	0.0003	169.73	164.79
Collectors	0.7503	NA	NA
Main Collectors	0.9485	NA	NA
Interceptors	0.9485	NA	NA
After Treatment	1.0425	NA	NA
Baixada Santista			
Connections	0.0020	113.53	29.26
Collectors	0.1106	NA	NA
Main Collectors	0.1573	NA	NA
Interceptors	0.1672	NA	NA
After Treatment	0.2686	NA	NA
Interior: Large & Medium Cities (CMG)			
Connections	0.0062	256.44	246.58
Collectors	0.1677	NA	NA
Main Collectors	0.2315	NA	NA
Interceptors	0.3039	NA	NA
After Treatment	0.4170	NA	NA
Interior: Small Communities (CPP)			
Connections	0.0069	173.13	166.47
Collectors	0.4513	NA	NA
Main Collectors	0.5683	NA	NA
Interceptors	0.5871	NA	NA
After Treatment	0.6767	NA	NA

divergences between the LRMC and the level of tariffs in the large and medium cities of the Interior, they are relatively small. The major differences occur in SABESP's small communities where the LRMC exceeds average tariff levels by more than 50%. However, such differences are not an immediate cause for concern, given the preponderance of low-income consumers in those centers and the fact that they account for a relatively small proportion (13%) of SABESP's total market.

TABLE 12.12 SABESP's Tariff Structure as of January 1989

Category	Minimum Monthly Charge (1) US$ / Consumer-Month		Monthly Water Consumption (MWC)						Estimated Average Tariff US$ / m³	
			10 < MWC < 20 US$ / m³		20 < MWC < 50 US$ / m³		50 < MWC US$ / m³			
	Water	Sewerage	Water	Sewerage	Water	Sewerage	Water	Sewerage	Water	Sewerage
RMSP										
Bulk Sale Contracts									0.1451	NA
Special Contracts									0.9238	0.7698
Final Consumers									0.3785	0.3849
- Domestic	1.5325	1.5325	0.3012	0.3012	0.5297	0.5297	0.7698	0.7698		
- Commercial	1.7636	1.7636	0.3463	0.3463	0.6092	0.6092	0.8853	0.8853		
- Industrial	1.9932	1.9932	0.3915	0.3915	0.6887	0.6887	1.0008	1.0008		
Baixada Santista										
Final Consumers									0.3250	0.3130
- Domestic	1.5325	1.5325	0.2952	0.2952	0.5144	0.5144	0.7490	0.7490		
- Commercial	1.7636	1.7636	0.3395	0.3395	0.5917	0.5917	0.8613	0.8613		
- Industrial	1.9932	1.9932	0.3837	0.3837	0.6689	0.6689	0.9737	0.9737		
- Boats	NA	NA	2.7520	NA	2.7520	NA	2.7520	NA		
- Ships	NA	NA	2.9512	NA	2.9512	NA	2.9512	NA		
Interior										
Final Consumers									0.2853	0.2248
- Domestic	1.5325	1.2293	0.2591	0.2073	0.4533	0.3627	0.6581	0.5265		
- Commercial	1.7636	1.4115	0.2981	0.2384	0.5214	0.4171	0.7568	0.6055		
- Industrial	1.9932	1.5945	0.3370	0.2696	0.5893	0.4714	0.8565	0.6843		
- Boats	NA	NA	2.7520	NA	2.7520	NA	2.7520	NA		
- Ships	NA	NA	2.9512	NA	2.9512	NA	2.9512	NA		

TABLE 12.13   SABESP's Costs, Tariffs and Subsidies as of January 1989

Category	Marginal Cost			Average Tariff		Financial Subsidy (Overcharge) (1)		Economic Subsidy (Overcharge) (2)		
	Water US$ / m³	W & SC (3) US$ / m³	W&SC&ET (4) US$ / m³	Water US$ / m³	W&SC&ET US$ / m³	Water %	W&SC&ET %	Water %	W & SC %	W&SC&ET %
RMSP: Integrated System										
Bulk Sale Consumers	0.1901	NA	NA	0.1451	NA	56.7	NA	23.7	NA	NA
Consumers with Special Contracts:										
- Served From a Treatment Plant	0.1442	0.4310	0.5498	0.9238	1.6937	(175.7)	(144.5)	(540.6)	(293.0)	(208.0)
- Served From a Primary Distribution Pipe	0.2221	0.5089	0.6277	0.9238	1.6937	(175.7)	(144.5)	(315.9)	(232.8)	(169.8)
- Served From a Secondary Distribution Pipe	0.2938	0.5806	0.6994	0.9238	1.6937	(175.7)	(144.5)	(214.4)	(191.7)	(142.2)
- Served From a Small Connection	0.3452	0.6320	0.7508	0.9238	1.6937	(175.7)	(144.5)	(167.6)	(168.0)	(125.6)
Final Consumers (Small Connections):										
- Domestic	0.3452	0.6320	0.7508	0.3785	0.7634	(13.0)	(10.2)	(9.7)	(20.8)	(1.7)
- Commercial	0.3452	0.6320	0.7508	0.3785	0.7634	(13.0)	(10.2)	(9.7)	(20.8)	(1.7)
- Industrial	0.3452	0.6320	0.7508	0.3785	0.7634	(13.0)	(10.2)	(9.7)	(20.8)	(1.7)
RMSP: Isolated Systems										
Final Consumers (Small Connections):										
- Domestic	0.5426	1.4911	1.5428	0.3785	0.7634	(13.0)	(10.2)	30.2	48.8	50.5
- Commercial	0.5426	1.4911	1.5428	0.3785	0.7634	(13.0)	(10.2)	30.2	48.8	50.5
- Industrial	0.5426	1.4911	1.5428	0.3785	0.7634	(13.0)	(10.2)	30.2	48.8	50.5
Baixada Santista										
Final Consumers (Small Connections):										
- Domestic	0.4497	0.6070	0.6682	0.3250	0.6380	3.0	7.9	27.7	(5.1)	4.5
- Commercial	0.4497	0.6070	0.6682	0.3250	0.6380	3.0	7.9	27.7	(5.1)	4.5
- Industrial	0.4497	0.6070	0.6682	0.3250	0.6380	3.0	7.9	27.7	(5.1)	4.5
- Boats	NA	NA	NA	NA	NA					
- Ships	NA	NA	NA	NA	NA					

TABLE 12.13 (continued)

Category	Marginal Cost			Average Tariff		Financial Subsidy (Overcharge) (1)		Economic Subsidy (Overcharge) (2)		
	Water US$ / m³	W & SC (3) US$ / m³	W&SC&ET (4) US$ / m³	Water US$ / m³	W&SC&ET US$ / m³	Water %	W&SC&ET %	Water %	W & SC %	W&SC&ET %
Interior: Large & Medium Cities (CMG)										
Final Consumers (Small Connections):										
- Domestic	0.3440	0.5755	0.6775	0.2853	0.5101	14.8	26.3	17.1	11.4	24.7
- Commercial	0.3440	0.5755	0.6775	0.2853	0.5101	14.8	26.3	17.1	11.4	24.7
- Industrial	0.3440	0.5755	0.6775	0.2853	0.5101	14.8	26.3	17.1	11.4	24.7
- Boats	NA	NA	NA	NA	NA					
- Ships	NA	NA	NA	NA	NA					
Interior: Small Communities (CPP)										
Final Consumers (Small Connections):										
- Domestic	0.6318	1.2001	1.2597	0.2853	0.5101	14.8	26.3	54.8	57.5	59.5
- Commercial	0.6318	1.2001	1.2597	0.2853	0.5101	14.8	26.3	54.8	57.5	59.5
- Industrial	0.6318	1.2001	1.2597	0.2853	0.5101	14.8	26.3	54.8	57.5	59.5
- Boats	NA	NA	NA	NA	NA					
- Ships	NA	NA	NA	NA	NA					

(1) Financial subsidies (FS) are defined as follows: $FS_i = (1-AT_i/AT)*100$, where: FS_i = Financial Subsidy (Overcharge) given to consumer classified in category i; AT_i = Average Tariff for consumers classified in category i; and AT = SABESP's Average Tariff (US$ 0.3351/m³ for water and US$ 0.6926/m³ for W&CS&ET).

(2) Economic subsidies (ES) are defined as follows: $ES_i = (1-AT_i/MC_i)*100$, where: ES_i = Economic Subsidy (Overcharge) given to consumers classified in category i; AT_i = Average Tariff for consumers classified in category i; and MC_i = Marginal Cost associated with consumer classified in category i.

(3) W&SC stands for water supplied and sewage collected.

(4) W&SC&ET stands for water supplied and sewage collected and effluent treated.

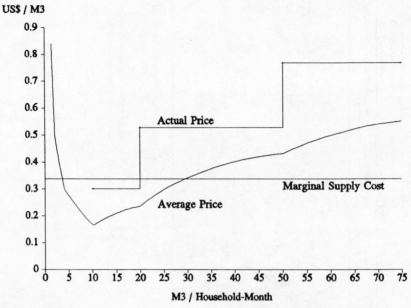

Figure 12.3 Residential Average Price, Marginal Cost and Price Structure in the RMSP

SABESP's consumers face a minimum monthly charge (MMC) for a minimum consumption level followed by a system of increasing block tariffs, in line with the Brazilian practice described in Section 12.1. This tariff schedule translates into a set of average prices that decreases sharply until a minimum point is reached at a monthly consumption of $10m^3$, and then begins to increase. Figure 12.3 illustrates this behavior for the case of residential consumers in the RMSP, and simultaneously shows the relationship of this curve with prices of the different blocks and with the corresponding marginal costs of supply. The consumption level at which average tariffs equal marginal costs varies greatly between consumer categories and regions, being usually about 25 to 35 m^3 for small consumers. However, where subsidies are large, equality is reached only at a very high consumption level, for example, in the small communities of the Interior this parity is achieved at 577 m^3 per residential customer.

With regard to low-income households, the minimum consumption level or MCL (typically $10m^3$ per month) is intended to provide consumers with a quantity of water sufficient to satisfy basic needs and maintain minimum health and sanitary conditions. The NTL provides that the minimum monthly charge (MMC) for this MCL (in the case of residential consumers) should not exceed about US\$ 2.42 for water and about US\$ 3.46 for water and sewerage combined. In fact, most Brazilian SWCs charge well below this legal limit for the MCL (about half on average), so that water and sewerage charges are affordable even to the poorest segments of the population. In the case of SABESP, the MMC for water and sewerage has represented under 5% of *one* minimum salary with only rare exceptions, since 1977 (1 minimum salary = US$ 60.42 in December 1988). In addition, SABESP does not charge a connection fee for service consisting of one tap and minimum flow. Tariff increases since January 1988 have pushed the MMC to near 6% of one minimum salary, or 2% of the three minimum salaries defined as the poverty income level. Domestic consumers in the Interior face a slightly smaller MMC. A rule-of-thumb sometimes used previously had been to keep water and sanitation charges under 5% of three minimum salaries.

Summary of Tariff Deficiencies

In summary, from our knowledge of appropriate pricing strategies and the effects of tariff setting previously explained in Chapter 7, we can see that SABESP's existing tariff structure has four main deficiencies which need to be addressed in the longer term.

First, the relative prices charged to different consumers within the non-residential category are not based on marginal costs. As a group, non-residential consumers pay more than the LRMC. Such a policy has the advantage that it facilitates the cross-subsidization of service to lower-income residential consumers, but the same result could be achieved with a more rational tariff structure.

Second, the distinction between residential and non-residential consumers is entirely arbitrary, bearing no relationship to the marginal cost of supply. This type of price discrimination could result in economic inefficiency as well as inequity.

Third, the system of increasing block tariffs, while typical of many developing countries as one means of encouraging water conservation and implementing cross-subsidies from higher to lower income consumers, may not be achieving the desired result. Recent evidence suggests that a significant proportion of the cross-subsidy is enjoyed by medium- and high-income consumers, while some of the poorest consumers are charged high effective rates, due to their very low consumption (and mandatory fixed charge). This is due to the fact that a large proportion of the consumer population are using less than 10 m^3, whilst in effect paying for the extra water, which is sold to larger consumers at a lower price than might otherwise be appropriate if the tariff regime was more equitable.

Fourth, the rates for combined water and sewerage service in the RMSP appear to be above the corresponding LRMC, which in principle could provide a source of financing for São Paulo's ambitious program to clean up its polluted waterways. The rate could act as a tax for environmental management. However, before firm practical conclusions can be drawn, a more refined calculation of LRMC is required, and consideration needs to be given to the potential and rationale which might exist for alternative sources of financing.

References

Accorsi and Associados LTDA. 1987. *Avaliacao das Normas e Criterios de Fixacao de Tarifas no Setor de Saneamento: Uma Analise dos Objetivos de Equidade, SANEPAR -- CEF (BNH).* Curitiba.

De Azevedo, J.C. Chaves, and V.L. Bazzanella. 1984.2. *Modelo de Estrutura Tarifaria, Convenio de Cooperacao Tecnica BNH/OPAS de 22/12/81.* Rio de Janeiro.

13

Philippines: Management of Groundwater Depletion and Saline Intrusion

Water Resource Management in the Philippines

In this chapter, we examine a policy-oriented case study of groundwater pollution management in Manila.

The Metropolitan Waterworks and Sewerage System and Groundwater Use

The provision of water supply and sanitation services in the Philippines has improved considerably over the past two decades. The current sector institutions were established and overall objectives, strategies and development plans defined in 1972. By the end of 1987, about 63 % of the population had access to safe water, including 31% which was served by piped systems. Although absolute service levels are improving, the quality of service in the areas covered is often poor, with low water pressures throughout and rationed service in some areas (World Bank 1986).

Institutional Arrangements

The National Water Resources Council (NWRC) is responsible for formulating policies for the water supply sector. The Metropolitan Waterworks and Sewerage System (MWSS) was established in 1972 to manage water supply and sewerage systems in or around Metropolitan Manila. The MWSS Service Area (MSA) of about 150,000 ha includes Manila and another 4 neighboring cities and 32 municipalities. The Local Water Utilities Administration (LWUA) provides technical and financial assistance for water supply and sanitation development to about 730 provincial cities with populations above 20,000 and, since 1987, to rural communities. Both MWSS and LWUA are semi-autonomous corporations under the Department of Public

Works and Highways (DPWH). The Health Department has a rural sanitation program and monitors drinking water quality.

Sector Financing

Sector development in Metropolitan Manila is financed through funds self-generated by MWSS, government equity contributions, and foreign or local loans. The Government's general policy is to develop systems on the basis of a community's financial ability and willingness to pay for them. Accordingly, individual house connections are usually provided in the larger metropolitan and provincial urban areas, and some standpipe systems on the basis of the willingness to pay for them. Wells with hand pumps are provided in the rural areas.

Due to the depressed economic conditions and political changes that occurred during 1984-86, investment in the sector declined, and water and sanitation services remained low. However, in 1987, the Government confirmed its commitment to sector development by adopting a Water Supply and Sanitation Master Plan which provides an integrated package of policies, programs and projects to be implemented in two stages: from 1988 to 1993 and from 1994 to the year 2000.

Groundwater Use

Groundwater use in the Manila area has grown so rapidly that for the last thirty years natural recharge was far exceeded, resulting in "mining" of the aquifer. This has had serious environmental consequences. Because of its geographical location, a devastating effect of this depletion is the encroachment of saline sea water into the coastal aquifer. As mentioned earlier, depletion of groundwater and the concurrent deterioration of water quality constitute a significant economic loss to the society as a whole. Added to this are the costs to the government and to individuals of subsidence that might occur at the surface due to consolidation of water bearing geological strata below. This has serious impacts on infrastructure in terms of roads and the structural integrity of buildings and pipelines, and also exacerbates risks of flooding. Each groundwater user will continue to impose external diseconomies or costs on all other existing and future users (Munasinghe 1984). These environmental externalities become more serious as the over-pumping of aquifers is allowed to continue.

On the other hand, curtailing the use of groundwater for existing industrial users would have a negative impact on industrial production and employment. As part of its development planning, the largest users of groundwater in depleted zones have been identified by MWSS, and adequate transmission and distribution facilities are planned to provide them with piped water. If the problems of groundwater depletion persist, especially after adequate piped water is provided by 1994, it would be necessary to enact legislation establishing more rigorous controls on water use, and allowing MWSS to charge for the use of groundwater, to reduce its excessive use and contribute to the financing of expanded water supply facilities in the MSA (World Bank 1989).

Models and Economic Analysis

The purpose of this section is to calculate the long-run economic costs of groundwater use, over and above the cost of extraction. These are additional external costs imposed by any given existing user on all other potential present and future groundwater users. All costs and prices are in constant mid-1984 terms, unless otherwise stated.

Groundwater Depletion Model

The physical model of the aquifer has been described elsewhere (MWSS 1983a) and all withdrawals in the Greater Manila Area (GMA) are assumed to be made from this common aquifer. For convenience, withdrawals from the aquifer are lumped together with no further spatial disaggregation. Following the earlier explanation in Chapter 5 and depiction in Figure 5.1, a more sophisticated approach might involve analysis of a progressively advancing saline intrusion front, and gradual salinization of wells in different zones, but the physical data currently available does not permit such discrimination.

On the basis of the rather limited data and reasonably realistic assumptions, two scenarios, as shown in Figure 13.1, are compared, to estimate externality costs. The first or depletion case (Curve ABEFI) is the base scenario that would prevail if present policies continued (MWSS 1983a,b). The conservation scenario (Curve AJFH) would be the result of a centrally managed groundwater extraction policy. Clearly, other scenarios are possible, but data unavailability does not permit further fine tuning. Nevertheless, the contrast between the above two cases is sharp enough to draw some valuable policy conclusions.

In the depletion case, we start with a withdrawal level of 730 Megaliters per day (MLD) in year 0 (1984), and then the pumping rate is assumed to remain constant until year 6 when the yield declines linearly down to 620 MLD in the year 16. Finally a very rapid decrease sets in with withdrawals dropping to zero by year 26, due to a progressive mining of the potable water. As explained in Appendix A.13.1 and illustrated in Figure 13.2, the average costs of withdrawals will rise linearly from US$ 0.13 per m^3 of water in year 0, to US$ 0.22 per m^3 in year 16, and finally to US$ 0.27 per m^3 in year 26.

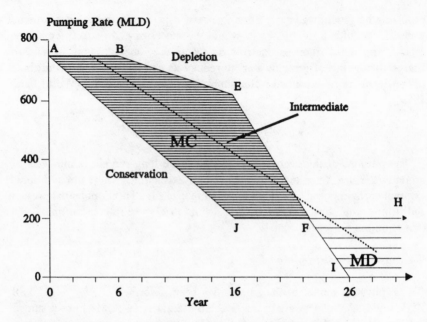

Figure 13.1 Alternative Scenarios for Groundwater Use in Manila

In contrast to the depletion case, we also explore a quasi- ideal conservation scenario in which groundwater use is controlled to eventually reach safe sustainable levels. The latter reflects a physical equilibrium stage where the sum of natural and artificial recharges equals total withdrawals. Although the conservation case is hypothetical it provides a useful practical benchmark for what might have been achieved with forethought and timely action initiated early enough. In this alternative, extraction rates are assumed to decline linearly from an initial 730 MLD in year 0 to 200 MLD in year 16, which is the estimated safe sustainable yield for potable water, based on the physical model of the aquifer. Once the equilibrium stage is reached, withdrawals can continue at this rate indefinitely into the future without mining the aquifer. The costs of pumping are estimated to remain constant at US\$ 0.13 per m^3 throughout (See Appendix A13)

Quantification of Economic Externality Costs

To compare the two cases, we make use of the fact that the total volume of water to be supplied (from both the aquifer and the MWSS system) is the same in each scenario. Thus, consumption benefits derived by water users in both cases are identical, and only the costs are different. As shown in Figure 13.1, the total water supplied is indicated by the area under the curve ABEFH.

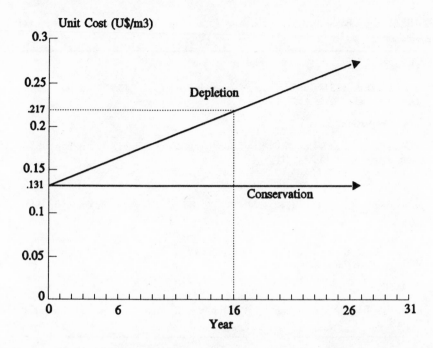

Figure 13.2 Long-Run Supply Costs for the Depletion and Conservation Scenarios

To meet the total demand, the MWSS system must supplement the groundwater supply with the amount MD (starting in year 23), in the depletion scenario. Similarly, to satisfy the same total demand, MWSS must supply the amount MC (starting in year 0), in the conservation case. The MWSS system draws water from sources other than the aquifer under consideration.

In Table 13.1, the costs of groundwater withdrawals in the depletion case are compared with the costs of pumping in the conservation case, including additional net costs to supplement the groundwater shortfall from MWSS pipeborne supplies, based on the average incremental cost or AIC of MWSS supply (see Appendix A13). The present discounted value of the difference in costs between the two cases is assumed to be a long-run measure of the economic externality costs (EC) incurred by following the depletion scenario, instead of the conservation case.

These additional externality costs are incurred because of the consumption pattern followed in the depletion case. The present discounted value of total groundwater withdrawals in this case is also shown in Table 13.1. The ratio UEC = EC/QD provides a measure of the long-run externality cost per m³ of groundwater withdrawn, and also serves as a guideline for a user charge that might be imposed on the depleters, to compensate for the resulting loss of

TABLE 13.1   Estimation of Economic Externality Costs Due to Groundwater
Depletion

(1) Depletion Case	
Present Discounted Value of Costs of Supplying Water (from Appendix Table A13.1)	406.87 (million US$)
(2) Conservation Case	
Present Discounted Value of Costs of Supplying Water (from Appendix Table A13.1)	377.56 (million US$)
(3) EC	
Difference in Costs: (1) - (2)	29.31 (million US$)
(4) QP	
Present Discounted Value of Total Groundwater Withdrawal in the Depletion Case	2444 (million m³)
(5) UEC	
Long-Run Economic Externality Costs Due to Depletion: (3) / (4)	0.012 (US$ / m³)

potential benefits (if the conservation scenario had been followed). On the
basis of the data available, the long-run externality cost estimate is given by
UEC = US$ 0.012 per m³ of groundwater pumped. We note that this average
value of UEC may be higher if estimated some years later. If UEC increased
over time as the aquifer became more depleted, this should be reflected in the
policy measures discussed below.

Policy Implications

While the physical model and groundwater extraction scenarios provide a
benchmark value for the externality costs of destroying the aquifer, very little
further information is available about the consumption patterns and economic
behavior (especially water demand curves) of groundwater users.
Nevertheless, it is possible to draw some policy conclusions, starting with a
simplified static analysis. The more dynamic aspects introduced later will not
change the essential logic of the arguments presented below.

A conventional downward sloping (private) demand curve for groundwater
is shown in Figure 13.3. DP represents the aggregate willingness-to-pay of
groundwater users, i.e., consumption volumes per year at various extraction
costs, and the area under this demand curve measures the benefits of water use

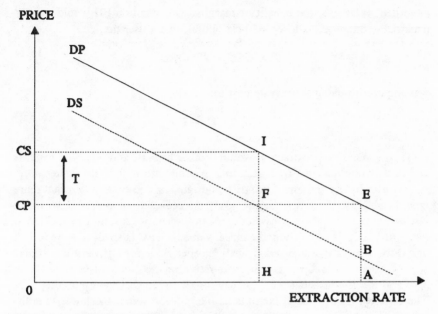

Figure 13.3 Groundwater Extraction and User Charges

based on consumer perceptions, excluding environmental and externality costs. Ideally, if there was full information about the future consequences of aquifer destruction and private well-owners had a good awareness of societal implications, the use of groundwater should be governed by a social demand curve, DS. This curve lies below DP because society has to incur an additional economic cost (like UEC, estimated earlier) for every m³ of groundwater extracted under the depletion scenario. The divergence between DP and DS could arise, for example, because a typical groundwater user may be ignorant or unconcerned about externalities. Alternatively, those who deplete most heavily in the early years and enjoy low extraction costs may not be the same persons who have to face the higher costs of pumping from a depleted aquifer in later years.

As mentioned earlier, the first best option for society would have been to somehow restrict groundwater pumping and enforce the conservation scenario. This would result in overall cost savings, UEC = US$ 0.012 per m³ over the period of analysis. However, such an outcome is unlikely since policy options should have been introduced many years ago to achieve this result. Under present policies, the depletion scenario will occur, and in a typical year users will extract a volume OA at a cost CP (Figure 13.3). There is an economic efficiency cost BE associated with the marginal unit of water used, because the extraction cost exceeds the consumption benefit to society. Ideally, if DS governed water use, the benefit of marginal consumption FH would exactly equal CP. Suppose, as a second best option, that a user tax:

$$T = UEC = IF = BE \qquad (13.1)$$

was imposed, raising the private cost to:

$$CS = CP + T \qquad (13.2)$$

Then groundwater extraction would decline by AH, and marginal benefits and costs would be equalized, resulting in economically efficient water use.

If we introduce the time dimension, our analysis becomes somewhat more complicated. As shown in Figure 13.1, the reduced pumping AH will give rise to an intermediate groundwater extraction scenario, resulting in a different value of UEC. Nevertheless, the initial value of UEC is small relative to CP, and if the elasticity of demand is small (steeper slope for DP), this adjustment will be small. Finally, through an iterative process, it will be possible to arrive at a self-consistent set of values for CS, CP, UEC and pumping rate. The efficient (second best) tax, TE, is likely to be somewhat lower than the original UEC. We note that more sophisticated dynamic analysis is possible, since the demand curve DP, the cost CP, and tax T can all vary over time. Furthermore, as the saline front gradually advances inland, greater spatial disaggregation also could be attempted if the data were available to determine extraction rates, costs and user charges by zone.

From the viewpoint of public finance, an average user charge of US\$ 0.012 per m³ will yield present valued revenues of about US\$ 29.31 million, in the depletion scenario. If UEC increased over time, then revenues would be greater. These resources could be used to develop alternative MWSS water resources to replace the failing aquifer.

Policy Options

General Rationale

Legally, all waters in the Philippines belong to the state, and the use of this water is a privilege granted to citizens, by the government. From the socioeconomic viewpoint, the water resources of the Philippines are a public good, to be allocated and utilized for the optimal benefits of the entire nation. The government has a special responsibility to regulate water use, particularly where shortages exist or are likely to occur in the future, if the prevailing patterns of use continue unchecked.

Groundwater use in the Greater Manila Area has grown rapidly over the last 30 years. As previously explained, the extraction rate exceeded the natural recharge many times, resulting in sharp declines of the water table and intrusion of sea water, especially in the coastal areas. Continued over-pumping will result in an economic loss to society due to increased pumping costs from the lower water table and due to the need to abandon wells as water quality steadily deteriorates further and further inland. Each current groundwater user is responsible for these external diseconomies imposed on all other existing and future users.

There is therefore, a strong case for the government to adopt rational policies for managing and controlling groundwater in the GMA. A soundly designed package of groundwater user charges and associated water resource management measures would help not only to restrict groundwater use in the GMA, but also to raise revenues so that alternative sources of water supply could be developed in the future (especially through extension of the MWSS pipeborne system), to supplement or replace (in the form of artificial recharges) declining groundwater availability.

Precedents for Groundwater Management and Existing Measures

Groundwater laws exist in developed countries such as the US (24 States), and in several developing countries like Mexico and Mali. Within the Philippines, charges are levied for developing and exploiting other natural resources such as minerals, forest products and water for electricity generation. The imposition of charges for the use of forest products, including timber and fuelwood, is particularly relevant, because like groundwater, forests are a renewable resource which can be damaged beyond the point of recovery through prolonged and uncontrolled over-exploitation. However, there are problems in implementing many of these regulations.

In the specific area of groundwater, several water districts like Cebu and Batangas have recently imposed user charges. Existing groundwater management measures relevant to the GMA are described in the Philippine Water Code (PWC) issued by the National Water Resources Council (NWRC), and the Republic Act No. 6234 of 19 June 1971, creating the MWSS. Thus, there are provisions for drilling and maintaining water wells, protection of water supply sources, filing fees, minimal user charges, and limits on withdrawal rates in relation to the distance between wells. However, the penalties are in general both inadequate and not sufficiently well enforced, to meet the crisis caused by the rapid depletion and salinization of groundwater resources in the GMA.

Policy Implementation Issues for
Environmental Management

There is clearly a need for a new package of groundwater management and control measures which is consistent with and supplements the existing laws mentioned above. The new measures should include the definition of critical groundwater areas in the GMA, licensing of well drillers, requirements for drilling permits, specifications for construction, maintenance, and sterilization of wells, metering and reporting requirements, user charges, limits on pumping (where necessary), the return of cooling water to the aquifer and contamination controls. Coordinated use of all policy instruments is important in to achieve the best results.

Drilling and Licensing Fees

All new well-owners ought to be charged a drilling fee to obtain the right to drill. In addition there should be an annual licensing fee, if the well is to be operated. These fees essentially provide a control mechanism whereby all existing and new wells appear on a government list, and their status is verified at least once a year. The approved permit to pump water should specify the construction specifications, allowable volume and the user fee to be paid, based on piezometric head and salt content of the groundwater. This will address the equity problem of private users accessing a public good in an unregulated manner.

Controls and Other Regulations

The government should adopt and impose a system for safe well abandonment. This is a difficult objective because it requires knowledge of all active wells. However, if all wells are abandoned properly by filling the bore completely from bottom to top with impermeable material (cement or clay), the protection of the fresh water part of the aquifer will be enhanced by lessening the likelihood of new points of downward flow of saline water. Had this procedure been followed since the early days of groundwater development in the GMA, the saline water would have progressed far less than is the case today. This is a form of aquifer protection.

In the critical areas characterized by a low piezometric head and/or a high salt concentration in the groundwater, a surcharge (in addition to the user charge), might be imposed on withdrawals above "normal requirements," if alternative MWSS supply is available. This is a demand tool designed to discourage abstraction.

Steps could also be taken to prevent man-made pollution of the aquifer. Rivers and stream channels, which feed the aquifer by percolation from their beddings, are the recipients of waste products from overland runoff, from effluent discharge of industries, city dumps and sanitary landfills. While provisions for pollution control already exist at the national level, regulations more specific to the GMA should be specified and strictly enforced. The fact that the aquifer is seriously depleted means that it has a much lower capacity to assimilate potentially harmful waste than was previously the case, and therefore must be protected from contaminant inflows wherever possible.

Conservation, Redistribution and Recharge

MWSS has operated a water development and distribution system based on its policy of conjunctive use of ground and surface waters. Groundwater is used in the outlying areas beyond the Central Distribution System (CDS), and it is used also within the existing CDS to supplement surface water. In 1980-81 it was estimated that groundwater contributed about 40 percent of the supplies for the GMA.

MWSS (1983b) reported that groundwater extraction in 1982 of 740 MLD would be reduced to about 615 MLD or less by the year 2000, and that the pumpage pattern would have been redistributed away from the overdeveloped so-called "cones of depression" in Valenzuela and Makati (see Figure 13.4). The report further stated that the probable progressive decline in groundwater pumpage in the GMA would continue into the next century, possibly stabilizing at a level of 200 MLD.

For all practical purposes, the existing depletion of groundwater storage extends over the entire GMA. Figure 13.4 is a map of the piezometric surface of the GMA for 1982 showing that the surface is below sea level in all but the extreme northeastern portion, which is less than 10 percent of the area. Furthermore, west of the North Expressway, the piezometric surface is from 40 to 100 meters below sea level. Between the provinces of Bulacan and Rizal on the one side and Manila Bay, the piezometric surface lies from 60 to 120 meters below sea level. From Makati to Pasig the level varies 100 to 140 meters below sea level. In most of the GMA the depletion of groundwater is widespread and severe, and the water levels are so low that the salt water intrusion will continue to damage the aquifer for years to come. Additionally, the withdrawal of groundwater from anywhere west of Laguna de Bay and southward, in adjoining Cavite Province has a negative effect on the piezometric surface in the GMA and eventually must be controlled.

Serious damage to the aquifer has been caused by salt-water intrusion laterally and downward along the coastal GMA from Valenzuela to Cavite City; in the Marikina Valley where there is upwelling from depths of 200 meters or more, and more recently, laterally along the boundary of Makati and Mandaluyong.

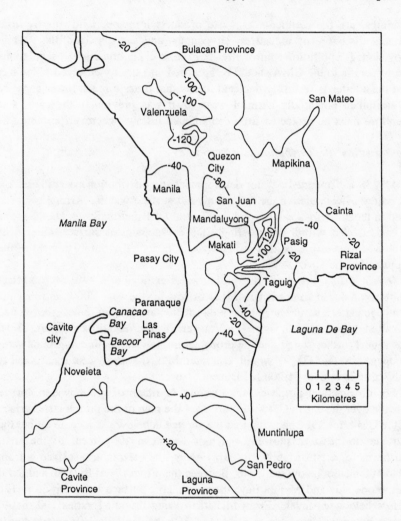

Figure 13.4 Map of Piezometric Surface (hydraulic head in meters below sea level) for the Manila Bay Aquifer System, Greater Manila Area, in 1982-3

In summary, the withdrawal of groundwater must be reduced and redistributed through the GMA, as soon as practicable. The highest priority areas to receive alternate water supplies and to reduce groundwater pumpage are Cavite City, the so-called Valenzuela cone, the Makati-Mandaluyong cone, Pasay City and Paranaque north of Sucat Road, and coastal Las Pinas. Cavite City will receive water from off-peninsula to the south in Cavite Province, causing a redistribution of groundwater pumpage to a more favorable area for withdrawal in the neighborhood of Noveleta. The other places named should be served by the newly developed surface water source, while groundwater pumpage reductions must be made concurrently. Levying a surcharge on the normal groundwater user fee on pumpage above some "normal level of depletion" can provide a strong incentive to the users of large volumes of water to reduce or eliminate groundwater withdrawals and purchase water from MWSS.

We conclude this section by examining recharge options (for a discussion of recharge see, e.g., Vaux 1985). Laguna de Bay is a large area to the southeast, serving as a source of fresh-water recharge to the aquifer, because of favorable differences in piezometric levels. Natural recharge also occurs from the highlands in the south, east and northeast, as well as some reaches of streams that cross the GMA during the rainy season. However, because of the relatively low permeability of the aquifer system in most of the GMA, it is believed that efforts to encourage additional natural recharge to the aquifer would be unsuccessful.

It would be worthwhile to experiment with artificial recharge wells in Makati, utilizing cooling water from the high-rise business establishments and apartment buildings, to replenish the aquifer. The used cooling water should be chemically compatible with the aquifer, and unused wells could be used as injection sites. If this experiment turned out to be successful, later experiments could be tried using water from the Central Distribution System (CDS) when it is available. At that time MWSS wells could be utilized as recharge wells. A similar experiment also could be tried along the coastal GMA to determine if a fresh-water mound or ridge could be built to control the inland migration of salt water. Finally, the government should monitor the water level and its quality in wells within the GMA, as groundwater pumpage is shifted away from the deep cones of depression.

Determining and Enforcing User Charges

Any realistic pricing framework must incorporate both economic efficiency and equity considerations (see Chapter 8). On sociopolitical grounds, there is a good case for distinguishing between household users who would be withdrawing relatively small amounts of water for their basic needs, and industrial and commercial well-owners who would be pumping large volumes of water as an input into a profit-making productive activity. This discrimination would apply only to the user charge since all well owners should be subject to drilling and licensing fees.

At the same time, users in the vicinity of the brackish interface (see Figure 13.1) have to be more cautious as to their extraction rate of the groundwater. Exceeding a critical maximum pumping rate causes a "sucking upward" or upconing of salt water, hence terminating the use of the well. The users close to the interface therefore will face an additional externality cost, i.e., income foregone associated with reduced pumping to avoid upconing. Due to excessive pumping by users located at some distance away from the interface, the salt water front will continue to progress inland forcing the closer users to gradually decrease their pumping rates and eventually to abandon their wells.

If information were available, spatial price discrimination or zoning (based on distance away from the brackish interface) might therefore be warranted. In the same context, one could argue for a dynamic pricing over time. However, no discrimination in the sense of "zoning" is considered in the present study, due to data limitations.

Household Users

Based on the sociopolitical argument that all citizens are entitled to their basic water needs, two basic alternative measures of relief from user charges for household well owners are proposed:

- exemption from the user charge up to 50 m^3 per month per household (based on basic needs allocation of 6 m^3 per capita per month, and assuming 8 persons per average household), with the normal user charge being levied on all pumpage exceeding 50 m^3 per month; and
- exemption from the user charge for all consumption, provided the well casing diameter is below some critical size (say 13 mm).

While both measures encourage conservation of groundwater, alternative (ii) would be easier to implement. It eliminates the need for metering, billing and collecting payments from a large number of small groundwater users.

Industrial and Commercial Users

This category of user who would be using the water for profitable activities should be charged the full rate (based initially on US$ 0.012 per m^3, estimated earlier), on all withdrawals.

Other User Charges

Earlier, certain areas were identified as critical zones, based on piezometric head and/or salt content of the groundwater. Therefore an additional surcharge on the normal user charge should be imposed, especially where alternative MWSS supply is available. The level of surcharge should be high enough to encourage the well owners to shift to MWSS supply. Additional charges may be imposed, based on the cost of disposal of groundwater that is pumped, including the actual costs of sewerage (where appropriate) and any other health or environmental costs associated with discharge.

As a basis for levying charges, there are three basic methods of determining the volume of water extracted from wells:

1) a water meter;
2) the electricity consumption; and
3) the pump capacity.

Of the three methods, the direct reading of a water meter is the best suited to a water utility like MWSS, where the organization has the trained manpower, local offices and procedures already in place. However, water meters can be tampered with to give erroneous readings, and therefore groundwater users should be persuaded to cooperate through a system of strong legal penalties. Also the decision to meter and the complexity of the installed device should be made after comparing whether the benefits of the metering exceed the costs (Munasinghe 1988).

The second best method would be power consumption data. This method requires skilled manpower, verified pump data and periodic readings from a dedicated electric meter. The records could be obtained from the power utility on a routine basis, or read directly by a water utility employee.

Using pump capacity as an indicator of water extracted entails some practical problems of proper control by the water utility. To compute the pumpage several technical data need to be obtained and requires the cooperation of the well owner. In the case of submerged pumps for instance, it would be impossible to verify anything about the size and horse power of an already submerged pump. This leaves the pump capacity the least attractive assessment method.

Each of these measures assumes that the MWSS can assemble a complete register of the characteristics and locations of all pumping installations accessing the aquifer, as a basis for a universal levy of tariffs and enforcement of pumping controls.

Conclusion

The GMA case study provides a good example showing how the neglect of long-run externality costs jeopardizes the availability and quality of groundwater resources. For the case when extraction rates exceed the combined natural and artificial recharge rates, the typical private groundwater user tends to be ignorant or unconcerned about the fact that the amount of groundwater that he or she pumps imposes external diseconomies or costs on all other existing and future users. In the GMA situation not only aquifer depletion, but also its resulting side effect of saline intrusion, worsens the long-term problem.

Among the measures that the Metropolitan Waterworks and Sewerage System (MWSS) could take to slow down the overall groundwater extraction rate, and hence safeguard water for future users and purposes, is a system of user charges. The determination of the user charge is based on the recognition that the use of groundwater should be governed by a social demand curve, which explicitly accounts for environmental and externality costs. In order to equalize marginal groundwater extraction costs and marginal consumption benefits to society, a user tax, equal to the long-run externality cost could be imposed per m^3 of groundwater withdrawn. A more detailed spatial and temporal disaggregation, considering the geographical advancing of the saline front and the depletion of the aquifer, should allow for a surcharge in addition to the defined user charge in critical zones.

It is the task of the government as a regulatory agency to systematically exploit and adequately regulate water use, particularly where shortages exist or are likely to occur in the future. In this regard, the imposition of taxes based on user charges should be only part of a combination of various groundwater demand management and control measures, in order to be effective in cutting down the groundwater use. A soundly designed package of groundwater resource measures would in addition help to raise revenues to develop alternative sources of water supply in the GMA to supplement or replace declining groundwater availability.

References

Munasinghe, M. 1988. *Contemporary Water Supply Efficiency and Pricing Issues in Developing Countries*. Paper Presented at the International Conference on Cost and Price of Water in Urban Areas. Paris, December 6-8.

_____. 1984. *Rationale and Economic Basis for a Groundwater User Charge Mechanism and Legislation. Metropolitan Waterworks and Sewerage System (MWSS) -- Final Report*. Manila.

MWSS. 1983a. *Groundwater Development MWSII Final Report (GWD)*. Metro Manila: Metropolitan Waterworks and Sewerage System.

_____. 1983b. *MWSII Water Demand and Tariff Study*. Manila: Metropolitan Waterworks and Sewerage System. pp. 61-3.

Vaux, H.J., Jr. 1985. "Economic Aspects of Groundwater Recharge." *Artificial Recharge of Groundwater*. T. Asano (ed.). London: Butterworths Press. pp. 703-718.

World Bank. 1989. *Angat Water Supply Optimization Project. Staff Appraisal Report No 7801-PH*. Washington DC: The World Bank.

_____. 1986. *Metropolitan Manila Water Distribution Project. Staff Appraisal Report No 5903-PH*. Washington DC: The World Bank.

Appendix 13
Economic Costs of Producing Water

Tables A13.1 to A13.5. provide detailed information on the production costs for:

- groundwater (depletion and conservation cases); and
- the MWSS public water supply.

The general approach used to estimate unit economic costs of water produced is to calculate the average incremental cost (AIC) of supply (see Chapter 7 for details).

$$AIC = \frac{Present\ value\ of\ incremental\ costs\ of\ producing\ water}{Present\ value\ of\ volume\ of\ incremental\ water\ produced}$$

TABLE A13.1 Groundwater Withdrawals and Supply Costs

	DEPLETION CASE						CONSERVATION CASE				
Year	Groundwater Withdrawals (MLD)	MWSS Supply (MLD)	Unit Cost of Production (1) (US$/m³)	Production Cost ('000 US$/day) Grw Wd	MWSS (3)	Total	Groundwater Withdrawals (MLD)	MWSS Supply (MLD)	Production Cost ('000 US$/day) Grw Wd (2)	MWSS (3)	Total
1984	730	0	0.131	95.9	0.0	95.9	730	0	95.9	0.0	95.9
85	730	0	0.137	100.1	0.0	100.1	697	33	91.6	7.6	99.2
86	730	0	0.142	103.8	0.0	103.8	664	66	87.3	15.4	102.6
87	730	0	0.148	107.9	0.0	107.9	631	99	82.9	23.0	105.9
88	730	0	0.152	111.6	0.0	111.6	598	132	78.6	30.6	109.2
89	730	0	0.159	115.8	0.0	115.8	565	165	74.3	38.3	112.6
1990	730	0	0.164	119.4	0.0	119.4	532	198	69.9	46.0	115.9
91	719	0	0.169	121.7	0.0	121.7	499	220	65.6	51.1	116.6
92	708	0	0.174	123.4	0.0	123.4	466	242	61.2	56.2	117.4
93	697	0	0.180	125.4	0.0	125.4	433	264	56.9	61.3	118.2
94	686	0	0.185	126.9	0.0	126.9	400	286	52.6	66.4	119.0
95	675	0	0.191	128.7	0.0	128.7	367	308	48.2	71.5	119.7
96	664	0	0.196	129.9	0.0	129.9	334	330	43.9	76.6	120.6
97	653	0	0.201	131.5	0.0	131.5	301	352	39.6	81.7	121.3
98	642	0	0.206	132.5	0.0	132.5	268	374	35.2	86.9	122.1
99	631	0	0.212	133.9	0.0	133.9	235	396	30.9	91.9	122.8
2000	620	0	0.217	134.6	0.0	134.6	200	420	26.3	97.5	123.8
01	558	0	0.223	124.4	0.0	124.4	200	358	26.3	83.1	109.4
02	496	0	0.228	113.0	0.0	113.0	200	296	26.3	68.7	95.0
03	434	0	0.234	101.4	0.0	101.4	200	234	26.3	54.4	80.6
04	372	0	0.239	88.7	0.0	88.7	200	172	26.3	39.9	66.2
05	310	0	0.244	75.7	0.0	75.7	200	110	26.3	25.6	51.9
06	248	0	0.249	61.9	0.0	61.9	200	48	26.3	11.1	37.4
07	186	14	0.255	46.0	3.3	49.3	200	0	26.3	0.0	26.3
08	124	64	0.260	32.2	14.9	47.1	200	0	26.3	0.0	26.3
09	62	138	0.266	16.5	32.1	48.6	200	0	26.3	0.0	26.3
2000 to INF	0	200	0.271	0.0	46.4	46.4	200	0	26.3	0.0	26.3

(1) Unit cost of Production is 0.217 US$ per m³ for Groundwater Withdrawal (Depletion Case in Year 2000), from Table A.13.3.
(2) Unit cost of Production is 0.132 US$ per m³ for Groundwater Withdrawal (Conservation Case), from Table A.13.2.
(3) Unit cost of Production is 0.23 US$ per m³ for MWSS Supply, from Table A.13.4.

Remark: Output is the same in both Depletion and Conservation cases.

TABLE A13.2   Initial Pumping Costs and Well Output in 1984

| | Costs | | Water Produced |
Year	Investment	Operating	(m^3)
0	92,857	9,400	179,050
1	0	9,400	179,050
2	0	9,400	179,050
3	5,100	9,400	179,050
4	0	9,400	179,050
5	5,100	9,400	179,050
6	2,607	9,400	179,050
7	5,100	9,400	179,050
8	0	9,400	179,050
9	16,900	9,400	179,050
10	0	9,400	179,050
11	7,707	9,400	179,050
12	0	9,400	179,050
13	5,100	9,400	179,050
14	0	9,400	179,050
15	5,100	9,400	179,050
16	2,607	9,400	179,050
17	5,100	9,400	179,050
18	11,800	9,400	179,050
19	5,100	9,400	179,050
Present Values in Year Zero (Discounted at 10%)	121,044	80,025	1,523,900

Unit Cost: (121,044 + 80,025) / 1,523,900 = 0.132 US$ / m³

Based on exchange rate 1 June 1984: 1 US$ = 14 Pesos

Well Characteristics in mid-1984:	Depth = 183 m Pumping rate = 0.454 cubic meter / min Total Dynamic Head (TDH) = 76 m Efficiency: 0.6 Capacity Factor: 50% Lifetime = 20 yrs

TABLE A13.3   Depletion Scenario: Pumping Costs and Well Output in 2000

| Year | Costs | | Water Produced (m³) |
	Investment	Operating	
0	92,857	12,614	179,050
1	0	12,614	179,050
2	0	12,614	179,050
3	5,100	12,614	179,050
4	0	12,614	179,050
5	5,100	12,614	179,050
Present Values in Year Zero (Discounted at 10%)	99,855	47,818	678,740

Unit Cost: $(99,855 + 47,818) / 678,740 = 0.217$ US\$ / m³

Based on exchange rate 1 June 1984: 1 US\$ = 14 Pesos

Well Characteristics in mid-2000 *(projected figures)*:   Depth = 183 m
Pumping rate = 0.681 cubic meter / min
Total Dynamic Head (TDH) = 116 m
Efficiency: 0.6
Capacity Factor: 50%
Lifetime = 6 yrs

Remark: Effects of groundwater depletion are lowered water table (increased TDH) and higher salinity (reduced lifetime).

TABLE A13.4   Average Incremental Cost (AIC) of MWSS Water Supply

The present values of production costs and volumes (from Table A13.5) discounted to 1984 at a rate of 10 percent per year, in constant mid-1984 prices:

1.	Capital Costs (million US\$)	632
2.	Operating costs (million US\$)	77
3.	Value of power and energy sales (million US\$)	59
4.	Net Present Value of costs (1+2-3) (million US\$)	650
5.	Water produced (million cubic meters)	2,801
6.	AIC of water produced (US\$/cubic meter)	0.23

TABLE A13.5 MWSS Costs and Production

| Year | Costs (millions US dollars) | | Production (million m³) |
	Investment	Operating	
1982	4.04	-	-
83	11.88	-	-
84	11.59	-	-
85	41.06	-	-
86	80.88	-	-
87	161.94	-	-
88	185.76	-	-
89	122.86	-	-
1990	43.26	4.86	9
91	52.08	6.14	80
92	56.97	7.53	160
93	53.84	9.04	247
94	52.54	10.53	336
95	56.39	12.16	439
96	43.30	13.89	541
97	35.68	15.66	648
98	34.70	16.61	697
99	-	16.61	697
2000-2030	-	16.61	697

About the Author

Mohan Munasinghe

Mohan Munasinghe was born in Sri Lanka, and has earned post-graduate degrees in engineering, physics and economics from Cambridge University, U.K., the Massachusetts Institute of Technology, USA, McGill University, Canada, and Concordia University, Canada.

He has received a number of international honours and prizes for outstanding research work and applications, and is the author of over 40 books and monographs, as well as several hundred technical papers on water, electric power, energy, environment, economics and information technology. He serves also on the editorial boards of several scholarly journals.

He is presently a Division Chief at the World Bank, Washington DC. During his 18 years with this institution, Professor Munasinghe has had field experience in most developing countries, and worked on electric power, environmental, petroleum, water, telecommunications, transport, urban and multi-purpose projects. From 1982 to 1986, he was the Senior Energy Advisor to the President of Sri Lanka, the Chairman of the Computer and Information Technology Council of Sri Lanka, and the President of the Sri Lanka Energy Managers Association (SLEMA), while on leave of absence from the World Bank.

He is a Fellow of the National Academy of Sciences, Sri Lanka, and has been active in a number of international think-tanks in the areas of energy, information technology and the environment -- serving as Chairman, Energy Research Group, IDRC-United Nations University, and Chairman, Committee on Computers and Informatics, Third World Academy of Sciences, Trieste, as well as member of several expert advisory panels of the National Academy of Sciences, USA. He has taught also in several Sri Lankan, Canadian and US universities, and conducted international training seminars for many senior developing country officials. Presently, he lectures to graduate students in energy and environmental management at the University of Pennsylvania.

Finally, he maintains a lively interest in sports, having formerly represented Sri Lanka (Junior Davis Cup) and Cambridge University in lawn tennis, and won several titles.